All the Best

[signature]

PICK® FOR PROFESSIONALS
ADVANCED METHODS AND TECHNIQUES

The PICK Library

Edited by Jonathan E. Sisk

The following additional books are in the Pick Library series:

PICK BASIC: A Programmer's Guide
by Jonathan E. Sisk

The PICK Perspective
by Ian Sandler

The PICK Pocket Guide
by Jonathan E. Sisk

PICK for the IBM PC and Compatibles
by John W. Winters, Ph.D. and Dale E. Winters

Programming with IBM PC BASIC and the PICK Database System
by David L. Clark

PICK®
FOR PROFESSIONALS
ADVANCED METHODS AND TECHNIQUES

Harvey E. Rodstein

TAB Professional and Reference Books

Division of TAB BOOKS Inc.

Blue Ridge Summit, PA

For my father, Bernard Rodstein, mathematician, philosopher, teacher, and a wonderful friend.

TPR books are published by TAB Professional and Reference Books, a Division of TAB BOOKS Inc. The TPR logo, consisting of the letters ''TPR'' within a large ''T,'' is a registered trademark of TAB BOOKS Inc.

FIRST EDITION
FIRST PRINTING

Library of Congress Cataloging-in-Publication Data

Rodstein, Harvey E.
   PICK for professionals : advanced methods and techniques / by
Harvey E. Rodstein.
     p.   cm.
   Reprint.
   ISBN 0-8306-0125-2
   1. PICK (Computer operating system)   I. Title.
QA76.76.063R635   1990
005.4'3—dc20   89-27496
                                                           CIP

TAB BOOKS Inc. offers software for sale. For information and a catalog, please contact TAB Software Department, Blue Ridge Summit, PA 17294-0850.

Questions regarding the content of this book should be addressed to:

Reader Inquiry Branch
TAB BOOKS Inc.
Blue Ridge Summit, PA 17294-0214

Vice President & Editorial Director: Larry Hager
Book Editor: Pat Mulholland-McCarty
Series Editor: Jonathan E. Sisk
Production: Katherine Brown

Contents

Foreword

PICK IS A WONDERFULLY RICH AND FLEXIBLE ENVIRONMENT FOR DEVELOPING DATA-base applications. It allows you to solve business problems in a small fraction of the time that it takes to use conventional operating systems and languages. Software written using PICK is normally three to ten times more efficient in its utilization of hardware resources than its competitors. PICK also offers an amazing degree of portability for the completed application. Most times it only takes one or two days to move your entire applica-tion to a different PICK system, supplied by any of the twenty or more PICK licensees, as your business needs change over time.

These benefits are easy to achieve, thanks to this book, even if you have little or no experience in designing computer applications or working with a relational database. This book provides real world examples of how to solve common PICK programming problems. It shows how to write code that is efficient and easy to use and maintain. More than that, this book teaches you how to design applications that will work efficiently on small PICK sys-tems with only a few users, and also on large PICK systems with several hundred users.

It is my belief that this book is destined to become a standard textbook for the PICK community. If you design or program PICK applications, you cannot fail to gain immea-surably from reading it.

Ian Sandler
Manager of PICK Research and Development
Sanyo/ICON Systems and Software Inc.

Acknowledgments

I WOULD LIKE TO THANK LYNNE KAUFFMAN, WILLIAM MEYERS, IAN SANDLER, Jonathan Sisk, and haneczka for their valuable contributions to this text. Lynne, thanks for the camera ready; Bill, thanks for the education on trees; Ian, thanks for the clarity; Jon, thanks for the exposure; and haneczka, thanks for the "you know what."

Introduction

THE PICK OPERATING SYSTEM IS AN INTEGRATED DATABASE AND STRING HANDLING environment which moves and processes data very well. Pick is not the "classic" version of an operating system, which is designed to control functions in a machine world and, subsequently, requires application programmers to deal with the hardware. Rather, Pick is designed to acknowledge the human mind. It exists in a purely software world in which thought is quite close to action. The programmer is free to think about the data application, rather than the computer hardware. Call it "The Instant Gratification Database Operating Environment."

The Pick system is currently available on a wide range of processors found on systems ranging in size from micros to mainframes. The ease at which applications software can be ported from one machine to the other is unsurpassed in the data processing industry. The average conversion effort can be measured in days.

It is the ease and speed at which applications can be prototyped, tested, implemented, and ported that makes Pick so very powerful and important. Applications, which once would require 100 programmers and take over three years to complete, now might take three programmers less than one year to complete. When using some of the newer application generators and fourth generation languages available in Pick, the prototyping phase can be reduced to weeks.

Pick exists in many flavors and under many guises. The "classic" Pick system which is currently available on PC XT and AT compatible machines is dubbed R83, for "Release 1983." This is Pick in its native *virtual mode*. The licensees who are currently offering compatible versions of R83 include ADDS/NCR, ALTOS, CIE SYSTEMS, FUJITSU, GENERAL AUTOMATION, and ICON/SANYO. Each has trodden a somewhat separate and sometimes diverging path of modification and enhancement. Thankfully, there are forces in action that are attempting to keep the lines closer if not completely parallel. One such standards organization is Pick Spectrum (formerly SMA, Spectrum Management Association.)

Pick has always been a tree with many branches. Its commercial beginnings were on the MICRODATA (McDONNELL DOUGLAS) machine under the marketing catch-word of REALITY. Label that R74. It was then ported to the HONEYWELL machine for ULTI-MATE. Label that R77.

Meanwhile, in the Pacific Northwest, a group of software jockeys called DEVCOM came up with "INFORMATION," a Pick look-alike environment written entirely in FOR-TRAN and Assembler controlled by the PRIMOS Operating System. This was the first case of the Pick data structure, retrieval language and processing languages being emulated on "top" of another operating system. The look-alike approach helped spawn REVELATION (on MSDOS) and UNIVERSE (on UNIX). Most recently, Pick was implemented under GUARDIAN on the TANDEM machine.

The advantage of these Pick-like environments is that any features that already exist in the host operating system are easy to include in the Pick environment. This includes extended arithmetic, networking, graphics, and CAD/CAM. This also makes other languages available such as COBOL, C and Pascal. The disadvantage is that the price performance is well below that of a native Pick implementation, because these other operating systems do not handle the resources of memory and disk as efficiently as Pick.

Pick R83 has also been implemented concurrently with other operating systems. An R83 compatible version is available as a guest of VM on IBM 360 architecture machines. Also available are versions of Pick that run as guests of other multiple operating system managers which allow MSDOS, UNIX and Pick to exist separately and simultaneously. This might be the ideal environment because each operating system can be used for the things it does best without the overhead of the look-alikes.

Unfortunately, Pick is not very well known in the data processing industry. Unlike AT&T's promotion of UNIX, the Pick system hasn't had the "big bucks" behind it to push it into industry-wide awareness. Despite this low profile, the Pick industry has experienced steady and strong growth based upon its merits, as well as word-of-mouth from an ever-increasing number of devoted users. Once a user is "spoiled" by how easy it is to do things in Pick, it is very difficult, if not impossible, to go back to the way things used to be done.

HOW ADVANCED ARE WE TALKING?

The most difficult task when laying out the contents of an advanced text is to decide what constitutes an advanced subject. At what point should an advanced text start and how deep should it go? After many hours of hair pulling, strong coffee, and arguments (discussions) with the editor, we decided that an advanced book should investigate the concerns and questions of the practicing Pick applications programmer by taking those subjects covered in an introductory text, provide more insight into their operation, provide more functional detail, and hopefully, raise more questions.

The choice of subjects for this text was heavily influenced by the many questions that I have been asked while teaching over the past few years. See if you recognize any of these.

- "How do you tune the database for optimum system performance?"
- "What changes can be made to my existing programs to make it run more efficiently?"

- "How can I use ACCESS more often and effectively so there is no need for a new program with every customer request?"
- "How do you design truly unattended and recoverable batch processes?"
- "What are some of the alternative ways of quick searching and indexing a data file without degrading the interactive users?"

Advanced techniques are more than just programming with PICK/BASIC. Rather, they are the integration of all the software features and functions available in the operating system. The Pick programmer should be as confident using PICK/BASIC as working in ACCESS, PROC or TCL. Each available language has its complement of strong points, as well as a set of weak points. It's a matter of picking the right tool for the right job.

WHO IS AN ADVANCED USER?

I know only a handful of people who can truly be called "Pick Experts." These ladies and gentlemen are the gurus of the operating system. They know the use of every bit and byte in the system. (Because they have the source code!)

The rest of us have to struggle through trial and error to gain the slightest tidbit of new knowledge with the system. Pick expertise is heavily dependent on time and experience. With enough time, one can do enough playing and experimenting to earn the title "Almost Expert."

The approach of this "almost expert" to writing this text is to share some of his experience. About five years ago, after almost seven years working with the Pick Operating System, I became aware of some relatively simple, but revolutionary concepts about designing and coding within the Pick environment. The approach taken in this text keeps these "revelations" in mind.

INTENTIONS

Knowledge of the Pick System is not something that is gained in one large dose. Any level of competence and comfort with a system comes by building layers of information. This can be likened to building a brick wall. Each layer of bricks contributes to the height and strength of the wall.

Advanced Pick Techniques provides the intermediate Pick user/programmer with the next step in the learning process. It is intended for the Pick programmer with at least one year of experience with the system and a working knowledge of the PICK/BASIC, ACCESS and PROC languages.

This text touches base with every language, function and command of the Pick operating system that should be of concern to the applications programmer. It is assumed that the reader has the recommended Pick experience. The "bootstrap" concepts of account, file, and item, or "how to log on" are not covered. However, it is impossible to wander through the system without touching upon some of these subjects. Reviews are intended to shed new light on a subject, without lingering on the fundamentals.

If you need more background on these subjects, please review the following recommended texts and references:

- *PICK/BASIC: A Programmer's Guide* by Jonathan Sisk, TAB Books
- *The Pick Perspective* by Ian Sandler, TAB Books
- *The Pick Pocket Guide* by Jonathan Sisk, TAB Books
- *Exploring the Pick Operating System*, by Jonathan Sisk and Steve Van Arsdale, Hayden Books, Division of Howard Sams, ISBN 0-672-48412-9

Upon first reading this text, take each chapter in sequence. You'll find there is some method to this madness. A handy reference or systems manual might be good supplemental reading for reinforcement of the syntax and fundamentals alluded to but not discussed in depth. This is an instructional text, not a reference manual.

WHAT TO EXPECT

The methods and techniques covered in this text are based on standards set forth by the Pick Spectrum and can be adapted to and prove useful for all implementations. The chapters contain sample file layouts and program listings (PICK/BASIC and ACCESS). The syntax for specific examples is compatible with most of the enhanced versions of releases prior to, and including R83. Where necessary, the equivalent ULTIMATE statement syntax is illustrated.

Here is a brief description of what one can expect within each chapter of this text.

Chapter 1, *The Pick Database*, discusses the hierarchy, access method, and structure of the Pick database. Item types are presented as they relate to the system structure. Next, the hashing algorithm is covered along with file group structures. The chapter winds up with the subject of disk frame types, linkages, and possible problems.

Chapter 2, *File Management*, continues the discussion of the Pick database. File management deals with the mechanics of maintaining data files. Topics include gathering statistics, determining file allocation (i.e. file sizing), and implementing file security.

Chapter 3, *A Closer Look at PICK/BASIC*, begins with a discussion of PICK/BASIC internals. This includes the PICK/BASIC compiler and object code items, and the distinction between compiler and runtime directives. There is also a section on how PICK/BASIC runtime manages variables in the descriptor table and free workspace.

The next section reviews the data string and array parsing commands. One example of PICK/BASIC programs shows how the elements of any string, even a command sentence, can be parsed and identified. Next, the subject turns to methods of array manipulation (dynamic and static), their relative efficiency and appropriate use. Finally, a review of programming standards is given. This includes the topics of structured coding and modular programming.

Chapter 4, *List Processing,* deals with the programmatic handling of lists. This chapter covers the techniques for handling ACCESS lists within PICK/BASIC and using PICK/BASIC to generate lists. The discussion includes techniques of maintaining chronological, correlated, ordered lists, for data history and cross-referencing. Included are examples of inverted list maintenance, linked lists, and a discussion of the nature of B-trees.

Chapter 5, *Process Control,* covers the subject of programs used to initiate unattended periodic routines such as day-end, month-end, or year-end procedures for performing data aging, or report generation. There are examples of process routines written in both PROC and PICK/BASIC leading to the inevitable comparisons. Subjects covered include parameter passing, output capturing, error logging and error recovery.

The chapter closes with an example of a TCL "shell" written in PICK/BASIC. Such programs are used to provide a secure environment in which users produce ad hoc reports and procedures without being given TCL privileges. Shells integrate the jobs of user security and process control while enhancing application functionality.

Chapter 6, *ACCESS Programming*, shows that ACCESS can be used as a viable alternative to PICK/BASIC in more than a few situations. The main issue of this chapter is the use of conversions and correlatives.

The chapter begins with an easy and practical method of standardizing file dictionary definitions, thereby eliminating the confusion of maintaining data definitions. The discussion turns to the use of conversions and correlatives for logical decisions, output formatting, targeting multi-values, performing arithmetic, doing table look-ups and generating break line totals. The chapter wraps up with directing the output of ACCESS to disk and tape, instead of the terminal or system printer. Included are examples of ACCESS as a batch update language, (REFORMAT).

Chapter 7, *Dictionary Driven Data Entry,* focuses on application development in a database operating environment where all data references are activated through, and controlled by file dictionaries. Such an approach serves to integrate all the elements of an application while forcing operational consistency. The bulk of the chapter is dedicated to a group of programs that can be used for generic dictionary-driven data input. These programs are provided to demonstrate the "home brewed" approach for integrating the functionality of PICK/BASIC and ACCESS.

Chapter 8, *The Virtual Machine*, brings to light how the system monitor manages system resources and discusses the system status commands—WHERE, WHAT, LISTU, and WHO. Familiarity with these status displays is invaluable for determining the condition of any process. The sample program STATUS, which allows process status to be monitored from the applications level, is provided for your amusement.

Finally, Chapter 9, is a short and sweet discussion of *Working in a Virtual Environment.* No programs and no examples, just a few well chosen words about the approach a programmer should take when designing and coding in the Pick Operating System.

The Pick Database

THE PICK SYSTEM IS REFERRED TO AS HAVING A RELATIONAL DATABASE, ALTHOUGH the structure does not fit the classic model of a relational database. A relational database uses precise mathematical calculations to build data relationships. The data from one or more record types is combined into two-dimensional relational tables. The classic approach ensures data redundancy for each new relationship and requires quite a bit of disk space and pre-processing time.

In contrast, the Pick Database is a flat file system which stores data using a single statistical access method. At the applications level, the storage and access of data elements can follow variable naming conventions, allowing relationships to be inferred by name rather than by proximity. Although the Pick database does not match the mathematical model for a relational database, it can perform as a relational database with none of the space and pre-processing overhead.

Whereas on most operating systems applications database management is performed by a programatically controlled "guest," database management is an integral part of the Pick operating system. The implementation of a database on any non-Pick machine requires a set of specialized programs which address the physical storage media under a variety of possible access methods. In order to provide varied methods of data update and retrieval within the same application, the programmer must choose the database manager that best fits the requirements at hand. Even then, the different elements of the same application might not be compatible.

The Pick operating system uses a "single thread" data storage and access method. Every level of the system hierarchy, (accounts, dictionaries, files) is handled in the same way. Everything is addressed as a named item within a file. This forces consistency while still allowing a variety of other access techniques to be emulated via the available high level languages. (PICK/BASIC is usually the language of choice. See Chapter 4, "List Processing" for the details.)

The first critical step in the development of any application is the design of the database. This is especially true under the Pick Operating System. An efficient application can only be implemented with an understanding of the "underpinnings" of the system database. It is with this in mind that this chapter is focused on a review of the Pick data storage schema and file access technique. The reader should already be familiar with the nature of accounts, files and items.

ITEMS IN THE SYSTEM HIERARCHY

Although the Pick database is considered flat, a hierarchical structure is implied based on the naming conventions and contents of the accounts, files and items. This hierarchical structure is illustrated in Fig. 1-1.

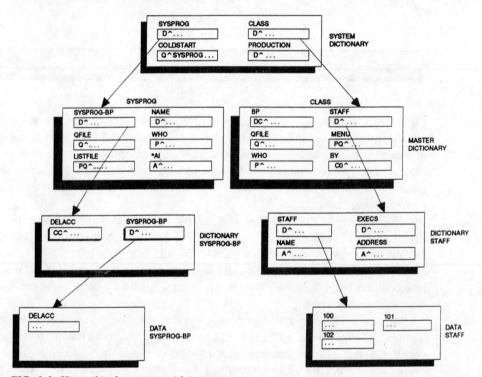

FIG. 1-1. Hierarchical structure with item types.

Items that reside at the system dictionary, account master dictionary and file dictionary levels are handled differently by the system depending on their contents. The *item type* is indicated by the first character of the first value position of the first attribute in the item.

2

Items with a "D" in the first attribute are used to define files. When these *D-pointer* items exist in the SYSTEM dictionary, they can define either account-level files or account master dictionaries. Other items that reside in an account's master dictionary can have a 'P' in the first attribute to define system processes or "verbs," an 'A', 'S' or 'X' to define default data definitions, or a 'C' to define the connectives used in ACCESS command sentences.

File Pointers

The SYSTEM dictionary is the first file allocated on the disk. SYSTEM is no different than any other file except that its address is stored in the ABS region (the *ABSolute code region* where the virtual assembler routines are stored) of the disk, instead of being a D-pointer item in another file. The system hierarchical relationship is based on the existence of file pointers in each of the subsequent file levels. The file D-pointers found at the account, master dictionary or file dictionary levels follow the same general format.

The "D," as shown in Fig. 1-2, stands for "data pointer." It can be modified by a combination of the "a" options. For example, a "DCY" indicates that a catalog type file definition is to be saved, but the contained items (cataloged or not) are not to be saved.

ID:filename

001 D$a\{a\}$		Where a can be:
	C-	Catalog type file.
		Contains lists and PICK/BASIC object code.
	X-	Skip this file during the SAVE process.
	Y-	Backup the file-defining item during SAVE.
		Don't save any of the data.
002 BASE		The FID of the first frame of primary space.
003 MODULO		The number of groups in the file matrix.
004 SEP		Separation. The number of frames per group.
005 L/RET		Retrieve lock codes. (See Chapter 2, "Security")
006 L/UPD		Update lock codes. (See Chapter 2, "Security")
007 PASSWORD		System level only.
008 SYS PRIV		System privilege level.
009 JUST		Justification.
010 MAX		Max length.
011 n/a		
012 n/a		
013 *(mod, sep)*		The modulo and separation used when the file is restored.

FIG. 1-2. D-pointer item layout.

The *base*, *modulo* and *separation*, also known as the BMS, are the active parameters used to map the location of items. Attributes 001-004 of a D-pointer item should never be touched in order to avoid catastrophic consequences. (D-pointer alteration is not possible on many of the new implementations.) Both attributes 7 and 8 are used only by account-defining items. Attribute 013 can be modified for file pointers at any level in the system, (Account Master Dictionary, file DICTionary, and file DATA). See Chapter 2, "File Management," under the heading "File Security."

Other file pointer items at the master dictionary level are used as synonym definitions for files residing in another or the current account. These items are called *Q-pointers* layed out in Fig. 1-3, because they contain a *Q* in the first position of attribute 001. The *target account name* resides in attribute 002, and the *target file name* in attribute 003. The rest of the item is optional.

ID:	*Synonym to the file name*
001	Q
002	*Account name*
003	*Actual file name*

FIG. 1-3. Q-pointer item layout.

In generic Pick, Q-pointers can only point to D-pointers. However, many implementations have altered this by allowing Q-pointers to point to other Q-pointers. This is potentially dangerous. Imagine a Q-pointer referencing another Q-pointer that points back to the original Q-pointer. This would cause the system to get caught in an infinite loop.

Verbs

While file D-pointers can be thought of as *static* pointers, which map data update and retrieval, verbs can be thought of as *dynamic* pointers because they invoke action by transferring the process to a virtual assembler mode.

Verb-defining items vary according to the type of verb, TCL-I, TCL-II, or ACCESS. The general form of verb item layouts is shown in Fig. 1-4.

The PG type verb is a special case in most implementations, which does not parse the sentence or interpret the options. The PQ type item, (PROC) is not considered a verb at all, because the presence of the Q causes the system to follow a completely different path. The rest of the options in attribute 001 are by convention only and might also differ between implementations.

The initial bytes in an ABS frame are reserved for branch commands that transfer control to code residing deeper in the frame. Entry points direct control to the required branch command. On firmware machines, the displacement of an entry point is calculated by the following formula:

$$displacement = (entry * 2) + 1$$

Entry point zero is at byte displacement 1, entry point 1 is at byte displacement 3, and so

ID: *verbname*

001 *Pa*		The *P* indicates a process.
		The *a* represents process special functions.
		A - output list
		C - change
		D - delete
		E - add
		L - list processing
		O - ignore TCL options
		G - retain the quotes in item-id's with embedded quotes.
		Z - all purpose
		Q - a PROC. The remaining verb layout does not apply.
002 *ennn*		Mode address 1. Where *nnn* is the ABS frame address in hex and the *e* is the entry point in the frame where execution is initiated.
003 *ennn*		Mode address 2.
004 *ennn*		Mode address 3.
005 *options*		The low level TCL-II options.
		C - Copy the item to process workspace.
		U - Update is permitted.
		P - Print the item-id's.
		N - New items allowed.

FIG. 1-4. Verb item standard layout.

on. This formula differs on software implementations, which use the following formula:

$$displacement = (entry * 4) + 2$$

The most useful information is the ABS frame address *nnn*. Using the TCL command XTD:

>XTD *nnn*

displays the decimal value of the hex number. For example,

>XTD FF

yields 255. To determine the layout of the system ABS, observe the verb items and record the FID's which are addressed. Attributes 2 and after indicate the initiating frames for each processing stage of the virtual assembler software.

TCL-I Verbs

An example of a TCL-I verb is as follows:

ID: WHO
001 P
002 10BB

The verb WHO transfers control to hex frame BB, entry point 1. Invoking the XTD command, >XTD BB, produces a result of 187. Therefore, the code which displays the port number and account name resides in ABS frame 187.

TCL-II Verbs

An example of a TCL-II verb is as follows:

```
ID: EDIT
001 PE
002 2
003 D
004
005 CUPN
```

The layout of a TCL-II verb is shown in Fig. 1-5.

ID: *verbname*

001   The P is modified by the special function parameter, E.

002   The first mode address for TCL-II is frame 2. Notice that when the entry point is left out, the default is zero. This transfers control to frame 2, entry point zero.

003   The second mode address where processing is transferred after the setup and housekeeping are initiated from frame 2. COPY transfers control to frame 8C, decimal FID 140.

004   The third mode where processing is transferred. Used by ACCESS.

005   All the processing options are in play:
C - Copy the item to process workspace.
U - Update is permitted.
P - Print the item-id's.
N - New items allowed.

FIG. 1-5. TCL-II verb item layout.

ACCESS Verbs

An example of an ACCESS verb is as follows:

```
ID: SORT
001 PA
002 35
003 4E
```

ACCESS verbs follow the same layout as TCL-II, without attribute 5 for special functions. Mode 1 specified in attribute 2 is the main ACCESS entry address, hex frame 35. The command

>XTD 35

indicates that the decimal FID is 53. This is where all the statement parsing, compilation and housekeeping is initiated.

FILE STRUCTURE

There is a single file access schema, which alleviates the need for a complex series of JCL instructions to attach a program to the correct file disk location and access technique. *Disk volume*, *cylinder* and *sector* are hardware terms that have no use to the Pick applications programmer.

Although an application references data by name, these mnemonics are translated into numeric identifiers which indicate a page on disk. Disk pages are called frames and the identifier is known as a *frame id* (FID). FID's are sequentially numbered from 1 to MAX-FID, the highest addressable frame on disk. These FID's are translated by the operating system into the corresponding hardware address including drive, cylinder, head, and sector.

Creation of these file matrices is performed by reserving a block of contiguous frames on the disk. The initial block of frames allocated to a file is called *primary space*. The Pick system is unique in that the data is not stored sequentially in a file. Sequential file organization makes it difficult for random access of the stored data without some kind of Indexed sequential access method (ISAM).

Instead, Pick files are *matrices*. A file matrix is illustrated in Fig. 1-6. The available disk space is divided into *buckets*. Each frame or block of frames is considered a unique entry in the matrix and is called a *group*. The number of groups allocated in primary space is called the *modulo* of the file. The number of primary frames allocated to each group is called the *separation*.

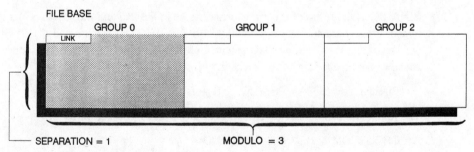

FIG. 1-6. The file matrix.

The Data Access Method

Data is written to, and read from a file using a direct data access method. Items are mapped to their unique statistical groups using a calculation called *hashing*. The hashing algorithm is a function of a unique string (the record key which is the item-id under Pick) and the modulo (the number of buckets) which produces the bucket or group address.

If the unique string is given the symbol ID, then the hashing function can be represented:

ID *mod* MODULO

A modulo hashing function is the remainder of a division. The binary equivalent of the unique string ID is divided by the modulo, producing a remainder within the range 0 through MODULO-1. The value of this remainder is equivalent to the file group number.

The hashing algorithm is demonstrated in Fig. 1-7, *PICK/BASIC routine* provided for demonstration purposes only. Because most versions of PICK/BASIC have definite arithmetic limits, this routine can result in negative numbers when long item-ids are used. Fortunately, the system does not depend on PICK/BASIC to perform hashing.

```
BINARYID = 0
IDLENGTH = LEN(ID)
FOR POSITION = 1 TO IDLENGTH
   BINARYID = SEQ(ID[POSITION,1]) + BINARYID*10
NEXT POSITION
GROUPNUM = REM(ID,MODULO)
FID = (GROUPNUM * SEPARATION) + BASE
```

FIG. 1-7. The hashing algorithm written in PICK/BASIC.

Before the modulo calculation can be performed, the ASCII item-id string must be converted to its binary equivalent. The routine which performs the conversion is as follows:

```
BINARYID = 0
IDLENGTH = LEN(ID)
FOR POSITION = 1 TO IDLENGTH
BINARYID = SEQ(ID[POSITION,1]) + BINARYID*10
NEXT POSITION
```

BINARYID, the result of this transformation, is initialized and the length of the ID determined. Each character, from POSITION 1 to IDLENGTH, is extracted. ID[POSITION,1] is then converted to its binary equivalent. In SEQ(ID[POSITION,1]) each subsequent digit is added to the binary sum of the preceding digits:

```
BINARYID = SEQ(ID[POSITION,1]) + BINARYID*10
```

The remainder can be calculated using the PICK/BASIC function REM:

```
GROUPNUM = REM(BINARYID,MODULO)
```

Please note that the synonym to the REM function is the MOD (Modulo) function. Both result in a remainder.

Next, the first FID, frame id, of the target group is calculated.

```
FID = (GROUPNUM * SEPARATION) + BASE
```

The first frame of the first group in primary file space is called the BASE of the file. The result of the hashing function (ID mod M) is first multiplied by the separation to allow for the size of each group, and the result is added to the file BASE. Once the FID of the group is determined, a sequential search through each frame in that group determines whether the item exists on the file. Remember, each group is statistically unique. A search occurs within the hashed group but not between groups.

During file creation, the system must find a contiguous block of frames from the overflow table. The size of the block is equal to the modulo times the separation.

BLOCKSIZE = MODULO * SEPARATION

There is a limit to the amount of data that can fit within the primary space of a group, but, virtually no limit to the amount of data in overflow. When the group overflows, the system retrieves additional frames from the overflow table and links them to the current end of the group, as shown in Fig. 1-8.

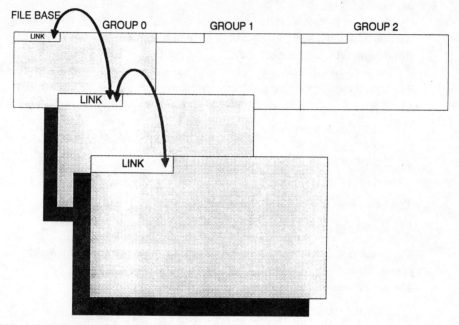

FIG. 1-8. Linked group overflow.

CAUTION: the more data in overflow, the slower retrievals and updates become and the greater the exposure to GFE's.

The hashing algorithm is designed to handle sequential numeric item-id's for the best possible spread across the file. However, it is not always possible or desirable to force all items to be sequentially numbered. So that randomly named items can get the best possible hashing, follow these simple rules:

- The hashing algorithm is right weighted. That is, the suffix of an item-id controls distribution more than the prefix. Item-id's with the same suffix will hash together in "clumps" and leave large open spaces in the file. Therefore, *never use the same item-id suffix*!

9

- Item-id's can be up to 48 characters in length. The characters at the beginning of the string have little or no significance as the length increases. Therefore, *keep item-id's short* (under 20 characters) *but DESCRIPTIVE* !

Group Data Formats

Items are not flat data records. Items are three-dimensional arrays. The dimensions of the array are referred to as attributes (fields) values (sub fields) and sub-values (sub-sub fields). *Attributes* are designated by attribute marks, ASCII character 254. *Values* are designated by value marks, ASCII character 253. *Sub-values* are designated as sub-value marks, ASCII character 252.

An item, as with all data on the Pick system, is a *string*. The system logically separates the fields and subfields of data in an item by counting the reserved system characters that designate the end of each field.

Now it's time to take a closer look at the way data items are stored within a frame. The logical item layout that most users are familiar with appears as follows:

```
ID: 100
001 BUGS BUNNY
002 AHOLE ON AVE J
003 BROOKLYN
004 NY
```

This same item in a physical layout looks like this:

```
100^BUGS BUNNY^AHOLE ON AVE J^BROOKLYN^NY
```

The layout of the item as it is stored within a file group is slightly more detailed. The item storage format is shown in Fig. 1-9.

The sample item is stored in a group like this:

```
002F100^BUGS BUNNY^AHOLE ON AVE J^BROOKLYN^NY^_
```

The length of the item is decimal 47, hex 2F.

The count field of an item typically consists of four ASCII characters which represent two hex bytes. The maximum hex number this can represent without going negative (setting the high order bit) is 7FFF (decimal 32,767). This is the artificial item size limit.

There is another type of item storage format called a pointer, or 'catalog' class item. *Pointer class items* store the body of the item in disk space other than primary space. This skirts the item size limitation. A 32K limit would not do for SELECTed and SAVEed lists or PICK/BASIC object code.

A small item, which resides in the file's primary space, defines the location on disk of the cataloged entry. The pointer item layout is shown in Fig. 1-10.

The CC type indicates a PICK/BASIC object item and the CL indicates a cataloged list. Attribute 4 is used only by a list. Indirect item storage is illustrated in Fig. 1-11.

Unfortunately, cataloged items cannot be accessed from PICK/BASIC. A READ statement retrieves the CL pointer and not the body of the item. However, list items can be

NNNNID ^ body of the item^_

where each element means:

NNNN   A 4-byte item length field. In generic implementations, the length is in ASCII-Hex format. This may differ on your system. The length includes not only the item, but also the count fields and the item terminating segment mark.

ID   A variable length character string which can be made up of any alphanumeric or punctuation characters. Notice that there is no delimiter between the count field and the item-id.

^   The caret or up-arrow represents an attribute mark. The first attribute mark sets off the item-id (attribute position 0) from the body of the item.

body   The body of the item is a variable length string with embedded attribute marks, value marks and sub value marks.

^_   An attribute mark followed by a segment mark. In hex; FEFF. This combination must terminate the item. The 4-byte item count includes the item terminating segment mark.

FIG. 1-9. Physical item layout.

ID:	*item identifier*	
001	CC *or* CL	
002	*Starting FID*	
003	*Number of frames*	
004	*Number of items in the list* (CL type only, null for CC)	
005	*Time Date Stamp*	

FIG. 1-10. Catalogued pointer item layout.

manipulated with EDIT as long as the FIL (file as a list) command is used. A word of caution: Due to the limitations of workspace, some implementations will not allow a list of over 32K bytes to be edited.

Extended Item Formats

In order to allow items that exceed the current 32K limit, the item formats must be altered. The method behind unlimited item size is similar to storing cataloged items. Any large item is stored in linked space outside of primary space. The body of the item is pointed to by a 10 to 15-byte entry in primary space.

In this approach, the system sets an artificial size limit to determine whether items are to be stored directly in primary space or indirectly in contiguous space. This limit varies

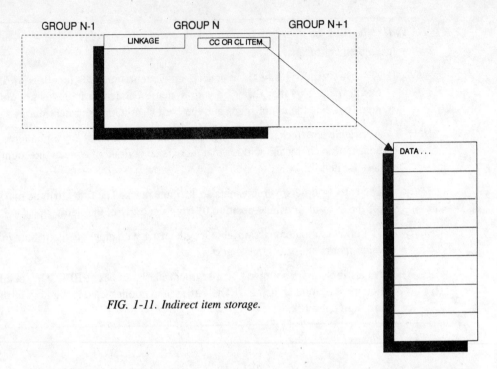

GROUP N-1   GROUP N   GROUP N+1

LINKAGE

CC OR CL ITEM

DATA . . .

FIG. 1-11. Indirect item storage.

according to the data frame size of the system. For argument sake, let's say the system has a 1024 byte data frame. The first 24 bytes are reserved for linkage and other functions, leaving 1K for data. Using a hypothetical item limit of 800 bytes, any item matching or exceeding 800 bytes will be stored outside of primary space.

The removal of large items from primary space reduces the amount of overflow that each group must have to maintain large items. This allows an item to grow without the application aborting. However, handling such large items will guarantee poor system thoughput. Be careful! This approach creates other problems with file optimization. (See Chapter 2, "File Management," under the heading "File Optimization").

Unfortunately, each vendor is implementing a different item-group format. The technique being distributed by a company called ACCUSOFT and made available on the CIE, ALTOS, GENERAL AUTOMATION, FUJITSU, and ICON implementations leaves the item length field in the same position and leaves the remainder of the item structure unchanged. The first two bytes of the item length fields are reserved for the item length in binary. The last two bytes are bit-mapped for specific flags used by the file manager.

The previously discussed item would look like this:

./..100^BUGS BUNNY^AHOLE ON AVE J^BROOKLYN^NY^

Looking at the length field (the first four bytes) in hex reveals:

002F8001

The length is still 2F, but there are 16 control bits for managing the state of the item. The bits are called item flags and are reserved as shown in Table 1-1. As can be observed from

Bit#	Description
0	always 1
1	reserved
2	1 if a D-pointer
3	reserved
4	1 if the D-pointer is deleted
5	1 if the D-pointer is updated
6	1 if the item is deleted
7	1 if the item is updated
8	reserved
9	1 if the item is binary
10	1 if the binary item is linked (not contiguous)
11	1 if the item is indirect
12	reserved
13	reserved
14	1 if the item size is odd
15	always 1

TABLE 1-1. Item Status Bits Layout.

the bit values, the system has a great deal of control over the current state of the item. In addition, items are not restricted to pure ASCII data anymore. Binary items can be maintained to hold object code from different compilers, pseudo DOS diskettes or any other "far out" extensions, which up until now have been impossible.

Another "trick" being played is that item sizes are forced to an even number. This prevents the length field from crossing frame boundaries and, thereby, simplifying the system file handling code, especially on hardware that requires memory references on even word boundaries. (That's almost all of the software machines.)

Different approaches to solving the same problem (but as effective) are available in Advanced Pick (a.k.a. Open Architecture) and on McDonnell Douglas and Ultimate machines. One thing is for sure; the debate is hot and heavy as to whose solution works the best.

Group Flux

Whenever an item is added, deleted or changed, the group in which the item resides is rearranged. As an item grows or shrinks, the items following it in the group are repositioned. There are two popular ways of handling a changing item in the group: 1) One way is to change the item in place, while compressing or expanding the rest of the group. 2) The other way is to remove the item, compress the group, and replace the item at the end of the group.

Whether the item retains its position in the group or it is removed and placed at the end of the group, there is a period of flux in which the change must "ripple" through all the linked frames. The longer the linked chain of frames in overflow, the more time it takes to retrieve from and update to a group. If there is a hiccup (power failure, hardware failure, or a hard system-level abort) while a group is in flux, then a Group Format Error (GFE) is highly probable. A GFE is reported whenever an item count field does not terminate on an item terminating segment mark.

Consider the case where process one is performing an ACCESS inquiry against a file while process two is updating the same file and both happen to address the same group at the same time. Process one may encounter a transient or "phantom" GFE. The GFE is reported because the inquiry process takes a "snapshot" of the group while it is in flux.

The transient GFE problem still exists on systems with releases compatible with R77 or before. Transient GFE's have been solved by most vendors either by forcing a lock during group update so that other processes cannot retrieve a group while it is in a state of flux, forcing a "read" lock (on McDonnell Douglas) or copying the group to workspace and reporting off the copy.

FRAME TYPES

Frames come in two flavors, linked and unlinked. *Unlinked* frames are used by assembler modes, found in the ABS section, and process control blocks. An unlinked frame uses every byte available within the frame for data. Unlinked frames are stand-alone entities. The size of the combined data must fit within the boundaries of the frame. Usually, unlinked frames hold binary information such as assembler opcodes and process counters, accumulators and registers.

Linked frames reserve an area called the linkage at the beginning of the frame. The *linkage* allows the system to find any remaining portions of data that exceed the frame size. The standard size of the linkage is 12 bytes long. However, the reserved area at the beginning of the linked frame varies in size according to the frame size. Twelve bytes are used in a 512 byte frame, 24 in a 1024 frame, 48 in a 2048, and 96 in a 4096 byte frame. In most of these cases, however, bytes 0 through 11 are used for linkage and the remaining bytes in the reserved area are used for specific non-linkage functions.

The linkage word stores its frame pointers and contiguous frame counts as binary-hexadecimal data. The rest of the frame is used to store ASCII strings, as illustrated in Fig. 1-12.

It can be said that "All the world's a string, and alphas, numerics and punctuation merely ASCII characters." The length of a string is not restricted to the boundaries of a frame. When a string of data exceeds frame boundaries, it must "overflow" into another available frame. Within a linked chain of frames, the linkage points to the frame following, as well as the frame preceding the current frame. A linked chain of frames can be made up of a set of randomly allocated or contiguously allocated frames. The linkage consists of four binary-hex fields. They are:

NNCF (Number of Next Contiguous Frames)   A 1-byte field used when a set of contiguous frames is logically linked. Indicates the number of frames which follow the current frame in a contiguous block. The value is zero if the block is not logically contiguous, meaning, the separation is one.

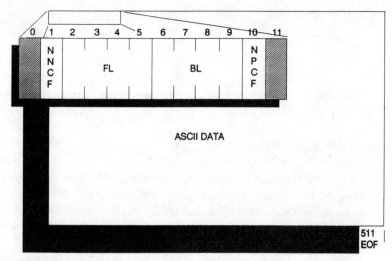

FIG. 1-12. Linked frame layout.

FL (Forward Link)   A 4-byte field which designates the next frame in the linked chain.

BL (Backward Link)   A 4-byte field which designates the previous frame in the linked chain.

NPCF (Number of Previous Contiguous Frames)   A 1-byte field used when a set of contiguous frames is logically linked. Indicates the number of frames that precede the current frame in a contiguous block. The value remains zero if the block is not logically contiguous.

Figure 1-13 displays a sample of the values in a linked chain of frames. Figure 1-14 illustrates a chain of linked frames. The first frame in a linked chain always has a backward link of zero. The last frame in a linked chain always has a forward link of zero. Notice that although frames 50789 through 50794 are contiguous, they are not considered logically contiguous.

Logically Contiguous Blocks

A *logically contiguous block* is a linked chain of physically contiguous frames where the linkage word of each frame indicates relative position within the block. NNCF is the

FID	NNCF	FORWARD LINK	BACKWARD LINK	NPCF
50623	0	50789	0	0
50789	0	50790	50623	0
50790	0	50791	50789	0
50791	0	50792	50790	0
50792	0	50793	50791	0
50793	0	50794	50792	0
50794	0	0	50793	0

FIG. 1-13. Linked chain values.

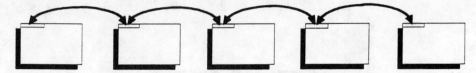

FIG. 1-14. Linked chain of frames.

number of frames that follow the current frame and NPCF is the number of frames that precede the current frame.

Although a block of frames is physically contiguous (a state that occurs after a full file restore) the frames may not be logically contiguous. Both the NNCF and NPCF remain zero. Because of the way that the Pick system utilizes this information, long strings can be traversed with fewer frame faults. As it turns out, logically contiguous blocks are preferable for efficiently storing and quickly traversing long data strings.

Within the virtual assembler, each process uses a set of index registers that reside in the primary control block. These registers are used as pointers to any byte position within a string. The register address indicates:

FID and DISPLACEMENT   The *FID* is the frame-id and the *displacement* is the number of bytes into the frame. A string position can be incremented by a pre-determined number of bytes. The virtual assembler mnemonic INC, increments a register position by a specified number of bytes. It looks like this:

    INC R15,D0

Where R15 is the register that is currently pointing to the beginning of the string and D0 is the accumulator reference that contains the incremental value.

Should the string exceed a frame in size, and the register is incremented to a position in the string that is three frames away, the intervening frames between the current register position and the final register position may or may not have to be read.

If the values of both the NNCF and NPCF are zero, all the intervening frames must be read. The system can only find a subsequent frame by following the FORWARD LINK to the next frame. Within 500 byte frames, traversing a 2000 byte string requires four frame faults.

Frames in a logically contiguous block not only have both FORWARD and BACKWARD links, but also indicate relative position within the block by using both NNCF, the next number of contiguous frames, and NPCF, the previous number of contiguous frames.

When the register is incremented by a value well beyond the current frame boundary, the system determines the number of frames away the end of the string resides, and reads the last frame of the string. The system "leap frogs" over strings which span multiple frames. Obviously, there is no advantage in traversing strings of two frames or less. Logically contiguous blocks are allocated within process workspace, saved ACCESS lists, BASIC object code items, or file groups with a separation greater than one. Figure 1-15 shows a block of seven logically contiguous frames. Notice that each frame keeps track of its relative position in the contiguous block, as shown in Fig. 1-16.

FID	NNCF	FORWARD LINK	BACKWARD LINK	PNCF
50788	6	50789	0	0
50789	5	50790	50788	1
50790	4	50791	50789	2
50791	3	50792	50790	3
50792	2	50793	50791	4
50793	1	50794	50792	5
50794	0	0	50793	6

FIG. 1-15. Logically contiguous block linkage values.

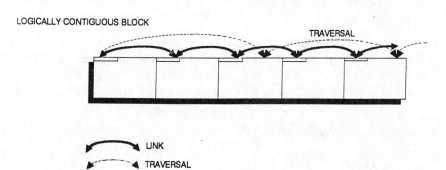

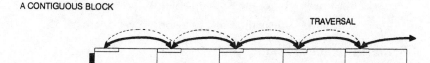

FIG. 1-16. Contiguous frames.

System Linkage Errors

There are a couple of system error messages that should make sense at this point. There isn't a lot that an applications programmer can do about them. But, if these occur, a better idea about what is happening is always an advantage.

Errors in Linked Frames

The wonderful thing about the Pick system is that when a register is incremented or decremented a number of bytes greater than the remaining number of bytes in the frame, the monitor automatically schedules a read of the next frame in the linked chain, and continues incrementing the register after the frame is read into memory. A read can only be scheduled if the next frame is known; the forward link. If the forward link is zero, the process runs into a virtual brick wall. The message is:

FORWARD LINK ZERO

Decrementing a register causes a similar message if the backward link happens to be zero.

BACKWARD LINK ZERO

For example, if an attempt to run any PICK/BASIC program immediately aborts with a FORWARD LINK ZERO! error and logging off and back on doesn't seem to clear up the problem, then it's a good bet that the links within process workspace have been corrupted. The only way to get around this is to make sure that the port is logged off and perform the command LINK-WS, to relink the workspace from another port. For example:

>LINK-WS   Links the workspace for all processes which are not logged on.

>LINK-WS 5   Links the workspace for the process on line 5.

>LINK-WS 5-15   Links the workspace for process 5 through 15.

Errors in Unlinked Frames

The message CROSSING FRAME LIMITS occurs when a register is incremented beyond the boundaries of an unlinked frame. This is something that should never be seen unless the programmer is delving into the virtual assembler. Otherwise, the ABS region might be corrupted. The command VERIFY-SYSTEM is used to make sure that all ABS frames are intact.

>VERIFY-SYSTEM   Calculates a check for every frame in ABS and compares it to a stored check sum value in the CHECK-SUM item found in the ERRMSG file. Each attribute in the CHECK-SUM item contains the expected check sum for the corresponding ABS frame.

If the system verifies but still aborts, call the dealer and raise hell.

The Overflow Table

The *overflow table* is the system's reservoir of unused disk frames. All processes must retrieve frames from and return frames to the overflow table. Only a single process at a time can alter the overflow table. Whenever a process accesses the table, it must lock the overflow table, or wait for another process to unlock the table and relinquish control. The current status of the overflow table can be reported by using the verb, POVF (print the overflow). The output of POVF is shown in Fig. 1-17. The following explains what happens when you invoke the POVF command:

>POVF   Displays the overflow table on the terminal.

>POVF (P)   Outputs the overflow table to the print spooler.

There are two major sections to the overflow table:

Contiguous blocks Indicated by the layout, StartFID- EndFID Blockcount. The available blocks of contiguous frames. These frames are used for file creation, saved ACCESS lists, PICK/BASIC object code, and, as a last resort, spooled print image and file overflow.

```
39805 (     15)
37531- 37536 :      6        38173- 38177 :      5
38560- 38564 :      5        39200- 39203 :      4
39223- 39226 :      4        39244- 39246 :      3
39434- 39441 :      8        39463- 39465 :      3
39467- 39469 :      3        39500- 39504 :      5
39523- 39528 :      6        39540- 39546 :      7
39578- 39580 :      3        39681- 39686 :      6
39692- 39695 :      4        39756- 39763 :      8
39784- 39790 :      7        39842- 39848 :      7
39870- 39875 :      6        41918- 41928 :     11
41961- 41969 :      9        41971- 41975 :      5
42078- 42112 :     35        42254- 42258 :      5
42265- 42271 :      7        42278- 42285 :      8
42328- 42355 :     28        42376- 42380 :      5
42395- 42451 :     57        42518- 42986 :    469
43027-111502 : 68476

        TOTAL NUMBER OF CONTIGUOUS FRAMES      : 69215
```

FIG. 1-17. Sample POVF output.

Linked overflow   Indicated by the layout, First FID (number of linked frames). These are the frames that could not be merged into the contiguous table. Linked overflow frames are retrieved one at a time and are used by file overflow, print spooling or any process that needs a single frame at a time.

The number of available entries in the contiguous table varies depending on the size of the frames on a particular implementation. The above example was generated on Pick release 2.1 on an AT clone, which uses 2K byte ABS frames.

Overflow Scenario

At this point, it would be helpful to describe the process of retrieving and returning overflow frames. The overflow table is constantly being modified by all routines that require additional workspace, file overflow, saved ACCESS lists, or print image spooling. On a system with many processes doing reporting, transaction updating or other file manipulation, the table can become fragmented in a matter of hours.

Primary file space and PICK/BASIC object code that need contiguous space, must retrieve frames from a large enough block in the contiguous table. If there is no contiguous block large enough to accommodate the request, then the process aborts with the message NOT ENOUGH DISK SPACE.

The majority of system routines require a single frame at a time. Single frame retrieval first attempts to extract a frame from the linked overflow portion of the table. If there are no linked frames available, the single frame is retrieved from the smallest contiguous block.

A newly restored system has no linked overflow, so all single frame extracts are from the contiguous portion of the table. No wonder fragmentation occurs almost immediately after a restore.

When a routine returns *frames* to *available overflow*, it first attempts to merge the frames into the contiguous table by checking if these frames fit at the beginning or end of existing blocks. If not, the frames are returned as a new contiguous entry. However, if the table is full, all returned frames can only be added to linked overflow. This is true whether the returned block is 1 or 100 frames. A 100 contiguous frame block is returned as if it were 100 single frames.

All R83 compatible systems store overflow as a flat table in a single frame of ABS, (frame 127 on most implementations). The amount of room in the contiguous table is directly related to the size of the frame. The newest versions of the Pick operating system (Open Architecture) handles the overflow table as a *balanced tree* (B-tree) that improves the process of table alteration. Frames can be more easily returned as contiguous blocks, more quickly retrieved, and the table size is effectively unlimited.

Because the overflow table is constantly being modified, the frame that it resides in is flagged write-required but is seldom the least recently used frame. This leads to a situation where the overflow table in physical memory does not match the overflow table on disk. Should the system decide to "take a dive" before memory can be flushed to disk, the stage becomes set for a corrupted database.

Corrupted databases usually manifest themselves as *group format errors* (GFEs). Any situation that can prevent the disk from being updated properly can create a GFE. The corruption of the overflow table is probably the most serious.

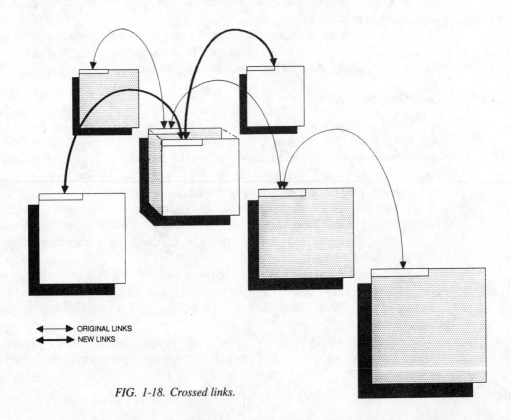

◄━━━► ORIGINAL LINKS
◄━━━► NEW LINKS

FIG. 1-18. Crossed links.

FID	NNCF	FORWARD LINK	BACKWARD LINK	PNCF
50623	0	50789	0	0
50789	0	50790	50623	0
50790	0	50791	50789	0
50791	0	78079	78078	0
78079	0	78080	50791	0
78080	0	0	78079	0

FIG. 1-19. *Crossed linkage values.*

Under this circumstance, during a system boot, the disk resident version of the overflow table is paged into memory. This version does not match the version lost during the system crash. None of the changes that occurred just prior to the crash are reflected in this version of the overflow table. Any routine that begins processing may extract overflow frames that are not truly available, thereby stepping on good data. This manifests itself in crossed linkages, shown in Fig. 1-18, where spooled print data crosses file overflow, or even worse, where two separate files have crossed overflow linkages. The crossed linkage valves are shown in Fig. 1-19.

This scenario should not scare anyone off. If a system is well maintained by periodic full saves and restores and power outages are prevented by the use of line conditioning equipment and uninterrupted power supplies, then this situation will never occur. However, if a user insists on not using UPS and line conditioners and the system experiences a power outage, then wish him or her good luck and try to get away quickly and quietly.

File Management

N O MATTER HOW WELL A DATABASE IS INITIALLY DESIGNED, SYSTEM INTEGRITY and throughput is heavily dependent on how well the database is maintained. A neglected database not only wreaks havoc with the speed at which data is retrieved and updated, but also increases the potential for database corruption.

The task of monitoring the state of the database usually falls to that special someone in the position of database administrator. (A position that Dick Pick calls the "Data Mama.") This person should be responsible for all database control tasks including monitoring the daily file statistics, file sizing, system growth, and system security.

This chapter is divided into four sections. The first covers the verbs for gathering database statistics and provides some insight in how to interpret them. The second discusses methods for file optimization in relation to file usage. The third provides a couple of step-by-step file sizing examples and an automated sizing routine. Finally, the fourth covers methods for implementing file and system security.

DATABASE STATISTICS

Statistics can be gathered for an entire system, individual accounts, or single files. All of the following verbs gather current statistics and display a potentially confusing amount of data.

Individual File Statistics

The four verbs covered in this section are STAT, GROUP, ITEM, and ISTAT. There are the ACCESS and TCL verbs available for reporting statistics on a single file. In fact, statistics gathering on large files can seriously degrade performance and take excessive amounts of time. Information on large files should depend on the statistics gathered during FILE-SAVE.

The use of these verbs is optional but proves quite helpful in gathering information about troublesome files. A troublesome file is a very large file or one that contains items that do not fit the basic rules of design.

- Item-ids should be sequential, right-weighted strings.
- Item size should be consistent and well within frame boundaries.

These rules are difficult to follow when dealing with text items (WP items, PICK/BASIC source code items, PROCS) which require random naming conventions and exceed the data frame size.

The STAT Verb

The ACCESS verb STAT uses the following syntax:

>STAT *filename* {*itemlist*} {*sellist*} {*modlist*} {*(options)*}

This outputs the total byte count, the item count, and the average bytes per item that meet the specified selection criteria. Performing STAT against the entire test file STAFF yields the following results:

STAT STAFF

STATISTICS OF STAFF :
TOTAL = 25569 AVERAGE = 87.26 COUNT = 293

The total bytes counted may vary slightly from the BYTES reported by the SAVE process. The byte count reported in the file statistics comes to 25862, while the STAT verb reports 25569. The STAT count gives a result which is 293 bytes less than the result of any other process. Coincidentally, one character per item is overlooked. The reason for this is that the SAVE process counts all characters in an item, including the 4-byte count field and all the embedded delimiters. The STAT verb counts all these characters except one—the *item-terminating segment mark* (xFF).

The GROUP Verb

The GROUP command provides statistics for every group in a specified file. However, GROUP does not provide a summary of the overall statistics. The following examples show the use of the GROUP command and options:

>GROUP STAFF

```
9907
005B 766
005F 128
005F 172
005F 645
0060 414
0056 33
005B 480
0056 55
0058 634
005A 403
0057 106
0053 601
0060 700
0032 205
0059 304
005F 656
0060 557
0059 88
0065 722
0050 117
0060 348
005F 502
005F 293
0049 22
0054 183
25 ITEMS 2222 BYTES 4/222 FRAMES
```

FIG. 2-1. First group of the GROUP statistics output.

Gathers hashing statistics for the groups in the STAFF file. Any file name can be specified. Outputs each groups base FID, item-id{s} and the size of each item. The summary line shows the total group size, item count, and frames in overflow.

> GROUP STAFF (N

Activates NOPAGE function on output to terminal.

> GROUP STAFF (P

Directs output to system printer, via spooler.

> GROUP STAFF (S

Suppresses output of item-id's.

The output of the GROUP command, shown in Fig. 2-1, is layed out in the following manner:

- The frame id (FID) of the primary frame of each group is displayed. In this case, 9907 is the FID of the first frame of primary space in the file STAFF. 9907 also happens to be the BASE frame of STAFF.

- The two column listing is the four digit number is the hexadecimal ITEM COUNT, the length of each item and the corresponding item-id presented in the order that they stored in the group. This provides a look at the "neighborhood" for each group. The first item in this group is item '766' which is hex 5B long.

- The group summary line indicates:

ii ITEMS *bbbb* BYTES *o/bbbb* FRAMES

> - *ii* ITEMS represents the number of items in the group. There are 25 items in this group.

> - *bbbb* BYTES indicates the total number of bytes in the group. There are 2,222 bytes in this group.

> - *o/bbbb* FRAMES summarizes the amount of overflow in the group. The number (o) preceding the slash (/) is the number of overflow frames. There are 4 overflow frames in the sample group. This number is only the overflow frames and does not include the primary frames. The number (bbbb) following the slash indicates the number of bytes used in the last frame of the group.

The ITEM Verb

The ITEM verb uses the system hashing algorithm to report the statistics for a specific group based on a specified item-id. This allows you to see the "neighborhood" of any item. The following examples show the use of the ITEM verb and options:

> > ITEM STAFF

Outputs the base FID of the group to which the specified item-id hashes, and a list of all item-id's that are currently hashed to the same group. The summary line shows the total group size, item count, and frames in overflow.

> > ITEM STAFF (N

Activates NOPAGE function on output to terminal.

> > ITEM STAFF (P

Directs output to system printer, via the spooler.

> > ITEM STAFF (S

Suppresses output of item-id's. Shows Checking for the item '101' in the file STAFF yields the output shown in Fig. 2-2. Notice that items '101' and '200' are at the bottom of the group. This indicates that these items have been recently modified. For more information on file updating, see the paragraph entitled "Group Flux" in Section 1 of Chapter 1, "File Structure."

The output layout of the ITEM verb is identical to the output of the GROUP verb except that the statistics are reported for only that group in which the item is found.

```
                                    >ITEM STAFF 101

                                    101
                                    9913
                                    0052 156
                                    0050 2
                                    0052 310
                                    0052 332
                                    0052 387
                                    0052 420
                                    0052 464
                                    005B 167
                                    005B 189
   FIG. 2-2. Sample ITEM output.    005B 409
                                    005B 838
                                    005B 915
                                    005B 959
                                    005B 970
                                    0060 112
                                    0060 475
                                    0060 508
                                    005F 72
                                    0064 706
                                    0058 805
                                    0050 101
                                    0076 200
                                    22 ITEMS 1978 BYTES 3/478 FRAMES
```

The ISTAT Verb

The ISTAT Verb displays the hashing distribution and summary statistics for the indicated file. An important goal for sizing any file is to achieve a flat distribution of the data. ISTAT proves useful for visualizing the item distribution.

> ISTAT STAFF

Outputs the item hashing distribution, based on the current modulo of the STAFF file.

> ISTAT STAFF (S

Suppresses display of the group histogram.
The current distribution of the STAFF file STAFF is shown in Fig. 2-3. And the distribution of the BP file is shown in Fig. 2-4.
Each line of the file histogram displays a summary of each group.

```
FRAMES BYTES ITMS
    nn    bbbb  ii *> > > > > > > > > > > > > > >
    nn
```

```
>ISTAT STAFF

FILE= STAFF MODULO= 11 SEPAR= 1      14:48:03  18 JUN 1988
FRAMES BYTES ITMS
      5    2222  25 *>>>>>>>>>>>>>>>>>>>>>>>>>
      5    2497  29 *>>>>>>>>>>>>>>>>>>>>>>>>>>>>>
      5    2344  26 *>>>>>>>>>>>>>>>>>>>>>>>>>>
      5    2481  28 *>>>>>>>>>>>>>>>>>>>>>>>>>>>>
      5    2106  24 *>>>>>>>>>>>>>>>>>>>>>>>>
      5    2361  27 *>>>>>>>>>>>>>>>>>>>>>>>>>>>
      4    1978  22 *>>>>>>>>>>>>>>>>>>>>>>
      6    2574  29 *>>>>>>>>>>>>>>>>>>>>>>>>>>>>>
      5    2399  27 *>>>>>>>>>>>>>>>>>>>>>>>>>>>
      5    2170  25 *>>>>>>>>>>>>>>>>>>>>>>>>>
      6    2730  31 *>>>>>>>>>>>>>>>>>>>>>>>>>>>>>>>
     56

ITEM COUNT=       293, BYTE COUNT=   25862, AVG. BYTES/ITEM=88.2
AVG. ITEMS/GROUP=26.6, STD. DEVIATION= 2.5, AVG.BYTES/GROUP=2351.0
```

FIG. 2-3. Sample ISTAT output for file STAFF.

```
>ISTAT BP

FILE= BP MODULO= 11 SEPAR= 1                  14:48:18  18 JUN 1988
FRAMES BYTES ITMS
      7    3118   8 *>>>>>>>>
     11    5014   6 *>>>>>>
     14    6954   6 *>>>>>>
     24   11612   9 *>>>>>>>>>
      8    3705   4 *>>>>
      7    3174   3 *>>>
     17    8482  10 *>>>>>>>>>>
     15    7171   9 *>>>>>>>>>
      8    3866   6 *>>>>>>
      8    3975   5 *>>>>>
     15    7446   6 *>>>>>>
    134

ITEM COUNT=        72, BYTE COUNT=   64517, AVG. BYTES/ITEM=  896.0
AVG. ITEMS/GROUP= 6.5, STD. DEVIATION= 2.2, AVG. BYTES/GROUP= 5865.1.
```

FIG. 2-4. Sample ISTAT for file BP.

The column headings are as follows:

- FRAMES   Indicates the number of frames used by each group. The FRAMES
           column totaled indicates the number of data occupied frames. The
           overflow frames can be determined by:
           OVERFLW = FRAMES − (MODULO*SEPAR)
- BYTES   Indicates the number of characters in each group.
- ITMS   The number of items in each group.

The following is the statistics summary line:

```
ITEM COUNT= nnn,  BYTE COUNT= bbbbb, AVG. BYTES/ITEM=b.b
AVG. ITEMS/GROUP=i.i, STD. DEVIATION=n.n, AVG.BYTES/GROUP=b.b
```

The elements of the ISTAT summary line are:

- ITEM COUNT   The total number of items in the file.
- BYTE COUNT   The total number of bytes in the file.
- AVG. BYTES/ITEM   The average number of bytes per item.
- AVG. ITEMS/GROUP   The average number of items per group. This is a result of the current file modulo and separation and gives a good indication of the file overflow.
- STD. DEVIATION   The standard deviation is based on the variance of the ITEMS/GROUP.
- AVG. BYTES/GROUP   The average number of bytes per group.

Here is a quick word about the STD. DEVIATION. The word is insignificant. "Why?" Standard deviation is based on the variance of the number of items per group, (not the number of bytes per group.) The best item distribution finds an equivalent number of items in every group of the file. As a result, the ideal standard deviation for a Pick file should be zero. However, a flat distribution of items can exist in an extremely undersized file. The standard deviation of a sampling of one group is always zero. Therefore, a file with 10,000 items using a modulo and separation of 1,1 has a standard deviation of 0.

The even distribution of items across a file is dependent on a single item design factor; item-id. The previous example for the file STAFF, Fig. 2-4, used randomly assigned numeric item id's. The next example, Fig. 2-5, shows the statistics for the same file. But, the item-id's have been reassigned as sequential numerics, forcing items to be hashed to different groups. The difference in distribution is apparent in the standard deviation.

```
FILE= STAFF MODULO= 11 SEPAR= 1              15:22:21  23 JUL 1988
FRAMES BYTES ITMS
      5   2411   27 *>>>>>>>>>>>>>>>>>>>>>>>>>>>
      5   2313   26 *>>>>>>>>>>>>>>>>>>>>>>>>>>
      5   2296   26 *>>>>>>>>>>>>>>>>>>>>>>>>>>
      5   2320   26 *>>>>>>>>>>>>>>>>>>>>>>>>>>
      5   2296   26 *>>>>>>>>>>>>>>>>>>>>>>>>>>
      5   2427   27 *>>>>>>>>>>>>>>>>>>>>>>>>>>>
      5   2422   27 *>>>>>>>>>>>>>>>>>>>>>>>>>>>
      5   2334   27 *>>>>>>>>>>>>>>>>>>>>>>>>>>>
      5   2372   27 *>>>>>>>>>>>>>>>>>>>>>>>>>>>
      5   2391   27 *>>>>>>>>>>>>>>>>>>>>>>>>>>>
      5   2312   27 *>>>>>>>>>>>>>>>>>>>>>>>>>>>
     55
```

```
ITEM COUNT=        293, BYTE COUNT=      25894, AVG. BYTES/ITEM=      88.3
AVG. ITEMS/GROUP=26.6, STD. DEVIATION=    .5, AVG. BYTES/GROUP=   2354.0.
```

FIG. 2-5. Sample ISTAT distribution with sequential item-ids.

Before the subject deviates from ISTAT, there are a couple of things to be aware of. First, ISTAT must pass through every frame of the file. This can take quite a while if the file is large. Second, on systems with fixed process workspace, ISTAT can only be used on files with modules up to 16,000 groups. Beyond that there isn't enough space to gather the statistics. Systems with floating workspace no longer have this problem. However, be aware that the hashing algorithm begins to introduce an aberration in the distribution (even with properly designed item-ids) as modules increase beyond 16K groups.

System and Account Statistics

The SAVE verb gathers current statistics for individual or all accounts. SAVE is used by the FILE-SAVE and ACCOUNT-SAVE processes to perform a formatted system save. The following is the general syntax:

>SAVE { (*options*) }

Invokes the system save processor. This verb is invoked by both the FILE-SAVE and ACCOUNT-SAVE process.

Some implementations require the following syntax:

>SAVE SYSTEM SYSTEM (*options*)

Pick R83 on the PC XT/AT simply requires:

>SAVE (*options*)

Please consult the system manuals for any differences. The available options are:

Option	Description
D	Saves data files.
F	Outputs filenames. When omitted, only SYSTEM-level names are displayed.
G	Log GFE's as they are encountered. Normally, GFE's cause the save process to require operator intervention for each occurrence. On many implementations (not all) this "fixes" any GFE's encountered.
I	Individual account (used in ACCOUNT-SAVE). The SAVE process prompts for entry of the account name.
N	No overflow space is required.
P	Outputs filenames to system printer.
R	Resets "group-changed flags" after saving. Optionally for use with the U option on incremental saves. ULTIMATE only!
S	Creates file statistics in STAT-FILE.
T	Outputs to magnetic tape.
U	Saves only the groups that have been changed since the last "full" save. See also the "R" option. ULTIMATE only!

Z   Indicates that tape should be created in SYS-GEN file order, rather than "regular" file order. This permits contents of system to be transferred to a different system. ULTIMATE only!

Different option combinations allow the SAVE processor to perform any of the following functions:

> SAVE (DIFT   Copy the contents of a single account to the magnetic tape. Display the file names as they are saved.

> SAVE (DFST   Copy contents of entire system to magnetic tape and produce file statistics data.

> SAVE (TUFD   Copy contents of CHANGED groups to magnetic tape (incremental FILE-SAVE).

> SAVE (DFGT   Copy the contents of the entire system to magnetic tape and fix GFE's encountered.

> SAVE (DFS   Gather statistics for the entire system. Save all data files, display the file names, and build statistics to the file STAT-FILE. Notice that since the T option is not used, there is no output to tape. "DFS" can be thought as an acronym for "dummy file save."

When the "S" option is used, the STAT-FILE is automatically cleared. If there is anything important in STAT-FILE, it better be copied to another file prior to performing any SAVE. Beware, the FILE-SAVE process always uses the "S"option modifying the SAVE verb. However, FILE-SAVE does provide the user with the option of whether or not to print the statistics report. It's a good idea to always print the file statistics.

A word about the "G" option. Please, don't believe that it can actually *fix* GFEs. There is no such thing as a GFE fix unless an amputation can be considered a cure for gangrene. The SAVE process truncates the offending group and skips writing it to tape. Beware, if the "G" is used without the "S," there is no record of the data loss unless the system happens to log the GFEs.

Interpreting File Statistics

The file statistics report is one of the most important parts of the daily FILE-SAVE procedure. However, nothing is useful unless it is understood. Figure 2-6 is an excerpt from a file statistics report showing the allocation of the files STAFF and BP.

NAME.......	BASE	M	S	....SIZE	ITEMS.	FRAMES	AV/ITM	FRM/GP	%UT.	PAD..	GFE
STAFF	9900	7	1	2,860	60	10	47	1.4	57	2,140	
STAFF*STAFF	9907	11	1	25,862	293	59	88	5.3	87	3,638	
BP	9411	11	1	3,136	69	11	45	1.0	57	2,364	
BP*BP	9422	11	1	64,517	72	134	896	12.1	96	2,483	

FIG. 2-6. Sample file statistics output.

The column headers are as follows:

Column Header	Description
NAME	The name of the file. A single name, such as STAFF, represents the DICT of the file. Two names separated by an asterisk indicate first the DICT name and the DATA area name. STAFF*STAFF represents the DATA area named STAFF defined within the DICT of STAFF. Another example might be STAFF*EXECS where STAFF is the DICT and EXECS is the DATA area.
BASE M S	The current base, modulo and separation of the file.
SIZE	The total number of data bytes. This includes the system delimiters and the item count field.
ITEMS	The total number of items in the file.
FRAMES	The total number of frames occupied by the file.
AV/ITM	The average number of bytes per item.
FRM/GP	The average number of frames in each group.
%UT	The percent of utilization. This is the ratio of the total number of data bytes to the total number of bytes within the frames being used.
PAD	The number of unused bytes within used frames.
GFE	The count of group format errors found in the file.

The gathered file statistics are stored in a file called the STAT-FILE. The file statistics report is an ACCESS formatted report of these items. Each item is assigned a unique item-id based on the position the file is found on the magnetic media. The item-id may or may not appear on the statistics report. The general form of the item-id is:

Reel# del *File#*

The indicator "del" is a delimiter separating the reel number (Reel#) and the file number (File#). For more detail on the STAT-FILE, see the SIZER program later in this chapter.

Utilization

Utilization indicates how much "head-room" is left in the file. The %UT (percent of utilization) is the ratio of the total number of data bytes (SIZE) to the total number of bytes available within the FRAMES used. The equation is:

Bytes available = *Frame size* * FRAMES

On the IBM AT implementation, there are 500 data bytes available per frame. In the case of the DATA file STAFF;

Bytes available = 500 * 59 = 29,500 bytes

The file is using 60 frames or 30K of disk space. The actual data SIZE is only 25,525 bytes. The ratio of 25,525 to 30,000 is the percent utilization.

%UT = 25,862 / 29,500 = .8766 or 88%

The *PAD* is the number of unused bytes in used frames. In this case, the PAD is 4,475 bytes.

3,638 / 29,500 = .1233 Or approximately 12%

The percent utilization is the inverse of the pad.

%UT = 100 − %PAD

Notice that these figures are ratios of totals, and are calculated independent of the current modulo and separation. Therefore, the percentage of utilization can be misleading. Utilization should be viewed from two perspectives in order to sort out potentially confusing points.

First, an interactively growing file must have room to grow without falling into extensive overflow. These files are best sized with a PAD proportional to the predicted growth. As an interactive file's utilization approaches 80%, it is time for reallocation.

Second, a static file seldom or very slowly grows. Interactive update and retrieval speed is not the important issue. The goal with this type of file is to use disk space as efficiently as possible. These files are targeted for utilization of over 90 percent. The next important factor in determining file allocation is the current amount of file overflow.

Overflow

How extensively a file is overflowed can be determined by either noting the average number of frames per group (FRM/GP) or by calculating the ratio of total overflow frames to total frames used. In either case, the results must be taken with a grain of salt. This grain of salt is called the *average bytes per item*, (AV/ITM). Files with items much smaller than a frame can be allocated with a minimum of overflow. Files with item sizes that approach or exceed a frame boundary seldom remain in primary space.

There is an item length threshold that varies according to frame size making it difficult to achieve efficient utilization of disk space. For example, using the ubiquitous 500-byte data frame, consider a file with items which approach and exceed 350 bytes. One item per group leaves 150 bytes free. Two items fill the first frame but leave the overflow frame with 300 unused bytes. Three items fill to the second frame of overflow, leaving the last frame with 450 unused bytes. The %UTIL in this kind of file can vary greatly and the percent of overflow proves misleading.

To determine the ratio of overflow frames, the number of frames in primary space must be compared to the total number of frames actually used. Primary space is calculated easily enough by multiplying the modulo by the separation:

Primary Frames = *Modulo * Separation*

Now, determine the number of frames in overflow.

Overflow Frames = *Total FRAMES − Primary*

And finally the ratio;

Overflow Ratio = *Overflow Frames / FRAMES used*

In the example above, the STAFF file has an average of 5.4 frames per group. In the case of the DATA section of the STAFF file;

Primary = 11 * 1 = 11
Frames = 59
Overflow Frames = 59 − 11 = 48 frames
Overflow ratio = 48/59 = .8135 or 81%

The disk utilization of an interactive file should be in the range of 50 to 60 percent. This leaves plenty of room for growth. However, utilization in a dynamic file is only meaningful if the amount of overflow is restricted.

Because the average item size in the STAFF file is 88 bytes, well under a frame, and the STAFF file is used extensively for interactive retrieval and update, 82% overflow can be considered excessive.

The BP file has 12.1 frames per group with an average itemsize of 896 bytes. In the case of the DATA section of the BP file;

Primary = 11 * 1 = 11
Frames = 134
Overflow Frames = 134 − 11 = 123 frames
Overflow ratio = 123/134 = .9179 or 92%

Due to the nature of a PICK/BASIC source code file, the size of each item can vary greatly. Average item size itself can be misleading if the range of item sizes is wide. Sizes range from 30 bytes to well over 3,000 bytes. Under these conditions, an average of 896 bytes is not a good indication of item size. In such a case, an item size value closer to 3,000 would be a better guess.

In a 500 bytes per frame environment, 3,000 bytes takes up 6 frames. Overflow is unavoidable due to the size of the items. Because 3,000 bytes is well above the size of a frame, the best possible overflow would be at least 6 frames. An average of 12.1 frames per group is a little over twice as much as would be expected for an interactive file, but is close to acceptable for a static file with large items. Therefore, a utilization of 92% is right in the ball park for this file. The priority for sizing a static file is efficient disk utilization and not the speed of interactive update.

FILE OPTIMIZATION

Both the initial file design and subsequent file allocation are critical to the performance of any Pick-based application. Unfortunately, not everyone has the luxury to redesign the database on an existing system. Therefore, the first and simplest course of action is to ensure that item-ids are assigned names that at least provide a chance for an even distribution. At the risk of being redundant (see Chapter 1), the main rule for assigning item-ids is:

Never use the same suffix!

If text items require identical extensions such as ---.BAK or ---.OLD, then reverse the order of the item-id. Make the extensions a prefix rather than a suffix. Therefore item-ids should follow the convention; OLD.---- or BAK.----.

The main course of action, which is available to all system users, is to ensure the correct file allocation. In fact, proper file size is the single most important factor in optimizing system throughput. Deciding how and when to initially allocate and then reallocate file space has traditionally caused some confusion and much consternation. In many cases, the answer has been to let the system do it via an automatic sizing routine.

An automatic routine can take the tedium away from scanning file statistics. It can look at the current statistical data and provide a new modulo and separation. However, calculating a file size is the mechanical, easy part. Determining which files need resizing is more difficult. The procedure for qualifying a file for reallocation is the most important task. An automatic sizing routine is a tool. And a tool is only as good as the skill of the user.

The problem is that an automatic file sizing routine does not know your database. A blanket resizing can be more of a hindrance than a help. Instead, run a sizing report without actually implementing the suggested sizes. An automatic routine should only provide suggestions. So, the task of file sizing falls back into the lap of trusty ol' Data Mama.

Determining File Usage

Files can be described as having traits that are either static or dynamic.

Static files are created, filled with data, and then repeatedly retrieved. Files that hold historical information may be considered static. Static files remain unchanged and therefore need not take part in a periodic resizing. Retrieval of a data in a static file is mainly for either interactive inquiry and/or ACCESS reporting.

Dynamic files are constantly growing or grow to a maximum, periodically cleared, and then refilled. Files used in a transactional environment are considered dynamic. Action against an interactive file is for both interactive update and inquiry. The secret to speedy retrieval and update from a dynamic file is the allocation of items per group allowing the system to get in and out of the file group quickly. This means there are few frames in any group. Group flux is restricted to 1 or 2 frames or at least the size of the largest item.

Well, so much for fantasy. Files that exist at either end of the spectrum are easy to deal with, because once a size is determined, changes seldom have to be made. Whether a file no longer grows or grows at a slow rate, it can be considered static.

File Reallocation

The hardest part about doing file reallocation is doing it the first time—and sometimes the second time. The trick is to get the database sizing under control. File usage can only be determined by reviewing file statistics on a weekly and monthly basis. The first few passes require a good many files to be expanded and contracted. Once the database has "settled" down, resizing should only occur on a handful of dynamic files.

If the size of each file is well below available physical memory, there is no significant difference in speed between restores with allocations and restores without reallocation. However, if the file size exceeds physical memory, restores with reallocation take roughly a factor of N longer than restoring without reallocation, where N is the number of items per group.

The great difference between restores with and without reallocation has to do with the order in which the SAVE process writes the data to tape. Because SAVE starts at the first group of a file and works its way through the groups in order of occurrence, the items on tape are clustered in the order that they exist in the file groups. A restore without reallocation fills each group in turn without needing to re-hash every item. The corresponding disk frames are read into memory, filled with data, and written to disk. The frames in each group are no longer needed once the group is filled. However, a restore with reallocation requires that every item be hashed to a new group. This tends to increase the number of frames that must be in memory and subsequently written to disk. After memory is initially filled, each frame fault requires a frame write, as well as a read. In a file that has 20 items per group, a restore which normally takes six hours would theoretically end up taking 5 days.

The following is a list of rules for sizing databases:

- Restores with reallocation of large files should be performed no more than two or three times a year.

- Don't bother to adjust a big file by a factor less than 20 percent of the current size. Any gains in throughtput prove to be insignificant.

- Ensure that there is extra space for growing files so that reallocation does not have to occur too often.

The fly in any file sizing ointment is a file that keeps growing and growing beyond any reasonably projected maximum. This may be either a large on-line transaction file that retains all history or a single "bucket" history file where all related history is dumped into large items.

Sizing an ever-growing file is also known as fighting a losing battle. These file types must be sized for 6 months to a year down the road. Although periodic full system saves and restores are essential for system health, constant resizing of large files during restore is not practical in a production environment.

A facility must be designed to allow periodic archival and purge of the "on-line" database. Periodically copying data to archive files and purging old business from current files keeps all file sizes at predictable and manageable levels. Associated files grow until the end of a period, and then they are once again cleared. File size can easily be predicted for the maximum file growth.

Downsizing should never be done as part of a file sizing regime. Downsizing is usually done solely when getting the database "in-hand."

- Run a test reallocation report prior to any periodic closing process which purges data. Allocation of disk space must reflect the "inflated" data requirements.

- Periodic archive and purge routines are not a luxury, they are a necessity.

Creating a new file always has an element of adventure. All you need to know is the average (or maximum) size of each item and the number of items projected for a known period of time. This point in time is called a *size review period*. File statistics are reviewed and alterations are recommended. This process has a heavy, techno-term, "trial and error." This is especially true when disk space is tight or if the projected modulo exceeds 64K groups. Most implementations do not allow such large modulos. Anyway, as stated previously, the hashing algorithm falls apart with modulos that get this large.

Packaged sizing or strict adherence to any "rule of thumb" does not solve the problem. The only solution is to downsize the file modulo so that hashing remains consistent and the distribution is even. So, don't be afraid to make special cases for very large files. Try reducing the modulo and increasing the separation to compact the file into less diskspace.

If you know the database and have asked all the right question concerning projected data retention, then an educated guess can be made. However, "packaged" application software must be generic and is usually distributed with a default size for all files. This leaves the task of file size tuning and qualification up to the user.

Using Multiple Data Areas

A good rule to follow for gaining optimum throughput and file allocation is to never keep more data in a single file than is absolutely necessary. This prevents the overhead of carrying a lot of useless garbage (out of date or unrelated data) around with every SELECT or other file sampling process. It also makes it much easier to size these files.

The approach to minimizing the amount of data stored in a single file is dependent on the ability of Pick file dictionaries to contain pointers to multiple data areas. The items in each data area follow identical layouts so that they can share the central defining dictionary.

Multiple data levels can be used to divide a file into distinct demographic or chronological entities. Rather than creating both the dictionary and data levels of a file in a single step, the dictionary and data levels are create dseparately. The general form is:

```
CREATE-FILE DICT filename mod,sep
CREATE-FILE DATA filename,dataname1 mod,sep
CREATE-FILE DATA filename,dataname2 mod,sep
CREATE-FILE DATA filename,datanamen mod,sep
```

Any reference to a single data area is expressed using the file name:

```
filename,dataname
```

Consider a mail order application where the main MAIL.ORDER file can contain in excess of 500,000 items. Each of these items has an average item size of 200 bytes, bringing the total size of the file to an excess of 100 megabytes. This would require a modulo (on a 500 byte frame system) of over 200,000 groups. This size file is cumbersome in all respects. Imagine the time needed to do a simple listing of all the items in region 5:

```
LIST MAIL.ORDER WITH REGION = "5'
```

Within this hypothetical mail order system, the main data demographic is geographical region. All retrieval and update is performed by region. Because a majority of the processing is done on each region separately, why not divide this file into separate regional data areas under a single MAIL.ORDER dictionary?

If the MAIL.ORDER file is divided into 10 regions, the average size of each file shrinks to 10 megabytes. The modulo of each data area becomes 20,000, well within the maximum limits:

```
CREATE-FILE DICT MAIL.ORDER 11,1
CREATE-FILE DATA MAIL.ORDER,REG1 20001
CREATE-FILE DATA MAIL.ORDER,REG2 20001
...
CREATE-FILE DATA MAIL.ORDER,REG10 20001
```

A report of items in region 5 does not require all the unrelated items to be processed. The command sentence now looks like this:

```
LIST MAIL.ORDER,REG5
```

Multiple data areas are also useful for archive and purge procedures. In this case, the data area containing the current information can retain the same name as the dictionary:

```
LIST filename
```

When the data area name matches the dictionary name, this is the same as saying:

```
LIST filename,filename
```

On each closing, a new data section is created based on some portion of the closing date as follows:

```
CREATE-FILE DATA filename,CLOSEJAN8modulo,separation
```

The data items are removed from the current file (purged) and placed in the history data area (Archive). Since the history is actually being kept in separate files, it is easy to T-DUMP the oldest ones to tape to make more room on the disk.

```
T-DUMP filename,CLOSEJAN77
DELETE-FILE DATA filename,CLOSEJAN77
```

Consolidating Data

There is a potential downside to this approach when it comes to consolidated reporting. Because the required information is spread between separate data areas, summarizing information requires extra work. To allow for consolidated reporting, each data area must be summarized, and the resulting information moved to a set of unique items in a separate SUMMARY data area. Once every current data area has been summarized and moved, the consolidated report can be generated from the SUMMARY file. To allow more control, a new SUMMARY area may be created for each consolidated reporting period, thereby, creating an on-line consolidated history. This approach is quite viable, especially when consolidated reporting is needed only once a quarter or once a year.

NOTE: The REFORMAT command is great for performing data summary and movement. See Chapter 6, "Access Programming."

FILE SIZING EXAMPLES

Here are a couple of practical approaches for choosing a file size. Breaking from tradition is always fun and sometimes dangerous. The two diverse methods are designed more for the user still living in the 500-byte world. The first method will suffice for all others.

Method 1: Interactive

The goals for sizing an interactive file are to;

- Provide room to grow
- Allow quick update and retrieval

which manifests itself in the file as;

- Little to no overflow
  (Maximum two frames if item sizes allow)
- 50-60% utilization.

Choosing Modulo

When actually calculating a new modulo, the only information needed is the AV/ITMS (average bytes per item) the ITEMS (number of items) and the size of a data frame (a system standard). The current SIZE is important, but it can be determined by multiplying the AV/ITMS by the ITEMS.

$$SIZE = AV/ITM * ITEMS$$

The goal in choosing a modulo for an interactive file is to keep each group below a frame in size. When items are small (as a transaction should be) it is easy to fit many into a frame without overflow. The best allocation for large items is one per group. GOOD LUCK! Handling large items in a system with unlimited item sizes is a bit different and will be discussed in "sizing files with unlimited item sizes."

Step1: Calculating possible modulo 1, MOD1:

$$MOD1 = SIZE / (Bytes\ per\ Frame)$$

In the case of the file STAFF; assuming a 500 byte data frame; the calculation looks like this:

$$MOD1 = 25,862 / 500 = 51.724$$

Using 500 bytes per frame assumes that the file is at a maximum and targets a utilization of over 85 percent. Growth is planned by using the projected number of items, not the current number. A utilization goal of 50 percent means that each frame is approximately half empty. Therefore, the file can effectively double in size before another reallocation is necessary.

Increasing the number of items by 50 percent achieves a utilization of 66 percent, as shown in Table 2-1. For a projected utilization of 50 percent, the projected number of items must be increased by 100 percent.

ITEMS = 293 + 293*(1.00) = 586 items

The average number of bytes per item (AV/ITMS) is 88. Therefore,

SIZE = 586 * 88 = 51568 bytes

and then,

MOD1 = 51568 / 500 = 105.136

Step 2:   Calculating possible modulo 2, MOD2:

MOD2 = *ITEMS*

The second possible modulo is the number of projected items. This covers the case of average item sizes which exceed a frame size. The projected number of items is used for possible modulo 2.

MOD2 = 586

The final task is to compare MOD1 and MOD2. The smaller of the two is closest to the best modulo. When item size is below the frame size, MOD1 is the smaller of the two. As items approach and exceed frame size, MOD2 becomes the smaller number.

MOD = *MOD1*, since MOD1 is less than MOD2.
MOD = *105*

There is an important rule for choosing a modulo:

Modulo must not be divisible by 5 or 2.

Growth	Target Utilization
.25	80%
.50	66%
1.00	50%
1.50	40%
2.00	33%

TABLE 2-1. Growth vs. Utilization.

Projected ITEMS = ITEMS + ITEMS*(growth)

This rule ensures that hashing will arrive at the best spread of items within a file. This should be obvious since the hashing algorithm multiplies each successive character in the item-id by 10. Any other numbers used for the modulo can leave many empty groups while forcing other groups into excessive overflow.

By the way, the old argument about prime number being the best is losing weight. Extensive studies at Pick Systems (performed personally by Mr. Pick) show that prime numbers are no better for hashing than modulos that are odd and not divisible by five. The now choice for the modulo is,

MOD = 107

Modulo 107 is the next highest prime number above 105. The decision can be confirmed by using the verb HASH-TEST.

The distribution resulting from a different modulo can be displayed by using HASH-TEST. The output of HASH-TEST is identical to ISTAT, except that it produces a report based on the predicted modulo, not the current. HASH-TEST need not be run every time a new file size is chosen. However, it is a good tool to diagnose the more difficult (poorly designed) files. The syntax for HASH-TEST is:

>HASH-TEST filename {itemlist} {sellist} {(options)}
TEST MODULO:modulo <cr>

This outputs the item hashing distribution of all items meeting the selection criteria with a test modulo, entered by operator. The option available is:

S Suppresses display of histogram.

The following invokes a test distribution on the new modulo:

>HASH-TEST STAFF (S
TEST MODULO: 107

Using the S option to supress the histogram generates the following:

```
FILE= STAFF MODULO= 107 SEPAR= 1                   15:18:18 18 JUN 1988
FRAMES BYTES ITMS
   109
ITEM COUNT=        293, BYTE COUNT=      25862,   AVG.    BYTES/
                                                          ITEM=     88.2.
AVG. ITEMS/GROUP=   2.7, STD. DEVIATION=  1.4, AVG. BYTES/GROUP=  241.7.
```

The average bytes per group is just less than 250, half the frame size. Our percent of utilization should be around the 50 percent mark. Calculate the percent utilization:

TOTAL FRAMES	= 109
Bytes available	= 109 * 500 = 54500 bytes
SIZE or BYTE COUNT	= 25862 bytes
%UTilization	= 25862 / 54500 = .4745 or 48%

Forty-eight percent utilization is close enough for rock and roll. However, there are still two frames of overflow. The STAFF file is using randomly assigned numeric item-id's. Even the best laid plans can't prevent overflow if the item-id's are not sequential and the same length.

Choosing Separation

The separation is chosen only when and where it is appropriate. If your system does not support the separation parameter, then don't use one. Anyway, separation is useless when frame sizes exceed 1K bytes.

The separation has nothing to do with the randomization of data within a file. Separation is simply the number of frames allocated to each group in primary space. Separation is a parameter that has gone by the wayside in many implementations. This is especially true of system with a minimum of 2048 bytes per frame. The larger the data frame size, the less the need for separations greater than 1. However, systems that still use 512-byte data frames can still get some benefit from higher separations.

For the world of the 500 byte frame, separation can be used to increase database integrity. Because overflow is inevitable when average item sizes exceed 500 bytes, separation is used to pre-allocate overflow so the overflow table is fragmented less, and the data can be kept in logically contiguous blocks.

Separation is also useful when sizing large files which have a calculated modulo of over 64K groups. Most implementations do not support modulos larger than this, so the modulo must be reduced and the separation increased to pre-allocate the predicted and inevitable overflow space.

Back to the case at hand. If the average item size is well below the size of a frame, then the number of bytes per group is below a frame size. So, the number of frames per group will not be over 1. Therefore, a separation of 1 is appropriate.

If the item size exceeds the frame size, overflow is guaranteed. The best possible distribution is 1 item per group. In this case, separation is equal to the number of frames occupied by the average item:

SEPAR = 1 + INT(AV/ITM / 500)

If you know the average size of a group, why force all the items into linked overflow? Keep it in contiguous space.

Method 2: Sizing a Static or Batch File

Method 2 is only appropriate for those systems which still use 500 byte data frames and do not have unlimited item size. All other systems can use method 1 and simply target utilization.

The goal of sizing a batch file is to achieve a high percentage utilization with a minimal amount of overflow. This optimum condition can easily be reached when item sizes are well below a frame. As item sizes approach frame sizes, it gets increasingly difficult to fill a frame without overflowing and wasting space in the next frame. There is a problem with 500 byte frames that does not crop up as soon in large frames. The larger the frame,

TABLE 2-2. *Static and Large Item File Sizing Chart.*

(This chart assumes 500 bytes of data per frame)

Avg Item Size	Avg Items per Group	Avg Bytes per Group	Min Separ
20	22.0	440	1
35	13.0	455	1
50	9.0	450	1
75	12.0	900	2
100	9.0	900	2
125	7.5	937	2
150	6.0	900	2
175	8.0	1400	3
200	7.0	1400	3
250	5.8	1450	3
300	6.4	1920	4
350	5.5	1925	4
400	4.8	1920	4
500	3.8	1900	4
1000	3.0	3000	6
5000	1.0	5000	10

the larger the average item sizes can be without requiring overflow. Also, there is a side benefit. ACCESS selects work faster.

Choosing Modulo

Choose a modulo using this chart (gratefully lifted from ancient, rainbow colored documentation). You'll find that this gives a very even spread of items across the file and achieves a utilization in excess of 90 percent.

Step 1 Using the average item size, select the number of items in a group, as presented in Table 2-2.

Step 2 Calculate the modulo using the formula:

Number of Items / Items per group = approximate modulo

Step 3 Choose the minimum separation.

Separation and Large Items

Separation can be used to optimize throughput when handling groups of large items. This marvelous feature can be directly attributed to the fact that each frame in a contiguous group knows its relative position to the other frames.

As previously described, the linkage word indicates the number of frames that are preceding and following the current frame in a contiguous block. This is used whenever a register is incremented any number of bytes beyond the current frame boundary. Rather than having to read all the frames within the linked chain, the system can jump across the logically contiguous block and directly address the frame where the end of the string resides.

Compare the group layout of linked versus logically contiguous frames in a case where the average item size is 1,900 bytes (4 500-byte frames), as shown in Fig. 2-7.

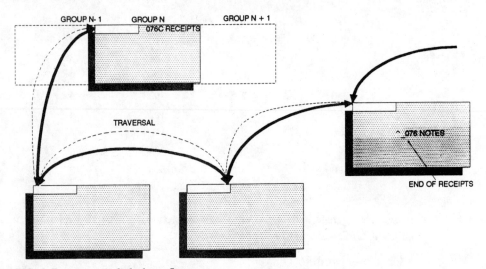

FIG. 2-7. A group in linked overflow.

To retrieve the item 'NOTES', which is the second item in the group, the system must pass through the entire first item, 'RECEIPTS'. In a chain of linked frames, all the frames occupied by the first item must be read. This requires four frame faults. Now take a look at the same file group using a separation of four, as shown in Fig. 2-8.

Because these frames are logically contiguous, the system needs only to read the first frame and the last frame of NOTES, requiring two frame faults.

Compare Techniques: Method1 versus Method2

Both methods can give the same result when the average size of the items is below a threshold of 75 bytes, the predicted number of bytes per group can remain well within a 500 byte frame boundary. However, the results become quite different as item sizes approach the 500 byte limit.

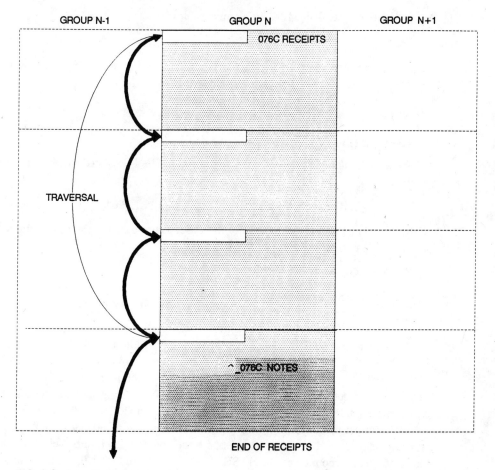

FIG. 2-8. A contiguous group.

Consider a hypothetical case where the average bytes per item, AV/ITM, is 350 and the projected number of items, ITEMS, is 1000. The total number of bytes, SIZE, is calculated as follows:

$$SIZE = AV/ITM * ITEMS = 350,000$$

Using Method 1

The following shows how a solution is reached using Method 1:

M1 = 350,000 / 500 = 700

The next odd number not divisible by 5 is,

M1 = 701

Because the number of items is 1000,

M2 = 1000

M1 is definitely less than M2. Not by much, but it is less.

MODULO = 701

Because the average item size is below a frame, the separation is 1. So, the new size suggestion is

701,1

Using Method 2

An average item size of 350 yields from the table a predicted number of items per group of 5.5.

MODULO = *ITEMS* / *items per group* = 1000 / 5.5 = 181.8181

A MODULO of 181 is close enough for this case. The separation can be determined from the "Min Separation" column.

SEPARATION = 4

The new suggested file size is:

181,4

Method 1 reserves 701 frames of primary space, while method 2 reserves (181 * 4) 724 frames. Without using separation, method 2 reserves only 181 frames.

A "perfect" test file is used for this example. All the items are the same size. The item-id's are sequential, left-filled zero numerics. Performing test hashing on this file indicates the total number of frames used by each method. The only discrepancy is the average bytes per item. The test was performed for items with 350 bytes of data. Each item also contains at least 13 bytes of overhead for the count and delimiter fields. The average size of 363 that is reported on the HASH-TEST statistics in Fig. 2-9, includes these bytes.

The histogram is suppressed in interests of brevity and page space. This file, sized for interactive use, requires 1000 frames. Notice that the average bytes per group is just over 500, but because of the item size, 99 frames are still forced into overflow.

```
FILE= TEST2 MODULO= 701 SEPAR= 1                08:23:08  21 JUN 1988
FRAMES BYTES ITMS
  1000

ITEM COUNT=      1000, BYTE COUNT=   363000, AVG. BYTES/ITEM=    363.0
AVG. ITEMS/GROUP= 1.4, STD. DEVIATION=   .4, AVG. BYTES/GROUP=   517.8.
```

FIG. 2-9. HASH-TEST using method 1.

The batch sizing uses a total of 819 frames. The average bytes per group is just over 2000. If a separation of 4 is chosen, then primary space is 732 frames. The number of linked overflow frames is (819-732) 89 frames. The average items per group, 5.5, is "right-on" as predicted by the chart. Overall, method 2, shown in Fig. 2-10, uses fewer frames than method 1.

```
FILE= TEST2 MODULO= 181 SEPAR= 1              08:22:22  21 JUN 1988
FRAMES BYTES ITMS
   819

ITEM COUNT=        1000, BYTE COUNT=   363000, AVG. BYTES/ITEM=    363.0
AVG. ITEMS/GROUP=  5.5, STD. DEVIATION=    .5, AVG. BYTES/GROUP= 2005.5.
```

FIG. 2-10. HASH-TEST using method 2.

Sizing with Unlimited Item Size

As described in Chapter 1, unlimited item sizes are handled by storing these items indirectly off primary space. Instead, a 10 to 15-byte pointer is stored in the primary space.

Usually, items are stored in primary space until they grow above the system designated threshold. This size threshold is directly related to the size of a frame. If the frame can hold 1000 bytes of data, the size threshold may be around 800 bytes. Items that are 799 bytes long are stored in primary space. Items that are 800 bytes long are stored in contiguous blocks outside of primary space.

This creates a new view of large items. Sizing on systems with unlimited item sizes is quite different from sizing on the "classic" Pick system. For example, consider a file which has 50 items, each in excess of 5000 bytes. On a system that stores large items indirectly, each item takes up a maximum of 15 bytes in primary space. The calculation of the total SIZE calculation is concerned only with this pointer item.

SIZE = *bytes per item * number of items* = 15 * 50 = 750
MOD1 = 750 / 1000 *bytes per frame* = .75 or 1
MOD2 = *number of items* = 1000

MOD1 is definitely less than MOD2. Therefore the MODULO and SEPARATION for such a file would be:

1,1

On a system without unlimited item size, this file needs a MODULO close to 1000 (the item size exceeds a frame size so MOD2 is definitely less than any calculated MOD1) and a SEPARATION of over 10.

Although unlimited item sizes solves the problem of handling large items, it makes statistics more difficult to read and allocation difficult to predict without an automated system process. Try to figure out a correct file size when the average size of an item is right on the threshold. Some items are kept in primary space, while others are stored indirectly. As these new systems become more and more accepted, file allocation by hand will become less and less common.

Implementing New File Sizes

The way the user goes about implementing new sizes is up to individual needs. In most cases, placing the new modulo and separation in attribute 13 of the D-pointer is sufficient. The next full restore will take care of the reallocation. However, sometimes it is necessary to resize files immediately without waiting for a full save and restore.

One method is to create a file with the new modulo and separation, copy over the contents of the original file, and delete the original file. There are many variations to creating a new file. This method can only be used if there is enough disk space to simultaneously support two copies of the file. In the next example, the data portion is being resized. Therefore, only the data portion has to be dealt with. The file name is STAFF and the data resides in the data area name STAFF.

1) First, create a new data area in STAFF called RESIZE.

   >CREATE-FILE DATA STAFF,RESIZE newmod,newsep

2) Then, copy the contents of STAFF,STAFF to STAFF,RESIZE.

   >COPY STAFF,STAFF *
   TO:(STAFF,RESIZE

3) Next, delete the original data area.

   >DELETE-FILE DATA STAFF,STAFF

Now, the task gets a little more difficult. The new data area STAFF,RESIZE must be renamed STAFF,STAFF. Some implementations have a verb called RENAME-FILE or COPY-FILE that performs this task. More often, this must be developed by the user. All that needs to be done is to copy the D-pointer item, RESIZE, in the DICT of STAFF to a new D-pointer item named STAFF, and delete the original pointer.

The above technique works just dandy on generic Pick. However, on a growing number of implementations, the COPY process excludes D-pointers from being copied and EDIT does not allow attributes 1-4 in D-pointers to be altered. This is a very good thing. Otherwise, pointers would easily be wiped out left and right. To accomplish the task at hand, the system must be "fooled" into thinking that the D-pointer is not a file defining item. Is this dangerous? YOU BET!

1) First, use the verb :SWE, which switches the D in a D-pointer to an E, effectively turning the pointer into an unclassified item.

   :SWE DICT STAFF RESIZE

2) Then, copy the item to its new name. Notice the D option to delete on the copy.

   >COPY DICT STAFF RESIZE (D
   TO:STAFF

3) Now, change the D-pointer back into a pointer type item. The verb to use is :SWD.

   >:SWD DICT STAFF STAFF

The above can be automated within PROC or PICK/BASIC. Most implementations still don't restrict PICK/BASIC programs from accessing and writing D-pointers.

The possible dangers of the above procedures cause many system analysts to refuse to even attempt it. Unfortunately, there is no other alternative on many systems. However, the advent of a new verb, COPY-FILE, has made the use of the :SWE obsolete. The COPY-FILE verb is a TCL-II verb which is used to rename or move existing files and follows the same syntax as the COPY verb. To perform the resizing of the STAFF file, enter the following commands:

1) First you enter the following:

```
>COPY-FILE DICT STAFF STAFF
TO:OLDSTAFF
```

The COPY-FILE verb automatically deletes the original item when the copy is complete. There is now a data section called OLDSTAFF on the dictionary of STAFF.

2) The new STAFF data section can now be created as follows:

```
>CREATE-FILE DATA STAFF,STAFF newmod,newsep
```

3) Now, the data in the old data section can be copied to the new data section.

```
>COPY DATA STAFF,OLDSTAFF *
TO:(DATA STAFF
```

4) When the copy is complete, the old data section can be deleted.

```
>DELETE-FILE DATA STAFF,OLDSTAFF
```

The last way to implement a new size on a single file is to T-DUMP the file to tape, delete the original file, create the new file, and T-LOAD the data. This is by far the easiest, safest and fastest method.

The Sizer Program

Figure 2-11 is a semi-automatic sizing routine. It is designed to interrogate the STAT-FILE by account or per file. After the statistics records are retrieved, SIZER displays the current statistics including percent utilization and overflow. The sizing algorithm is based on file usage (transaction or batch) and the predicted growth factor.

```
    SIZER
001 *PROGRAM SIZER
002 *Resize files according to STAT-FILE and file type
003 *H.E.Rodstein Computer Consultants (C) 1988,89
004 *
005 PROMPT ''
006 *
007 OPEN 'MD' TO MD ELSE STOP 201,'MD'
008 OPEN 'STAT-FILE' TO STAT.FILE ELSE STOP 201,'STAT-FILE'
009 *
010 EQU FRAMESIZE TO 500 ;* Change as appropriate
011 *
```

FIG. 2-11. The SIZER program listing.

```
012 CNT = 0
013 QREC = ''
014 QFILE = 'RFQFILE'
015 EOS = @(-3)
016 EOL = @(-4)
017 *
018 SCR.DISPLAY = @(10,4):'* Determining Modulo and Separation *'
019 SCR.DISPLAY = SCR.DISPLAY:@(10,7): 'Account Name     ='
020 SCR.DISPLAY = SCR.DISPLAY:@(10,8): 'File Name        ='
021 SCR.DISPLAY = SCR.DISPLAY:@(10,9): 'Avg Item Size    ='
022 SCR.DISPLAY = SCR.DISPLAY:@(10,10):'Item Count       ='
023 SCR.DISPLAY = SCR.DISPLAY:@(10,11):'Modulo           ='
024 SCR.DISPLAY = SCR.DISPLAY:@(10,12):'Separation       ='
025 SCR.DISPLAY = SCR.DISPLAY:@(10,13):'Frames Used      ='
026 SCR.DISPLAY = SCR.DISPLAY:@(10,14):'Size (Bytes)     ='
027 SCR.DISPLAY = SCR.DISPLAY:@(10,15):'% Utilized       ='
028 SCR.DISPLAY = SCR.DISPLAY:@(10,16):'New Mod,Sep      ='
029 *
030 1 * Select stat items to be processed
031 *
032 PRINT @(-1):@(10,0):@(-13):'File Sizing':@(-14):
033 PRINT @(10,18):EOS:'Enter (S)ingle file, (A)ccount files, e(X)it ':
034 INPUT FUNCTION,1:
035 FUNCTION = OCONV(FUNCTION,'MCU')
036 *
037 BEGIN CASE
038   CASE FUNCTION = 'X'
039     GOTO 90
040   CASE FUNCTION = 'A'
041     PRINT @(10,19):EOL:"Enter ACCOUNT or (*) for All " :
042     INPUT ANS
043     IF ANS = '' THEN GOTO 1
044     IF ANS = '*' THEN ANS = ''
045     ANS = OCONV(ANS,'MCU')
046     EXECUTE 'SSELECT STAT-FILE BY *A1 WITH *A1 = "':ANS:']"'
047 * GET(MSG.,1) ERR ELSE ERR = ''
048     ERR = SYSTEM(17)
049     IF ERR = 401 THEN GOTO 1
050   CASE FUNCTION = 'S'
051     PRINT @(10,19):EOL:"Enter ACCOUNT*FILE*FILE ":
052     INPUT ANS
053     IF ANS = '' THEN GOTO 1
054     ANS = OCONV(ANS,'MCU')
055     EXECUTE 'SELECT STAT-FILE WITH *A1 = "':ANS:'"'
056 * GET(MSG.,1) ERR ELSE ERR = ''
057     ERR = SYSTEM(17)
058     IF ERR = 401 THEN GOTO 1
059   CASE 1
060     GOTO 1
061 END CASE
062 PRINT SCR.DISPLAY:
063 *
064 10 * Get the next STAT-FILE item-id ...
```

FIG. 2-11 continues.

```
065 *
066 READNEXT ID ELSE
067     PRINT @(10,20):EOS:'COMPLETE... ':CNT:' files resized'
068     PRINT @(10,21):'Press Any Key to Continue ':
069     INPUT ANS,1:
070     GOTO 1
071 END
072 * ... and the record
073 READ REC FROM STAT.FILE,ID ELSE GOTO 10
074 LIN     = REC<1>
075 ACCT    = FIELD(LIN,'*',1)
076 DICT.FN = FIELD(LIN,'*',2)
077 IF ACCT = DICT.FN THEN GOTO 10
078 DATA.FN = FIELD(LIN,'*',3)
079 MODULO  = REC<4>
080 SEPAR   = REC<5>
081 FRAMES  = REC<12>
082 ITMCNT  = REC<6>
083 TOTAL.BYTES = REC<7>
084 *
085 * Point to the other accounts MD
086 * or DICT level "D" (data) pointers.
087 *
088 QREC<1> = 'Q'
089 QREC<2> = ACCT
090 QREC<9> = 'L'
091 QREC<10> = '10'
092 *
093 IF DATA.FN = '' THEN
094   * Point to the target account's MD
095   QREC<3> = ''
096   ERR = 'MD ':ACCT
097   XFN = DICT.FN
098 END ELSE
099   * Point to the target file DICT
100   * to retrieve DATA level pointer
101   QREC<3> = DICT.FN:',':DATA.FN
102   ERR = 'DICT ':DICT.FN
103   XFN = DATA.FN
104 END
105 WRITE QREC ON MD,QFILE
106 OPEN 'DICT',QFILE TO POINTER.FILE ELSE STOP 201,ERR
107 READ POINTER FROM POINTER.FILE,XFN ELSE GOTO 10
108 IF POINTER<1> = 'Q' THEN GOTO 10 ;* NO Q pointers
109 *
110 * Calculate the summary info.
111 *
112 UTIL = TOTAL.BYTES/(FRAMES*FRAMESIZE)
113 IF ITMSIZ THEN ITMSIZ=INT(TOTAL.BYTES/ITMCNT) ELSE ITMSIZ=0
114 PRIMARY = MODULO*SEPAR
115 OVERFLOW= FRAMES-PRIMARY
116 PCOVER  = OVERFLOW/FRAMES * 100
117 *
```

FIG. 2-11 continues.

```
118 * Display it.
119 *
120 PRINT @(29,7):EOL:ACCT:
121 PRINT @(29,8):EOL:DICT.FN:
122 IF DATA.FN # '' THEN PRINT ',':DATA.FN:
123 PRINT @(29,9):EOL:ITMSIZ:
124 PRINT @(29,10):EOL:ITMCNT:
125 PRINT @(29,11):EOL:MODULO:
126 PRINT @(29,12):EOL:SEPAR:
127 PRINT @(29,13):EOL:FRAMES        "L#10":
128 PRINT 'Primary Space' 'L#16':PRIMARY:
129 PRINT @(29,14):EOL:TOTAL.BYTES "L#10":
130 PRINT 'Overflow''L#16':OVERFLOW:
131 PRINT @(29,15):EOL:ICONV(UTIL,"MR2")"L#10":
132 PRINT '%Overflow''L#16':PCOVER:
133 PRINT @(29,16):EOS:
134 *
135 LOOP
136   PRINT @(10,18):'Size as a (T)ransaction or (B)atch file, ':
137   PRINT '(S)kip or E(X)it ':
138   INPUT TYPE,1:
139   TYPE = OCONV(TYPE,'MCU')
140 UNTIL TYPE # '' AND INDEX('SXTB',TYPE,1) DO REPEAT
141 IF TYPE = 'S' THEN GOTO 10
142 IF TYPE = 'X' THEN
143   GOSUB 1000 ;*BLEED ANY ACTIVE LIST
144   GOTO 1
145 END
146 IF TYPE='B' AND FRAMESIZE>500 THEN TYPE='T'
147 *
148 LOOP
149  PRINT @(10,19):'Enter a percentage (in decimal) growth factor ':
150   INPUT FAC
151 UNTIL (FAC='') OR NUM(FAC) DO REPEAT
152 IF FAC = '' THEN FAC = 0
153 *
154 * Find the MODULO
155 *
156 ITMCNT = ITMCNT + INT((ITMCNT*FAC)+.5) ;* GROWTH
157 BEGIN CASE
158  CASE TYPE = 'B'
159    BEGIN CASE
160      CASE ITMSIZ >= 3000 ; BYTEPERGROUP = ITMSIZ
161      CASE ITMSIZ >= 1000 ; BYTEPERGROUP = 3000
162      CASE ITMSIZ >=  500 ; BYTEPERGROUP = 1900
163      CASE ITMSIZ >=  400 ; BYTEPERGROUP = 1920
164      CASE ITMSIZ >=  350 ; BYTEPERGROUP = 1925
165      CASE ITMSIZ >=  300 ; BYTEPERGROUP = 1920
166      CASE ITMSIZ >=  250 ; BYTEPERGROUP = 1450
167      CASE ITMSIZ >=  200 ; BYTEPERGROUP = 1400
168      CASE ITMSIZ >=  175 ; BYTEPERGROUP = 1400
169      CASE ITMSIZ >=  150 ; BYTEPERGROUP =  900
170      CASE ITMSIZ >=  125 ; BYTEPERGROUP =  937
```

FIG. 2-11 continues.

```
171     CASE ITMSIZ >=  100 ; BYTEPERGROUP =  900
172     CASE ITMSIZ >=   50 ; BYTEPERGROUP =  450
173     CASE ITMSIZ >=   35 ; BYTEPERGROUP =  455
174     CASE ITMSIZ >=   20 ; BYTEPERGROUP =  440
175     CASE 1               ; BYTEPERGROUP =  440
176     END CASE
177     MODULO = INT(ITMCNT/(BYTEPERGROUP/ITMSIZ))
178     SEPAR = INT((BYTEPERGROUP/FRAMESIZE)+.5)
179   CASE TYPE = 'T'
180     BYTEPERGROUP = FRAMESIZE
181     MODULO = INT(ITMCNT/(BYTEPERGROUP/ITMSIZ))
182     IF ITMCNT < MODULO THEN MODULO = ITMCNT
183     SEPAR = 1 + INT((ITMSIZ/FRAMESIZE))
184 END CASE
185 *
186 * PRIME NUMBER
187 *
188 PRIME = 0
189 FOR J = MODULO TO J+1 UNTIL PRIME
190   IF REM(J,2) THEN
191     DENOM = 3
192     MAX.DIV = INT(SQRT(J))+1
193     LOOP UNTIL DENOM>=MAX.DIV OR NOT(REM(J,DENOM)) DO
194       DENOM = DENOM + 2
195     REPEAT
196     IF DENOM >= MAX.DIV THEN
197       MODULO = J
198       PRIME = 1
199     END
200   END
201 NEXT J
202 *
203 50 * Display the new MODULO and Separation.
204 *
205 PRINT @(29,16):MODULO:',':SEPAR
206 *
207 POINTER<13> = '(':MODULO:',':SEPAR:')'
208 *
209 *PRINT @(10,17):'Pointer    --> ': POINTER :
210 *
211 PRINT @(10,21):"Press (U)pdate, (S)kip, or e(X)It ":
212 INPUT ANS,1:
213 ANS = OCONV(ANS,'MCU')
214 BEGIN CASE
215   CASE ANS = 'X'
216     GOSUB 1000 ;* BLEED THE LIST
217     GOTO 1
218   CASE ANS = 'S'
219     GOTO 10
220 END CASE
221 *
222 WRITE POINTER ON POINTER.FILE,XFN
223 CRT ' Updated!'
```

FIG. 2-11 continues.

```
224 RQM
225 CNT = CNT + 1
226 GOTO 10
227 *
228 90 *
229 *
230 PRINT @(10,19):EOS:'File Re-Allocation Complete.  ':
231 PRINT CNT:' file(s) resized.'
232 STOP
233 *
234 *
235 * Subroutines
236 *
237 1000 * Bleed remaianing elements in an active list
238 *
239 ELIST = 0
240 LOOP
241     READNEXT ID ELSE ELIST = 1
242 UNTIL ELIST DO REPEAT
243 RETURN
244 *
245 *
246 END
```

FIG. 2-11 ends.

Program Highlights

SIZER must be able to update attribute 13 of the targeted file D-pointer item. There-fore, a Q-pointer item has to be created to address the file level where the D-pointer resides. To resize a dictionary level file, the D-pointer item in the account MD must be modified. To resize the DATA level, the D-pointer in the current file dictionary must be altered:

```
    PAYABLES
001 D
002 13445
003 29
004 1
005
006
007
008
009 L
010 10
011
012
013 (91,1)
```

SIZER's first task is to select the items in STAT-FILE. Then ACCESS SELECT is exe-cuted in order to create an active list of statistics items.

ID:*reel*:*seqn*	The *reel* is the reel number of the tape or diskette. The *sequence* is the numeric file tape position number.
001 *fname*	A unique file identifier made up of the account, file dictionary, and data level names. ACC*DICTNAME*DATANAME.
002 *level*	The level of the file in the system hierarchy. 1 is an account MD, 2 is a file DICT and 3 is file DATA.
003 *base*	The base FID of the file. The first frame in the first group of a file.
004 *modulo*	The file modulo.
005 *sep*	The file separation.
006 *items*	The number of items in the file.
007 *size*	The total number of data bytes.
010 *mx/gp*	The maximum number of items in a group.
011 *mn/gp*	The minimum number of items in a group.
021 *gfe*	The number of GFE's found in the file.
022 *dcovr*	The number of frames taken up by cataloged DC file type items.

FIG. 2-12. *STAT-FILE item layout.*

Because the STAT-FILE items are keyed by tape position, and not by file name, selection criteria uses the generic definition item-id, *A1, to ensure that the file name in attribute 1 is always addressed. Figure 2-12 shows the layout for the STAT-FILE item.

File names which are a single name, such as CLASS, contain the statistics for the master dictionary of the CLASS account. File names containing the account name and a file DICT name, such as CLASS*STAFF, contain the statistics for the DICT of STAFF. File names containing three designations, such as CLASS*STAFF*STAFF or CLASS-*STAFF*EXECS, hold the statistics for each DATA level file.

The code for selecting an *(A)ccount* is:

```
EXECUTE 'SSELECT STAT-FILE BY *A1 WITH *A1 = " ":ANS:']"'
```

If the value of ANS is "CLASS," then the statement is read as:

```
SSELECT STAT-FILE BY *A1 WITH *A1 = "CLASS]"
```

ANS can also include the file DICT and DATA level names. Using a search value of CLASS*STAFF produces select statistics items for files CLASS*STAFF, CLASS*STAFF*STAFF and CLASS*STAFF*EXECS.

The code for selecting a *(S)ingle* file is:

```
055 EXECUTE 'SELECT STAT-FILE WITH *A1 = " ":ANS:'"'
```

This is a literal search for the statistics item having a value in attribute 1 that matches the value of ANS. After any SELECT, it is necessary to determine whether the select was successful. The item-id of the error message is returned after the EXECUTE.

```
047 *GET(MSG.) ERR ELSE ERR = ''
048 ERR = SYSTEM(17)
049 IF ERR = 401 THEN GOTO 1
```

The comment line 047 contains the required syntax for ULTIMATE machines. The SYSTEM(17) function is for all other Pick users.

Each item is read:

```
066 READNEXT ID ELSE
067 .....
071 END
073 READ REC FROM STAT.FILE,ID ELSE GOTO 10
```

The account name, DICT file name, and DATA file name are parsed.

```
074 LIN      = REC<1>
075 ACCT     = FIELD(LIN,'*',1)
076 DICT.FN  = FIELD(LIN,'*',2)
077 IF ACCT  = DICT.FN THEN GOTO 10
078 DATA.FN  = FIELD(LIN,'*',3)
```

A pointer is established to the proper file level.

```
088 QREC<1> = 'Q'
089 QREC<2> = ACCT
090 QREC<9> = 'L'
091 QREC<10> = '10'
092 *
093 IF DATA.FN = '' THEN
094     * Point to the target account's MD
095     QREC<3> = ''
096     ERR = 'MD ':ACCT
097     XFN = DICT.FN
098 END ELSE
099     * Point to the target file DICT
100     * to retrieve DATA level pointer
101     QREC<3> = DICT.FN:',':DATA.FN
102     ERR = 'DICT ':DICT.FN
103     XFN = DATA.FN
104 END
105 WRITE QREC ON MD,QFILE
106 OPEN 'DICT',QFILE TO POINTER.FILE ELSE STOP 201,ERR
```

A Q-file item is interactively created to point to the file containing the targeted D-pointer item. Once the Q-item is written to the local MD, the PICK/BASIC program can then open it to the file variable, POINTER-FILE, using the file name in variable, QFILE. The variable XFN is the item-id of the D-pointer. XFN means "cross file name."

Once the first file name is retrieved and the pointers set up, SIZER needs to know the file use type; (T)ransactional or(B)atch. Transaction files are sized using sizing method 1. Batch files are sized using an approximation of the chart in method 2. However, if the frame size exceeds 500 bytes, the transactional method is forced. (FRAMESIZE is equated to 500 at the beginning of the program.) For example:

```
146 IF TYPE = 'B' AND FRAMESIZE > 500 THEN TYPE = 'T'
```

The growth factor is requested and the projected item count is calculated.

```
156 ITMCNT = ITMCNT + INT((ITMCNT*FAC) + .5) ;* GROWTH
```

The possible modulo and separation is determined based on the file type. Batch file types choose the variable BYTESPERGROUP from a CASE table based on the average item size.

```
177    MODULO = INT(ITMCNT/(BYTEPERGROUP/ITMSIZ))
178    SEPAR = INT((BYTEPERGROUP/FRAMESIZE) + .5)
```

Transaction file types use the standard "rule of thumb."

```
180    BYTEPERGROUP = FRAMESIZE
181    MODULO = INT(ITMCNT/(BYTEPERGROUP/ITMSIZ))
182    IF ITMCNT < MODULO THEN MODULO = ITMCNT
183    SEPAR = 1 + INT((ITMSIZ/FRAMESIZE))
```

The modulo is rounded to the next highest prime number. Ok, prime number modulos are also fine. Anyway, it's always good to have a prime number routine somewhere in the system, even though it isn't especially needed in this case.

```
188 PRIME = 0
189 FOR J = MODULO TO J + 1 UNTIL PRIME
    ....
201 NEXT J
```

After the modulo and separation are determined, attribute 13 of the pointer array is updated.

```
207 POINTER<13> = '(':MODULO:',':SEPAR:')'
```

This is harmless unless the (U)pdate option is chosen. (U)pdate writes the altered D-pointer back to the XFN file.

```
222 WRITE POINTER ON POINTER.FILE,XFN
223 CRT ' Updated!'
```

SECURITY

The goal of system wide file security is to ensure database integrity. In the ideal world, security controls the user session from logon until logoff. Here is a laundry list of system functions that allow security to be implemented.

- Encrypted passwords for each user.
- Automatic logging of system usage.
- Ability to define user privilege levels.
- Ability to test for port number and user account name under program control.
- Update and retrieval codes to control access and updating of files.
- Ability to restrict user access to security-sensitive commands and processes.
- Inherent capabilities of protecting data integrity by preventing simultaneous updates to data.

The inherent file security in the Pick operating system has been traditionally overlooked. Most methods used for operator control and file update/retrieval have been written at the applications level, ignoring many of the system-provided methods. All of the above points can be implemented by using system provided features without a special database and without applications level coding.

Account Security Parameters

Each account has a set of security parameters, a profile, associated with it. These parameters can be found in the account definition item in the SYSTEM dictionary, as shown in Fig. 2-13. The security related attributes are L/RET, L/UPD, PASS, PRIV, and

ID: *Account Name*	
001 D	A file pointer item defining the account's Master Dictionary.
002 BASE	FID of the first frame of primary space.
003 MOD	Modulo of the account MD.
004 SEP	Separation of the account MD.
005 L/RET	Retrieval lock(s).
006 L/UPD	Update lock(s).
007 PASS	Encrypted password.
008 PRIV	System privilege level.
009 FLAGS	Additional account profile flags.
010 MAX	Column length for ACCESS.

FIG. 2-13. Account definition item layout.

FLAGS. Most of these parameters can be specified at CREATE-ACCOUNT time. If not, they can be added later. Here is a brief review of the security parameters.

Password

The password may or may not be encrypted depending, again, on the implementation. The algorithm used on the generic versions of Pick differs from the one used on ULTIMATE. The major difference is that the generic algorithm is a one-way encryption routine producing an 8 digit hexadecimal code.

There is no unique way to work backwards. Passwords can be changed for any account by using the verb PASSWORD in the SYSPROG account. PASSWORD is a PICK/BASIC program which uses a system user exit to perform the encryption. For example:

```
INPASSWORD = OCONV(PASSWORD,'U3060')
```

System Privilege

The generic system privilege levels are 0, 1, and 2. Newer implementations also support a level 3. Certain system level functions are restricted depending on the privilege level. Updating an account MD or using the magnetic tape is restricted to users with at least a system privilege of SYS1. Use of debugger commands other than END, OFF, G and P is restricted to users with a level of at least SYS2. FILE-SAVE and RESTORE, assembly level programming, and DUMP are also restricted to level 2 or above.

SYSPROG is the only account that has *no* security. This does not mean that anyone can point to SYSPROG. On the contrary. It means that SYSYPROG can point to anything on the system without going through security. This is important when doing system wide saves and restores. The newly implemented SYS3 privilege level is equivalent to SYSPROG. It overrides all security.

Flags

The additional security flags reside in attribute 9; the justification field for ACCESS. The value for these flags can be L, R, or U; the normal ACCESS values. However, in a system dictionary pointer, these values take on new meanings.

Value	*Description*
L	Indicates that there are no special options.
R	Indicates the restart option. This prevents the debugger command END from returning a process to TCL. Instead, the account logon PROC is reinvoked.
U	Indicates that the accounting file, ACC, is to be updated with connect time statistics when the user logs off the system.
B	Indicates that BREAK is disabled during the entire logon session. B is only available on a limited number of implementations.

The U flag can be used in conjunction with the L or the R. For example, a specification of RU means restart and update the ACC file, while LU means update the ACC file but allow BREAK and END to go to TCL.

As mentioned earlier, the ACC file contains items that indicate an active user. These items use the PCB as the item-id and contain the account name, the time and date of logon. These items are interrogated by the LISTU and WHO verbs.

ACC is also used to keep track of connect time statistics. All the time and date information is stored in internal format as correlated multi-valued lists. Figure 2-14 shows the ACC item layout. The ACC file is reported by the command LISTACC. There is no reason why a customized PICK/BASIC routine cannot access this information for more elaborate accounting requirements.

The Charge-To Verb

CHARGE-TO is a TCL command which allows a new item to be created in the ACC file to a combination of the account name and the charged user.

The current logon session charges are updated to the ACC file and a new item is created in the ACC file using the following item-id layout.

ID: *Accountname*Userid#Portnumber*

The following CHARGE-TO command executed on port 5 in the account PRODUCTION creates an ACC entry with the item-id: PRODUCTION*GEORGE#5.

> CHARGE-TO GEORGE

Update/Retrieval Locks

Now that the preliminaries are over, let's get down to business. Update and retrieval locks can be quite useful for controlling the availability of files within or between accounts.

ID: *Accountname#Portnumber*

001 not used	
002 not used	
003 not used	
004 Dates logged on	This field is multi-valued.
005 Times logged on	Times are sub-valued within the same date.
006 Connect time	The time in seconds that the user was logged onto the specific account. Again, sub-valued within the same date value.
007 Charge-units	The CPU usage for this session.
008 Printer pages	The number of pages sent to the line printer during this session.

FIG. 2-14. ACC item layout.

Primary Lock Codes

As specified in the SYSTEM item layout, *retrieval locks* are placed in attribute 5 of the defining item and *update locks* are placed in attribute 6. Retrieval locks by themselves are sufficient to lock all access to a file. You can't update anything if you can't retrieve it. Update locks do not block retrieval. To keep things straight and easy, the update and retrieval locks should match. Anything more extensive is left to the creativity and patience of the reader.

The Update/Retrieval lock mechanism is based on a lock code match, as shown in Fig. 2-15. The lock code for the account PRODUCTION is XXX and the lock code for DEVELOPMENT is YYY. These obviously do not match. Therefore, anyone on the PRODUCTION setting a Q-pointer to a file on the DEVELOPMENT account, or visa-versa, will either get the message:

    [210] FILE aaaa IS ACCESS PROTECTED

or

    [201] aaaa IS NOT A FILE NAME

Again, this depends on the implementation. Error message 201 is preferable to 210, because it isn't a good idea to let the user know whether the attempted file exists or not.

		PRODUCTION	DEVELOPMENT
	001	D	D
	002	13445	17765
	003	29	29
FIG. 2-15. Account definition items with	004	1	1
single lock codes.	005	XXX	YYY
	006	XXX	YYY
	007	PASS1	PASS2
	008	SYS1	SYS2
	009	RU	LU
	010	10	10

Notice that the PRODUCTION account has a SYS1 privilege, while the DEVELOPMENT account has SYS2 privilege. In addition, the R in attribute 009 of the PRODUCTION D-pointer prevents the users from using the debugger to enter TCL. Both accounts update the ACC file.

The lock code comparison does not have to match the entire string. For example, if the DEVELOPMENT account had a lockcode of YYX and the PRODUCTION account had a code of YY, Q-pointers to PRODUCTION from DEVELOPMENT would allow access, while a Q-pointer to DEVELOPMENT from PRODUCTION would not.

Secondary Lock Codes

Lock codes can be multi-valued, as shown in Fig. 2-16. The first value is considered the *primary lock code*. This prevents the access of any file within an account from another account without the same lock code. The remaining values are *secondary lock codes*. Secondary lock codes allow the user to access any account or file that has any of these codes as a primary lock.

```
         PRODUCTION              DEVELOPMENT
001   D                       D
002   13445                   17765
003   29                      29
004   1                       1                          FIG. 2-16. Account definitions with
005   XXX                     YYY]XXX                    multi-valued lock codes.
006   XXX                     YYY]XXX
007   PASS1                   PASS2
008   SYS2                    SYS0
009   RU                      LU
010   10                      10
```

The DEVELOPMENT account has a primary lock code of XXX. DEVELOPMENT can access any account with a primary code of XXX or YYY. Therefore, DEVELOPMENT can update and retrieve files on the PRODUCTION account, while PRODUCTION remains locked out of the DEVELOPMENT account.

The locks in a SYSTEM account defining item can also be used to define a user's *file access profile*. Because attributes 005 and 006 can be used for Update/Retrieval locks within any D-pointer item, security control can apply to the file DICT and DATA levels. For example, a file called SALARIES exists on the PRODUCTION account. The D-pointer in the MD of PRODUCTION is shown in Fig. 2-17. Any attempt to list the SALARIES file while logged onto the PRODUCTION account results in the message:

[E201] 'SALARIES' IS NOT A FILE NAME

However, anyone on the DEVELOPMENT account can point to and list the SALARIES file in PRODUCTION.

```
         SALARIES
001   D
002   23445
003   11
004   1
005   YYY              FIG. 2-17. File D-pointer with lock codes.
006   YYY
007
008
009   L
010   10
```

Using Synonym Accounts

Here is a way to identify each user while providing individual user profiles without a mass of high level coding: *Synonym items*. They are allowed in the SYSTEM dictionary and can be used as alternate logon paths, as shown in Fig. 2-18. Notice that all the security parameters can be individually assigned to a each synonym.

To ensure security, application users are restricted from logging onto any D-pointer type accounts. These are considered more as central directories rather than interactive accounts. System support and maintenance personnel are the only users who are given the passwords of these accounts.

ID: *Synonym Name*	
001 Q	Standard Q-pointer designation.
002 Account	The account name.
003	Not Used.
004	Not Used.
005 L/RET	Retrieval lock(s).
006 L/UPD	Update lock(s).
007 PASS	Encrypted password.
008 PRIV	System privilege level.
009 FLAGS	Additional account profile flags.
010 MAX	Column length for ACCESS.

FIG. 2-18. *Account synonym definition item layout.*

Common users must be defined to the system by creating a Q-pointer account synonym item for each individual operator. This allows encrypted passwords for each system user and the ability to track each user via the ACC file.

In addition, each operator initiates a unique logon path. Logon paths and functional menus can be very easily implemented for both groups and individual users. Figure 2-19 is an example of the SYSTEM Dictionary items. PRODUCTION is the primary directory. SAMR and SALLYS are users.

	PRODUCTION	SAMR	SALLYS
001	D	Q	Q
002	13445	PRODUCTION	PRODUCTION
003	29		
004	1		
005			
006			
007	PASS1	PASS2	PASS3
008	SYS2	SYS0	SYS1
009	L	RU	RU
010	10	10	10

FIG. 2-19. *Definition item and user synonyms.*

Notice that the passwords and system privileges are different for each user. Also, attribute 009 utilizes the R to force are start of the logon path when END is typed in the debugger.

Providing users with separate synonym definitions also allows each to be given individual update/retrieval locks, as shown in Fig. 2-20. In this case, SAMR and SALLYS can both retrieve information from PRODUCTION. However, SAMR can also access infor-

	PRODUCTION	SAMR	SALLYS
001	D	Q	Q
002	13445	PRODUCTION	PRODUCTION
003	19		
004	1		
005	XYZ	XYZ]ZZZ	XYZ]AAA
006	XYZ	XYZ]ZZZ	XYZ]AAA
007	PASS1	PASS2	PASS3
008	SYS2	SYS0	SYS1
009	L	RU	RU
010	10	10	10

FIG. 2-20. Synonyms with update/retrieval locks.

mation from any account with ZZZ as a primary lock. SALLYS does not have the ZZZ keyword and therefore is restricted from such an account.

In addition, any file within an account can have a primary lock code in attributes 005 and 006 of the defining D-pointer, as shown in Fig. 2-21. Consider the file called SALARIES in the PRODUCTION account. In this case, SALLYS can access the SALARIES file, but SAMR cannot.

	SALARIES
001	D
002	66666
003	347
004	1
005	AAA
006	AAA
007	
008	
009	L
010	10

FIG. 2-21. File D-pointer with lock codes.

Simplifying the Security Process

Here is a simple scheme for giving the operators a 10-level rating of security and allowing each file on an account to also be given a security rating.

As shown in Fig. 2-22, the major account 'PRODUCTION' has access to all levels. Only those users responsible for maintenance and coding can logon to PRODUCTION. SAMR has a level 3 clearance and SALLYS has a level 6 clearance.

The files SALARIES, EMPLOYEES, and EXECUTIVES are in the PRODUCTION Account. The PRODUCTION MD entries are shown in Fig. 2-23.

NOTE: Locks can be used in both the DICT and DATA level D-pointers. SAMR can only access the EMPLOYEES file while SALLY can access both EMPLOYEES and EXECUTIVES. Neither can access SALARIES.

Potential Problems

The use of update and retrieval locks can get quite complex when several sets of users are using the same system. The previous schema should help to alleviate some of the potentially confusing situations.

	PRODUCTION	SAMR	SALLYS
001	D	Q	Q
002	13445	PRODUCTION	PRODUCTION
003	29		
004	1		
005	0]1]2]3]4]5]6]7]8]9	0]1]2]3	0]1]2]3]4]5]6
006	0]1]2]3]4]5]6]7]8]9	0]1]2]3	0]1]2]3]4]5]6
007	PASS1	PASS2	PASS3
008	SYS2	SYS0	SYS1
009	L	RU	RU
010	10	10	10

FIG. 2-22. 10 level security lock schema.

	SALARIES	EMPLOYEES	EXECUTIVES
001	D	D	D
002	34555	67889	55667
003	3	7	11
004	1	1	1
005	9	3	6
006	9	3	6
007			
008			
009	L	L	L
010	10	10	10

FIG. 2-23. File D-pointers with security level assignments.

Unfortunately, on most implementations, whenever a PICK/BASIC routine attempts to update a protected file, it immediately returns to TCL. This is not a desired effect, especially when the whole purpose is to keep people out of TCL. (The correct system response to such an attempt should be a PICK/BASIC runtime error.) This can be avoided if updates are not attempted before reads.

It is also a good idea to keep the update and retrieval locks matched. If a file is open for retrieval but locked for update, then the write attempt can send the process to TCL. If update and retrieval locks are matched, then the situation should not be encountered.

Users and Directories

Many of the new implementations of the Pick system are diverging from the classic structure of accounts. In generic Pick, a user identifier and an account directory are inexorably tied together. Even when using synonym accounts, the user needs to LOGTO a different synonym for each new account master dictionary that is required.

To get around this problem, the new approach separates the contents of the master dictionary into two separate locations, a file directory and a user vocabulary. All users are separately defined and are given a password, privilege level, lock schema, and associated vocabulary of verbs that can be used. Once the user has been identified by the system, any number of file directories (master dictionaries) can be attached or detached without losing the current user identity. Variations of this approach are presently available on Advanced Pick as well as on PRIME Information, CIE and ICON.

Logon Security Programs

For the rest of us, there must be some way to identify users at the application level. A *logon security routine* prompts for a unique operator identifier, looks it up in a security file, optionally requires another password, and then chooses an appropriate execution path.

Application-dependent security places the entire job of user accounting, intra-file security, and system integration into the hands of the applications programmer. System level security becomes useless, because operators share logon accounts and therefore all security parameters.

The following is a simple PICK/BASIC program for interrogating security parameters such as port number, account name, and requiring a user identifier.

A Sample Logon Security Program

Figure 2-24 is a simple security program that can be invoked by a logon PROC. The program interrogates a file named USERS, which contains an item for each valid system user. In this case, USERS are keyed by a short alphabetic user-id. Each user-identifying item contains an encrypted password and the user's security level (0-9.) The choice of the number of security levels is arbitrary.

	NAME	PASSWORD	LEVEL
001	A	A	A
002	00	1	3
003			
004			
005			
006			
007			
008			
009	L	L	R
010	10	10	3

FIG. 2-24. Users file dictionary items.

As it stands, any other routine that needs to interrogate the user's security level will have to re-read the USERS file. When a logon security program is implemented as a part of an integrated application, the security information should be made available through a COMMON variable block.

Program Highlights

The user is given a maximum number of retries to enter the USER code and its associated password. MAX.TRY indicates that the retry limit is three. All user responses are forced to uppercase with the "MCU" conversion. The passwords are kept on file in encrypted format by using the user exit, "U3060." The current port number and account name is retrieved by the user exit, "U50BB." All the OCONV calls and the RETRY limit are EQUATED to synonym names to make the code self documenting.

```
013 EQU MAX.TRY TO 3
014 EQU ENCRYPT TO 'U3060', WHOM TO 'U50BB'
015 EQU UPPER TO 'MCU'
```

```
      USER.LOGON
001 PROGRAM USER.LOGON
002 * LOGON SECURITY ROUTINE
003 * (c) 1988 H.E.Rodstein Computer Consulting
004 * Harvey Eric Rodstein
005 *
006 PROMPT ':'
007 *
008 EQU AM   TO CHAR(254)
009 EQU VM   TO CHAR(253)
010 EQU NILL TO CHAR(0)
011 EQU ESC  TO CHAR(27)
012 *
013 EQU MAX.TRY TO 3
014 EQU ENCRYPT TO 'U3060', WHOM TO 'U50BB'
015 EQU UPPER   TO 'MCU'
016 *
017 DIM SECURE.REC(3)
018 EQU INPASSWORD TO SECURE.REC(1)
019 EQU LEVEL      TO SECURE.REC(2)
020 *
021 BREAK OFF
022 *
023 WHO       = OCONV(0,WHOM)
024 PORT      = FIELD(WHO,' ',1)
025 ACCOUNT   = FIELD(WHO,' ',2)
026 PASSFLAG  = 0
027 MAT SECURE.REC = ''
028 *
029 OPEN 'USERS' TO USERS.FILE ELSE
030   PRINT 'USERS FILE DOES NOT EXIST'
031   CHAIN 'OFF'
032 END
033 *
034 PRINT @(-1):
035 FOR TRY = 1 TO MAX.TRY UNTIL PASSFLAG
036  PRINT @(10,10):'Enter user id  ':@(-4):
037  INPUT USERID
038  USERID = OCONV(USERID,UPPER)
039  MATREAD SECURE.REC FROM USERS.FILE,USERID THEN PASSFLAG = 1 ELSE
040     PRINT @(10,14):'Invalid User Id':@(-4):
041     PASSFLAG = 0
042  END
043 NEXT TRY
044 IF NOT(PASSFLAG) THEN GOTO 1000 ;* Security failure
045 PRINT @(10,14):@(-4):
046 *
047 IF INPASSWORD # '' THEN
048   PASSFLAG = 0
049   FOR TRY = 1 TO MAX.TRY UNTIL PASSFLAG
050    PRINT @(10,12):'Enter password ':@(-4):
051    ECHO OFF
052    INPUT PASSWORD
```

FIG. 2-25. USER security LOGON program listing.

```
053     ECHO ON
054     PASSFLAG=(INPASSWORD=OCONV(PASSWORD,UPPER:VM:ENCRYPT))
055     IF NOT(PASSFLAG) THEN PRINT @(10,14):'Password?':@(-4):
056   NEXT TRY
057     IF NOT(PASSFLAG) THEN GOTO 1000 ;* Security failure
058 END
059 PRINT @(10,14):'Passed security checkpoint':@(-4):
060 BREAK LEVEL>5
061 EXECUTE 'CHARGE-TO ':USERID
062 STOP
063 *
064 1000 * Security Failure
065 *
066 PRINT @(10,14):'Retry Limit Exceeded':@(-4):
067 CHAIN 'OFF'
068 *
069 END
```

FIG. 2-25 ends.

SECURE.REC is the dimensioned variable into which the USER item is read. Synonym names are equated to each array entry to increase the readability of the program. INPASSWORD makes more sense than SECURE.REC(1).

```
017 DIM SECURE.REC(3)
018 EQU INPASSWORD  TO SECURE.REC(1)
019 EQU LEVEL       TO SECURE.REC(2)
```

The break key is disabled to prevent the user from using the break key to get around security.

```
021 BREAK OFF
```

Next, the current port and account name are retrieved with the user exit "U50BB." This produces output identical to the TCL command WHO.

```
NN ACCOUNT    where NN is the port number and ACCOUNT is the account
              name. The parameters are separated by a space.
```

The variables PORT and ACCOUNT must be parsed from the variable WHO by using the FIELD function.

```
022 *
023 WHO  = OCONV(0,WHOM)
024 PORT = FIELD(WHO,' ',1)
025 ACCOUNT = FIELD(WHO,' ',2)
```

The file USERS is opened to the file variable USERS.FILE. A missing USERS file indicates that any log on attempt is to be aborted. The command CHAIN "OFF" logs off the user. This is one of the few cases that a CHAIN is easy to follow.

```
029  OPEN 'USERS' TO USERS.FILE ELSE
030    PRINT 'USERS FILE DOES NOT EXIST'
```

```
031     CHAIN 'OFF'
032 END
```

The following FOR..NEXT..UNTIL kills two birds with one stone. The incremented counter, TRY, gives the user MAX.TRY a certain number of times to enter a valid user identification, USERID. If the USERID is a valid item-id on the file USERS then PASSFLAG is set to true (1) and the FOR..NEXT loop is terminated.

```
035 FOR TRY = 1 TO MAX.TRY UNTIL PASSFLAG
036     PRINT @(10,10): 'Enter user id ':@(-4):
037     INPUT USERID
038     USERID = OCONV(USERID,UPPER)
039     MATREAD SECURE.REC FROM USERS.FILE,USERID THEN PASSFLAG = 1
ELSE
040         PRINT @(10,14): 'Invalid User Id':@(-4):
041         PASSFLAG = 0
042     END
043 NEXT TRY
044 IF NOT(PASSFLAG) THEN GOTO 1000
```

After the loop is exited by either TRY being incremented greater than the maximum or by a valid USERID being entered, PASSFLAG is checked for a false condition. If PASSFLAG has not been set, the program branches to the security failure routine at statement label 1000.

```
063 1000 * Security Failure
064 *
065 PRINT @(10,14): 'Retry Limit Exceeded':@(-4):
066 CHAIN 'OFF'
```

The error message is displayed and the user is automatically logged off the account.

Once the correct USERID is entered, the user password is requested. The password routine is executed only if a user password exists.

```
047 IF INPASSWORD # '' THEN
048     PASSFLAG = 0
049     FOR TRY = 1 TO MAX.TRY UNTIL PASSFLAG
050         PRINT @(10,12): 'Enter password ':@(-4):
051         ECHO OFF
052         INPUT PASSWORD
053         ECHO ON
054         PASSFLAG = (INPASSWORD = OCONV(PASSWORD,UPPER:VM:ENCRYPT))
055         IF NOT(PASSFLAG) THEN PRINT @(10,14): 'Password?':@(-4):
056     NEXT TRY
057     IF NOT(PASSFLAG) THEN GOTO 1000 ;* Security failure
058 END
```

Terminal echo is disabled when inputing the password.

```
051    ECHO OFF
052    INPUT PASSWORD
053    ECHO ON
```

Password encryption is a one-way street. The entered password must be encrypted before it is compared to INPASSWORD. PASSFLAG is set true if the correct password is entered. Take a closer look at line 54.

```
054    PASSFLAG = (INPASSWORD = OCONV(PASSWORD,UPPER:VM:ENCRYPT))
```

PASSFLAG is generated by the Boolean expression:

```
(INPASSWORD = OCONV(PASSWORD,UPPER:VM:ENCRYPT))
```

This checks to see if the stored encrypted password, INPASSWORD, is equal to the encrypted version of the entered PASSWORD. If true, PASSFLAG is set to one, otherwise PASSFLAG is set to zero.

The function, OCONV(PASSWORD,UPPER:VM:ENCRYPT)), passes the value of PASSWORD, first through the "MCU" (Mask Character Upper Case) conversion, and then though the encryption user exit.

After the number of TRYs have been exhausted, PASSFLAG is checked for a false condition and the user is automatically logged off.

```
057    IF NOT(PASSFLAG) THEN GOTO 1000 ;* Security failure
```

Finally, once the security is passed, the BREAK key is enabled or disabled according to the security level.

```
060 BREAK LEVEL[15
061 EXECUTE 'CHARGE-TO ':USERID
062 STOP
```

If the LEVEL is greater than 5, the BREAK key is enabled. Otherwise, the BREAK key is disabled. This form of the BREAK command follows PICK R83 conventions.

```
BREAK expression
```

A true expression enables BREAK, false disables BREAK. The BREAK key may or may not be re-enabled when STOP is performed, depending on the implementation. Again, experimentation provides the answer.

Finally, CHARGE-TO is executed based on the USERID.

```
061 EXECUTE 'CHARGE-TO ':USERID
```

This creates an item in the accounting file charged to ACCOUNTNAME*USERID. With a current account name of PRODUCTION and a USERID value of HER, the accounting item-id is PRODUCTION*HER.

Other Security Measures

After all this, only the surface of the security issue has been brushed. Here are some other suggestions for implementing applications security:

- *Encrypted data fields*. This prevents unwanted and unauthorized perusement of financial summaries or personnel records.

- *Encrypted program source*. This helps to prevent the application package from proliferating without the consent of those who developed it.

- *Hidden program source*. This is the simplest way to prevent programs from being "ripped off." Just deliver the object code.

A Closer Look
at PICK/BASIC

PICK/BASIC IS A HYBRID OF A COMPILED AND AN INTERPRETED LANGUAGE. UNLIKE compilers which translate, optimize and assemble source code statements into machine readable microcode, the PICK/BASIC compiler translates source code into an intermediate language made up of high-level opcodes similar in concept to Pascal p-code. The generated meta code is then interpreted during PICK/BASIC runtime. This meta code is also called the generated "object."

The Compiler

The generic implementation of the PICK/BASIC compiler has two major passes. Since engineers love to change things, the compiler on each implementation may do much the same job in four or more passes, or in a single pass. But, after all is said and done, the critical tasks remain the same.

In the first pass, the syntax of each line is checked, variables are assigned entries in the descriptor table, and statement labels are assigned byte displacements from the beginning of the object code item. Descriptor entries are discussed at length in the next section, "Variable Management." In the second pass, branch locations are resolved. The statement label byte displacements are "plugged" into the corresponding GOTO and GOSUB statements.

For GOTO and GOSUB branch statements to work efficiently during PICK/BASIC runtime, (known as the Basic Runtime Package or BRP), the object code must be stored in a block of logically contiguous frames. A logically contiguous block allows the system to "leap frog" between frames when a byte displacement is indicated. The GOTO and

GOSUB statements would be painfully slow if every frame between the current position and the destination had to be read. For example, if a GOSUB is encountered in the first frame of the object code and the destination statement label is 10 frames away, the system needs only 1 additional frame fault to perform the branch. The same branch in a chain of non-contiguous frames would require 10 frame faults to complete the branch.

In releases R77 and after, PICK/BASIC object code is stored as a cataloged item in the dictionary of the file where the source code resides. The object code item is allocated a logically contiguous block addressed by a pointer item stored in the primary space of the file dictionary, as shown in Fig. 3-1.

ID: *program name*

001 CC

002 *starting FID*   The first frame location of the object code.

003 *number of frames*   The number of frames in the contiguous block.

004 n/a

005 *Time Date*   The time and date the programs were last compiled.

FIG. 3-1. PICK/BASIC object pointer item.

NOTE: In a system that supports unlimited item sizes, the object code pointer is hidden in the file dictionary. In other words, there is no discernable item which provides the above information to the user. Object pointers are only available to the system.

Shared Runtime

PICK/BASIC runtime code is re-entrant. *Re-entrancy* means that the object code frames in memory are shared by all processes running the same program. On releases R77 and after, PICK/BASIC runtime is re-entrant regardless of whether the program is invoked by the RUN verb or by a cataloged program name. The CATALOG verb is used to write the program name as a verb in the current master dictionary. Re-compilation automatically overwrites the previously generated object item with the newly generated object. Re-cataloging is not necessary.

On releases of the Pick Operating System that pre-date R77, the object code is written back to the same file data area under a new item-id made up of the original program name prefixed with a dollar-sign, $. These object items are stored in linked overflow like any other item. The RUN verb forces the object code to be copied to a logically contiguous block of process workspace before beginning runtime. Each process running the same program requires an individual copy of the object code in its own process workspace. Therefore, ten users running the same program end up with ten copies of the object code competing for physical memory.

In this pre-R77 environment, (still in effect on the McDonnell Douglas implementation), CATALOG not only writes a verb to the currrent master dictionary, but also allocates a logically contiguous block of frames for the program object. The cataloged object item is addressed by a pointer item stored in a SYSTEM level file called POINTER-FILE. Only cataloged entries invoked by the cataloged program name are re-entrant.

Each time the program is compiled, the dollar-sign version of the object item is overwritten, leaving the cataloged version unchanged. In order to update the re-entrant version, the CATALOG verb must be envoked after each compilation.

The Onlyme Program

There are specific programming cases, (periodic data aging or consolidation routines) where multiple processes simultaneously running the same program can corrupt the final result. The worst case occurs when these routines update current data files with their results.

One way to prevent processes from stepping on each other's toes is to prevent re-entrancy. Multiple users can be prevented from running the same program by the use of the PICK/BASIC runtime locks. There are usually 64, (0-63) shared system bytes which a program can set or clear using the LOCK or the UNLOCK statement.

Figure 3-2 is a simple example of a program containing a routine that can only be run by a single process at a time.

Program Highlights

Subroutine 1000 is the routine which is accessible to a single process at one time. Subroutine 1000 simply executes the command LIST-LOCKS so that the set lock can be verified. The current port number should appear in the lock 1 position.

The *retry loop* is written as a structure FOR..NEXT..UNTIL to allow two conditions for termination; either the retries are exceeded or the system lock is successful. For example:

```
008  EQU RETRY TO 5
....
017  SUCCESS = 0 ;* Init a retry success flag
018  FOR TRY = 1 TO RETRY UNTIL SUCCESS
019      * Attempt to LOCK number 1
020      LOCK 1 THEN
021          SUCCESS = 1
          ...
024      END ELSE
          ...
027      END
028  NEXT TRY
```

The LOCK command uses the general form:

LOCK *n* THEN..ELSE

```
      ONLYME
001 *PROGRAM ONLYME
002 *Demonstrate Execution Locks
003 *
004 *
005 *
006 PROMPT ''
007 *
008 EQU RETRY TO 5
009 *
010 10 * Main
011 *
012 PRINT 'Press <cr> to continue or (Q)uit ':
013 INPUT ANS
014 ANS = OCONV(ANS[1,1],'MCU')
015 IF ANS = 'Q' THEN STOP
016 *
017 SUCCESS = 0   ;* Init a retry success flag
018 FOR TRY = 1 TO RETRY UNTIL SUCCESS
019    * Attempt to LOCK number 1
020    LOCK 1 THEN
021       SUCCESS = 1   ;* Successful
022       GOSUB 1000    ;* Lock successful, perform the routine
023       UNLOCK 1      ;* Clear the lock
024    END ELSE
025       PRINT 'Try #':TRY:', the routine is locked...':
026       SLEEP 2   ;* Delay for 2 seconds before retrying
027    END
028 NEXT TRY
029 *
030 GOTO 10    ;* Restart
031 *
032 *
033 * Subroutine
034 *
035 1000 * Any ol' thang
036 *
037 PRINT 'A success!!!!!'
038 EXECUTE 'LIST-LOCKS'
039 RQM
040 PRINT 'Time for a nap!'
041 SLEEP 20
042 RETURN
043 *
044 END
```

FIG. 3-2. ONLYME program listing.

where *n* is a number between 0 and 63, inclusive. If the LOCK is successful, the THEN clause is taken. If the LOCK has already been set by another process, the ELSE clause is taken.

If the LOCK can be set, SUCCESS is set to true and subroutine 1000 is performed.

```
021   SUCCESS = 1
```

```
022   GOSUB 1000
023   UNLOCK 1
```

Upon completion of the subroutine, the lock is cleared by the command UNLOCK using the general form:

```
UNLOCK n
```

If the lock is unsuccessful, the number of the try is printed and the process sleeps for 2 seconds until another try is attempted.

```
025   PRINT 'Try #':TRY:', the routine is locked...':
026   SLEEP 2 ;* Delay for 2 seconds before retrying
```

The SLEEP command is available as a PICK/BASIC command to generic Pick only. Other systems have to execute the TCL command as follows:

```
EXECUTE "SLEEP 2"
```

An alternative method is to use the Release Quantum (RQM) command. This command gives up the current process timeslice. The process is reactivated the next time the monitor passes it in the Select Next User (SNU) queue. RQM is often used in place of a SLEEP 1, since Releases R83 and before treat the PICK/BASIC statements RQM and SLEEP identically, even though this shouldn't be the case. This is being changed on newer implementations.

In this example, two RQM's would be a good substitute for the SLEEP 2 command:

```
RQM;RQM
```

VARIABLE MANAGEMENT

PICK/BASIC keeps track of variables and their contents by dividing the virtual workspace into three entities:

- the *descriptor table*, containing a descriptor entry for each variable,
- *free workspace area*, where data strings are kept,
- and the *buffer table*, which keeps track of unused free workspace.

The Descriptor Table

The descriptor table is used to keep track of the value of variables during PICK/BASIC runtime. As each variable is encountered by the PICK/BASIC compiler, a ten-byte descriptor is reserved in the table. The descriptor table is initialized at runtime and the descriptors are filled in "on-the-fly."

The descriptor table is actually a string, (no suprise by now) requiring each descriptor to be addressed as a displacement from the beginning of the table. The descriptor table is stored in logically contiguous space so that any displacement into the table can be addresses in no more than 2 frame faults.

As with all strings in the Pick system, the descriptor table has a size limitation of approximately 32,000 bytes. Since each descriptor uses 10 bytes, the maximum number of possible descriptors is around 3,200.

The 32K string limit is imposed by the fact that PICK/BASIC object code jumps are a two-byte opcode followed by a two-byte address:

Address	Description
06 addr	unconditional jump
0A addr	branch if true
0B addr	branch if false

The maximum positive number which can be kept in 2 bytes is7F, or approximately 32K. Therefore, jumping forward 40,000 bytes would generate a jump backward of 24,000 bytes. (64k(xFF) – 40k = 24k)

NOTE: Sometimes PICK/BASIC apparently runs slowly due to the overhead of Pick's virtual memory management. For each variable data reference, the system must check to see if the descriptor is in memory or not. (See Chapter 8, "The Virtual Machine.")

Descriptor Table Layout

The first two bytes of a descriptor contain the descriptor type. The contents of the remainder of the descriptor varies according to the descriptor type. The descriptor contents can be binary numbers, ASCII strings, file pointers or cataloged subroutine pointers.

Descriptor Type	Description
Binary numeric	is held as a 6-byte binary number.
File variable	is stored as the file BASE, MODULO and SEPARATION. The number of bytes for each can vary between implementations.
Subroutine name	is a 6-byte pointer to the first frame of the subroutine object code.
ASCII string	is stored in two different ways, depending on string length:
	• If the string is 8 bytes or less in length (including the string terminating segment mark, (xff,) CHAR (255)), then the string is stored as part of the descriptor entry.
	• If the string exceeds 8 bytes, the descriptor holds a 6-byte pointer which designates the location of the string in free workspace.
Select variable	is a 6-byte pointer to the beginning of an active select list. Select variables are assigned by the SELECT TO "selectvariable" command or by any form of PASSLIST or RTNLIST modifier in an EXECUTE statement.

Variable Declaration and Typing

PICK/BASIC does not require a specific variable declaration section. There is no compiler or runtime requirement concerning placement of variable initializing statements.

Variable assignments are usually placed where they make the most sense in the logic of the program. However, it is important to always assign an initial value to a variable before referencing it. A variable referenced on the right side of an equal sign (=) or used in a PRINT statement prior to initialization causes PICK/BASIC runtime to display the non-fatal warning message:

[B10] VARIABLE HAS NOT BEEN ASSIGNED A VALUE; ZERO USED!

To provide a sense of order and, in the long run, to improve readability and maintainability of a program, variables should be initialized in some pseudo working storage section placed at the beginning of the source item. This is a completely voluntary restraint.

Here are samples of variable assignment statements which generate different descriptor types:

Statement	*Generates*
STRING = "ABD"	A literal string
NUMBER = 255	A numeric constant
STRING = NUMBER : " IS THE STRING"	Any compound string
NUMBER = NUMBER − 10	An arithmetic or Logical expression
TRUE = NUMBER > 200	
OPEN "STAFF TO STAFF.FILE ELSE..	A file variable
CALL VALIDATE(STRING)	A Subroutine name
SELECT FILE TO LIST	A select variable.

PICK/BASIC types the contents of variables based on the assignment statement. Binary numerics are designated as numeric constants, ASCII strings are designated as literals delimited by a double-quote ("), a single-quote ('), or a backslash (\), file variables are defined in OPEN statements, and subroutine names are defined in CALL statements.

PICK/BASIC does not restrict variable usage based on whether the variable is defined as a binary numeric or an ASCII string. For example, a numeric constant is indicated by the statement:

NUMBER = 255

The value of NUMBER is stored as a 6 byte binary number. An ASCII numeric string can be assigned by the statement:

SNUMBER = "255"

The value of SNUMBER is stored as a 3-byte ASCII string. If the statement,

PRINT NUMBER

is encountered, the PICK/BASIC runtime automatically converts the binary number to its ASCII equivalent before printing. The opposite occurs if the following statement is executed.

ANSWER = SNUMBER * 3

The string variable SNUMBER is converted to its binary numeric equivalent before the calculation is performed. The result of the statement is a binary value.

The obvious advantage to non-typed variables is that the applications programmer's job is simplified. The not-so-obvious disadvantage is the potential system overhead. Each variable reference must be qualified and, if necessary, converted before the statement can be performed.

If the code is layed out carefully, data conversions should have little impact on throughput. In fact, with proper variable initialization, Pick actually does less data conversion than most classical systems. The only exception to this is when numerics are stored in dynamic arrays. This kills the performance of any system.

When a variable containing an ASCII string is used in a statement that requires a binary numeric value, PICK/BASIC runtime attempts to convert the string into an equivalent binary numeric value. The conversion cannot be performed if the string contains characters other than ASCII numerics, (0-9.) An attempt to convert a non-numeric ASCII string to an equivalent binary numeric value results in the non-fatal warning:

[B16] NON-NUMERIC DATA WHERE NUMERIC DATA REQUIRED; ZERO USED!

It is not a good idea to leave a warning message unaddressed. Spurious zeros being used in any calculations can produce highly inaccurate results. Sometimes, the zero can compound the problem and produce another error.

[B24] DIVIDE BY ZERO ILLEGAL; ZERO USED!

Beware of the PICK/BASIC runtime option of S, which should be known as the "Sue-Me" option. Here is an example of its use:

>RUN BP TEST (S

Option S suppresses the messages, but does not prevent the zero from being used as the value of the variable. This is not a desirable circumstance if it happens to occur in a month-end aging routine. The S option is also known as the lazy programmers method of removing unwanted warning messages. Such techniques indicate that a rewarding career in fast food awaits this programmer. The moral of this story is:

Fix the problem, don't just hide it!

A better way to handle these warning messages is to use the PICK/BASIC runtime option of E. For example:

>RUN BP TEST (E

The E option forces runtime to enter the PICK/BASIC debugger whenever a warning message is generated. This is far less haphazard than trying to catch the warning message by hitting the BREAK key at the right time.

RULE: If a variable is to be used solely for arithmetic calculation or any other numeric function, then the variable should be initialized as a numeric constant. If the variable is to be used strictly as a string, then the variable should be initialized as an ASCII string.

Conversion of the data storage type can be forced. For example, the variable, SNUMBER, which contains an ASCII numeric string, can be converted to a binary numeric by using a dummy arithmetic statement.

```
SNUMBER = "255"          ;* SNUMBER is a string
NUMBER  = SNUMBER + 0 ;* NUMBER is a binary numeric.
```

Conversely, a binary numeric can be converted to an ASCII string with a dummy string statement.

```
SNUMBER = NUMBER : "" ; SNUMBER is a numeric string.
```

Free Workspace

Free workspace is used by those strings which exceed 8 bytes in length. (The 8-byte length includes the string terminating segment mark, (xFF), CHAR (255)). The descriptor table entry contains a pointer to the string in free workspace, rather than the string itself. Free workspace is divided into manageable storage buffers which may vary in size between implementations. Generically, workspace is allocated in increments of 50, 150, and 250 byte buffers.

As a string grows beyond the 8-byte maximum for storage in the Descriptor Table, a 50-byte buffer is allocated in free workspace. This gives the string some "headroom" to grow without having to allocate a new buffer. As the string grows beyond 50 bytes, a 150-byte buffer is allocated and the previously used 50-byte buffer is freed for later use. As the string exceeds 150 bytes, a 250-byte buffer is allocated. Strings which exceed 250-bytes are allocated multiples of 250-byte buffers. The Descriptor Table is illustrated in Fig. 3-3.

At the start of PICK/BASIC runtime, the free workspace is one large contiguous block. As new buffers are allocated and old buffers discarded, free workspace fragments. If a string requires a buffer size or a combination of buffers that is not contiguously available, the runtime process initiates a procedure known as "garbage collection." *Garbage collection* packs all used buffers to the beginning of workspace in order to free a large enough chunk of contiguous workspace. If, after garbage collection, a large enough contiguous block still cannot be found, PICK/BASIC runtime aborts with the message:

```
[B28] NOT ENOUGH WORKSPACE
```

Some of the newer systems, which have floating workspace, do not abort at this time. Instead, more workspace is attached to the process, and the program continues. This permits the development of behemoth programs, which prove cumbersome to maintain and modify. This also allows PICK/BASIC runtime to "eat up" all the available overflow on disk. Consider this another case where poor design and sloppy programming can exist without fault.

CAUTION: The more often a process is forced to garbage collect, the slower it runs. The greater the number of large strings handled simultaneously within a PICK/BASIC program, the lesser the amount of free workspace is available, and the more often garbage collection is required. This is an important reason for reusing a variable that is used to hold a long string. When long strings are handled individually in this manner, workspace

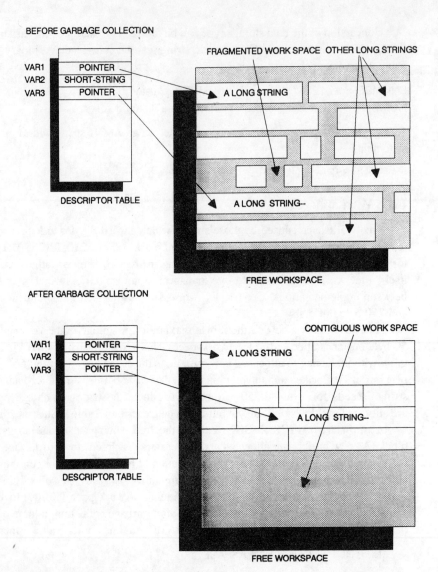

FIG. 3-3. The descriptor table and free workspace.

is allocated more efficiently (the buffers are probably already allocated) and the program performs at optimum efficiency.

Descriptor Allocation

Variables are allocated descriptors based on a priority determined by whether the variable usage is common, simple or dimensioned. Common variables are allocated their own set of descriptors at the beginning of the descriptor table and share the same overflow pool with normal variables. Descriptors in the common block are shared by the main program and all external subroutines.

NOTE: Some of the newer implementations offer a named common area. This allows variable contents to remain intact for a complete logon session. Named common has its own descriptor table and string overflow pool. The table and overflow space are established by the first program referencing the named common area and returned to the overflow table when the user logs off.

Each subroutine call appends a block of locally defined simple and dimensioned descriptors to the table. When local variables are passed to a subroutine, the corresponding descriptors are copied to the next level of the descriptor block, as shown in Fig. 3-4. Strings that are held in free workspace remain untouched; only the pointer data is moved.

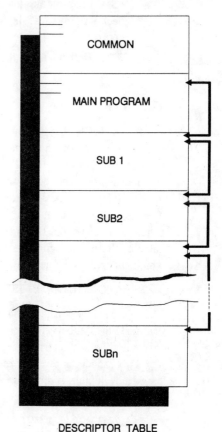

FIG. 3-4. Subroutine parameter passing.

DESCRIPTOR TABLE

This is how everything is supposed to work. However, beware of this scenario. The main routine calls a subroutine as follows:

```
CALL SUB(X,Y,X)
```

The subroutine looks like this:

```
SUBROUTINE SUB(A,B,C)
C = 1
RETURN
```

This is one of the major causes for PICK/BASIC runtime aborts from the garbage collection routine.

The more variables passed to an external subroutine, the longer the transfer takes. In integrated software packages which require 50 or more variables to be shared between the programs, such overhead has to be avoided. Here's where the COMMON statement comes to good use. Common variables can be shared among the levels of subroutine without movement of the descriptors.

- It is important that when the common variables are used, the main routine and all related subroutines have matching COMMON statements. If the common area declaration varies, the descriptor table may become corrupted causing runtime to abort.

- 3,200 descriptors is the combined limit of the main routine and related subroutines.

The Symbol Table

As the PICK/BASIC compiler allocates descriptors, it also builds a cross reference table which indicates the variable name and corresponding displacement in the descriptor table. This cross reference is called the *symbol table*.

The symbol table is not required for runtime. However, the symbol table is required for the PICK/BASIC debugger to be useful during runtime. Within most of the Pick implementations, the symbol table is automatically generated and tagged on to the end of the generated object code. If, for security reasons, the PICK/BASIC variables are not interrogated or altered through the debugger, the program must be compiled using the (S) option, which suppresses the generation of the symbol table.

```
>BASIC BP MCOMPTEST (S
```

The debugger is still available (END, OFF, G) but useless for tracking down program errors. If the debugger is to be deactivated during runtime, the BREAK ON/OFF statements are the best alternatives.

This process is reversed on McDonnell Douglas machines. The symbol table is suppressed by default. If the symbol table is needed (the debugger is required), then the compiler (M) option must be used.

```
>BASIC BP MCOMPTEST (M
```

The (M) option exists on both generic Pick and McDonnell Douglas. In generic Pick, the (M) option simply displays the variable allocation on the descriptor table. On McDonnell Douglas, the (M) option generates the symbol table and displays the variable allocation.

Reporting Descriptor Allocation

To demonstrate variable assignment, the program MCOMPTEST, shown in Fig. 3-5, is compiled with not only the (M) option to generate a map, but also with the (L) option to generate a listing, and the (P) option to direct the output to the print spooler.

```
001 *PROGRAM MCOMPTEST
002 *TEST THE (M) COMPILE OPTION AND SHOW THE DESCRIPTOR TABLE
003 *
004 *
005 COMMON CVAR1,CVAR2,CVAR3
006 *
007 DIM LOCARRAY(10)
008 MAT LOCARRAY = 0
009 10 *
010 PRINT 'ENTER FACTOR ':
011 INPUT FACTOR
012 IF FACTOR = ''  OR NOT(NUM(FACTOR)) THEN STOP
013 *
014 FOR CNT = 1 TO 10
015    LOCARRAY(CNT) = LOCARRAY(CNT) + FACTOR
016 NEXT CNT
017 *
018 FOR CNT = 1 TO 10
019    PRINT LOCARRAY(CNT)
020 NEXT CNT
021 *
022 GOTO 10
023 END
```

C030	CVAR1	C040	CVAR2	C050	CVAR3	080	LOCARRAY
060	FACTOR	070	CNT				

```
025  10
FRAMES LINES
 01  001-020
```

Program 'MCOMPTEST' compiled. 1 frame/s used.

FIG. 3-5. Compiler Output using the (M,L,P) options.

Program Highlights

The common statement,

COMMON CVAR1,CVAR2,CVAR3

allocates 3 variables to the common area. The use of the C in the variable names is an arbitrary convention used in the sample program. These variables are designated in the (M)apped output as:

C030 CVAR1   C040 CVAR2   C050 CVAR3

The C preceding the descriptor displacements is the system indication that these are common. This indicates that the variable CVAR1 is at displacement 30 from the beginning of the table, CVAR2 is at displacement 40 and CVAR3 is at displacement 50.

The local simple variables, FACTOR and CNT are defined in the next available descriptor table entries in the order in which they were encountered in the source program.

The dimensioned array LOCARRAY begins at displacement 80. This array actually takes up displacements, 80, 90, 100, 110,120, 130, 140, 150, 160, and 170 since it has 10 entries.

The first available descriptor entry is at displacement 30. This is due to the fact that the first entries are reserved for the following default descriptors:

- *FV   The first descriptor is the default file variable. The PICK/BASIC OPEN, READ, and WRITE statements do not require a file variable to be specified. The most recently open file which has not been assigned a file variable is held in this descriptor.

- *SV   The second descriptor is the default active list. The READNEXT command gets the next item-id from this list unless a select variable is specified in the internal SELECT TO and retrieved with the READNEXT FROM commands. See the chapter "List Processing" for more details.

The output for statement lable 10,

```
025   10
```

indicates that statement label 10 is at a 25-byte displacement within the generated object code.

Finally, the map shows equivalent lines of source code which are compiled into the object frames. This is handy for optimizing loops which may cross frame boundaries.

```
FRAMES LINES
  01   001-020
  02   021-023
```

There may be a bug in this portion of the report. On Pick PC release R83, the lines of the source code in the last frame of the object are not reported. This is probably due to the fact that the last frames of object code contain the symbol table, which is not yet completed.

ARRAYS AND STRINGS

An array is the most useful means of structuring data within a program. PICK/BASIC provides two flavors of array management, dynamic and static (dimensioned). Because a majority of the code written in Pick deals with data in arrays, it is important to be familiar with the nature of these arrays.

Dynamic Arrays

Dynamic arrays are data strings which use the standard system delimiters—(attribute, value, and subvalue marks—as field delimiters. A string is a string is a string. Redundant, isn't it? That's the way it is in the Pick system. Strings are arrays of ASCII characters, whether made up of a single logical data entity or a series of logical entities. The character used to delimit data entities (fields) within a string can be any unique ASCII character that is not used as part of the data.

Dynamic array strings are, essentially, no different than any other variable data string being addressed in a PICK/BASIC program.

- Dynamic array are treated as a single variable containing an ASCII string requiring a single descriptor table entry.
- The maximum array length cannot exceed 32,000 bytes on most releases.

The word dynamic means "in motion, changing." The number of entries varies and does not have to be declared to the PICK/BASIC compiler or runtime. The power of dynamic arrays lies in the use of the special intrinsic functions provided in PICK/BASIC. These functions allow any element in a string to be addressed by three dimensions—attribute, value, and subvalue.

Intrinsic Function Review

The dynamic array intrinsic functions are presented in two formats, the traditional and contemporary. The *traditional* intrinsic function formats have existed since the inception of dynamic arrays in the Pick system and are found on all implementations. The *contemporary* versions were first implemented by Microdata Corporation back in the late 70's. Since then, most of the implementations have adopted the contemporary versions. However, the only way to be sure is to experiment with the different forms.

Element Extraction

Any element on the array can be addressed and retrieved through the EXTRACT function. The variable named ARRAYcontains the dynamic array string:

```
ELEMENT = EXTRACT(ARRAY,attr#,val#,subval#)
```

Or, in the more contemporary form which is compatible on all machines:

```
ELEMENT = ARRAY<attr#,val#,subval#>
```

Element Replacement

Any element on the array can be addressed and replaced using the REPLACE function:

```
ARRAY = REPLACE(ARRAY,attr#,val#,subval#,DATUM)
```

Or, in the contemporary format:

```
ARRAY<attr#,val#,subval#> = DATUM
```

RULE: *for both extract and replace; use the contemporary version!* It works on all implementations and increases the readablility of the code.

A position indicator of -1, designates a replace at the end of the array. This does not replace the last entry. Rather, a new entry is tagged on the end.

```
ARRAY<-1> = DATUM
```

The statement above adds the string in DATUM as a new attribute at the end of the array string, ARRAY. Here are some other examples:

```
ARRAY<2,-1> = DATUM
```

adds a new value to the end of the multivalue list in attribute two.

```
ARRAY<1,3,-1> = DATUM
```

adds a new subvalue to the end of the subvalue list in value three of attribute one. The -1 indicator works the same with the INSERT function.

Be careful when appending a null entry at the end of an array. It doesn't work. In most cases, null values have to be added to the end of an array string by concatenating the delimiter character as follows:

```
ARRAY = ARRAY : CHAR(254)
```

Element Insertion

Elements can be inserted at any position on a dynamic array. The relative position is changed for elements at the same level (attribute, value or subvalue), which follow the insert position. ARRAY is the array variable and DATUM is the string to insert:

```
ARRAY = INSERT(ARRAY,attr#,val#,subval#,DATUM)
```

The lowest level addressed determines the level of the insert.

```
ARRAY = INSERT(ARRAY,1,0,0,DATUM)
```

The following statement inserts the contents of VALUE before the first attribute of the array, ARRAY:

```
ARRAY = INSERT(ARRAY,3,1,0,DATUM)
```

The following statement inserts the string in DATUM before the first value of the third attribute in the array, ARRAY. The contemporary format is easier to read:

```
INS DATUM BEFORE ARRAY<attr#,val#,subval#>
```

Here are the same intrinsic functions as above expressed in the contemporary form:

```
INS DATUM BEFORE ARRAY<1>
INS DATUM BEFORE ARRAY<3,1>
```

The contemporary INSERT is available on most of the new implementations. Use it if it is available. However, for the sake of compatibility, the traditional version is used exclusively in this text.

A position indicator of -1, like that of a REPLACE statement, tags an entry at the end of the array. The following statement adds the string in DATUM as a new attribute at the end of the array string, ARRAY:

    ARRAY = INSERT(ARRAY, − 1,0,0,DATUM)

The next statement adds a new value to the end of the multivalue list in attribute two.

    ARRAY = INSERT(ARRAY,2, − 1,0,DATUM)

The next statement adds a new subvalue to the end of the subvalue list in value three of attribute three.

    ARRAY = INSERT(ARRAY,1,3, − 1,DATUM)

Once again, be careful when inserting a null element to the end of an array. If it doesn't work, use string concatenation.

Element Deletion

Any element can be deleted from a dynamic array:

    ARRAY = DELETE(ARRAY,*attr#,val#,subval#*)

The contemporary format is clearer:

    DEL ARRAY < *attr#,val#subval#* >

Again, this syntax is available on most, but not all of the implementations.

Please note that the DELETE function physically removes the targeted attribute, value or subvalue along with the referenced delimiter. This should not be confused with the action of replacing an entry with a null string:

    DEL ARRAY<3> vs ARRAY<3> = ''

The latter does not change the relative positions of the attributes; the DEL does.

Null Array Elements

Whenever a dynamic array is written to the disk using the WRITE statement, the trailing null attribute elements are trimmed. For example, consider the following string:

    this]is^a^string^^^

The trailing attribute marks are stripped. Embedded nulls are left intact. Consider the following string:

    this^is^a^test^^^

The trailing attributes are stripped, but the embedded null second attribute remains unchanged. Finally, consider the following array string:

    this]is]a]^^]^^

Only the trailing attributes are stripped. The remaining value marks are left untouched.

Locating Array Elements

Any element in a dynamic array can be searched for and the current position reported:

LOCATE(DATUM,ARRAY;POSITION) THEN... ELSE...

This command searches for the string DATUM in every attribute of the array ARRAY. DATUM is compared to the entire attribute. If the string is found on ARRAY, the THEN clause is taken and the value of POSITION is the matching attribute number. The ELSE clause is taken when the string is not found in the array.

If the criteria for the search is to compare each value within an attribute, then the attribute containing the multivalued list must be designated:

LOCATE(DATUM,ARRAY,2;POSITION) THEN.. ELSE..

In this case, POSITION is set to the matching value position number.

Subvalue lists reside within a value. Therefore, the value position must be included in the statement.

LOCATE(DATUM,ARRAY,1,3;POSITION) THEN... ELSE..

The above locates a subvalue in value three of attribute 1. POSITION is set to the subvalue position number.

LOCATE is the driving tool for maintaining dynamic ordered lists in a PICK/BASIC program. Because the statement is conditional, elements can be added or removed from the list depending on whether they already exist or not.

The contemporary syntax yields a far friendlier statement. The delimiter search is based on the position indicated in the dynamic reference (<amc,vmc,svmc>). The absence of a dynamic reference designates an attribute search. The use of a dynamic amc reference (<amc>) designates a value search. The use of both an amc and vmc reference (<amc,vmc>) designates a subvalue search.

LOCATE DATUM IN ARRAY,1 SETTING POSITION THEN...ELSE...

or

LOCATE DATUM IN ARRAY<2>,1 SETTING POSITION THEN..ELSE...

or

LOCATE DATUM IN ARRAY<1,3>,1 SETTING POSITION THEN..ELSE.

The first statement locates the attribute containing the string DATUM on the array ARRAY starting from the first attribute. The (,1) indicates the search starting position. If it had been a (,3) then the search would have started at attribute 3.

The second statement locates the value containing the string DATUM, starting at the first value in the second attribute of ARRAY.

The third statement locates the subvalue containing DATUM in the third value in the first attribute of ARRAY. The search begins at the first subvalue.

Once again, the contemporary version is not yet available on all implementations.

Dimensioned Arrays

Dimensioned arrays are static arrays that must be declared in the source program by the DIMENSION compiler directive. A descriptor is allocated for each array entry:

DIM ITEM(10)
DIM TABLE(5,2)

Each array generates 10 descriptors. Each entry in a dimensioned array is allocated a separate descriptor. Because a descriptor can be used to define any data type, a dimensioned array be used as a matrix of file variables, subroutine pointers, binary numbers, simple ASCII strings or dynamic arrays. A descriptor array is illustrated in Fig. 3-6.

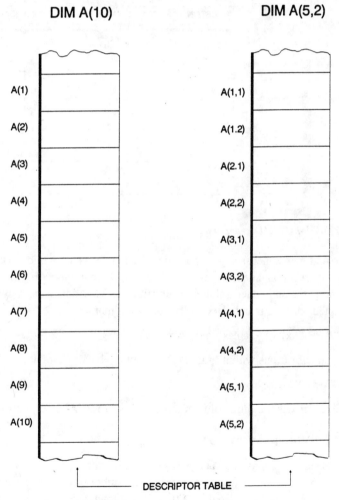

FIG. 3-6. Dimensioned array descriptors.

When an item is read using MATREAD, the attributes are parsed to corresponding array entries, as shown in Fig. 3-7. (MATREAD only works with 1 dimensional arrays.)

```
DIM ARRAY(5)
MATREAD ARRAY FROM FILE,ID ELSE STOP
```

Each attribute becomes a separate variable. Compare this to the case where the READ statement is used to retrieve the entire item into a single variable. As the item length crosses frame boundaries, the difference in handling an item in a dimensioned array versus a single dynamic array can be drastic. ARRAY(2) is attribute 2 of the item MATREAD into ARRAY.

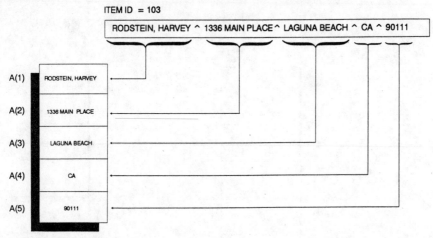

FIG. 3-7. MATREAD item parse.

A dimensioned array is potentially a matrix of dynamic arrays. If the item being MATREAD contains multivalued attributes, the corresponding dimensioned array entry contains the embedded value and subvalue marks. Addressing a dynamic value in a subscripted variable is indicated in the following manner:

```
ARRAY(x{,y})<amc{,vmc{,svmc}w1
```

The specifications within braces ({}) are optional. For example:

```
ARRAY(2)<1,3>
```

This addresses the third value in dimensioned array, ARRAY, entry number 2.

Dimensioned Array Limits

Because dimensioned arrays reserve a descriptor per entry, the maximum number of array entries cannot exceed the maximum number of descriptors available to a program. For example, an array sized at 100 by 100, shown as:

```
DIM A(100,100)
```

requires 10,000 descriptors. This is quite a bit more than the maximum of 3,200.

Arrays Larger Than an Item

A mismatched array size, where the number of attributes in an item is less than the number of entries in the dimensioned array, causes no problems unless the number of descriptors is close to the 3,200 maximum. It is often good practice to design some "head room" in a dimensioned array so that as new attributes are added, the DIM statements do not have to be modified. The MATREAD parses an item until the last attribute is encountered and initializes the trailing locations to null. The MATWRITE rebuilds the item string and strips any trailing null attributes.

It is important to make sure that the dimensioned array is initialized to all null strings before the MATREAD, (MAT A = ''). If the array is not initialized, the system assumes that each element contains a zero (VARIABLE UNASSIGED, ZERO USED!). This eliminates the problem of extra attributes containing zeros being appended to an item on the next MATWRITE.

Arrays Smaller Than an Item

The next case of mismatched array size occurs when an item is parsed and read into an array smaller than the number of attributes in the item. The attributes are parsed into their corresponding array elements until the last entry is reached. At this point, the remaining attributes are bunched into the last descriptor in the array. This is all well and good as long as no references are made to the last array entry. Any references to the last array entry are fatal to PICK/BASIC runtime. Array subscripts less than the last entry perform normally.

The MATWRITE rebuilds the entire item from the array (including the orphan string in the last entry) and writes it to the file. This technique of dimensioning an array smaller than an item is useful for parsing only the first few attributes while leaving the remainder of the item untouched. This is advantageous only if the first few attributes are needed and the rest of the item can be carried around as baggage.

CAUTION: The best way to destroy the integrity of a database is to enter strings of data containing attribute marks into array elements in the middle of a data structure, then MATWRITE that structure. All the attributes beyond that point in the array are shifted down an equivalent number of attribute positions.

The Mat Statement

Every entry in a dimensioned array can be set to the same value by using the MAT statement:

```
DIM A(10)
MAT A = ''
```

This sets every entry in the array A to a null string without having to brute force the code:

```
DIM A(10)
FOR I = 1 TO 10
  A(I) = ''
NEXT I
```

The MAT command can be used to set corresponding values of one array to another. For example:

```
DIM A(10),B(10)
MAT A = ''
MAT B = MAT A
```

This is proper as long as the receiving array is the same size or larger than the source array. For example:

```
DIM A(10),B(12),C(5,2)
```

The following statements are valid:

```
MAT B = MAT A
MAT A = MAT C
```

If the receiving array is smaller than the source array, only those corresponding descriptors are copied between the arrays. The remaining entries are untouched. When equating single and two dimensional arrays, the number of entries is the determining factor, not the array dimensions. That is why A and C can be equated. Both have 10 entries.

However, this statement is invalid:

```
MAT A = MAT B
```

Array A is smaller than B making this statement unacceptable and causing a PICK/BASIC runtime abort.

NOTE: Depending on the size of the array, the MAT statement may take a little extra time to perform. This can make the initialization of a large dimensioned array noticeably slow. However, there are circumstances that make it more efficient to accept slower setup in order to allow more efficient data manipulation. Read on!

Dynamic vs. Dimensioned Arrays

Although dynamic array intrinsic functions are powerful, they can lure the programmer into a trap which becomes quicksand for the application. Each time a dynamic reference is made to an array element, the system must scan from the beginning of the array string, counting delimiters, until the targeted element is found. This can cause a considerable amount of overhead, especially if the string crosses frame boundaries. For example, in the following FOR..NEXT loop:

```
CNT = DCOUNT(LIST,VM)
FOR I = 1 to CNT
  PRINT LIST<1,VM>
NEXT I
```

Each time a multivalue element is extracted and printed from the array LIST, the system must scan from the beginning of the array to locate the specified entry.

The number of "worst-case" frame faults generated by repetitively addressing subsequent entries in a dynamic array depends on a number of factors, including the number of data references in a frame, the number of frames occupied by the string, and the amount of physical memory available.

Crossing a frame boundary when scanning a string does not, in itself, mean that a frame fault occurs. The frame, or frames, may already be in memory. However, reducing the number of frame boundaries crossed does reduce the number of possible frame faults.

The number of frame boundaries crossed can be figured out. To reference any field in a string N frames from the beginning requires N-1 frame boundaries to be crossed. Notice that frame 1 is not being counted because it is the starting point. If frame 1 is paged out between each process, then it too generates a frame fault. However, in this case only frame boundary crossings are being calculated.

Letting R represent the number of dynamic references per frame, (this can be thought of as extracts per frame), the number of crossed frame boundaries is:

$$B = R * (N - 1)$$

B is the number of crossed frame boundaries. Repetitive extracts, as in the above FOR..NEXT loop, makes B the summation of $(R*(N-1))$ for frames from 1 to the last frame in the linked chain.

Table 3-1 is a brief chart of the frame boundaries crossed versus the size of the string, assuming that each extract is approximately 50 bytes long. In a 500-byte data frame, the value of R is equal to 10.

	String size (in frames)	Crossed Frame boundaries
	1	0
TABLE 3-1. Possible Frame Boundary Crossings when Scanning a Dynamic Array.	2	10
	3	30
	4	60
	5	100
	6	150
	7	210

Arrays under 1 frame show no significant overhead. As array sizes grow, (or, for that matter, the size of any string), the number of frame boundary crossings and therefore the number of possible frame faults increase.

When a frame boundary is crossed without a disk read, the overhead is still considerable due to the fact that the system must detach the pointing register, looks for the new frame in memory, and re-attach the register to the new frame. Even when frame boundaries are not crossed, there is still a measurable amount of overhead for the system to scan for each array reference.

Array Scanning Example

This is an effective demonstration of the way system throughput can be significantly affected by the choice of the array used in a PICK/BASIC program. Consider an application where each item is made up of a set of correlated multivalued lists, as shown in Fig. 3-8.

```
ID: DocumentNumber
001 122]323]345]222].......111]333
002 222]123]232]232].......321]544
003 922]234]233]111].......121]433
...
...
030 245]566]765]899].......123]444
```

FIG. 3-8. Sample item with multi-valued lists.

Each item has, on the average, 30 attributes, and each attribute has 100 values. Each attribute is approximately 300 bytes long, which makes each item between 9K and 10K bytes long. The file contains 1000 items.

The task of the programmer is to break the item into a series of fixed length data records. This is often a requirement when interfacing via tape or communications to non-Pick systems.

The records are made up of the correlated values in each of the attributes. That is, the first values of every attribute are concatenated to form the first record, the second values form the second record, and so on.

Now, take a look at the skeletal structure of the code that might be used to perform the item parsing, as shown in Fig. 3-9. The dynamic reference extracts the value and concatenates it to the end of the record. Each time that this statement is performed, the system is forced to scan from the beginning of the string. This can potentially cause performance problems.

```
READ ITEM FROM FILE,ID ELSE STOP
FOR VMC = 1 to 100
     RECORD = ''
     FOR AMC = 1 to 30
          DATFLD = ITEM<AMC,VMC>
          RECORD = RECORD : DATFLD "R%4"
     NEXT AMC
     ..
NEXT VMC
```

FIG. 3-9. Parse the multi-valued item using dynamic functions.

Take a look at the number of bytes scanned for each pass through the AMC loop. (Each attribute is approximately 300 bytes long.) When AMC is 1, the scan is effectively zero. But when AMC is 2, the scan is 300, when AMC is 3, the scan is 600, when AMC is 4, the scan is 900 and so on. This can be represented as the summation of

$(AMC-1)*300$ for AMC from 1 to 30. For example:

```
TOTAL = 0
FOR AMC = 1 TO 30
 TOTAL = TOTAL + (AMC-1)*300
NEXT AMC
PRINT TOTAL
```

This routine generates the total number of bytes scanned for the first value pass alone. One hundred records are built per item. The approximate number of bytes scanned to parse the first item into 100 records is 13,050,000. Now consider the processing overhead for 1000 items. This puts the figure over 13 billion bytes.

The goal in any Pick program is to avoid repetitive handling of long strings and, thereby, reduce the number of required frame faults. The solution is to force the system to parse the attributes of the item into a series of separate, smaller strings by using the MATREAD statement. The same program is re-written in Fig. 3-10.

```
DIM ITEM(30)
MATREAD ITEM FROM FILE,ID ELSE STOP
FOR VMC = 1 to 100
     RECORD = ''
     FOR AMC = 1 to 30
          DATFLD = ITEM(AMC)<1,VMC>
          RECORD = RECORD : DATFLD "R%4"
     NEXT AMC
       ..
NEXT VMC
```

FIG. 3-10. Parse the multi-valued item using both dynamic and static references.

The only significant change is that the variable ITEM is now a dimensioned array. The MATREAD statement parses the attributes to separate descriptors, thereby alleviating the requirement to scan all preceding attributes before addressing the targeted attribute and value. The statement for retrieving a value from the targeted attribute is:

```
DATFLD = ITEM(AMC)<1,VMC>
```

The subscripted variable reference ITEM(AMC) addresses the parsed attribute. The dynamic reference <1,VMC> extracts the value. When MATREAD parses the attributes to separate array entries, each is treated as a single attribute. Hence, the need for the attribute designator of one.

The first pass to build the first record requires an insignificant amount of data scanning resulting in a byte scan of effectively zero. In fact, the first 100 records parsed from the first item does not need to scan more than 130,500 bytes. This is still approximately 13 times more than the actual item size, but significantly less than what is required when handling the item as a single dynamic array.

Conclusions

Comparative speed of the file IO commands is not the only factor for choosing them. Even though MATREAD may take twice as long as READ, and MATWRITE may take three times as long as WRITE, the overall efficiency of the program is based on the string sizes being handled during processing.

In an application with large items, dynamic arrays are a wonderful way to degrade system throughput. The suggested way to handle file IO is to use the MATREAD and MATWRITE statements for items that exceed frame size. If items are under a frame in length, then the dynamic READ and WRITE may be used with little noticeable degradation. The choices that the programmer has to make are heavily dependent on the initial database design.

Item size in itself is not the limiting factor. In the ideal world, each attribute should be under a frame size for the best throughput. Assume that an application is running on a machine with enough memory to accommodate a 50K item. If all the data in this item is needed at one time, a MATREAD can read and parse the item in 2 or 3 seconds. If this data is spread out into 10 separate items of 5K each, it might take over 20 or 30 seconds to perform all these reads.

However, if the application dictates that this 50K byte of details is made up of individual parts, which are usually retrieved and manipulated separately, then breaking it up into multiple items is a much better approach. There is no need to carry around all that unrelated data in the same item.

Data String Parsing

The power of PICK/BASIC is its ability to handle variable length ASCII strings. As described above, there is a set of powerful intrinsic functions for parsing strings which use the standard system delimiters to mark substrings, (fields in a dynamic array). There is also a set of powerful functions for extracting data fields from strings delimited by any unique ASCII character. These include the FIELD, COL1, COL2, and INDEX intrinsic functions. Mastering these string functions is as important as becoming comfortable with the dynamic array instrinsics. This is especially true when converting other data types and formats to Pick.

In this section, two examples are presented. The first demonstrates inserting, deleting, and replacing entries from a string that uses asterisks (*) as field delimiters. The second example demonstrates that any string using any delimiter can be parsed and evaluated. The string is an ACCESS sentence which the PICK/BASIC program pre-parses and displays the data reference elements prior to passing the sentence to TCL.

Parsing Example 1

Emulating dynamic functions on an ASCII string delimited by asterisks (*) is shown in Fig. 3-11.

```
    PARSE1
001 *PROGRAM PARSE1
002 *Emulate dynmaic functions using string functions
003 *Harvey E. Rodstein
004 *
005 *
006 PROMPT ''
007 EQU DEL TO '*'
008 EQU BEL TO CHAR(7)
009 *
010 STRING = ''
011 *
012 1 * Function Menu
013 *
014 PRINT @(-1):'String Functions':
015 PRINT @(1,2):'String = ':STRING:
016 PRINT @(1,4):'I)NSERT'
017 PRINT @(1,5):'D)ELETE':
018 PRINT @(1,6):'R)EPLACE':
019 PRINT @(1,7):'C)LEAR':
020 PRINT @(1,8):'Q)UIT':
021 LOOP
022    PRINT @(1,11):'Enter choice ':@(-4):
023    INPUT ANS,1:
024    ANS = OCONV(ANS,'MCU')
025    BRANCH = INDEX('IDRCQ',ANS,1)
026 UNTIL ANS # '' AND BRANCH DO REPEAT
027 IF BRANCH = 5 THEN
028     PRINT @(-1):
029     STOP
030 END
031 DELCNT = DCOUNT(STRING,DEL)
032 ON BRANCH GOSUB 100,200,300,400
033 GOTO 1
034 *
035 *
036 100 * Insert an entry
037 *
038 PRINT @(1,12):'Enter value to insert ':
039 INPUT VALUE
040 IF VALUE = '' OR VALUE = 'QUIT' THEN RETURN
041 GOSUB 1000 ;* Get field position
042 IF POS = '' OR POS[1,1] = 'Q' THEN RETURN
043 IF POS>DELCNT THEN
044     IF NOT(DELCNT) THEN DELCNT = 1
045     STRING=STRING:STR(DEL,(POS-DELCNT))
046     STRING = STRING:VALUE
047 END ELSE
048     STARTINS = INDEX(STRING,DEL,POS-1)
049     STRING = STRING[1,STARTINS]:VALUE:'*':STRING[STARTINS+1,32000]
050 END
051 RETURN
052 *
```

FIG. 3-11. PARSE1 program listing.

```
053 200 * Delete
054 *
055 GOSUB 1000
056 IF POS = '' OR POS[1,1] = 'Q' THEN RETURN
057 VALUE = FIELD(STRING,DEL,POS)
058 STRING = STRING[1,COL1()]:STRING[COL2()+1,32000]
059 RETURN
060 *
061 *
062 300 * Replace
063 *
064 PRINT @(1,12):'Enter value string to use for the replace ':
065 INPUT VALUE
066 IF VALUE = '' OR VALUE = 'QUIT' THEN RETURN
067 GOSUB 1000 ;* Get field position
068 IF POS = '' OR POS[1,1] = 'Q' THEN RETURN
069 IF POS>DELCNT THEN
070    IF NOT(DELCNT) THEN DELCNT = 1
071    STRING=STRING:STR(DEL,(POS-DELCNT))
072    STRING = STRING:VALUE
073 END ELSE
074    SEARCHVAL = FIELD(STRING,DEL,POS)
075    STRING = STRING[1,COL1()]:VALUE:STRING[COL2(),32000]
076 END
077 RETURN
078 *
079 *
080 400 * Clear it
081 *
082 STRING = ''
083 RETURN
084 *
085 *
086 1000 * Get field position
087 *
088 LOOP
089    PRINT @(1,13):'Enter field position ':
090    INPUT POS
091    POS = OCONV(POS,'MCU')
092 UNTIL NUM(POS) OR POS[1,1] ='Q' DO
093    PRINT BEL:
094 REPEAT
095 RETURN
096 *
097 END
```

FIG. 3-11 ends.

Program Highlights

PARSE1 initializes its test string, STRING, to null and displays a menu to allow fields to be inserted (I), deleted (D), replaced (R), or the whole string cleared (C). The menu option is prompted for and validated by the following code:

```
021 LOOP
```

```
022      PRINT @(1,11): 'Enter choice ':@(-4):
023      INPUT ANS,1:
024      ANS = OCONV(ANS,'MCU')
025      BRANCH = INDEX('IDRCQ',ANS,1)
026 UNTIL ANS # '' AND BRANCH DO REPEAT
```

To allow case insensitivity, the answer is forced to uppercase:

```
ANS = OCONV(ANS,'MCU')
```

Next, ANS is converted to an equivalent sequence number based on the INDEX function:

```
BRANCH = INDEX('IDRCQ',ANS,1)
```

An answer of I, D, R, C, or Q generates a value between 1 and 5, respectively. The Q condition (5) is handled as a bailout prior to the branch. The remaining numeric values of BRANCH can now be used in an index GOSUB statement as follows:

```
032 ON BRANCH GOSUB 100,200,300,400
```

Each subroutine needs to know the current number of fields, DELCNT, in order to parse the string. So that the code need not be repeated in every subroutine, DELCNT is determined before the branch is taken:

```
031 DELCNT = DCOUNT(STRING,DEL)
```

Choosing I)nsert   An insert is controlled by subroutine 100. The user is prompted for the value string and position of the insert. Subroutine 1000 is a generalized subroutine to prompt for the field position.

Before the insert can be performed, there are some statistics about the string that you must know. If this string had been a dynamic array, this setup work would automatically be taken care of by the dynamic array intrinsic functions. Because this string is not a dynamic array, it is up to the programmer to do the work.

First, the current number of fields is already stored in DELCNT. It must be determined whether the targeted insert position (POS) exists or the string must be padded to the position.

```
043 IF POS>DELCNT THEN
044      IF NOT(DELCNT) THEN DELCNT = 1
045      STRING=STRING:STR(DEL,(POS-DELCNT))
046      STRING = STRING:VALUE
047 END ELSE
048      STARTINS = INDEX(STRING,DEL,POS-1)
049      STRING STRING[1,STARTINS]:VALUE:'*':STRING[STARTINS+1,32000]
050 END
```

If the targeted position is greater than the current number of fields, then the string must be padded to the correct number of delimiters.

To address the initial case when the string is null and the number of delimiters is zero, the DELCNT is forced to 1 because the minimum number of fields must be 1. The delimiter padding is performed by the statement:

STRING = STRING:STR(DEL,(POS – DELCNT))

The length of the padded delimiters is equal to the difference between the targeted position and the current number of fields. Once the string is padded with delimiters, the value to be inserted can be added to the end of the string:

STRING = STRING:VALUE

However, if the position of the insert is within the body of the string, padding is not required. First, the starting position for the insert must be determined:

STARTINS = INDEX(STRING,DEL,POS – 1)

The number of delimiters in a string is one less than the number of fields. Therefore, the starting character position for the insert begins at POS – 1. Here the INDEX function proves useful not for validation but to determine the character position of the delimiter preceding the field for the targeted insert. All that is left is to rebuild the string with the inserted value. The variable TAIL controls whether the insert is performed at the end or within the body of the string:

STRING = STRING[1,STARTINS]:VALUE:'*':STRING[STARTINS + 1,32000]

In order to embed VALUE within the body of the string, the string preceding the insertion must be extracted:

STRING[1,STARTINS]

This string must then be concatenated with the data value along with an extra delimiter,

VALUE:'*'

and then with the remainder of the string:

STRING[STARTINS + 1,32000]

The length indication of 32,000 in the text extract statement should handle any size string. The system scans to the string terminating segment mark, not the full 32,000 characters. If this seems distasteful, the number of characters remaining in the string can be calculated within the statement as follows:

STRING[STARTINS + 1,LEN(STRING) – STARTINS – 1]

The length function requires the overhead of scanning the entire string for the length, but may eliminate the possibility on some systems of an over-scan of the string. An over-scan is manifested by an unpredictable garbage at the end of the rebuilt string. If the insert requires padding to be accomplished, the new value is simply tagged on the end of the padded string:

STRING = STRING[1,STARTINS]:VALUE

Choosing D)elete The delete code is a bit easier than the insert. All the program needs to know is the field position to be deleted. This is placed in the variable POS as before. The string must be rebuilt from the substring preceding and following the field in question. The FIELD function takes care of all the information needed.

```
057 VALUE = FIELD(STRING,DEL,POS)
```

The actual contents of VALUE is not important. What is important is the "side effect" functions available after a FIELD statement. The COL1( ) function provides the column position of the delimiter preceding the field, and COL2( ) provides the column position of the delimiter following the field. Armed with this information, the string can be rebuilt without the targeted field by the following statement:

```
058 STRING = STRING[1,COL1( )]:STRING[COL2( )+1,32000]
```

The first part of the string is extracted up to and including the delimiter preceding the field to be deleted:

```
STRING[1,COL1( )]
```

The remainder of the string is extracted beginning at the column position just following the field terminating delimiter.

```
STRING[COL2( )+1,32000]
```

These two components are concatenated to produce the newstring.

Choosing R)eplace Deciding on the method of replacement, like insert, depends on whether or not the string must be padded. If the addressed field position is greater than the delimiter count, the string must be padded and value tagged to the end:

```
070  IF NOT(DELCNT) THEN DELCNT = 1
071  STRING = STRING:STR(DEL,(POS − DELCNT))
072  STRING = STRING:VALUE
```

If the replace takes place in the body of the string, padding is not required. The variable SEARCHVAL is not important. Again, what is important are the functions, COL1( ) and COL2( ).

```
074 SEARCHVAL = FIELD(STRING,DEL,POS)
075 STRING = STRING[1,COL1( )]:VALUE:STRING[COL2( ),32000]
```

The string is rebuilt in the same way that the delete is performed, except the new value is concatenated between the string preceding and following SEARCHVAL.

Choosing C)lear Clearing a string is accomplished by setting the variable equal to a null string.

```
STRING = ''
```

Parsing Example 2

An ACCESS statement is like any other data string. The fields of the string are words delimited by spaces. The purpose of the routine listed in Fig. 3-12 is to identify the key words in the ACCESS sentence. This example program accepts input of an ACCESS sentence and pre-parses the data references to make sure everything is kosher. Because this program can identify the data definitions as well as the filename and verb, an additional level of security can be added by placing a similar routine between the user and TCL.

```
        PARSE2
001 *PROGRAM PARSE2
002 *Parse an ACCESS sentence and display major compenents
003 *Harvey E. Rodstein
004 *
005 *
006 PROMPT ':'
007 EQU DEL TO ' '
008 EQU BEL TO CHAR(7)
009 EQU AM  TO CHAR(254)
010 *
011 OPEN 'MD' TO MD ELSE STOP 201,'MD'
012 *
013 * Main Routine
014 *
015 LOOP
016   CRT 'Enter an ACCESS sentence or "QUIT" to stop '
017   INPUT SENTENCE
018   SENTENCE = OCONV(TRIM(SENTENCE),'MCU')
019 UNTIL SENTENCE = 'QUIT' DO
020   IF SENTENCE # '' THEN GOSUB 1000 ;* PARSEIT
021 REPEAT
022 *
023 STOP
024 *
025 *
026 1000 * PARSEIT
027 *
028 * VERB
029 *
030 VERB = FIELD(SENTENCE,DEL,1)
031 READ CHECKITEM FROM MD,VERB THEN
032      ERROR = CHECKITEM[1,1]#'P'
033 END ELSE ERROR = 1
034 IF ERROR THEN
035   CRT 'A BAD VERB "':VERB:'"'
036   RETURN
037 END
038 *
039 * FILENAME
040 *
041 WORDCNT = DCOUNT(SENTENCE,DEL) ; * Count the words
```

FIG. 3-12. PARSE2 program listing.

```
042 FOUND = 0
043 FOR POS = 2 TO WORDCNT UNTIL FOUND
044    WORD = FIELD(SENTENCE,DEL,POS)
045    OPEN 'DICT',WORD TO DICTFILE THEN FOUND = 1
046 NEXT POS
047 IF FOUND THEN
048    FILENAME = WORD
049 END ELSE
050    CRT 'FILE NAME "':WORD:'" IS NOT FOUND'
051    RETURN
052 END
053 *
054 * DATA DEFINITIONS
055 *
056 DEFARRAY = '' ;* Initialize data def array
057 ERROR = 0
058 FOR POS = 2 TO WORDCNT UNTIL ERROR
059    WORD = FIELD(SENTENCE,DEL,POS)
060    FOUND = 1
061    READ DATADEF FROM DICTFILE,WORD ELSE
062        READ DATADEF FROM MD,WORD ELSE FOUND = 0
063    END
064    IF FOUND THEN
065      IF INDEX('AS',DATADEF[1,1],1) THEN DEFARRAY<-1>=WORD
066    END
067 NEXT POS
068 *
069 * DISPLAY THE RESULTS
070 *
071 CRT STR('=',25)
072 CRT 'VERB = ':VERB
073 CRT 'FILE = ':FILENAME
074 CRT 'DEFS = ':
075 CNT = DCOUNT(DEFARRAY,AM)
076 FOR POS = 1 TO CNT
077      CRT DEFARRAY<POS>:" ":
078 NEXT POS
079 CRT
080 CRT STR('=',25)
081 RETURN
082 *
083 END
```

FIG. 3-12 ends.

Program Highlights

Once the sentence is INPUT, the string, SENTENCE, is converted to its simplest format. That is, the string is trimmed of leading, trailing and spurious embedded spaces, (using the TRIM function), and all alphabetic characters are forced to all uppercase. This is a good practice to become familiar with in order to ensure the entry of consistent data.

```
018   SENTENCE = OCONV(TRIM(SENTENCE),'MCU')
```

If the sentence is not the command "QUIT", then the words of the sentence are ready to be parsed by subroutine 1000. Subroutine 1000 has three major tasks:

- Identify the verb
- Identify the file
- Identify all data definitions

Identifying the Verb   The verb is the easiest of the words to extract because it must be the first word of the sentence. The FIELD function is used to perform the extraction of the first word:

```
030 VERB = FIELD(SENTENCE,DEL,1)
```

The potential verb is then verified by attempting to read the verb item from the master dictionary and verifying whether the item begins with a "P."

```
031 READ CHECKITEM FROM MD,VERB THEN
032    ERROR = CHECKITEM[1,1]#'P'
033 END ELSE ERROR = 1
```

Remember from Chapter 1 that all verbs in R83 have a "P" in the first position of attribute one of the verb defining item.

The following is a good example of the "stand-alone" capability of a logical statement:

```
CHECKITEM[1,1]#'P'
```

The following relational statement evaluates to a one if true (the first character of the CHECKITEM is not a "P"), and zero if false (if it is equal to a "P"). The result is placed in the variable ERROR. If the item does not exist in the master dictionary, then the ELSE clause is taken and the error flag, ERROR, is forced to a one, true.

```
034 IF ERROR THEN
035    CRT 'A BAD VERB "':VERB:'"'
036    RETURN
037 END
```

The error flag is then checked to see if either condition has set it to true. If so, the verb is bad and the process returns.

Identifying the File   Identifying the file is a bit more complex, because any word at any position following the verb is potentially the file name. The first thing to do is count the number of words in the sentence:

```
041 WORDCNT = DCOUNT(SENTENCE,DEL) ; * Count the words
```

Remember, words in a sentence are simply fields delimited by spaces.

The next task is to loop through every word in the sentence until a file name is found. The variable FOUND is used as a flag to indicate success.

```
042 FOUND = 0
```

The loop is a FOR..NEXT from word position 2 thought the maximum number of words. If the file is found, then the loop terminates before the rest of the words are processed.

```
043 FOR POS = 2 TO WORDCNT UNTIL FOUND
...
...
046 NEXT POS
```

The simplest way to determine whether the word is a valid file name is to attempt to open the dictionary of the file. Already having the dictionary open proves useful later on when validating the data definition items. The word is extracted using the FIELD function and then used in an OPEN statement. If the OPEN is successful, the flag FOUND is set and the loop terminated:

```
044 WORD = FIELD(SENTENCE,DEL,POS)
045 OPEN 'DICT',WORD TO DICTFILE THEN FOUND = 1
```

After the loop completes, the FOUND flag is double checked. If the filename is found, then FILENAME contains the value of the last word checked. If the file is not found, the parsing attempt is terminated.

```
047 IF FOUND THEN
048     FILENAME = WORD
049 END ELSE
050     CRT 'FILE NAME "':WORD:'" IS NOT FOUND'
051     RETURN
052 END
```

Identifying Data Definitions   More than one data definition is possible in the sentence. Therefore, a dynamic array of definition names is built as the sentence is parsed. The array DEFARRAY is initialized before proceeding:

```
056 DEFARRAY = '' ;* Initialize data def array
```

A loop is initiated that processes every word in the sentence from position 2 until all the words are processed or an unidentified word is found. Unidentified words may be flagged by the variable ERROR:

```
057 ERROR = 0
058 FOR POS = 2 TO WORDCNT UNTIL ERROR
...
...
067 NEXT POS
```

Every data definition word in an ACCESS sentence must reside in either the file dictionary or in the account master dictionary. The word is tested by using it as an item-id to attempt a read from the file dictionary. Upon failure, a second read attempt is made, but this time, from the master dictionary. The flag FOUND is initially set to true. If the word is not found in either file, the flag FOUND is reset to false.

```
059 WORD = FIELD(SENTENCE,DEL,POS)
060 FOUND = 1
061 READ DATADEF FROM DICTFILE,WORD ELSE
062    READ DATADEF FROM MD,WORD ELSE FOUND = 0
063 END
```

If the word is found, the first character of the first attribute is tested for an A or an S, indicating a valid data definition item. An X type is not valid because it is a protected attribute:

```
064 IF FOUND THEN
065    IF INDEX('AS',DATADEF[1,1],1) THEN DEFARRAY< -1> =WORD
066 END
```

If the word is a valid definition, it is added to the DATADEF array. The INDEX function proves useful as an implied OR, testing for the value of the first character in DATADEF.

This example takes the first step of identifying the major elements of a command sentence. Once the file and data definitions are isolated, there is nothing to stop the programmer from checking these words against a security file to determine whether they are within the security limits of the user. This simply requires another level of read from a security file to determine whether access is to be restricted.

Advanced Parsing Commands

All of the string handling commands previously mentioned (string parsing and dynamic arrays) have one thing in common; they all must start at the beginning of the string and count delimiters before extracting any data.

The use of a dimensioned array is a great way of breaking strings down to their lowest common denominator before processing. The only commands generically available to perform this are MATREAD, to parse each attribute during a read, and MATWRITE, to rebuild the string from the matrix parts and write.

The newer implementations are providing extended intrinsic functions which can parse a string into a dimensioned array and then rebuild a string based on any delimiter character.

The syntax demonstrated here is courtesy of the late Rod Burns and John Drumheller who invented them for the Prime Information implementation. (By the way, they also invented EXECUTE and PICK/BASIC subroutine calls from data dictionary items.) The following functions seem to be popping up on most of today's implementations.

The MATPARSE Command

The MATPARSE command allows any string to be parsed and distributed to a dimensioned array based on any delimiter character. The general form is:

MATPARSE *dimarray* FROM *string*,delimiter

The *dimarray* is any previously dimensioned array, the *string* is any valid string expression, and the *delimiter* is any string of one or more characters, (system delimiters included).

```
DIM ARRAY(10)
STRING = 'THIS IS A TEST'
MATPARSE ARRAY FROM STRING," "
```

There is also another function, INMAT( ), which is a byproduct of the MATPARSE command. This function indicates the number of fields parsed in the last MATPARSE executed. This is quite helpful to limit a processing loop on the dimensioned array. If these commands had been available for the PARSE2 program, the code may have looked like this:

```
DIM WORDMAT(200)
MATPARSE WORDMAT FROM SENTENCE,DEL
WORDCNT = INMAT( )
FOUND = 0
FOR POS = 2 TO WORDCNT UNTIL FOUND
 WORD = WORDMAT(POS)
 OPEN 'DICT',WORD TO DICTFILE THEN FOUND = 1
NEXT POS
```

The MATBUILD Command

In order to complete the set of intrinsic parsing commands, the system needs a function to rebuild a string from a dimensioned matrix. This function is called MATBUILD. The general form is:

MATBUILD *string* FROM *dimarray,delimiter*

Where *string* is the variable name to hold the built string, *dimarray* is the dimensioned array name, and *delimiter* is one or more characters to delimit the elements of the resulting string.

The REMOVE Command

The REMOVE command allows an array to be scanned from the beginning to the end without repositioning to the beginning of the array between each extraction. Each time REMOVE is performed, a pointer is incremented to the end of the last element and retained for the next time. The general form looks like this:

REMOVE *string* FROM *dynamicarray* AT *loc* SETTING *delimflag*

The variable indicated by *string* is the substring removed from the array, *dynamicarray*.

The location, *loc*, is the position of the delimiter character which terminates the substring in the array. The location is initialized to zero prior to the first execution of REMOVE. From then on, *loc* should not be referenced unless to reinitialize it to zero. The delimiter flag, *delimflag,* is set to a numeric value based on the system delimiter encountered. The delimiter flag values are:

Value	Description
0	End of the string
2	CHAR(254), an attribute mark
3	CHAR(253), a value mark
4	CHAR(252), a subvalue mark
5	CHAR(251)
6	CHAR(250)

The REMOVE function passes back a value for *string* when any one of these delimiters is encountered. For example, consider the following dynamic array:

```
ARRAY = SMITH, JOHN^123 MAIN]APT 3C^SANTA ANA^CA
```

Note that the caret (^) represents an attribute mark, and the bracket (]) represents a value mark. A routine to process this string, using REMOVE, might look as follows:

```
LOC = 0
LOOP
    REMOVE STRING FROM ARRAY AT LOC SETTING DFLAG
WHILE DFLAG AND STRING#'' DO
    PRINT "Dflag = ":DFLAG:" Loc = ":Loc:" String = ":STRING
REPEAT
```

Notice that LOC is initialized to zero before entering the loop. The loop terminates only when both the DFLAG is zero and the STRING is null. The results of this routine look like this:

```
Dflag = 2 Loc  = 12 String  = SMITH, JOHN
Dflag = 3 Loc  = 21 String  = 123 MAIN
Dflag = 2 Loc  = 28 String  = APT 3C
Dflag = 2 Loc  = 38 String  = SANTA ANA
Dflag = 0 Loc  = 40 String  = CA
Dflag = 0 Loc  = 40 String  =
```

Because the REMOVE statement triggers on every delimiter, it is probably better used on consistently delimited strings where there is only one level of delimiter. In the hypothetical multivalued array LIST, the old method of processing the array is:

```
CNT = DCOUNT(LIST,VM)
FOR I = 1 to CNT
    PRINT LIST
NEXT I
```

This can be substituted with the following:

```
CNT = DCOUNT(LIST,VM)
FOR I = 1 to CNT
    REMOVE STRING FROM LIST AT LOC SETTING DFLAG
    PRINT STRING
NEXT I
```

This works only if there are no subvalues embedded in the values.

One word of caution before departing from this subject. Elements must not be replaced, deleted or inserted onto the dynamic array while looping through and using the REMOVE statement. If a change to the array is required, the location variable must be reset to zero, and the loop restarted from the beginning.

PROGRAMMING STANDARDS

The subject of programming standards is a touchy one because there are no hard and fast rules dictated by the operating system. The result of development efforts range from highly standardized to completely chaotic. It really depends on whether a shop dictates certain rules or leaves the decision completely up to the programmers. From there, it depends on whether or not the programmers communicate to each other. (The most difficult communication task in any system is the one between human beings.) What follows is a discussion of the main topics of system standardization. Notice that it all comes down to self discipline.

Structure

PICK/BASIC program source can run the gamut from highly structured to completely anarchical. The system makes no restriction. It is up to the programmer to use self-imposed rules for program structure. Otherwise, the results are difficult to maintain and alter.

Large, unstructured programs are maintenance nightmares. Imagine wading through a thousand lines of unstructured, "goto ridden" code to make a two or three byte change, only to discover that the modification of that single statement has caused the program logic to fall apart like a house of playing cards.

The 90-10 rule applies to writing any application. 90 percent of the code is used 10 percent of the time. Efficiency is not the hallmark of the first pass of any coding effort, rather it is maintainability. The efficiency "hot spots" can be tackled after the application is up and running.

Within the source item, a simple structure must be implemented to force consistency. This structure begins with an initialization section, which includes constants setup, variable declaration, and file opening statements. Next comes the main part of the program. The last section covers internal subroutines. Adhering to this structure makes program enhancement and support a much less hectic task. The programmer can control the "look" of the program by following a few simple procedures.

Statement Labels

Make statement labels stand out by always labeling a comment line rather than a command line. For example:

```
10 * The main routine
   *
PRINT X
```

Rather than,

```
10 PRINT X
```

If alphanumeric labels are allowed, USE THEM! They make the resulting code eminently more readable and easier to handle. Ever try to keep numeric statement labels in sequence? For example:

```
MAINPART: *
*
PRINT X
```

Indentation

Indent logical levels for readability. PICK/BASIC does not trigger logical levels by the columnar position of the statement. The end of a level must be indicated to the compiler with the END, NEXT, or REPEAT statements. Proper indentation, whether manually or automatically maintained is important for readability. This is cumbersome to read:

```
FOR I = 1 to 100
PRINT I
IF I > 50 THEN
  PRINT 'UPPER'
END ELSE
  PRINT LOWER
END
NEXT I
```

This is much easier to read and much prettier.

```
FOR I = 1 to 100
    PRINT I
    IF I > 50 THEN
        PRINT 'UPPER'
    END ELSE
        PRINT LOWER
    END
NEXT I
```

Semicolons

Multiple statements on one line are difficult to read and separate in case of a compile or BRP (runtime) error. Use only with simple initializations, such as:

```
X = 0 ; Y = 0 ; Z = 0
```

Semicolons are also useful for in-line comments, especially for describing cryptic variables, such as:

```
X = 0 ;* Initialize the occurance counter
```

Structured Loops

The heated debate about program efficiency is usually centered around "branching" (GOTO) logic versus "fall through" (structured loops) logic. The answer is, "six of one, half a dozen of the other."

Structured loops are great for "short loops." That is, loops that span no more than a page or two of a program listing. "Long" structured loops prove to be cumbersome. Loops are considered long when they contain code that crosses three or more pages of the program listing. Even if all the correct indentation is used, the task of reading a loop which starts on one page and ends pages later gets quite confusing and frustrating.

GOTO logic should only be used when it makes the code more readable. GOTOs are always better than "long" structured loops. The flavors of structured loops are:

```
LOOP....WHILE or LOOP...UNTIL
```

and

```
FOR...NEXT...UNTIL or FOR...NEXT...WHILE
```

The LOOP Statement

The first standard form of the loop statement is:

```
LOOP
   {statement(s)}
UNTIL logicalexpression DO
   {statement(s)}
REPEAT
```

The statements between the LOOP and UNTIL are performed UNTIL the indicated logical expression evaluates to true, (any positive integer). Program execution continues after the REPEAT statement. The statements within the DO...REPEAT are performed only if the logical expression evaluates as false, zero. The second standard form is:

```
LOOP
   {statement(s)}
WHILE logicalexpression DO
   {statement(s)}
REPEAT
```

The statements between LOOP and WHILE are performed and the logical expression is evaluated. If the expression is true, the statements within the DO . . . REPEAT are performed and the LOOP starts over. When the logical expression evaluates as false, the LOOP terminates, (DO..REPEAT is not performed), and program execution continues after the REPEAT statement.

Figure 3-13 compares two coding techniques for validating terminal input. The first uses the structured LOOP. The second example is the same procedure coded using a GOTO. It really depends on what is familiar to you. However, the structured approach is preferable in most cases.

The structured approach:

```
LOOP
   PRINT @(1,13):'Enter field position ':
   INPUT POS
   POS = OCONV(POS,'MCU')
UNTIL NUM(POS) OR POS[1,1] ='Q' DO
   PRINT BEL:
REPEAT
```

The GOTO approach:

```
500 *
PRINT @(1,13):'Enter field position ':
INPUT POS
POS = OCONV(POS,'MCU')
IF NUM(POS) OR POS[1,1] ='Q' ELSE
   PRINT BEL:
   GOTO 500
END
```

FIG. 3-13. Comparative looping techniques.

LOOPS can be "unbalanced," meaning that the statements to be performed can be entirely between the LOOP and UNTIL or WHILE, or entirely between the DO . . . REPEAT. This is demonstrated in Fig. 3-14.

```
COUNTER = 1
LOOP UNTIL COUNTER > 20 DO
   PRINT COUNTER
   COUNTER = COUNTER + 1
REPEAT
```

FIG. 3-14. Two examples of unbalanced loops.

```
ENDOFLIST = 0
LOOP
   READNEXT ID THEN
      PRINT ID
   END ELSE ENDOFLIST = 1
UNTIL ENDOFLIST DO REPEAT
```

RULE: The one thing that should never, (that's NEVER!), be done in a structured loop is GOTO. In many structured languages a GOTO from a structured loop has the same potential problems as a GOTO from a subroutine. As is the nature of Pick, such coding practices are forgiven and work without a hitch. However, using a GOTO from a structured loop is like using "ain't" in a graduate English composition. It's just bad grammar. Using a GOTO from an internal subroutine can be fatal.

To terminate a structured routine, flag variables are quite handy as 'drop-out' indicators in the WHILE or UNTIL modifiers. Figure 3-15 compares two methods of terminating a LOOP statement.

The proper way:

```
DEAD = 0
LOOP UNTIL DEAD DO
     FOOD = GATHER OR BUY OR KILL
     CALL EAT(FOOD)
     DEAD = (FOOD='POISON")
REPEAT
IF DEAD THEN GOTO BURYIT
```

The messy way:

```
ALIVE = 1
LOOP
     FOOD = GATHER OR BUY OR KILL
     CALL EAT(FOOD)
     ALIVE = (FOOD='LOW CHOLESTEROL')
     IF ALIVE THEN GOTO 200
UNTIL DEAD DO REPEAT
200 IF NOT(ALIVE) THEN GOTO BURYIT
```

FIG. 3-15. Terminating a LOOP statement.

The reason for remaining consistent when using a structured loop is to ensure that there is only one way in and one way out. There is no confusion where the loop starts and ends.

The FOR . . . NEXT Statement

The FOR . . NEXT loop is a determinate loop. The loop is inherently controlled by a count value. The general form is:

```
FOR variable = startcount TO endcount
    statement(s)
NEXT variable
```

The *variable* is incremented by a default value of one until the value of *endcount* is exceeded. Each time the NEXT statement is encountered, control passes back to the FOR line. The variable is incremented and tested against the *endcount*. If the variable is greater than the *endcount*, program control passes to the statement following the NEXT line. For example:

```
FOR I = 1 to 10
  PRINT I
NEXT I
```

The above example prints the value of I from 1 to 10. The value of I is 11 when the FOR..NEXT loop terminates.

The indicators for the start count and end count can be any numeric constant, variable, or function. A function, such as a COUNT, DCOUNT, or INDEX, used to indicate the end count is executed at each pass through the loop. The preferred form removes the function from the loop statement and places it in a variable prior to initiating the loop. This is demonstrated in Fig. 3-16.

The slow way:

```
FOR I = 1 TO DCOUNT(ARRAY,CHAR(254))
  PRINT ARRAY<I>
NEXT I
```

The preferred way:

FIG. 3-16. FOR..NEXT with string functions.

```
CNT = DCOUNT(ARRAY,CHAR(254))
FOR I = 1 TO CNT
  PRINT ARRAY<I>
NEXT I
```

Writing code in the first form causes the number of attribute marks to be counted every time through the loop. It is preferable to first place the result of the function in a variable, then use the variable in the FOR..NEXT loop.

The STEP modifier allows the incremental value to change. The general form is:

```
FOR variable = startcount TO endcount STEP value
  statement(s)
NEXT variable
```

For example, this routine prints the values 1, 3, 5, 7, and 9. The value of I is 11 upon termination of the loop.

```
FOR I = 1 TO 10 STEP 2
  PRINT I
NEXT I
```

A FOR..NEXT construct is not limited to positive increments. The loop can be used to count down a series of numbers by using a negative STEP modifier.

```
FOR I = 10 to 1 STEP −1
  PRINT I
NEXT I
```

The FOR..NEXT loop can be modified by an UNTIL or WHILE clause in the form:

FOR *variable* = *startnumber* TO *endnumber* UNTIL *expression*

...

NEXT *variable*

or

FOR *variable* = *startnumber* TO *endnumber* WHILE *expression*

...

NEXT *variable*

The FOR..NEXT has multiple conditions for terminating the loop. Either the counter exceeds the maximum or the logical expression becomes true or false depending on the use of a UNTIL or WHILE clause, respectively. There is enough variation in this that there should be no need for spurious GOTO's.

RULE: As with any structured loop, NEVER GOTO out of a FOR...NEXT. This is bad grammar!

The following compares an example of an archical code to the structured approach. Up to this point in the hypothetical program, a multivalued dynamic array is read into the variable ARRAY. The program prints each entry until a null entry is encountered.

In Fig. 3-17, the maximum number of entries in the multivalued list is counted by the first statement.

```
MAX = DCOUNT(ARRAY,CHAR(254))
```

The BAD Way:

```
FOR I = 1 TO 9999
   VALUE = ARRAY<1,I>
   IF VALUE = '' THEN GOTO 20 ELSE PRINT VALUE
NEXT I
20 *
```

The Preferred Way:

```
MAX = DCOUNT(ARRAY,CHAR(254))
ENDOFLIST = 0
FOR I = 1 TO MAX UNTIL ENDOFLIST
   VALUE = ARRAY<1,I>
   ENDOFLIST = (VALUE = '')
   IF NOT(ENDOFLIST) THEN PRINT VALUE
NEXT I
```

FIG. 3-17. Terminating a FOR..NEXT loop.

The FOR..NEXT loop is indicated as:

FOR I = 1 TO MAX UNTIL ENDOFLIST

...

NEXT I

The two conditionals are included to respond if the maximum number of entries is exhausted or a null entry is found. The value of ENDOFLIST is true or false based on the statement:

```
ENDOFLIST = (VALUE = '')
```

If the contents of VALUE is null then ENDOFLIST is true.

CAUTION: Evaluating the maximum array entries via the DCOUNT function takes some overhead but sometime preferable to terminating the loop when a null value is encountered. If the list contains embedded null entries, the loop terminates prematurely. This is the case in the following routine:

```
I = 1
LOOP
  VALUE = ARRAY<1,I>
UNTIL VALUE = '' DO
  PRINT VALUE
  I = I + 1
REPEAT
```

The EXIT command has been added for those programmers who feel the need to embed a condition which branches out of a structured loop. The EXIT command terminates the loop at any point and continues execution after the NEXT or REPEAT statements.

```
FOR I = 1 TO 9999
  VALUE = ARRAY<1,I>
  IF VALUE = '' THEN EXIT ELSE PRINT VALUE
NEXT I
```

Structured Conditional: The Case Statement

The CASE statement is a highly readable, easy to modify construct for deciding action on a variable that has a wide range of instances. The standard forms are:

```
BEGIN CASE
  CASE logicalexpression ; statement ; statement ...
  CASE logicalexpression ; statement ; statement ...
  ....
END CASE
```

or

```
BEGIN  CASE
  CASE  logicalexpression
      statement
      statement ...
  CASE  logicalexpression
      statement
  ....
END CASE
```

Each case is tested in-turn until the first true logical expression is encountered. The statements within the true CASE are performed and program control continues following the END CASE statement. CASE's are easily added and removed while maintaining the same program flow. The following examples in Fig. 3-18 are derived from the SIZER program found in Chapter 2. Figure 3-19 compares the multiple alternatives to the CASE statement using the IF..THEN..ELSE.

```
BEGIN CASE
      CASE ITMSIZ >= 3000 ; BYTEPERGROUP = ITMSIZ
      CASE ITMSIZ >= 1000 ; BYTEPERGROUP = 3000
      CASE ITMSIZ >=  500 ; BYTEPERGROUP = 1900
      CASE ITMSIZ >=  400 ; BYTEPERGROUP = 1920
      ......
      CASE ITMSIZ >=  100 ; BYTEPERGROUP =  900
      CASE ITMSIZ >=   50 ; BYTEPERGROUP =  450
      CASE ITMSIZ >=   35 ; BYTEPERGROUP =  455
      CASE ITMSIZ >=   20 ; BYTEPERGROUP =  440
      CASE 1              ; BYTEPERGROUP =  440
END CASE
```

FIG. 3-18. A sample case construct.

Alternative method 1:

```
IF ITMSIZ >= 3000 THEN BYTEPERGROUP = ITMSIZ
IF ITMSIZ >= 1000 THEN BYTEPERGROUP = 3000
IF ITMSIZ >=  500 THEN BYTEPERGROUP = 1900
....
IF ITMSIZ >=   35 THEN BYTEPERGROUP = 455 ELSE BYTEPERGROUP = 440
```

Alternative method 2:

```
IF ITMSIZ >=    0 THEN BYTEPERGROUP = 440
IF ITMSIZ >=   35 THEN BYTEPRGROUP = 455
..
..
IF ITMSIZ >=  500 THEN BYTEPERGROUP = 1900
IF ITMSIZ >= 1000 THEN BYTEPERGROUP = 3000
IF ITMSIZ >= 3000 THEN BYTEPERGROUP = ITMSIZ
```

Alternative method 3:

```
IF ITMSIZ >= 3000 THEN BYTEPERGROUP = ITMSIZ; GOTO 20
IF ITMSIZ >= 1000 THEN BYTEPERGROUP = 3000  ; GOTO 20
IF ITMSIZ >=  500 THEN BYTEPERGROUP = 1900  ; GOTO 20
....
IF ITMSIZ >=   35 THEN BYTEPERGROUP = 455 ELSE BYTEPERGROUP = 440
20 *
```

FIG. 3-19. Alternative IF..THEN constructs.

The trouble with the first alternative structure is that after the first true conditional is encountered, the remaining conditional tests must still be performed. In this case, the logic would fail completely because any ITMSIZ greater than or equal to 3000 is also greater than or equal to the remaining conditions. These conditional statements must be rearranged from smallest to largest to account for this logical error.

The second method still requires more work than is absolutely necessary. Consider the next method using GOTO's to branch around the redundant code. If the use of the GOTO still leaves a queezy feeling, a nested conditional structure as shown in Fig. 3-20 can be substituted. The first true condition should eliminate the remaining conditions.

```
IF ITMSIZ >= 3000 THEN BYTEPERGROUP = ITMSIZ ELSE
   IF ITMSIZ >= 1000 THEN BYTEPERGROUP = 3000 ELSE
      IF ITMSIZ >=  500 THEN BYTEPERGROUP = 1900  ELSE
         IF ITMSIZ >=  400 THEN BYTEPERGROUP = 1920 ELSE
            ....
            IF ITMSIZ >= 35 THEN BYTEPERGROUP = 455 ELSE
               BYTEPERGROUP = 440
            END
         END
      END
   END
END
```

FIG. 3-20. The nested IF..THEN construct.

Apparently, nested IF..THEN's are a good solution. Except when the nested conditional starts getting beyond two levels deep in logic. The task of counting END statements is always a challenge.

The obvious conclusion is to use the CASE statement. CASE runs no faster or slower than a nested conditional and the construct is far easier to read!

Indexed Branching

Indexed branching is one of the most efficient ways to direct program flow without using complex IF..THEN..ELSE logic or building a large CASE statement. The general form is:

ON *value* GOTO *label1,label2,...,labeln*

or

ON *value* GOSUB *label1,label2,...,labeln*

In one statement, the decision can be made for an N-way branch. The restriction is that the indexed value must be a sequential numeric. If the value is 1, then the branch is taken to label 1, value 2, to label 2 and so on. A value of zero causes the statement to act as a no-op and processing continues with the statement immediately following.

Compare the CASE statement with an indexed GOSUB in Fig. 3-21. Using the CASE statement, in the worst case where the value of V is 4, the system must step through three levels of logic tests before branching to subroutine 400. The time to determine the branch location in an ON..GOSUB is essentially the same for all values of V.

```
BEGIN CASE
    CASE V = 1 ; GOSUB 100
    CASE V = 2 ; GOSUB 200
    CASE V = 3 ; GOSUB 300
    CASE V = 4 ; GOSUB 400
END CASE
```

FIG. 3-21. Indexed branching.

An indexed branch:

```
ON V GOSUB 100,200,300,400
```

What happens if an indexed branch is to be used but the value of V is not a sequential numeric? There are several ways to convert the value to a numeric. The simplest way is when the value of V is a single alpha character.

For the following example, the value of V can be an A, B, C, or D. The value can be translated into a sequential numeric by using the following INDEX function:

```
INDEX('ABCD',V,1)
```

The result of the INDEX function is 1 for an A, 2 for a B, 3 for a C and 4 for a D. Any other value of V generates a zero result. The INDEX function is used to translate the alpha value of V to a sequential number used in the index branch statement as follows:

```
ON INDEX('ABCD',V,1) GOSUB 100,200,300,400
```

This is a very powerful and efficient statement compared to the amount of coding that would be required with the standard IF..THEN or CASE structure.

Modularized Code

Modularized coding is an approach which serves to consolidate commonly used routines. A library of commonly used routines alleviates the need to re-invent the wheel every time a program is written. It also forces consistency in style and variable usage. Modular routines also allow special processing to be isolated from the mainline of the program. An application becomes machine independent when tasks such as disk and terminal IO are handled in separate free-standing routines.

Program modification is made to the modules and not to the main program logic path. The entire procedure of isolating a routine, modifying, testing and implementing is easier when the change is within a 50 to 100 line program versus a 5000 line program. The resulting application can be ported from one machine to the other with comparative ease and control.

Included Code Segments

One method of implementing modular routines can be done by including at compile time, specified items which contain PICK/BASIC code segments. These code segments are compiled in-line with the object code generated from the original source item. The PICK/BASIC compiler directive for including code segments is:

    INCLUDE {*filename*} *item-id*

If the file name is not specified, then the item is retrieved from the source item file. Please note that the name on the directive varies between implementations. Here are all the variations; INCLUDE, $INCLUDE, INSERT, and $INSERT. The specification of the file name and item-id is identical.

Included code segments are very useful for standardizing program preambles. A *preamble* takes care of initialization including setting up a common descriptor area, program constants, device characteristics and database references.

In a large, integrated application, much of the code used in a preamble is normally repeated in hundreds of programs. If a change is required in the number or order of entries in a common area, every program with the common statement must be first modified and then re-compiled. Removing such code from the mainline of the program and placing it into a single shared code segment makes the job of modification easier and much quicker. All that needs to be done is the modification of the single code segment item followed by a re-compilation of the programs in the package.

Figures 3-22 through 3-26 are some examples of code segments stored in a file named CODELIB. *Equated constants* shown in Fig. 3-22, are good contenders for included code. Most every program in an integrated package needs them; so why not include them in a single line of code rather than re-entering this in every program.

```
    CONSTANTS
001 *
002 * STANDARD CONSTANTS
003 *
004 EQU BEL  TO CHAR(7)
005 EQU LF   TO CHAR(10)
006 EQU FF   TO CHAR(12)
007 EQU CR   TO CHAR(13)
008 EQU ESC  TO CHAR(27)
009 EQU DEL  TO CHAR(127)
010 EQU ESCC TO CHAR(251)
011 EQU AM   TO CHAR(254)
012 EQU VM   TO CHAR(253)
013 EQU SVM  TO CHAR(252)
014 *
```

FIG. 3-22. Included constants (EQUATES) code segment.

Figure 3-23 is a sample of an included segment that combines a common area and standard equates. This is the common area used by the INPUT program discussed later in this text.

Figure 3-24 shows how terminal characteristics can be set up via a code segment rather than calling it as a subroutine.

Figure 3-25 shows how code segments can be used to establish file driven device controls that are not inherently part of the operating system. Printers, for example, can have their control sequences stored in a shared file called PRINTER.TYPES. The type of

```
      INPUT.COMMONS
001 *
002 * COMMON VARIABLES AND CONSTANTS FOR THE 'INPUT' PROGRAM
003 *
004 COMMON DATADEF(75),DSPFIELD(75),ITEM(75),ITEMID,IDDEF
005 COMMON ARGS,ACTIVELIST,FORMFLAG,COMPILE,PAGELIMITS
006 COMMON DATAFILE,DICTFILE,FILENAME
007 COMMON FIRSTROW,LASTROW
008 COMMON TERMDEPTH,TERMWIDTH,TERMTYPE
009 COMMON PAGENO,PAGES
010 *
011 EQU TAB          TO CHAR(9)
012 EQU CR           TO CHAR(13)
013 EQU LF           TO CHAR(10)
014 EQU ESC          TO CHAR(251)
015 EQU ESCC         TO CHAR(27)
016 EQU SP           TO CHAR(32)
017 EQU AM           TO CHAR(254)
018 EQU VM           TO CHAR(253)
019 EQU SVM          TO CHAR(252)
020 EQU BELL         TO CHAR(7)
021 EQU BACKSPACE    TO CHAR(8)
```

FIG. 3-23. COMMONS code segment for the INPUT program.

```
      TERMINAL
001 *
002 * TERMINAL CHARACTERISTICS
003 *
004 WHO     = OCONV(0,'U50BB')
005 PORT    = FIELD(WHO,' ',1)
006 ACCOUNT = FIELD(WHO,' ',2)
007 PORT    = STR(0,3-LEN(PORT)):PORT
008 *
009 CLS = @(-1)
010 EOS = @(-3)
011 EOL = @(-4)
012 RON = @(-13)
013 ROF = @(-14)
014 *
015 TERMTYPE  = SYSTEM(7)     ;* TERMINAL TYPE
016 PAGEWIDTH = SYSTEM(2)     ;* PAGE WIDTH (TERM)
017 PAGEDEPTH = SYSTEM(3)     ;* PAGE DEPTH (TERM)
018 *
```

FIG. 3-24. Terminal characteristics code segment.

printer being used can be keyed off a number of elements including the port number. As you can see, any file type can be standardized in an included code segment. The example in Fig. 3-26 standardizes the methods of addressing the STAFF file in an application. Notice how the equates are used to allow names to be associated with the item attribute positions. All the overhead of opening the file and defining and initializing the dimensioned array is performed in the code segment. All the applications programmer has to do is INCLUDE it and get on with the business at hand.

```
001 *
002 * PRINTER TYPES CONTROL
003 *
004 DIM PCODES(10)
005 OPEN 'PRINTER.TYPES' TO PRINTER.TYPES ELSE STOP
006 *
007 EQU CPI .12   TO PCODES(1)
008 EQU CPI .10   TO PCODES(2)
009 EQU LETTER.Q TO PCODES(3)
010 EQU NORMAL.Q TO PCODES(4)
  ...
NNN EQU GOTHIC TO PCODES(10)
```

FIG. 3-25. Printer control code segment.

```
    FILE.STAFF
001 *
002 * FILE 'STAFF' SETUP
003 *
004 OPEN 'STAFF' TO STAFF.FILE ELSE STOP 201,'STAFF'
005 *
006 DIM STAFF.ITEM(10)
007 MAT STAFF.ITEM = ''
008 *
009 EQU STAFF.NAME     TO STAFF.ITEM(1)
010 EQU STAFF.ADDRESS TO STAFF.ITEM(2)
011 EQU STAFF.CITY     TO STAFF.ITEM(3)
012 EQU STAFF.STATE    TO STAFF.ITEM(4)
013 EQU STAFF.ZIP      TO STAFF.ITEM(5)
014 EQU STAFF.PHONE    TO STAFF.ITEM(6)
015 EQU STAFF.SALARY   TO STAFF.ITEM(7)
016 *
```

FIG. 3-26. File setup code segment.

Compiler Options for Handling Included Code

When a program that uses included code segments is compiled, the line counter is not incremented until the entire segment is merged with the mainline and compiled. The compiler does not generate the usual end-of-line characters for lines within the entire segment.

This "feature" allows programs with included code to be compiled and debugged without having to extrapolate the actual line positions of any coding errors. However, if there is an error in the included segment, the line of the INCLUDE statement is reported regardless of how long the code segment happens to be.

The I option is used when it is required that the end-of-line characters be inserted at the end of every line of the included code segments:

>BASIC BP TEST (I

Now the compiler and BRP, (including the PICK/BASIC DEBUGGER) treat the included code segment as if it was written in-line with the source program.

There is one more problem. The programmer needs a listing of the source code with the code segments and line indicators corresponding to the compiler and BRP messages.

The compile option of L is used to generate a listing of the expanded program. To preserve this listing for the programmers use and for posterity, the P (printer) option should also be specified:

```
>BASIC BP TEST (I,L,P
```

The above command generates an expanded listing of the source code to the system printer via the spooler. Be careful. This should not open the door for using executable code in included code segments. That is the purpose of subroutines.

Subroutines

Subroutines are used to modularize code used by the Basic Runtime Package (BRP). Unlike an INCLUDE, which reads a code segment at compile time and includes it in-line with the generated object code, subroutines are activated at PICK/BASIC runtime; suspending the current routine, stacking the return location, and passing parameters. Therefore, subroutines require a significant amount of overhead.

Internal subroutines reside within the body of the main program item and are activated by the command GOSUB while external subroutines reside in separate items and are activated by the CALL statement.

Execution of any subroutine "pushes" the location of the line of code following the GOSUB command onto a return stack, and transfers control to the location of the specified statement label. Each subsequent GOSUB pushes the next return location onto the stack. When the RETURN command is performed, the stack is "popped." That is, the top location of the stack is removed from the stack and program control is transferred to the location stored at the top of the stack. The main through put cost of external subroutines is that of parameter passing. COMMON alleviates the need to pass a large number of variables between levels of subroutines.

Also be careful of multiple levels of subroutine CALLs. The first subroutine call forces PICK/BASIC runtime to:

1) Read the catalog pointer from the MD.
2) Read the file pointer containing the object code.
3) Read the object code pointer from the DICTionary of the file.
4) Save the address of the subroutine for subsequent calls. (Stored in the subroutine variable.)
5) Call the subroutine.

This process has to be repeated for each new subroutine called. Re-calling an already addressed subroutine does not require the same overhead.

Testing Subroutine Levels Program

The number of stack entries possible on release 2.2 of Pick on the AT is currently 199. This varies between implementations and can be tested by writing a program which breaks the first rule of using subroutines:

Never GOTO out of a subroutine!!!!

Figure 3-27 lists a sample program that can be used to determine the maximum number of subroutine levels available on any implementation.

```
        SUBLEVELS
001 *PROGRAM SUBLEVELS
002 * TEST THE MAXIMUM NUMBER OF SUB LEVELS BEFORE ABORT
003 *
004 LEVEL = 0
005 PRINT 'LEVEL ':
006 *
007 10 * START
008 *
009 GOSUB 100
010 STOP
011 *
012 100 * SUBROUTINE
013 *
014 LEVEL = LEVEL + 1
015 PRINT LEVEL 'L#5':
016 GOTO 10
017 *
018 END
```

FIG. 3-27. SUBLEVELS *test program listing.*

Unlike a structured loop, which forgives the periodic GOTO or any other sloppy structure, a subroutine which never gets the chance to return can cause a program to abort with the message:

[B31] STACK OVERFLOW!

Another major no-no is the use of the CHAIN command from a subroutine. A CHAIN from an external subroutine can lead to many unpredictable errors. The CHAIN statement is a system-wide GOTO. If GOTO logic is difficult to maintain within a program, just think of the nightmare of system-wide jumps with no rhyme or obvious reason.

Repetitive Subroutine Calls

How and when a subroutine is repetitively called can effect the overall throughput of a program. Consider an interactive program which calls a subroutine just prior to and after each field is prompted. Unless this is an intense "heads-down" data entry situation, a 5 millisecond run versus a 15 millisecond run, (inferring that the subroutine is already memory resident), is transparent to the operator. In the situation where the number of iterations is in the hundreds, thousands, or more; a subroutine call at every pass can have a significant effect on speed.

RULE: For repetitive tasks, code multiple iterations within the subroutine. Do not call the routine for each pass through the loop.

```
                          SUBTEST
                      001 * PROGRAM SUBTEST
                      002 *
                      003 MAX = 0
                      004 LOOP MAX = MAX + 1000 UNTIL MAX > 10000 DO
                      005      *
                      006      T1 = SYSTEM(9)
                      007      C = 0
                      008      FOR I = 1 TO MAX
                      009          GOSUB 1000
                      010      NEXT I
                      011      T2 = T1 - SYSTEM(9)
                      012      PRINT MAX:" 1 ":T2
                      013      *
                      014      T1 = SYSTEM(9)
                      015      GOSUB 2000
                      016      T3 = T1 - SYSTEM(9)
                      017      PRINT MAX:" 2 ":T3
                      018      *
                      019      PRINT 'IMPROVEMENT ':(T2-T3)/T2
                      020      PRINT
                      021 REPEAT
                      022 STOP
                      023 *
                      024 *
                      025 1000 *
                      026 *
                      027 C = C + 1
                      028 RETURN
                      029 *
                      030 2000 *
                      031 *
                      032 C = 0
                      033 FOR I = 1 TO MAX
                      034     C = C + 1
                      035 NEXT I
                      036 RETURN
                      037 *
                      038 END
```

FIG. 3-28. SUBTEST program listing (test subroutine levels).

The program listed in Fig. 3-28 tests the difference in overhead between repetitively calling an internal subroutine each time through a loop or calling it once by placing the loop within the subroutine.

Program Highlights

The SUBTEST program tests performing an internal subroutine a MAX number of times through a loop versus a similar loop performed within another subroutine. Tests are performed using the MAX values of 1,000 to 10,000 in incremental values of 1,000. This is indicated in the LOOP statement as follows:

```
003 MAX = 0
004 LOOP MAX = MAX + 1000 UNTIL MAX > 10000 DO
```

...
```
021   REPEAT
```

The first test performed is the subroutine call on every pass through the FOR..NEXT loop:

```
006   T1 = SYSTEM(9)
007   C = 0
008   FOR I = 1 TO MAX
009      GOSUB 1000
010   NEXT I
011   T2 = T1 – SYSTEM(9)
012   PRINT MAX:" 1 ":T2
```

The SYSTEM(9) function retrieves the total number of CPU units in milliseconds used since logging on. The CPU value is retrieved before the loop and then used to calculate the number of CPU milliseconds elapsed after the loop:

```
T2 = T1 – SYSTEM(9)
```

The second test performs a single subroutine call and processes the entire loop within subroutine 2000.

```
014   T1 = SYSTEM(9)
015   GOSUB 2000
016   T3 = T1 – SYSTEM(9)
017   PRINT MAX:" 2 ":T3
```

Again, the CPU usage is calculated using the SYSTEM (9) function.

```
T3 = T1 – SYSTEM(9)
```

The percent increase in CPU usage of the second test over the first test is then calculated and displayed.

```
0019   PRINT 'IMPROVEMENT ':(T2 – T3)/T2
```

Running this program on an AT clone with a 12 MHz clock using Pick Release 2.2 yields an average improvement of 30 percent comparing test routine 2 to test routine 1.

Rules for Maintaining Subroutines

The following list describes command statements and points to keep in mind when using them.

Function	*Rule*
COMMON	Every program called from the mainline using a COMMON statement, must also have identical COMMON statements. If the number and position of the COMMON variables change with each program, the descriptor table may end up being "shifted," causing unpredictable errors.

CLEAR	DO NOT USE. The CLEAR statement sets all descriptors to a binary zero value. Not a good move in the middle of a program. Not a preferred move anywhere.
RETURN TO	The dreaded combination of a RETURN and a GOTO to alleviate the problem of STACK OVERFLOW ABORTS. If GOTO's are hard to follow, try this on for size!
CHAIN or ENTER	Any chained logic is difficult to follow. Consider this a system-wide GOTO and stay away from it.
PRECISION	The PRECISION statement must exist in the main routine and all subroutines to prevent a runtime abort.
INDIRECT CALLS	Otherwise known as the CALL @ command. Placing the value subtest in a variable called X and then indirectly using the value of X as indicated as:

```
X = "SUBTEST"
CALL @X
```

Use indirect calls sparingly if at all. It's great for parameterizing routines for general use, but increases the difficulty of tracking down the correct subroutine in case of an error and is drastically slower (almost 10 to 1) than a direct CALL. Each call of the same subroutine requires all the overhead of the initial call since the subroutine pointer is not stored.

User Defined Functions

Here is a little icing on the modular programming cake. The latest and greatest new feature to be offered by some of the vendors is the ability to create user defined functions ala C or PASCAL. The general form is as follows:

```
FUNCTION functionname(@arg, @arg...)
        statements
        statements
        .....

        RETURN expression
END
```

The indicators *@arg* are special references used within the function. These receive the result of the expressions passed to the function in the function call. Function definitions must reside at the beginning of the source item, as with all like structured programs. Functions are called as follows:

functionname(expression, expression...., expression)

Each normal PICK/BASIC expression produces a result which is passed to the corresponding @arg indicator. Within the function, the @arg's cannot be modified. *@arg = anything* is invalid and will not compile.

```
FUNCTION PRIME(@NUMBER)
    PRIMEOK = 0
    RESULT = @NUMBER
    FOR J = RESULT TO J+1 UNTIL PRIMEOK
        IF REM(J,2) THEN
            DNOM = 3
            MAX.DIV = INT(SQRT(J))+1
            LOOP UNTIL DNOM>=MAX.DIV OR NOT(REM(J,DNOM)) DO
                DOM = DNOM + 2
            REPEAT
            IF DNOM >= MAX.DIV THEN
                RESULT = J
                PRIMEOK = 1
            END
        END
    NEXT J
    RETURN RESULT
END
INPUT N
PRINT PRIME(N)
```

FIG. 3-29. Prime number FUNCTION listing.

The **RETURN** statement is expressed in the form:

RETURN *expression*

The **FUNCTION** returns the result of the *expression*. For example:

RETURN @VALUE*10

If the value of @VALUE is 20, then the result of the following function call is 200.

X = *functionname*(VAL)

The variable X contains the result, 200.

Figure 3-29 demonstrates a sample function which calculates a prime number. Functions can be shared among programs by placing them in a central code library (CODELIB is a good name) and then including them in the source code using an INCLUDE, $INCLUDE, $INSERT or whatever is available.

List Processing

Now you could say, "all the world's a list." Earlier in this text, it was stated that "all the world's a string;" same concept. In the Pick system, a list is any string of characters containing fields delimited by any one of the system delimiters; attribute, value or subvalue mark.

ACCESS can be used to select valid data and pass the active list of item-ids to another ACCESS, TCL-II or PICK/BASIC routine. The active list can also be saved and repeatedly recalled for processing. An advantage to relegating the task of pre-processing to ACCESS is the ability to order and restrict the items that the PICK/BASIC program (or subsequent system routine) must process. The decision as to which items are included is made within the logic of ACCESS, thereby allowing the PICK/BASIC program logic to be much simpler.

However, ACCESS is not the only process which can build lists. PICK/BASIC can be used as a stand-alone process to generate lists and write them as standard items. Any attribute within an item is a potential list delimited by value and subvalue marks. An *item* is essentially a list of attributes. An example of an item stored list is a multivalued attribute containing part numbers in an invoice. The same invoice item can contain correlated lists of quantities and prices. Item stored lists are also used for data cross reference.

This chapter covers the techniques for building, processing, searching, and maintaining lists both pre-processed by ACCESS and passed to PICK/BASIC as well as lists handled completely through PICK/BASIC.

SELECTING LISTS

This discussion begins with accessing lists in PICK/BASIC. Lists saved via the SAVE-LIST verb presently cannot be read as an item into a PICK/BASIC program. However, the differences between a cataloged list item and a standard item are disappearing as unlimited item size is being implemented. In fact, unlimited item size versions have no lists. They just have big and little items. Therefore, lists can be processed as easily as normal items. However, in "classic" Pick, PICK/BASIC programs must address a list using the READNEXT statement.

EXECUTEing an ACCESS SELECT

The EXECUTE statement allows the ACCESS SELECT to be processed without leaving the control of a PICK/BASIC program. Prior to the availability of the EXECUTE statement, a PROC was necessary in order to prompt the operator for the required variable information, build and perform the ACCESS SELECT sentence, and then run the PICK/BASIC program. Applications written under these constraints are riddled with PROCs and PICK/BASIC programs, all passing data back and forth, all dependent on each other, and, subsequently, proving to be a support nightmare. Through the EXECUTE statement, all functionality can be kept under the control of a single PICK/BASIC program.

When an ACCESS SELECT statement is EXECUTED, the active list is immediately available to the READNEXT statement in the PICK/BASIC program. It is important that the file addressed in the ACCESS statement match the file being opened in the PICK/BASIC program, as shown in Fig. 4-1. Otherwise, the ever popular GIGO (garbage-in, garbage-out) condition is inevitable.

```
OPEN 'STAFF' TO STAFF.FILE ELSE STOP 201,'STAFF'
EXECUTE 'SSELECT STAFF BY NAME WITH STATE = "CA"'
ENDLIST = 0
LOOP
      READNEXT ID ELSE ENDLIST = 1
UNTIL ENDLIST DO
      READ REC FROM STAFF.FILE,ID THEN
          .....
          ...
      END
REPEAT
```

FIG. 4-1. ACCESS SELECT in PICK/BASIC.

If the programmer is feeling particularly lazy, there is no need to go through the whole process of opening the file and reading the items. An ACCESS SELECT can be used to retrieve the required data.

A SELECT is not restricted to building lists of item-ids. By simply indicating an output-list in the ACCESS sentence, the SELECT output generates a list containing the specified data elements. Consider the following statement:

```
SSELECT STAFF BY NAME WITH STATE = "CA" NAME
```

The output-list, NAME, produces a list of names, not item-id's, in the form:

```
001   AARON, HANK
002   EINSTEIN, ALBERT
003   LAZLO, VICTOR
004   MOUSE, MINNIE
...
...
```

The PICK/BASIC program can be used to display the selected names in any format chosen, as is demonstrated in Fig. 4-2.

```
EXECUTE 'SSELECT STAFF BY NAME WITH STATE = "CA" NAME'
ENDLIST = 0
LOOP
     READNEXT NAME ELSE ENDLIST = 1
UNTIL ENDLIST DO
     PRINT NAME "L#25":" ":
REPEAT
```

FIG. 4-2. Printing ACCESS SELECT data from PICK/BASIC (without OPEN).

The following ACCESS command sentence produces an output-list containing more than one data value. Each output column generates a separate attribute in the list.

```
SSELECT STAFF BY NAME WITH STATE = "CA" NAME ADDRESS
```

This produces a list in the form:

```
001   AARON, HANK
002   11 BASEBALL BLVD.
003   EINSTEIN, ALBERT
004   EMC2 SUBATOMIC LANE
005   LAZLO, VICTOR
006   5769 CASABLANCA AVE.
007   MOUSE, MINNIE
008   3 MAIN ST.
...
...
```

This assumes that none of the attributes are multivalued.

Figure 4-3 demonstrates how this ACCESS list can be used to format a report without a file OPEN or READ.

Passing Lists Between Execute Levels

The EXECUTE method used by generic Pick systems (R83) and compatibles is relatively easy to use. An active list can either be used by the READNEXT statement, as shown above, or passed to another EXECUTEd TCL, ACCCESS or PICK/BASIC program.

```
        EXECUTE 'SSELECT STAFF BY NAME WITH STATE = "CA" NAME ADDRESS'
        ENDLIST = 0
        LOOP
             READNEXT NAME THEN
                     READNEXT ADDRESS ELSE ENDLIST = 1
             END ELSE ENDLIST = 1
        UNTIL ENDLIST DO
             PRINT NAME "L#25":ADDRESS "L#25"
        REPEAT
```

FIG. 4-3. PICK/BASIC formatted output (without OPEN).

```
    EXECUTE 'SSELECT STAFF'
    EXECUTE 'RUN BP APROG'
```

or

```
    EXECUTE 'SSELECT STAFF BY STATE'
    EXECUTE 'T-DUMP STATE'
```

The active list of STAFF item-ids can now be retrieved by the APROG program or sent to magnetic media via the T-DUMP verb. This is possible because of the method by which the EXECUTE is implemented. All EXECUTES are performed on the same TCL level. However, certain implementations of EXECUTE handle execution levels in a different manner. The result is that the active list is made available to the READNEXT in the program, but is not available to a subsequent EXECUTE. (Ultimate is one of the culprits.)

For example, the following statements work in "classic" Pick.

```
    EXECUTE 'SSELECT STAFF BY STATE'
    EXECUTE 'SAVE-LIST BYSTATE'
```

In incompatible implementations, each EXECUTE level attaches a full new process workspace. Whenever an active list is generated, it is passed back to the level that executed the select, thereby making the list available to the READNEXT statement. However, in the case of two EXECUTES back-to-back, the second EXECUTE is performed at the higher TCL level which no longer has a pointer to the active list. In this case, the list must be specifically passed between the levels.

Following Pick Spectrum (SMA) standards, the syntax for passing an active list requires a PASSLIST and RTNLIST clause appended to the EXECUTE statement:

```
    EXECUTE 'SSELECT STAFF BY STATE' RTNLIST STATELIST
    EXECUTE 'SAVE-LIST BYSTATE' PASSLIST STATELIST
```

STATELIST is assigned an entry in the descriptor table which points to the active list in virtual memory. This is also required when using GET-LIST in the form:

```
    EXECUTE 'GET-LIST BYSTATE' RTNLIST STATELIST
    EXECUTE 'RUN BP APROG' PASSLIST STATELIST
```

Please consult the system manuals that came with your system for the availability of these commands and subsequent compatibility.

These same statements on the Ultimate implementation require the use of a specific "redirection clause" in the form:

```
EXECUTE 'GET-LIST BYSTATE,//SELECT. > STATELIST
EXECUTE 'RUN BP APROG',//SELECT. < STATELIST
```

Comparatively archaic, but powerful nonetheless. There will be more about these type of redirection clauses in Chapter 5, "Process Control."

Whether or not the list variable can be referenced as a dynamic array depends on the implementation. In systems that use unlimited item sizes, the list can be written as an item without the use of the SAVE-LIST verb. Just be careful parsing these items with standard dynamic intrinsic functions. Remember, the longer the lists, the slower throughput becomes.

Another method of passing an active list in an EXECUTE is to use the DATA statement much like the STON command is used in PROC. Any data in the stack is passed to the next command.

```
DATA 'RUN BP APROG'
EXECUTE 'SSELECT STAFF'
```

Exploded Sorts

The BY-EXP modifier allows an attribute with a multivalued list to be broken apart and reported in the correct sequence along with the rest of the items in the file. Consider these sample items in Fig. 4-4 and their corresponding data definition items in the INVOICE file.

INVOICE data items:

```
ID: 100              200              300
001 255          001 354          001 655
002 W23]Q55]Z32  002 E34]A12      002 T11]B12]F11
003 1]1]2        003 2]1          003 3]2]2
```

INVOICE data definition items:

```
ID: CUSTOMER         PART.NUM         QTY
001 A            001 A            001 A
002 1            002 2            002 3
...
009 R            009 L            009 R
010 5            010 5            010 8
```

FIG. 4-4. Sample INVOICE data and definitions for BY-EXP.

Generating an ACCESS command sentence to process an exploded sort based on the part number is straightforward. Figure 4-5 illustrates the ACCESS command sentence and the corresponding output.

```
>SORT INVOICE BY-EXP PART.NUM. PART.NUM
```

Which produces the following output:

INVOICE..PART.NUM

200	A12
300	B12
200	E34
300	F11
100	Q55
300	T11
100	W23
100	Z32

FIG. 4-5. BY-EXP example.

A SSELECT generates a list of item-id's in the same order.

001	200
002	300
003	200
004	300
005	100
006	300
007	100
008	100

Subsequent READNEXT's in a PICK/BASIC program re-read the same item-id as many times as it appears in the list. There must be some way of letting the program know which entry in the value list is the active entry. There is!

When a BY-EXP modifier is used within a SSELECT, the resulting list contains more than just the item-id's. Consider the next ACCESS statement:

```
>SSELECT INVOICE BY-EXP PART.NUM
```

This produces an active list which looks like this:

001	200]002
002	300]002
003	200]001
004	300]003
005	100]002
006	300]001
007	100]001
008	100]003

The right bracket (]) represents a value mark. Each line in the list contains the item-id value-marked with the value-mark count of the part number which controlled the position in the list. Compare this list to the previous example of the report and the results become apparent.

Now all that is needed is a way to tell the PICK/BASIC program which value-mark count is being used. This is accomplished using the READNEXT statement with a syntactical extension. The general form is:

```
READNEXT ID,VMC THEN... ELSE...
```

The item-id is placed into the variable represented by ID and the value-mark count is stored in the variable represented by VMC. A simple routine which uses this method is illustrated in Fig. 4-6.

```
DIM REC(10)
OPEN 'INVOICE' TO INVOICE.FILE ELSE STOP 201,'INVOICE'
EXECUTE 'SSELECT INVOICE BY-EXP PART.NUM'
ENDLIST = 0
LOOP
     READNEXT ID,VMC ELSE ENDLIST = 1
UNTIL ENDLIST DO
     MAT REC = ''
     MATREAD REC FROM INVOICE.FILE,ID THEN
        PRINT 'PART   ':REC(2)<1,VMC>
        PRINT 'SOLD   ':REC(3)<1,VMC>:' UNITS'
        PRINT
     END
REPEAT
```

FIG. 4-6. PICK/BASIC routine to process an exploded sort.

CAUTION: BY-EXP sorts only work in simple cases. Null values and A and F correlatives can cause strange system aborts and silly answers.

PICK/BASIC Internal Selects

Items in a file do not have to be pre-sampled by ACCESS. There is a SELECT statement available in PICK/BASIC that provides an active list for the READNEXT statement.

The internal SELECT works differently than an ACCESS SELECT. ACCESS requires the entire file space to be searched before the list is finalized. This allows the entries in the list to be sequenced and logically selected before being passed to the program.

The internal PICK/BASIC SELECT builds a sub-list of every item in a group as each group is encountered. The entries on the sub-list are accessed by each subsequent READNEXT statement. When a sub-list is exhausted, the next group in the file is scanned and another sub-list is produced. This continues until the end of the file is reached.

The advantage to a PICK/BASIC SELECT over an ACCESS SELECT is that there is no delay time before the program starts processing. The file can be processed effectively in a single pass. This gives a great gain in throughput if every item must be processed and the order of processing is not important. However, if only a small portion of the file must be processed and the order in which it is presented is critical, then an ACCESS select is worth the wait.

There is a situation where an internal SELECT must not be used. This has to do with updating items back to the same file under new item-id's. When an item is read, assigned a new item-id and re-written to a file, the system may hash the item to a new group. There is no problem if the group is one that has already been scanned by the internal SELECT. If the new group is not one that has been scanned, the program ends up re-reading and processing the same item, potentially causing unrecoverable errors in the data.

As with many "features" of the Pick system, this may not be true on every implementation (ICON for one). However, to remain consistent and to prevent the possibility of this kind of data corruption, don't update the same file that is being scanned with a PICK/BASIC SELECT statement.

Using Select to Scan a Dynamic Array

The SELECT statement can also be used to treat a dynamic array as an active list. This is a great trick to increase the efficiency of handling dynamic arrays. Subsequent entries in the list can be extracted without having to re-scan the entire array. The general form is:

SELECT *dynamicarray* TO *listvariable*

Each entry from the array *dynamicarray* can be extracted in-turn by referencing *listvariable* in a READNEXT statement. The READNEXT needs the FROM modifier in the form:

READNEXT *var* FROM *listvariable* THEN.. ELSE...

The variable *var* is where the next extracted element is placed. The only restriction is that the dynamic array must use attribute marks as the delimiter because active system lists use the attribute mark by default. Also, note that the READNEXT can only extract entries in one direction. That is, the list can be scanned forward, not backward. In addition, entries should not be inserted or deleted from the dynamic array while within the READNEXT loop.

Multiple Active Lists

More than one selected list can be active at one time within a PICK/BASIC program by marking each list with a descriptor called the list variable.

In standard Pick, active lists can be assigned a list variable by using the SELECT..TO statement. If the entire file is required, then the SELECT statement is sufficient. If the resulting lists must be in sequence and restricted to specific selection criteria, the SELECT can be used in conjunction with an executed ACCESS statement. The general form of the PICK/BASIC SELECT..TO is as follows:

SELECT *filevar* TO *listvariable*

The indicator *filevar* represents a file variable, and the *listvariable* indicates the list pointer variable. Remember, a list variable can only be referenced via a READNEXT and not as a dynamic array.

NOTE: Default lists are almost as much of a nuisance as default file variables. The code reads much better using SELECT..TO and READNEXT...FROM and is much easier to maintain.

Performing a PICK/BASIC SELECT while a list is active, causes the internal SELECT to be overridden by the active list. An active list can be previously generated at TCL, from a PROC or executed within the same PICK/BASIC program. A SELECT..TO statement following each EXECUTE of an ACCESS SELECT command sentence, subsequently assigns each active list to a different list variable.

Figure 4-7 sets up two active lists, one referenced by the list variable, ALIST, and the other referenced by the list variable, BLIST.

```
OPEN 'AFILE' TO AFILE ELSE STOP 201,'AFILE'
OPEN 'BFILE' TO BFILE ELSE STOP 201,'BFILE'
EXECUTE 'SSELECT AFILE BY DEFA WITH DEFB > "1000"'
SELECT AFILE TO ALIST
EXECUTE 'SSELECT BFILE BY BDEF'
SELECT BFILE TO BLIST
```

FIG. 4-7. Multiple active lists in a PICK/BASIC program.

Elements can be extracted from a specific active list by using the READNEXT.. FROM statement in the form:

READNEXT *var* FROM *listvariable* THEN... ELSE...

The *var* indicator represents the variable into which each list element is placed and *listvariable* is the addressed list variable.

The LFILES Program

Figure 4-8 is a sample PICK/BASIC program for demonstrating the use of multiple active lists. This routine can be used to replace LISTFILES. An active list of "D" pointers is built from the master dictionary. Each file pointer element is used to select the data level elements defined within each file dictionary.

Program Highlights

The first task of LFILES is to select the master dictionary to retrieve a sorted list of all 'D' and 'Q' type pointers. This is accomplished by the following code:

```
025 GETFILES = \SSELECT MD BY D/CODE WITH D/CODE = \:CODES
026 EXECUTE GETFILES CAPTURING DUMMY
027 IF NOT(SYSTEM(11)) THEN STOP
028 SELECT MD TO DICTLIST
```

The SELECT statement is initialized as a variable, GETFILES, strictly for the purpose of readability. Otherwise, the statement line would wrap to the next print line and look rather messy.

The variable, CODES, is the implied, or value list of the type of pointers to be used in

```
      LFILES
001 PROGRAM LFILES
002 * List Account DICT and DATA files
003 * H.E.Rodstein
004 * Oct 8, 1988
005 *
006 PROMPT ''
007 *
008 DIM POINTER(15)
009 OPEN 'MD' TO MD ELSE STOP 201,'MD'
010 EQU PCODE TO POINTER(1)
011 EQU BASE  TO POINTER(2)
012 EQU MOD   TO POINTER(3)
013 EQU SEP   TO POINTER(4)
014 *
015 CODES=\"D""DC""DX""DY""DZ""Q"\
016 *
017 * Setup Page and Column Header
018 *
019 H="Page 'PN'   ****MD*** File Defining Items     'DLL'
020 H=H:"Dict Name....."""L#15" : "Code.""L#5"
021 H=H:"Mod......."""L#10" : "Sep.""L#4" : SPACE(6)
022 H=H:"Data Name....."""L#15" : "Code.""L#5"
023 H=H:"Mod......."""L#10" : "Sep.""L#4" : "'L'"
024 *
025 GETFILES = \SSELECT MD BY D/CODE WITH D/CODE = \:CODES
026 EXECUTE GETFILES CAPTURING DUMMY
027 IF NOT(SYSTEM(11)) THEN STOP
028 SELECT MD TO DICTLIST
029 *
030 HEADING H
031 *
032 ENDDICTS=0
033 LOOP
034   READNEXT DICTNAME FROM DICTLIST ELSE ENDDICTS=1
035 UNTIL ENDDICTS DO
036   OPEN 'DICT',DICTNAME TO DICTFILE THEN
037     GOSUB 1000 ;* Get and Print Pointers
038   END
039 REPEAT
040 STOP
041 *
042 *
043 * Subroutines
044 *
045 1000 *  Get and Print Pointers at all levels
046 *
047 MAT POINTER=''
048 MATREAD POINTER FROM MD,DICTNAME THEN
049   *
050   PRINT DICTNAME"L#15" : PCODE"L#5" :
051   PRINT MOD"L#10" : SEP"L#4" : SPACE(6) :
052   *
```

FIG. 4-8. LFILES program listing (continues).

```
053    IF PCODE#'Q' THEN
054      GETDAT=\SSELECT DICT \:DICTNAME:\ BY D/CODE\
055      GETDAT=GETDAT:\ WITH D/CODE = \:CODES
056      EXECUTE GETDAT CAPTURING DUMMY
057      IF SYSTEM(11) THEN
058         SELECT DICTFILE TO DATALIST
059         DATACNT=0
060         ENDDATA=0
061         LOOP
062            READNEXT DATANAME FROM DATALIST ELSE ENDDATA=1
063         UNTIL ENDDATA DO
064            GOSUB 2000 ; * Get and Print Data Pointers
065            DATACNT=DATACNT+1
066         REPEAT
067      END ELSE PRINT   ; * Next Print Line
068    END ELSE PRINT      ; * Next Print Line
069 END
070 RETURN
071 *
072 *
073 2000 * Get and Print Data Pointers
074 *
075 MATREAD POINTER FROM DICTFILE,DATANAME THEN
076    *
077    IF DATACNT THEN PRINT SPACE(40):
078    PRINT DATANAME"L#15" : PCODE"L#5" :
079    PRINT MOD"L#10" : SEP"L#4"
080    *
081 END ELSE
082    PRINT
083 END
084 RETURN
085 *
086 END
```

FIG. 4-8 ends.

the SELECT sentence selection criteria. Again, this is strictly for the purpose of readability.

```
015 CODES = \ "D""DX""DZ""Q" \
```

The CAPTURING clause in the EXECUTE statement is used to hush the output of the number of items selected. CAPTURING re-directs to a variable, (DUMMY in this case), the print output which would normally go to the terminal screen. The CAPTURING clause is discussed at length in Chapter 5, "Process Control."

Immediately following the EXECUTE, the existence of an active list is verified by the SYSTEM(11) (not available on Ultimate) function. If there is no active list, (no items present), the program terminates. If there is an active list, it is assigned the list variable, DICTLIST, by the statement:

```
028 SELECT MD TO DICTLIST
```

The program must now read each D or Q pointer item-id from the master dictionary and select all the D-pointers found in the file DICT:

```
032 ENDDICTS = 0
033 LOOP
034   READNEXT DICTNAME FROM DICTLIST ELSE ENDDICTS = 1
035 UNTIL ENDDICTS DO
036   OPEN 'DICT',DICTNAME TO DICTFILE THEN
037   GOSUB 1000 ;* Get and Print Pointers
038   END
039 REPEAT
040 STOP
```

Subroutine 1000 prints the DICT pointer and then calls subroutine 2000 to print the DATA pointers. However, subroutine 1000 is not called unless the DICT of the file can first be opened. Otherwise, the loop continues and reads the next DICT pointer selected from the master dictionary.

Subroutine 1000 attempts to read the DICT pointer from the MD. If the read is successful, the pointer code, base, modulo and separation are printed. Notice that the data-names—PCODE, BASE, MOD and SEP—are EQUATED in the initialization section of the program.

The DATA level pointers are not listed if the DICT pointer is a 'Q' type. D-pointers in the file DICT are selected and assigned to a new list variable, DATALIST:

```
054   GETDAT = \ SSELECT DICT \:DICTNAME:\ BY D/CODE \
055   GETDAT = GETDAT:\ WITH D/CODE  =  \:CODES
056   EXECUTE GETDAT CAPTURING DUMMY
057   IF  SYSTEM(11) THEN
058     SELECT DICTFILE TO DATALIST
          ...
          ...
067   END ELSE PRINT ; * Next Print Line
```

Once DATALIST is active, the READNEXT loop uses the pointer item-ids to retrieve and print each D-pointer defining a DATA level.

```
059   DATACNT = 0
060   ENDDATA = 0
061   LOOP
062     READNEXT DATANAME FROM DATALIST ELSE ENDDATA = 1
063   UNTIL ENDDATA DO
064     GOSUB 2000 ; * Get and Print Data Pointers
065     DATACNT = DATACNT + 1
066   REPEAT
```

Subroutine 2000 takes care of reading and displaying the DATA level pointer. The counter, DATCNT, is used to determine the amount of indentation for each new DATA level.

Other Methods of Addressing Multiple Lists

Not every implementation supports the SELECT..TO following the EXECUTE. If not, the system may support the RTNLIST and PASSLIST modifiers to the EXECUTE statement. These allow the list variable to be assigned in a single statement, rather than in two. The initial select statement in the LFILES program can be rewritten as follows:

```
GETFILES = \ SSELECT MD BY D/CODE WITH D/CODE = \:CODES
EXECUTE GETFILES CAPTURING DUMMY RTNLIST DICTLIST
```

There is no need for the additional SELECT..TO statement. ULTIMATE users must depend on their special brand of EXECUTE redirection clause to assign a list variable:

```
GETFILES = \ SSELECT MD BY D/CODE WITH D/CODE = \:CODES
EXECUTE GETFILES,//OUT. > DUMMY,//SELECT. > DICTLIST
```

Notice the multiple redirection clauses in both cases. If this gets too confusing, Ultimate redirection clauses can be placed on the next line as follows:

```
EXECUTE GETFILES,
    //OUT. > DUMMY,
    //SELECT. > DICTLIST
```

ORDERED LISTS

Ordered lists are any set of elements maintained in a chronological or sorted sequence. An ordered list can be expressed generally as,

(e1, e2, e3, ... en

where *ei* is an element of the set. Examples of ordered lists are the months of the year,

JANUARY, FEBRUARY, MARCH, APRIL, MAY....

or the ascent of man,

APE, HOMO ERECTUS, NEANDERTHAL, CRO MAGNON, HOMO SAPIEN

or Reagan's years as president,

1980, 1981, 1982, 1983, 1984, 1985, 1986, 1987, 1988

or Ben Casey's universal words,

MAN, WOMAN, BIRTH, DEATH, INFINITY

This section deals with methods used to build and maintain ordered lists in PICK/ BASIC. It is important to be familiar with the dynamic array intrinsic functions before continuing with this section. The range of functions are used, (EXTRACT, REPLACE, INSERT, DELETE and LOCATE.) Remember, any string delimited by the standard system delimiters is considered a list and such a list can be treated as a dynamic array.

Stack Lists

One of the simplest applications of a dynamic array is to emulate dynamic stacks. *Stacks* are ordered lists which are especially useful for keeping track of chronological events. To be more specific, there are two types of stacks demonstrated in this section, *last-in first-out* (LIFO), and *first-in first-out* (FIFO).

LIFO stacks are also called "pushdown" stacks. All insertions and deletions on a LIFO stack are made to the "top" of the stack. Each new insertion to the top of the stack pushes down the remaining elements. Each removal from the top "pops up" the remaining elements. LIFO stacks make the most recent occurrence the first element available. LIFO stacks can be used to keep track of "pathways" through an application or simply for monitoring occurrences of any process.

An effective use of a LIFO stack is demonstrated in the SHELL program found in Chapter 5, "Process Control." This stack keeps track of every TCL command sentence entered. The TCL stack can be recalled later for processing of any stored entry.

FIFO stacks are also known as queues because they service the data which is "first come, first served." Insertions are made at the "rear" of the queue and removals are made from the "front." FIFO stacks are useful for keeping track of multiple requests to be serviced by a single process.

A FIFO stack might be used in a transaction logging routine which works in the "background." Each "foreground" process adds a new processing request to the end of a processing queue item stored in a shared system location. The logging routine reads the queue item, removes the first entry and re-writes the queue item. (Be aware that each process addressing the queue item must lock it prior to modification.)

The program in Fig. 4-9 serves as a very simple illustration of the commands needed to maintain an array as either a LIFO or a FIFO stack.

```
      LIFO.FIFO
001 *PROGRAM LIFO.FIFO
002 *USE A MULTI-VALUED LIST TO EMULATE A STACK
003 *
004 *
005 *
006 PROMPT ''
007 EQU VM TO CHAR(253)
008 TYPES = 'LIFO':VM:'FIFO'
009 *
010 1 * Check for stack type
011 *
012 STACK = ''
013 PRINT @(-1):'DYNAMIC ARRAYS AS STACKS':
014 PRINT @(1,2):'1) LIFO':
015 PRINT @(1,3):'2) FIFO':
016 PRINT @(1,4):'3) QUIT':
017 LOOP
018    PRINT @(1,6):'Enter choice ':@(-4):
019    INPUT ANS,1:
020 UNTIL ANS # '' AND INDEX('123',ANS,1) DO REPEAT
```

FIG. 4-9. LIFO.FIFO program listing (continues).

```
021 IF ANS = '3' THEN
022    PRINT @(-1):
023    STOP
024 END
025 STACKTYPE = TYPES<1,ANS>
026 *
027 10 * Display current STACK and ask for a new ENTRY
028 *
029 PRINT @(-1):STACKTYPE:' Stack':
030 PRINT @(1,1):'STACK = ':STACK:
031 PRINT @(1,4):'1) PUSH':
032 PRINT @(1,5):'2) POP':
033 PRINT @(1,6):'3) QUIT':
034 LOOP
035    PRINT @(1,8):'Enter choice ':@(-4):
036    INPUT ANS,1:
037 UNTIL ANS # '' AND INDEX('123',ANS,1) DO REPEAT
038 *
039 IF ANS = '3' THEN GOTO 1
040 *
041 ON ANS GOSUB 100,200
042 GOTO 10
043 *
044 100 * Push an entry onto the stack
045 *
046 PRINT @(1,10):'Enter value to push ':
047 INPUT STRING
048 IF STRING = '' OR STRING = 'QUIT' THEN RETURN
049 IF STACKTYPE = 'LIFO' THEN
050    STACK = INSERT(STACK,1,1;STRING) ;* INSERT at TOP
051 END ELSE
052    STACK<1,-1> = STRING ;* Tag on the end for FIFO
053 END
054 RETURN
055 *
056 *
057 200 * Pop the first entry
058 *
059 IF STACK<1> = '' THEN
060    PRINT @(1,10):'THE STACK IS EMPTY':
061 END ELSE
062    POPVALUE = STACK<1,1>        ;* Get the first value
063    STACK = DELETE(STACK,1,1)   ;* Delete it from the list
064    PRINT @(1,10):POPVALUE:' was popped from the stack'
065 END
066 PRINT ' Press any key to continue':;INPUT ANY,1:
067 RETURN
068 *
069 END
```

FIG. 4-9 ends.

Program Highlights

The example program, LIFO.FIFO, prompts the user to build either a LIFO or a FIFO stack using any free-form strings entered. If the answer is a valid menu choice, the variable STACKTYPE is set to the value LIFO or FIFO, depending on whether the answer is 1 or 2, respectively.

```
025 STACKTYPE = TYPES<1,ANS>
```

The STACKTYPE is retrieved from a short multivalued array that has been set up at the beginning of the program. The strings LIFO and FIFO are stored in positions which correspond to the value of ANS.

The TYPES array is built as any other data string. Initializing an array using concatenation is more efficient than repeatedly performing replaces.

```
007 EQU VM TO CHAR(253)
008 TYPES = 'LIFO':VM:'FIFO'
```

The action taken for menu options 1 and 2 are determined by the indexed GOSUB statement. A STACK push uses subroutine100. A STACK pop uses subroutine 200:

```
041 ON ANS GOSUB 100,200
042 GOTO 10
```

The STACK push first requests the value string to add to the array STACK. The statement used to push depends on whether the stack is LIFO, the value is inserted at the top of the array, or FIFO, the value is added to the end of the array. The dynamic INSERT function is perfect for adding to the LIFO stack, while the REPLACE function ($<1, -1>$ in contemporary syntax) serves well for the FIFO stack:

```
049  IF STACKTYPE = 'LIFO' THEN
050     STACK = INSERT(STACK,1,1;STRING) ;* INSERT at TOP
051  END ELSE
052     STACK<1,-1> = STRING ;* Tag on the end for FIFO
053  END
```

Both LIFO and FIFO stacks "pop" and entry from the "top" or "front" of the stack. The stack "pop" routine uses the EXTRACT function (again in contemporary syntax) to remove the first stack element and the DELETE function to delete it. All remaining entries "pop" up 1 position in the array STACK:

```
062 POPVALUE = STACK<1,1>   ;* Get the first value
063  STACK = DELETE(STACK,1,1)   ;* Delete it from the list
064  PRINT @(1,10):POPVALUE:' was popped from the stack'
```

Sorted Lists

This section covers the methods for maintaining a list in sorted order via the use of the LOCATE dynamic array function. To make it possible to maintain a list in sorted order, a sequence indicator is added to the LOCATE syntax.

```
LOCATE(DATUM,ARRAY;POSITION;"AL") THEN... ELSE...
```

The value of the sequence indicator may be:

AL   for ascending left-justified

DL   for descending left-justified

AR   for ascending right-justified

DR   for descending right-justified

As described in Chapter 3, the delimiter level for which DATUM is being located is determined by the numeric indicator following the ARRAY variable. The above case is searching for attributes.

If the search string is found, then the THEN clause is taken and the value of POSITION is set to the attribute position of the search string. If the string is not found, then the ELSE clause is taken and the value of POSITION is set to the attribute position where the string should reside to maintain the ordered list. Values and subvalues can be located by indicating the array element level to perform the search. For example:

```
LOCATE(DATUM,ARRAY,2;POSITION;"AL") THEN... ELSE...
```

This searches for values in attribute 2 of ARRAY.

```
LOCATE(DATUM,ARRAY,2,1;POSITION;"AL") THEN... ELSE...
```

This searches for subvalues in attribute 2, value 1 of ARRAY.

The previous LOCATE examples written in contemporary syntax are as follows:
Locating an attribute:
```
LOCATE DATUM IN ARRAY,1 BY "AL" SETTING POSITION ... THEN.. ELSE..
```

Locate a value:
```
LOCATE DATUM IN ARRAY<2>,1 BY "AL" SETTING POSITION ... THEN.. ELSE..
```

Locate a subvalue:
```
LOCATE DATUM IN ARRAY<2,1>,1 BY "AL" SETTING POSITION ... THEN.. ELSE..
```

The "BY" clause controls the sequence. The ",1" is required and indicates the starting attribute, value or subvalue of the search.

NOTE: The LOCATE does not sort an existing array, but, it allows new entries to be added at the correct position. The array in question must be initially null, or have a pre-sorted set of elements. Some implementations are now offering a new PICK/BASIC SORT function that follows the LOCATE syntax very closely. The SORT function allows existing arrays to be sorted in a single statement.

Locate Words Example

Figure 4-10 maintains an ordered list of words entered by the operator. The list is built in left-justified, ascending order. Each new word is inserted at the correct position on the list. If the word already exists, the operator is given the option to delete it.

```
       LOCATE.WORDS
001 *PROGRAM LOCATE.WORDS
002 *KEEP A MULTI-VALUED LIST OF NON-DUPLICATE WORDS
003 *
004 *
005 *
006 PROMPT ''
007 WORDLIST = ''
008 *
009 10 * Display current WORDLIST and ask for a new word
010 *
011 PRINT @(-1):@(1,10):'WORDLIST = ':WORDLIST:
012 LOOP
013    PRINT @(1,1):'Enter a word (Quit to Stop) ':@(-4):
014    INPUT WORD
015 UNTIL ALPHA(WORD) DO REPEAT
016 WORD = OCONV(WORD,'MCU') ;* Force to all upper case
017 IF WORD = 'X' OR WORD = 'QUIT' THEN STOP
018 * Locate the word and add it if not there
019 * Prompt for delete if it is.
020 LOCATE(WORD,WORDLIST,1;POSITION;"AL") THEN
021    PRINT @(1,2):WORD:' exists at value position ':POSITION
022    LOOP
023       PRINT @(1,4):'Delete it? ':
024       INPUT ANS
025       ANS = OCONV(ANS[1,1],'MCU')
026    UNTIL ANS#'' AND INDEX('YN',ANS,1) DO REPEAT
027    IF ANS = 'Y' THEN WORDLIST=DELETE(WORDLIST,1,POSITION)
028 END ELSE
029    WORDLIST=INSERT(WORDLIST,1,POSITION;WORD)
030 END
031 GOTO 10
032 *
033 END
```

FIG. 4-10. LOCATE.WORDS program listing.

Program Highlights

To ensure consistency and allow for a correctly sequenced list, each word that will be added to the list must be forced to uppercase via the MCU conversion.

```
016 WORD = OCONV(WORD,'MCU') ;* Force to all uppercase
```

The word is located on the array, WORDLIST, in ascending, left-justified order.

```
020 LOCATE(WORD,WORDLIST,1;POSITION;"AL") THEN
    .....
    .....
028 END ELSE
    .....
030 END
```

The THEN clause is taken if WORD is found in the multivalued array in attribute 1 of WORDLIST.

```
021     PRINT @(1,2):WORD:' exists at value position ':POSITION
022     LOOP
023       PRINT @(1,4):'Delete it? ':
024       INPUT ANS
025       ANS = OCONV(ANS[1,1],'MCU')
026     UNTIL ANS#'' AND INDEX('YN',ANS,1) DO REPEAT
```

The operator is prompted for whether or not to delete the existing entry. On line 25, the first character is stripped from the variable ANS.

ANS[1,1]

The result is forced to uppercase.

ANS = OCONV(ANS[1,1],'MCU')

And the new ANS is tested for in the LOOP..UNTIL statement.

INDEX('YN',ANS,1)

The INDEX function acts as an implied OR. It checks for the first occurrence of the value of ANS in the string 'YN.' Should ANS contain Y or N, the result would be 1 or 2, respectively. Both positive integers, and therefore true. INDEX generates a zero on any other value of ANS. Careful, a null string passes an INDEX. The UNTIL clause must also check for a non-null value in ANS.

If the answer is affirmative, the value at the indicated value position is deleted.

027 IF ANS = 'Y' THEN WORDLIST = DELETE(WORDLIST,1,POSITION)

If the LOCATE statement fails to find the word in WORDLIST, the ELSE clause is taken. The value of POSITION is the multivalue location of where the string should be inserted into the array.

029 WORDLIST = INSERT(WORDLIST,1,POSITION;WORD)

Correlated Lists

A single item may keep one or more attributes as multivalued lists. In the case of an invoice item holding information for each "line item,", each attribute contains a multi-valued list of part numbers, quantities, unit prices and, possibly, extended prices.

The lists are described as *correlated* because the nth entry on the list of part numbers references the nth entry on the quantity and price lists. An example is shown in Fig. 4-11. Whether each attribute is maintained as an ordered list, or a LIFO or FIFO stack, any action taken on one of the lists, must be repeated on all the lists. The job of maintaining the correlation must be "brute-forced" using the PICK/BASIC intrinsic functions. Figure 4-12 shows how you handle deleting a correlated list.

Invoice item format:

```
ID:    invoice#
…
…
mmm    partx]party]partz
nnn    qtyx]qtyy]qtyz
ooo    pricex]pricey]pricez
```

FIG. 4-11. Correlated lists.

Sample invoice item:

```
ID: UVC-001
001 THE ABC COMPANY
002 124 SESAME STREET
003 NEW YORK
004 NY
005 10019
006 111-23]440-99]677-99
007 10]1]3
008 1112]2345]2222
```

```
DIM INVOICE(10)
EQU VM TO CHAR(253)
...
MATREAD INVOICE FROM INVOIVES,INVID ELSE STOP 202
...
LINES = DCOUNT(INVOICE(6),VM)
...
* Delete a line item
INPUT LINENUM
FOR ATTR = 6 TO 8
    INVOICE(ATTR) = DELETE(INVOICE(ATTR),1,LINENUM)
NEXT ATTR
....
```

FIG. 4-12. Handling correlated list deletion.

LINKED LISTS

One of the major shortcomings of handling dynamic lists within PICK/BASIC is throughput. Short lists are alright, but, when lists start crossing frame boundaries, throughput begins to degrade geometrically. Consider the PICK/BASIC program which in Fig. 4-13 converts an ACCESS generated list into a standard item.

The crossed frame boundaries are not the only factor causing degradation. As the string in the variable LIST gets larger, old workspace buffers must be abandoned and new ones assigned. This also forces garbage collection. Not only is throughput adversely affected when building a large list in this manner, but it is also affected when traversing the list.

```
                SIMPLE.LIST
001 PROGRAM SIMPLE.LIST
002 * Demonstrate building a simple item list
003 * HER
004 * 10/05/88
005 *
006 *
007 OPEN "LISTS" TO LISTS ELSE STOP 201,'LISTS'
008 *
009 LIST = ''
010 *
011 EXECUTE "SSELECT MD"
012 *
013 EOL = 0
014 LOOP
015   READNEXT ID ELSE EOL = 1
016 UNTIL EOL DO
017   LIST<1,-1> = ID
018   CRT '*':
019 REPEAT
020 WRITE LIST ON LISTS,'MDLIST'
```

FIG. 4-13. SIMPLE.LIST program listing.

An effective solution to this problem is to break up the large list into a series of smaller lists (list nodes), each within a frame size. In order for a program to traverse the entire list, these smaller lists must somehow contain pointers to the previous and next items in the chain.

One approach to linked lists has the elements stored as a value-marked array in a single attribute of an item. Another attribute in the same item contains pointers to the lists that precede and follow the current item, as illustrated in Fig. 4-14. The possible format is shown in Fig. 4-15.

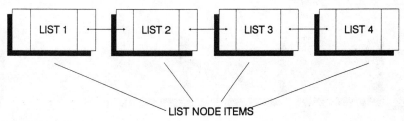

FIG. 4-14. Linked list.

ID: *listname.suffix*

001 *previous listname.suffix] next listname.suffix*

002 *element1] element2] ....] elementn*

FIG. 4-15. Linked list item possible layout.

The listname suffix used must be a unique identifier, such as a sequential number. This is simple enough for a one-time build of the linked chain with no modification. Maintaining such a design for an ordered list where elements need to be inserted and deleted is quite a bit more work than desired. As list elements grow beyond the maximum size or shrink below a minimum threshold, new list nodes must be added or deleted. The links in the preceding and following lists must be rebuilt. Figure 4-16 diagrams the modification process.

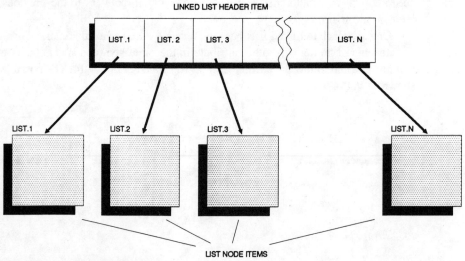

FIG. 4-16. Linked list node split.

An alternative method is to maintain a special header item, as shown in Fig. 4-17, which contains an ordered list of the item-ids of each list node. Any additions or deletions of list nodes requires the modification of the header item. The format of a header item is described in Fig. 4-18.

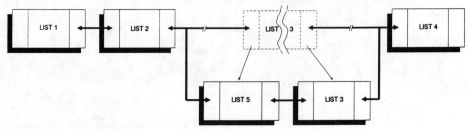

FIG. 4-17. A headered linked list.

ID: *listname*.HDR

001: *listname.suffix1*] *listname.suffix2*] ....] *listname.suffixn*

FIG. 4-18. Linked list header item.

The SIMPLE.LINKED.LIST Program

The next program, in Fig. 4-19, elaborates on the SIMPLE.LIST program by forcing a new list before the frame size is exceeded, (using a 500 byte frame). The list is given a unique identifier based on the port number and a sequential suffix. The lists are linked via a header item as described above.

```
          SIMPLE.LINKED.LIST
001 PROGRAM SIMPLE.LINKED.LIST
002 * Demonstrate building a simple linked list
003 * HER
004 * 10/05/88
005 *
006 *
007 OPEN "LISTS" TO LISTS ELSE STOP 201,'LISTS'
008 *
009 LIST = ''
010 LISTHDR = ''
011 LISTSEQ = 1
012 PORT = FIELD(OCONV(0,'U50BB'),' ',1)
013 *
014 EXECUTE "SSELECT MD"
015 *
016 EOL = 0
017 LOOP
018    READNEXT ID ELSE EOL = 1
019 UNTIL EOL DO
020    LIST<1,-1> = ID
021    CRT '*':
022    IF LEN(LIST) > 480 THEN
023       WRITE LIST ON LISTS,PORT:'.':LISTSEQ
024       LISTHDR<1,-1> = PORT:'.':LISTSEQ
025       LIST = ''
026       LISTSEQ = LISTSEQ + 1
027       CRT '-':
028    END
029 REPEAT
030 IF LIST # '' THEN
031    LISTHDR<1,-1> = PORT:'.':LISTSEQ
032    WRITE LIST ON LISTS,PORT:'.':LISTSEQ
033    CRT '-'
034 END ELSE CRT
035 WRITE LISTHDR ON LISTS,PORT:'.HDR'
036 STOP
```

FIG. 4-19. SIMPLE.LINK.LIST program listing.

Program Highlights

The general format of SIMPLE.LINKED.LIST is similar to SIMPLE.LIST except for a few wrinkles. First, the list name is determined by the current port number as retrieved in line 012:

```
012 PORT = FIELD(OCONV(0, 'U50BB'), ' ',1)
```

Second, as the LIST variable is built, the size is checked. Should the size exceed 480 bytes (to keep it under a frame boundary), the current LIST is written with a sequence tag, the LISTHDR is updated with the new list name, and LIST is reset to null:

```
022    IF LEN(LIST) > 480 THEN
023       WRITE LIST ON LISTS,PORT:'.':LISTSEQ
024       LISTHDR<1,-1> = PORT:'.':LISTSEQ
025       LIST = ''
026       LISTSEQ = LISTSEQ + 1
027       CRT    '-':
028    END
```

When the MD list is exhausted, the LIST item is checked for any other values. If it is not null, the last linked item list is written and the header item is updated.

```
030 IF LIST # '' THEN
031    LISTHDR<1,-1> = PORT:'.':LISTSEQ
032    WRITE LIST ON LISTS,PORT:'.':LISTSEQ
033    CRT '-'
034 END ELSE CRT
```

This linked list built program never has to deal with a list which exceeds a frame boundary. Compare the processing time of SIMPLE.LIST and SIMPLE.LINKED.LIST. The difference is dramatic.

Linking Linked Lists

Now that the linked lists are built, how can these be converted to an active ACCESS list to be fed to another process? The answer is: by using the QSELECT verb. QSELECT allows any list stored as an item to be made active for any TCL, ACCESS or PICK/BASIC process. The general form of QSELECT is:

QSELECT *filename* {*itemlist*} }(*amc*)}

The *itemlist* can be specified or implied from a previously active list. The option (amc) is the target attribute which contains a value-marked list of id's. If the option is omitted, an active list is built from all the attributes in the item. The series of linked item lists can be linked and fed to ACCESS by first entering:

QSELECT LISTS *listname*.HDR (1

and then:

QSELECT LISTS

The first statement activates a list of the header pointers. This active list is subsequently fed to the second statement which links and activates all the list items in the header. If a linked chain contains 10 list items, each of which contains 100 entries, the previous command sequence would generate the following messages:

```
>QSELECT LISTS TEST.HDR (1
[404] 10 ITEMS SELECTED

>QSELECT LISTS
[404] 1000 ITEMS SELECTED
```

The resulting active list can be saved with SAVE-LIST or used to drive any other process. These procedures can be placed in a PROC or PICK/BASIC program called LINK. Figure 4-20 compares the link PROC to the same process in PICK/BASIC. Either of these processes creates an active list from the header item and then subsequently from the list items.

The program in Fig. 4-21 is designed for those who speak ULTIMATE.

```
LINK PROC:

ID: LINK
001 PQ
002 HQSELECT LISTS
003 A\2
004 H.HDR
005 STON
006 HQSELECT LISTS
007 P
008 IF #S XNO ACTIVE LIST
009 HSAVE-LIST
010 A2
011 P


LINK Program:

ID: LINK
001 PROGRAM LINK
002 * Links lists and SAVES as LIST item.
003 * HER
004 *
005 *
006 PROMPT ''
007 INPUT LISTNAME
008 IF LISTNAME = '' THEN STOP
009 DATA 'QSELECT LISTS'
010 EXECUTE 'QSELECT LISTS ':LISTNAME:'.HDR'
011 IF NOT(SYSTEM(11)) THEN STOP
012 EXECUTE 'SAVE-LIST ':LISTNAME
```

FIG. 4-20. LINK routine for activating linked lists.

The LINKED.MAINT Subroutine

The subroutine in Fig. 4-22 is a more generalized routine for adding or deleting values to a linked ordered list. As in SIMPLE.LINKED.LIST, each list node is written as it exceeds a frame size and the new item-id is added to a list header item. The difference is

```
    ID: LINK.ULT
    001 * PROGRAM LINK.ULT
    002 * Links lists and SAVES as LIST item.
    003 *.HER
    004 *
    005 *
    006 PROMPT ''
    007 INPUT LISTNAME
    008 IF LISTNAME = '' THEN STOP
    009 ACTIVELIST = ''
    010 EXECUTE 'QSELECT LISTS':LISTNAME:'.HDR',
    011    //SELECT.>ACTIVELIST
    012 IF ACTIVELIST='' THEN STOP
    013 NEWLIST = ''
    014 EXECUTE 'QSELECT LISTS',
    015    //SELECT.<ACTIVELIST,//SELECT.>NEWLIST
    016 IF NEWLIST='' THEN STOP
    017 EXECUTE 'SAVE-LIST ':LISTNAME,//SELECT.<NEWLIST
```

FIG. 4-21. ULT.LINK listing.

```
    LINKED.MAINT
    001 SUBROUTINE LINKED.MAINT (VALUE,KEYWORD,LISTFILE,SEQ,ACTION)
    002 * Search a linked list for an item (works like LOCATE)
    003 * HER
    004 * 10/05/88
    005 *
    006 * VALUE is the list entry being added or deleted
    007 * KEYWORD is the secondary key which is being indexed
    008 * LISTFILE is the file variable for the LIST file
    009 * SEQ can be 'AL', 'AR', 'DL', 'DR'
    010 * ACTION is 'A'dd or 'D'elete
    011 *
    012 EQU FRAMESIZE TO 500
    013 EQU VM        TO CHAR(253)
    014 *
    015 IF SEQ = '' THEN SEQ = 'AR'
    016 HDRID = KEYWORD:'.HDR'
    017 READU LISTHDR FROM LISTFILE,HDRID ELSE
    018      GOSUB 5000 ;* Get next item-id suffix
    019      LISTHDR = KEYWORD:'.':NEXTSFX
    020 END
    021 *
    022 * Find the list segment
    023 *
    024 LISTSMAX = DCOUNT(LISTHDR,VM)
    025 POS      = 1
    026 DONE     = 0
    027 FOUND    = 0
    028 LOOP UNTIL DONE DO
    029      INDEXKEY = LISTHDR<1,POS>
    030      IF INDEXKEY # '' THEN
    031        READ LISTITEM FROM LISTFILE,INDEXKEY ELSE
    032            LISTITEM = ''
```

FIG. 4-22. LINKED.MAINT subroutine listing (continues).

```
033         END
034         MAXVMC = DCOUNT(LISTITEM,VM)
035         LOCATE(VALUE,LISTITEM,1;F;SEQ) THEN
036             FOUND = 1
037             DONE  = 1
038         END ELSE
039             IF F > MAXVMC AND POS < LISTSMAX THEN
040                 POS = POS + 1
041             END ELSE
042                 DONE = 1
043             END
044         END
045       END ELSE DONE = 1
046 REPEAT
047 *
048 1000 * Check and perform action
049 *
050 BEGIN CASE
051   CASE ACTION = 'D' AND FOUND
052       * Delete from list
053       LISTITEM = DELETE(LISTITEM,1,F)
054       IF LISTITEM = '' THEN
055           LISTHDR = DELETE(LISTHDR,1,POS)
056           IF LISTHDR = '' THEN
057               DELETE LISTFILE,HDRID
058           END ELSE
059               WRITE LISTHDR ON LISTFILE,HDRID
060           END
061           DELETE LISTFILE,INDEXKEY
062       END ELSE
063           WRITE LISTITEM ON LISTFILE,INDEXKEY
064       END
065   CASE ACTION = 'A' AND NOT(FOUND)
066       * Add to list
067       LISTITEM = INSERT(LISTITEM,1,F;VALUE)
068       LENITEM = LEN(LISTITEM<1>)
069       IF LENITEM > FRAMESIZE THEN
070           * Break it up
071           BRKPOS = COUNT(LISTITEM<1>[1,INT(FRAMESIZE/2)],VM)
072           BRKPOS = INDEX(LISTITEM<1>,VM,BRKPOS)
073           ITEM1 = LISTITEM<1>[1,BRKPOS-1]
074           ITEM2 = LISTITEM<1>[BRKPOS+1,LENITEM]
075           GOSUB 5000 ;* Get next item-id suffix
076           WRITE ITEM1 ON LISTFILE,INDEXKEY
077           NEWKEY = KEYWORD:'.':NEXTSFX
078           WRITE ITEM2 ON LISTFILE,NEWKEY
079           LISTHDR<1,POS> = INDEXKEY:VM:NEWKEY
080       END ELSE
081           WRITE LISTITEM ON LISTFILE,INDEXKEY
082       END
083       WRITE LISTHDR ON LISTFILE,HDRID
084 END CASE
085 RELEASE
086 RETURN
```

FIG. 4-22 continues.

```
087 *
088 *
089 5000 * Get next item-id suffix
090 *
091 READU NEXTSFX FROM LISTFILE,'NEXTSFX' ELSE NEXTSFX=1
092 WRITE NEXTSFX+1 ON LISTFILE,'NEXTSFX'
093 RETURN
094 END
```

FIG. 4-22 ends.

that this program keeps the list in sorted sequence based on a SEQ parameter passed to it. This supercedes the simpler case where each list is built in turn. Before an element can be added or deleted, each list mode must be searched in turn. This requires a series of READS and LOCATES until the value is found or verified non-existent.

As an element is added to or deleted from the ordered list, the linked items must be checked for size and then split or removed. These unique list suffixes are sequence numbers assigned by the program. When an item is split, the next available number is assigned as the list suffix, and the new element is inserted into the header item.

Program Highlights

The LINKED.MAINT subroutine is passed the following variables:

- VALUE is the item-id being searched for, but can be any unique value to be added or deleted from the list.

- KEYWORD is the list identifier. If this routine is used to maintain an inverted cross reference list, it is the item-id used for secondary index key.

- LISTFILE is the file variable to which the file holding the lists is opened.

- SEQ is the sorted sequence in which the list values are to be kept. The value of SEQ can be 'AL' (ascending left,) 'AR' (ascending right,) 'DL' (descending left,) or 'DR' (descending right.)

- ACTION can be A to add a new value to the list, or D to delete an existing value from the list.

Because the list items are restricted to the size of a data frame and each entry in the list is delimited by a value mark, these constants are defined at the offset:

```
012 EQU FRAMESIZE TO 500
013 EQU VM   TO CHAR(253)
```

The header list item-id is built from KEYWORD and an attempt is made to read the header list item from LISTFILE. If the header item does not exist, it's time to create it:

```
016 HDRID = KEYWORD:'.HDR'
017 READU LISTHDR FROM LISTFILE,HDRID ELSE
018    GOSUB 5000 ;* Get next list item suffix
019    LISTHDR = KEYWORD:'.':NEXTSFX
020 END
```

Subroutine 5000 is used as the standard routine to assign the next available suffix to a list item-id:

```
089  5000 * Get next list item suffix
090  *
091  READU NEXTSFX FROM LISTFILE,'NEXTSFX' ELSE NEXTSFX = 1
092  WRITE NEXTSFX + 1 ON LISTFILE,'NEXTSFX'
093  RETURN
```

The READU (read for update), is used to lock the group or item, depending on the implementation, so that no other process retrieves the count while the current one is using it. Once retrieved, the counter is incremented and updated to the NEXTSFX item. The WRITE automatically clears the lock.

The first major task at hand is to determine whether or not the search value, VALUE, exists within the linked lists. The function DCOUNT is used to determine the total number of lists in the linked chain:

```
024 LISTSMAX = DCOUNT(LISTHDR,VM)
```

The main loop looks through each consecutive list for the existence of VALUE:

```
028 LOOP UNTIL DONE DO
029      INDEXKEY = LISTHDR<1,POS>
030      IF INDEXKEY # '' THEN
031        READ LISTITEM FROM LISTFILE,INDEXKEY ELSE
032          LISTITEM = ''
033        END
034        MAXVMC = DCOUNT(LISTITEM,VM)
         .....
         .....
045      END ELSE DONE = 1
         .....
         .....
046 REPEAT
```

Each subsequent list node item-id (key) is extracted:

```
INDEXKEY = LISTHDR<1,POS>
```

If INDEXKEY is not null, an attempt is made to read the list item from LISTFILE. Once retrieved, the maximum number of elements in the list node is counted.

```
DCOUNT(LISTITEM,VM)
```

The LOCATE statement is used to make the initial determination of whether the search value already exists in the current list or not:

```
035      LOCATE(VALUE,LISTITEM,1;F;SEQ) THEN
036          FOUND = 1
037          DONE = 1
```

```
038        END ELSE
039            IF F > MAXVMC AND POS < LISTSMAX THEN
040                POS = POS + 1
041            END ELSE
042                DONE = 1
043            END
044        END
```

If VALUE is not found in the current list, the program must determine whether the search is over. The search is over if the end of the entire linked list is reached, or the value of POS is within the current list. A POS value within the current list states that VALUE does not exist. A POS value greater than the number of entries in the current list indicates that the search is not over and that VALUE must be in the next linked node.

```
IF F > MAXVMC AND POS < LISTSMAX THEN
```

This conditional checks to see if the next item list node should be read. If so, the pointer, POS, is incremented, otherwise the search is complete. Either way, the value of F indicates where the value is or should be in the last searched list. The CASE condition in routine 1000 is performed when the search is complete.

```
048  1000 * Check and perform action
049  *
050  BEGIN CASE
051      CASE ACTION = 'D' AND FOUND
052          * Delete from list
             ....
065      CASE ACTION = 'A' AND NOT(FOUND)
066          * Add to list
             ....
084  END CASE
085  RELEASE
086  RETURN
```

An entry cannot be deleted if the entry is not found. Likewise, an entry cannot be added if it already exists.

Adding a List Element   New list elements are inserted onto the current list node and the length is checked:

```
067  LISTITEM = INSERT(LISTITEM,1,F;VALUE)
068  LENITEM = LEN(LISTITEM<1>)
```

If the length exceeds the framesize, then the list node must be broken into two items, otherwise the current item is simply updated to the LISTFILE:

```
069      IF LENITEM > FRAMESIZE THEN
070          * Break it up
```

```
          .....
          .....
080       END ELSE
081           WRITE LISTITEM ON LISTFILE,INDEXKEY
082       END
```

The split is determined by first finding the element just before the midpoint of the item:

```
070       *  Break it up
071       BRKPOS = COUNT(LISTITEM<1>[1,INT(FRAMESIZE/2)],VM)
```

An approximate midpoint is determined and the first half of the list extracted by the function:

```
LISTITEM<1>[1,INT(FRAMESIZE/2)]
```

The number of value marks up to this point is then counted, using the compound expression:

```
COUNT(LISTITEM<1>[1,INT(FRAMESIZE/2)],VM)
```

The character position of the last value mark in the first half of the string is then determined by an **INDEX** function:

```
072   BRKPOS = INDEX(LISTITEM<1>,VM,BRKPOS)
```

The item is then split in two:

```
073   ITEM1 = LISTITEM<1>[1,BRKPOS–1]
074   ITEM2 = LISTITEM<1>[BRKPOS+1,LENITEM]
```

Now, the program must get the next node suffix for the new list node:

```
075   GOSUB 5000 ;* Get next node id
```

The two list nodes can now be updated to LISTFILE:

```
076   WRITE ITEM1 ON LISTFILE,INDEXKEY
077   NEWKEY = KEYWORD:'.':NEXTSFX
078   WRITE ITEM2 ON LISTFILE,NEWKEY
```

The new list node pointer is then added to the header list:

```
079   LISTHDR<1,POS> = INDEXKEY:VM:NEWKEY
```

In either case, node split or not, the list header is written back to the LISTFILE.

```
083   WRITE LISTHDR ON LISTFILE,HDRID
```

Delete a List Element   The located VALUE is deleted from its position in the current list node:

```
052   * Delete from list
053   LISTITEM = DELETE(LISTITEM,1,F)
```

Now, the list node must be checked to see if it is empty. If not, the list item is written to the LISTFILE. Notice that no attempt is made here to recombine the remaining list nodes.

```
054    IF  LISTITEM  =  '' THEN
          .....
062    END ELSE
063       WRITE LISTITEM ON LISTFILE,INDEXKEY
064    END
```

If the list node item ends up being empty, it must be deleted and removed from the header list. In addition, if the header list ends up being empty, it too must be deleted from LIST-FILE:

```
055    LISTHDR  =  DELETE(LISTHDR,1,POS)
056    IF  LISTHDR  =  '' THEN
057       DELETE LISTFILE,HDRID
058    END ELSE
059       WRITE LISTHDR ON LISTFILE,HDRID
060    END
061    DELETE LISTFILE,INDEXKEY
```

So much for this program. Have fun!

DATA CROSS REFERENCING

The most powerful use of lists maintained with programs is for cross-referencing data on keys other than the item-id. Cross-reference lists allow quick secondary key retrieval of data without the overhead of a lengthy ACCESS SELECT.

Inverted Lists

Inverted lists are a type of cross reference. Each list item is assigned an item-id using any substring from the referenced data item, (last name, city, state, zip.) The body of the index item is an attribute marked or value marked list of the item-id's. For example:

Consider a master data file named STAFF where there are three employees with the last name SMITH. The SMITH index list item, stored in the cross-reference file and named STAFF.XREF, is an inverted list item based on the last name. Refer to Fig. 4-23.

There is no particular reason why this list is multivalued. The STAFF.XREF item could just as well look like this:

```
ID:    SMITH
001    201
002    325
003    657
```

If a cross-reference item is to contain more than one list, multiple values are required.

Cross-reference lists, as they exist today, place the burden of creation and mainte-nance squarely on the shoulders of the application programmer. A routine for maintaining

STAFF File

```
ID: 201                    325                   657
001 SMITH, ALEXIS          SMITH, JOHN           SMITH, CORONA
002 14 Karet Blvd          13 Anonymous St       3 Ribbon Dr
003 Beverly Hills          Allentown             Omaha
004 Ca                     Pa                    Nb
```

STAFF.XREF File

```
ID: SMITH
001 201]325]657
```

FIG. 4-23. Inverted list.

the list items must be invoked each time an interactive routine modifies the master file. In addition, there should be a batch build routine which can rebuild the lists from scratch in case anything like a GFE occurs in the cross-reference file.

The BUILD.XREF Program

The program listed in Fig. 4-24 is a simple batch build routine which rebuilds all the inverted list for the STAFF file. Lists are created for multiple secondary keys including last name, state, zip code and area code.

```
     BUILD.XREF
001  PROGRAM BUILD.XREF
002  * Batch builds Staff file XREF Items
003  * 10/01/88
004  * HER,JES
005  *
006  EQU VM TO CHAR(253)
007  *
008  OPEN "STAFF" TO STAFF ELSE STOP 201,"STAFF"
009  OPEN "STAFF.XREF" TO STAFF.XREF ELSE STOP 201,"STAFF.XREF"
010  *
011  DIM STAFF.ITEM(13)
012  CLEARFILE STAFF.XREF
013  *
014  SELECT STAFF
015  KEYWORD = ""
016  ENDOFLIST = 0
017  LOOP
018     READNEXT ID ELSE ENDOFLIST = 1
019  UNTIL ENDOFLIST DO
020     MAT STAFF.ITEM = ""
021     MATREAD STAFF.ITEM FROM STAFF,ID THEN
022     *
023     * FIRST, CUSTOMER NAME FIELD (UPPER OR LOWER CASE)
```

FIG. 4-24. BUILD.XREF program listing (continues).

```
024        KEYWORD = OCONV(STAFF.ITEM(1),"MCU")
025        GOSUB 500
026   *  SECOND, STATE ABBREVIATION
027        KEYWORD = STAFF.ITEM(4)
028        GOSUB 500
029   *  THIRD, ZIP CODE
030        KEYWORD = STAFF.ITEM(5)
031        GOSUB 500
032   *  FOURTH, AREA CODE
033        KEYWORD = STAFF.ITEM(6)[1,3]
034        GOSUB 500
035     END
036 REPEAT
037 *
038 STOP
039 *
040 *
041 500 * STRIP GARBAGE FROM STRING AND WRITE XREF ITEM
042 *
043 DELIM = OCONV(KEYWORD,"MC/N":VM:"MC/A")[1,1]
044 KEYWORD = FIELD(KEYWORD,DELIM,1)
045 *
046 READ STAFF.XREF.ITEM FROM STAFF.XREF,KEYWORD ELSE
047        STAFF.XREF.ITEM = ''
048 END
049 *
050 PRINT KEYWORD
051 * STAFF.XREF.ITEM<1,-1> = ID
052 LOCATE(ID,STAFF.XREF.ITEM,1;F;"AR") ELSE
053   STAFF.XREF.ITEM = INSERT(STAFF.XREF.ITEM,1,F;ID)
054 WRITE STAFF.XREF.ITEM ON STAFF.XREF,KEYWORD
055 END
056 *
057 RETURN
058 *
059 END
```

FIG. 4-24 ends.

Program Highlights

File control is straightforward. Both the source data file, STAFF, and the cross-reference file, STAFF.XREF, must be opened. Because this program performs a full batch rebuild of the cross-reference data, the STAFF.XEF file must be initially cleared:

```
008 "STAFF" TO STAFF ELSE STOP 201,"STAFF"
009 OPEN "STAFF.XREF" TO STAFF.XREF ELSE STOP 201,"STAFF.XREF"
010 *
011 DIM STAFF.ITEM(13)
012 CLEARFILE STAFF.XREF
```

Because the order of retrieval is not important to this program, the STAFF file is selected via a PICK/BASIC SELECT statement. Each KEYWORD being used as the secondary key must be read as each data item is encountered:

```
014 SELECT STAFF
016 ENDOFLIST = 0
017 LOOP
018    READNEXT ID ELSE ENDOFLIST = 1
019 UNTIL ENDOFLIST DO
       ...
021    MATREAD STAFF.ITEM FROM STAFF,ID THEN
          ... Update the XREF file ...
035    END
036 REPEAT
```

Each keyword is extracted from the item and updated to the inverted list via the 500 subroutine:

```
022    *
023    * FIRST, CUSTOMER NAME FIELD (UPPER OR LOWER CASE)
024      KEYWORD = OCONV(STAFF.ITEM(1),"MCU")
025      GOSUB 500
026    * SECOND, STATE ABBREVIATION
027      KEYWORD = STAFF.ITEM(4)
028      GOSUB 500
029    * THIRD, ZIP CODE
030      KEYWORD = STAFF.ITEM(5)
031      GOSUB 500
032    * FOURTH, AREA CODE
033      KEYWORD = STAFF.ITEM(6)[1,3]
034      GOSUB 500
```

Subroutine 500 first processes each KEYWORD and passes only those characters leading up to the first non-alphanumeric:

```
043 DELIM = OCONV(KEYWORD,"MC/N":VM:"MC/A")[1,1]
```

KEYWORD is passed through a value-marked conversion string:

```
"MC/N":VM:"MC/A"
```

These mask character conversions first strip all non-numeric characters and then all non-alphabetic characters. For example, a comma (,) is left when the string "SMITH, JOHN" is passed through this conversion. The first character is extracted from the string of non-alphanumerics:

```
OCONV(.....)[1,1]
```

This character is used to delimit the end of the secondary key string. The new keyword is extracted from the original keyword:

```
044 KEYWORD = FIELD(KEYWORD,DELIM,1)
```

Once the cross-reference item, STAFF.XREF.ITEM, is retrieved from the STAFF.XREF file, the new item-id is added to the list. Notice that line 051 is commented out. This would maintain the list in a FIFO arrangement and not check for duplicate entries.

```
046   READ STAFF.XREF.ITEM FROM STAFF.XREF,KEYWORD ELSE
047        STAFF.XREF.ITEM = '
048   END
050   PRINT KEYWORD
051   * STAFF.XREF.ITEM<1,-1> = ID
```

The LOCATE statement allows the item-ids to be kept in sorted order:

```
052   LOCATE(ID,STAFF.XREF.ITEM,1;F;"AR") ELSE
053      STAFF.XREF.ITEM = INSERT(STAFF.XREF.ITEM,1,F;ID)
054      WRITE STAFF.XREF.ITEM ON STAFF.XREF,KEYWORD
055   END
```

Linked Inverted Lists

A single inverted list starts losing its attraction as the size of the list crosses frame boundaries. A major shortcoming is that many systems still have an upper limit of 32K per item. However, simple cross references are deadly to system performance even before it reaches the 32K size limits.

One solution is to maintain these lists in a linked item structure. This shouldn't change the main flow of the previous program. In fact, it shouldn't make a difference to the main programs of any application. As shown before, the code to add and delete any elements of a linked list or any type of cross reference can be "black boxed." Just determine which KEYWORD list is to be built and call the subroutine. BUILD.XREF needs only the LOCATE code removed. The altered subroutine 500 is illustrated in Fig. 4-25.

```
041 500 * STRIP GARBAGE FROM STRING AND WRITE XREF ITEM
042 *
043 DELIM = OCONV(KEYWORD,"MC/N":VM:"MC/A")[1,1]
044 KEYWORD = FIELD(KEYWORD,DELIM,1)
045 CALL LINKED.MAINT (ID,KEYWORD,STAFF.XREF,'AR','A')
046 CRT KEYWORD
047 *
048 RETURN
049 *
050 END
```

FIG. 4-25. Linked inverted list update.

ISAM Lists

An inverted list is a good solution for quickly retrieving any STAFF member whose last name is SMITH, but it is not designed to retrieve anyone whose last name starts with "S." One solution is to maintain linked lists used to reference data via an Indexed Sequential Access Method (ISAM).

ISAM is easy to emulate by not only adding a correlated data value list to the linked list header item, but also to each list node, as shown in Fig. 4-26. For example, if the linked list is kept in order of the first name, each entry in a list node has a corresponding data value of the name, and each element in the header contains a data value equivalent to the last data value of each node. Figure 4-27 shows the possible layout of an ISAM list header item.

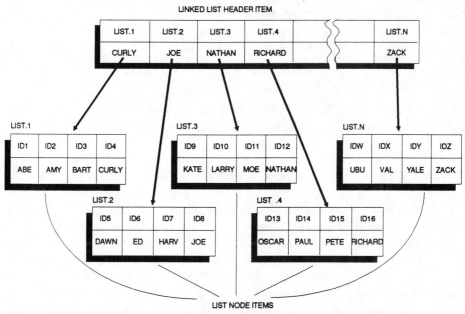

FIG. 4-26. ISAM linked list.

ID: *listname*.HDR

001 *listname.suffix1*] *listname.suffix2*] ....] *listname.suffixn*

002 *data value1*] *data value2*] ......] *data valuen*

FIG. 4-27. ISAM list header item.

The linked list can now be searched without having to sequentially process every list node, as shown in Fig. 4-28. The name value can be LOCATEd in attribute 002 of the ISAM header item. If the name value is found or not, the set variable contains the list position of the name equal to or higher than the search value. The corresponding list name in attribute 001 of the header identifies the node to be searched.

```
PROGRAM FIND.NODE
DIM ISAMHDR(2)
OPEN 'ISAMLISTS' TO LISTS ELSE STOP 201
...
INPUT LISTNAME
READ HEADREC FROM LISTS,LISTNAME:'.HDR' ELSE STOP 202
...
INPUT NAME
LOCATE(NAME,ISAMHDR(2),1;POS;"AL") ELSE NULL
LISTID = ISAMHDR(1)<1,POS>
...
```

FIG. 4-28. ISAM search for a linked list node.

Trees

The discussion now turns to the use of trees. *Data trees* are an efficient solution for indexed searches through large amounts of data that are based on any portion of a secondary key reference.

Although listing and program explanations are provided for building and maintaining linked and inverted lists, trees are approached at a higher level. What? What was that? Is there someone out there saying, "What a copout!"? Not in the least. There are so many different approaches to trees and so many different packages available, it is better to buy a package than try to "home-brew" one. Tree maintenance programs should be "black boxes" which are called when an addition or deletion is required. Better yet, tree maintenance should be an integral part of the system so that any read or write to the file automatically maintains the trees associated with that file. The only routines that the application programmer should have to address are those provided for tree traversal.

The simplest tree data structure is a binary tree. A *binary tree structure* is organized so that data is located along two possible paths. A tree database structure has a *root*, the base of the tree, and *nodes*, the point at which two possible branches can be taken.

A binary tree contains a single data value at each node. The search value is compared to the first node and the question is asked, "is the value being searched for greater than, less than, or equal to this value?" If it is greater than this value, the search continues down the tree to the right. If it is less than, the search continues down and to the left. The search process follows along the branches to the right or left child nodes and repeats the same comparison until the lowest level is reached. A binary tree is shown in Fig. 4-29.

Each node is made up of the data value and two pointers, one to the right sub-tree and one to left sub-tree. The number of branch levels that a tree breeds is called the "height" of the tree. The *height* of a tree determines the number of worst-case reads required to find a particular value.

One of the main disadvantages of a binary tree is that it can quickly become unbalanced. If the first node is ZEBRA, then the left child can grow quite large. If the first node is AARON, then the right child can become large. Binary trees require complex balancing routines to maintain efficiency.

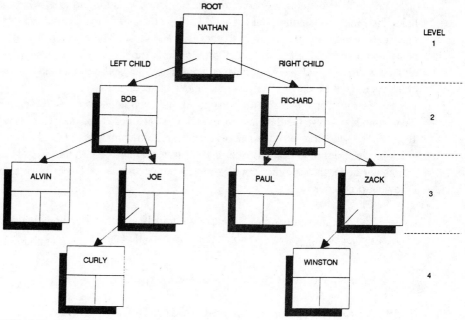

FIG. 4-29. Simple binary tree.

B-Trees

B-trees are self-balancing trees, (hence the name B-tree.) A *B-tree* is made up of basically the same elements as a binary tree, except that each node contains a list of values and a correlated list of pointers. Each pointer element designates the next level node-id, which contains the list of values less than the current value at the previous level. Each node contains N unique data values and N+1 pointer values. The last node of any branch is called the "failure" node, because no levels follow it. The B-tree structure is shown in Fig. 4-30.

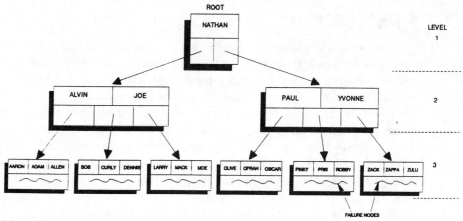

FIG. 4-30. B-tree structure.

The quickest method to search a list is not from beginning to end, which is the way linked lists must be handled, but to first divide the list into n smaller lists, which point to n other lists, which, in turn, point to n other lists and so on. The number of values searched is narrowed down by a factor of n as each node is traversed. This procedure is repeated until the value is found or a failure node is reached. Such a search method can handle a list of hundreds of thousands of entries in a matter of seconds.

For example, in a list of 1 million entries and each node contains 100 elements, then the first node narrows the database to 1 percent of the entire expanse. This gives us one in 10,000. The second level node narrows the search down to 1 in 100 and so on.

The strict definition of a B-tree is an m-way search tree, where m is the number of entries per node, that is either empty or has a height $>= 1$. A B-tree must also have the following properties:

- The root node must have at least two branches, (otherwise known as children).
- All nodes must have at least $m/2$ entries, where m is the maximum entries per node.
- Failure nodes must be at the same level in the tree.

For efficiency in Pick, each node should not exceed a frame size.

The B-trees that are commercially available come in two major flavors, those written in PICK/BASIC available to be loaded and retro-fitted to any application on any implementation, and those written in the Pick Virtual Assembler which are, for the most part, tied to a specific implementation.

A bit of controversy has arisen among the vendors concerning the method by which B-trees should be implemented. One faction says that the B-tree should be a separate index structure that follows all the rules of the standard Pick data access method. This is not unlike the way B-trees are handled from PICK/BASIC. The other faction says that the database should actually be handled as a B-tree, overriding the standard file access technique. Nothing has been agreed upon as a standard. Once again, application programmers must create their own.

B-Trees in PICK/BASIC

The B-tree nodes are a set of items kept in a file separate from the data file being referenced. Each node is assigned a sequential or other unique item identifier. The format is shown in Fig. 4-31. The root of a B-tree may point to or actually be the first node. It may contain information on how this tree is being maintained. Other tree definition parameters may be kept in the root item.e. For example, the sequence in which the tree is maintained. A sequence could be AL, AR, DL, or DR as used by the LOCATE function.

The item-id of the root can also be a variable. Rather than calling it ROOT, it may be called STAFF.NAME or STAFF.ZIP indicating the secondary key referenced by the tree. This allows multiple B-trees to be maintained in a single file. In order not to use the same nodes for different trees, a last used node-id counter is implemented to provide the next free item-id to any new nodes on any of the B-trees in the same file.

ID: ROOT

001 *First node pointer-id*

002 *Maximum number of entries per node*

FIG. 4-31. B-TREE root item layout.

The maximum number of node entries should be an even number. As the mode grows beyond the maximum, the value at the middle of the list becomes a central node and all values preceding it become a child node to the left and the values greater become a child to the right. A sample layout is shown in Fig. 4-32.

ID: *Node-id*

001 *pointer1] pointer2] ......] pointerN] pointerN + 1*

002 *val1] val2] ......] valN*

FIG. 4-32. Sample B-TREE node layout.

Each pointer is the node-id, which contains a list of values less than the corresponding value in attribute 002 of this node. Pointer1 points to the list of values less than val1 and pointerN points to a list of values less than valN. Pointer N + 1 points to the list of values greater than valN.

Whenever a node grows or shrinks so that the tree is weighted to the left or right, the central node must be changed for that portion of the sub-tree. Obviously, the code to maintain such a B-tree can get quite complex.

The values found in attribute 002 can be a combination of the keyed data value, (name, city, state, etc.) and the uniqueitem-id in the following form:

002 AGAMEMNON.101]AGAMEMNON.201]MARSUPIAL.233]ZEBRA.999

The period is some low ASCII character, preferably a CHAR(0). Each entry must be extracted and then parsed with the FIELD statement to remove the data value and the item-id. Otherwise, the key data value and the item-id reference can be kept on separate lines, with no repetition in the key value:

002 AGAMEMNON]MARSUPIEL]ZEBRA
003 101/201]233]999

Notice that a third attribute is added. This new correlated list contains the item-id references to the master file. Also notice that since AGAMEMNON occurs twice in the file, a subvalued list must be maintained.

Tree handling in PICK/BASIC is performed with the intrinsic functions; EXTRACT, REPLACE, DELETE, INSERT, and especially LOCATE. If the value is not found in the current node, (the ELSE clause of the LOCATE function), then the set variable contains the value-mark position the value greater than the search value. Translating that location to the correlated list of pointers gives the node-id of the child node so that the search can continue.

A feature of PICK/BASIC which makes B-tree handling relatively simple and quite powerful is the ability to call *recursive subroutines*. Because each node of a B-tree is handled exactly in the same manner, a single subroutine can be written to insert, delete, or search a node, and recursively call itself each time a new level pointer is found.

Please note that not all packages take advantage of recursive programming. The B-tree emulations—which are actually tree indexed, linked lists—can easily traverse the tree with no recursion. Oh well, programmers are as different as snowflakes. The point is that most of the available packages do the job fairly well. If none meet the mark for a particular job, the best decision is to purchase the package that comes with the source code. Modifications can then be made to meet individual requirements.

B-trees implemented in PICK/BASIC can be retrofitted to any application on any Pick-based machine with little or no change to the tree handling routines. However, all routines that access the master file must be modified to update the tree on each READ, WRITE and DELETE.

Any B-tree package should be accompanied by utilities for searching and traversing the tree. These routines should be able to perform the following functions:

- Get the next N entries on the tree
- Get the previous N entries on the tree
- Retrieve an exact match from the tree
- Retrieve the closest match from the tree

This chapter discusses a couple of sample recursive subroutines written to traverse a B-tree forward and backward. The B-tree structure was designed by Bill Meyers, who is one of many with a full B-tree utility package available. Thanks to him for so graciously allowing his B-tree design and traversal programs to be demonstrated here.

Figure 4-33 shows a sample root pointer and root node. The item-id of the root is the name of the file being referenced. This allows multiple trees to be maintained in the same file. Other B-tree packages allow for multiple keys in totally different manners. It is an important feature in order to prevent the need for many files to cross-reference the same master file. In Fig. 4-34, attribute 001 of the root points to the "root node," which has been given a sequential identifier of 3.

This node has a single value entry and two pointer entries. The first pointer value, 1, points to the left child node and the second value, 2, points to the right child node. Node-id's are assigned from a control item in the file which holds the next available sequential node-id.

The layout is exactly the same as the parent node, except that the child has 38 entries. This is also the failure node, because the pointer list is all nulls indicating that there are no children of this node.

```
Rootid: STAFF
001   3          Pointer to the node-id of level 1
002   48         N, the maximum number of entries per node
003   AL         The tree sequence.


Node:3
001   1                    Number of values in the node
002   NIXDORF, RICARDO.108 Name, CHAR(0), and item-id
003   1]2                  Lower level pointer list.
004   SAN QUENTIN          Data list.
```

FIG. 4-33. STAFF B-Tree sample root pointer and root node.

```
Node:    1
001      38
002      ALLEN, STEVE.009]BIRD, BIG.025]BOB,
         FARMER.046]BULLWINKLE,PERRY.021]CARLSON,
         FRED.291]CLAUS, SANTA.015]COLLINS, RUTH.155]CONNER,
         TOM.103]CYPHERS, HOWARD.075]DINGY, RUTH.011]DOE,
         JOHN.129]DUCK, DONALD.292]DUNKEN,
         DONUTS.079]FAIRCHILD, MAX.139]FRANKEL,
         NOAM.048]FUDDRUCKER, MOTHER.208]GORBACHEV,
         RAISA.047]HANSON, TERESA.044]HARTMAN,
         MARY.257]HERMAN, PEEWEE.258]HERMAN, WOODY.054]HUTTON,
         BETTY.117]HUTTON, E.F..116]JASON,
         HOCKEYPUCK.180]JETSON, GEORGE.206]JOHNSON,
         MARY.287]JONES,DICK.235]KELLOGG, IRVING.177]LADY,
         CHURCH.157]LARSON, NICHOLETTE.007]MERTZ,
         ETHEL.261]MERTZ, FRED.077]MOUSE, MICKEY   .022]MOUSE,
         MINNIE.049]MUNSTER, EDDIE.288]NEUMAN, ALFRED
         E.078]NICHOLSON, ANNETTE.095]NICHOLSON, JACK.062
003      ]]]]]]]]]]]]]]]]]]]]]]]]]]]]]]]]]]]]]]
004      44 SMOK-SMOK LANE]SEASAME STREET]6 CORN STALK
         WAY]HIGH FLY DRIVE]5460 IRVING]999 RAINDEER LANE]1519
         CHERBUSCO AVENUE]1100 - 23RD AVE]103 OXFORD ST]444
         WACKO DRIVE]456 CULLIGAN WAY]111 DUCK PLACE    ]34 SAN
         MIGUEL]1 MAGNIFICENT MILE]300 RAND BLVD]123 GOLF
         DR.]999 RED SQUARE]RT 1 BOX 147]123 MAIN ST]202 NUTSO
         AVE]12 JAZZ WAY]56 E 82ND ST]2001 WALL
         STREET]SOMEWHERE IN THE WOODS]AIRWAY 4]122 LOCUST
         STREET]123 4 PARKVIEW]825 NORTH SAN VICENTE]SNL
         STAGE]55 CULVER BLVD]300 RAND BLVD]1212 E
         BURBANK]DISNEY LANE]222 WINDSOR WAY]1313 MOCKINGBIRD
         LANE]123 MADDENING WAY]1 COURT CIRCLE]5 EASY PIECES
         WAY
```

FIG. 4-34. Left child node of STAFF B-Tree.

B-Tree Traversal Programs

This section contains a couple of programs that are used to traverse the above B-tree structure. They are provided to demonstrate the integration requirements for making B-trees part of the system. The first program, MAKELIST, is a higher level routine which builds linked lists from a B-tree based on prompted selection criteria. In this case, the selection criteria is the name of a STAFF member.

MAKELIST depends on the generalized subroutine, FKEYS, to pass back from the tree a predetermined number of values to be written as a linked list item.

Note the COMMON statement used in both routines. The COMMON statement is essential for throughput when calling possibly three or four levels of subroutines while needing to share the parameters. Standard parameter passing would noticeably hinder throughput. When retro-fitting B-trees to an existing application, these COMMON statements have to be placed in every routine which uses the B-tree update or search programs.

The MAKELIST Program

Figure 4-35 shows the MAKELIST program.

```
PROGRAM MAKELIST

    MAKELIST
001 PROGRAM MAKELIST
002 * Build Linked lists from a B-tree
003 * 1988 Harvey E. Rodstein and William K Meyer
004 *
005 COMMON TREEVARS(15)
006 *
007 EQU AM     TO CHAR(254)
008 EQU VM     TO CHAR(253)
009 EQU DELIM TO CHAR(0)
010 *
011 EQU TREE    TO TREEVARS(1)    ;* Tree file variable
012 EQU ROOTID  TO TREEVARS(2)    ;* Root identifier
013 EQU SKEY    TO TREEVARS(3)    ;* Search key
014 EQU INDAT   TO TREEVARS(4)    ;* Additional dat in the tree
015 EQU LOC.SEQ TO TREEVARS(5)    ;* The sorted sequence
016 EQU START   TO TREEVARS(6)    ;* Start value
017 EQU PREFIX  TO TREEVARS(7)    ;* Value prior to start key
018 EQU POSTFIX TO TREEVARS(8)    ;* Value after last key
019 EQU KEYS    TO TREEVARS(9)    ;* List of retrieved keys
020 EQU LINES   TO TREEVARS(10)   ;* Ongoing retrieval count
021 EQU NOMORE  TO TREEVARS(11)   ;* No more forward
022 EQU NOLESS  TO TREEVARS(12)   ;* No more backward
023 EQU RETFLG  TO TREEVARS(13)   ;* Flag end of search
024 EQU MAX     TO TREEVARS(14)   ;* Max entries to retrieve
025 EQU DATS    TO TREEVARS(15)   ;* List of data values
026 *
027 * The layout of each node
028 EQU NUM TO 1 ;* Number of entries in a node
029 EQU KEY TO 2 ;* Unique key list
030 EQU PTR TO 3 ;* Next node pointers
031 EQU DAT TO 4 ;* Additional data kept in the node
032 *
033 OPEN "BTREE" TO TREE ELSE STOP 201,"BTREE"
```

FIG. 4-35. MAKELIST program listing (continues).

```
034 OPEN "STAFF" TO STAFF ELSE STOP 201,"STAFF"
035 OPEN "LISTS" TO LISTS ELSE STOP 201,"LISTS"
036 *
037 ROOTID="STAFF"
038 PROMPT ":"
039 *
040 PORT = FIELD(OCONV(0,'U50BB'),' ',1)
041 LOOP
042   CRT "NAME (LAST,FIRST MI) ":
043   INPUT NAME
044   HEADNAME = PORT:'.':NAME
045   HEADLIST = ''
046 UNTIL NAME="" DO
047   PREFIX=NAME
048   START=PREFIX
049   MAX=50
050   RETFLG=0
051   NOMORE=0
052   LINES=0
053   L=LEN(PREFIX)
054   PAGE=0
055   POSTFIX=PREFIX[1,L-1]:CHAR(SEQ(PREFIX[L,1])+1)
056   IF PREFIX="*" THEN POSTFIX="["
057   SUFFIX=PREFIX[1,L-1]:CHAR(SEQ(PREFIX[L,1])-1):"[":VM
058   KEYS=SUFFIX
059   DATS=""
060   KLIST = ''
061   READ ROOT FROM TREE,ROOTID ELSE STOP "NO ROOT!"
062   LOC.SEQ=ROOT<3>
063   ROOT=ROOT<1>
064   CALL FKEYS(ROOT)
065   NOLESS=1
066   PAGE=PAGE+1
067   SEQ = 1
068   GOSUB 1000
069   LOOP
070     IF NOMORE THEN
071       CRT CHAR(7):"END of the list":
072       RQM
073     END ELSE
074       KEYS=KEYS<1,LINES+1>
075       DATS=DATS<1,LINES>
076       START=KEYS:"X"
077       LINES=0
078       RETFLG=0
079       READV ROOT FROM TREE,ROOTID,1 ELSE STOP "ROOT LOST!"
080         CALL FKEYS(ROOT)
081         PAGE=PAGE+1
082     END
083     GOSUB 1000
084   UNTIL NOMORE DO REPEAT
085   WRITE HEADLIST ON LISTS,HEADNAME
086 REPEAT
```

FIG. 4-35 continues.

```
087 *
088 STOP
089 *
090 *
091 1000 *
092 *
093 FOR II = 1 TO LINES
094     KLIST<-1>=FIELD(KEYS<1,II+1>,DELIM,2)
095 NEXT II
096 IF KLIST#'' THEN
097     WRITE KLIST ON LISTS,PORT:'.':SEQ
098     HEADLIST<-1> = PORT:'.':SEQ
099     SEQ = SEQ+1
100     CRT '-':
101     KLIST = ''
102 END
103 RETURN
104 *
105 END
```

FIG. 4-35 ends.

Program Highlights

The COMMON area is placed in a single dimensioned array.

```
005 COMMON TREEVARS(15)
```

This makes the statement short and sweet. Each entry in the array is given a name via the series of EQUATE statements that follow:

```
007 EQU AM        TO CHAR(254)
008 EQU VM        TO CHAR(253)
009 EQU DELIM  TO CHAR(0)
010 *
011 EQU TREE       TO TREEVARS(1)     ;* Tree file variable
012 EQU ROOTID   TO TREEVARS(2)     ;* Root identifier
013 EQU SKEY       TO TREEVARS(3)     ;* Search key
014 EQU INDAT     TO TREEVARS(4)     ;* Additional dat in the tree
015 EQU LOC.SEQ  TO TREEVARS(5)     ;* The sorted sequence
016 EQU START     TO TREEVARS(6)     ;* Start value
017 EQU PREFIX    TO TREEVARS(7)     ;* Value prior to start key
018 EQU POSTFIX  TO TREEVARS(8)     ;* Value after last key
019 EQU KEYS       TO TREEVARS(9)     ;* List of retrieved keys
020 EQU LINES      TO TREEVARS(10)   ;* Ongoing retrieval count
021 EQU NOMORE   TO TREEVARS(11)   ;* No more forward
022 EQU NOLESS   TO TREEVARS(12)   ;* No more backward
023 EQU RETFLG   TO TREEVARS(13)   ;* Flag end of search
024 EQU MAX        TO TREEVARS(14)   ;* Max entries to retrieve
025 EQU DATS       TO TREEVARS(15)   ;* List of data values
```

Also, the attribute position of the correlated lists in each node is named via an EQUATE:

```
027   * The layout of each node
028   EQU NUM TO 1   ;* Number of entries in a node
029   EQU KEY TO 2   ;* Unique key list
030   EQU PTR TO 3   ;* Next node pointers
031   EQU DAT TO 4   ;* Additional data kept in the node
```

The entire COMMON and EQUATE area is probably better placed in an INCLUDED code segment ("Don't do as I do, do as I say").

The value of ROOTID is hard coded in this example, but may be variable for a more generalized routine:

```
037 ROOTID = "STAFF"
```

Each linked list that is built is based on port number and a unique sequence number. The linked header item is based on the port number and the search criteria.

```
039 *
040   PORT = FIELD(OCONV(0, 'U50BB'),' ',1)
041   LOOP
042       CRT "NAME (LAST,FIRST MI) ":
043       INPUT NAME
044       HEADNAME = PORT:'.':NAME
045       HEADLIST = ''
046   UNTIL NAME = "" DO

      ......

      ......

085       WRITE HEADLIST ON LISTS,HEADNAME
086   REPEAT
```

The value of NAME does not have to be the entire name. It can be any number of the first characters in the name. For example, NAME can be SMITH for all employees with the last name SMITH, or it can be "S" for the employees whose last name starts with "S." The starting and ending limits of the tree search must be set up. This is accomplished by the following:

```
047       PREFIX = NAME
048       START = PREFIX
049       MAX = 50
050       RETFLG = 0
051       NOMORE = 0
052       LINES = 0
053       L = LEN(PREFIX)
054       PAGE = 0
055       POSTFIX = PREFIX[1,L – 1]:CHAR(SEQ(PREFIX[L,1]) + 1)
056       IF PREFIX = "*" THEN POSTFIX = "["
```

```
057      SUFFIX = PREFIX[1,L – 1]:CHAR(SEQ(PREFIX[L,1]) – 1):"[":VM
058      KEYS = SUFFIX
```

Both PREFIX and START are given the same NAME search value at the offset. START is, of course, the starting value of the search. The value of MAX is the maximum number of values to retrieve from the tree per linked list item. The value of POSTFIX is the ending value of the search. The statement increments the last character of the search string to 1 greater than the original value. First, all characters are extracted up to but not including the last character of the search string in PREFIX:

PREFIX[1,L – 1]

The last character of the search string is extracted by the following:

PREFIX[L,1]

Then the ASCII sequence is incremented by one:

SEQ(PREFIX[L,1]) + 1

The resulting decimal value is translated back to the corresponding ASCII character via the CHAR function.

CHAR(SEQ(PREFIX[L,1]) + 1)

A PREFIX of SMITH results in a POSTFIX of SMITI. However, if the search criteria is an asterisk, the end of the search is the last value in the tree.

056 IF PREFIX = "*" THEN POSTFIX = "["

The SUFFIX is being used as the string just prior to the search string. Here the last character in the string is decremented by one.

057 SUFFIX = PREFIX[1,L – 1]:CHAR(SEQ(PREFIX[L,1]) – 1):"[":VM

The PREFIX of SMITH results in s SUFFIX of SMITG.

The B-tree root is retrieved and the subroutine FKEYS is called to retrieve the first 50 entries on the tree which pass the search criteria.

```
060      KLIST = "
061      READ ROOT FROM TREE,ROOTID ELSE STOP "NO ROOT!"
062      LOC.SEQ = ROOT < 4 >
063      ROOT = ROOT < 1 >
064      CALL FKEYS(ROOT)
```

Subroutine 1000 writes the retrieved list and add the list-id to the linked list header.

```
067      SEQ = 1
068      GOSUB 1000
```

The remainder of the program takes care of the next 50 and so on until there are NOMORE entries in the B-tree that pass the search criteria.

```
```

```
069    LOOP
070      IF NOMORE THEN
071        CRT CHAR(7):@(0,23):"END of the list":
072        RQM
073      END ELSE
074        KEYS = KEYS<1,LINES+1>
075        DATS = DATS<1,LINES>
076        START = KEYS:"X"
077        LINES = 0
078        RETFLG = 0
079        READV ROOT FROM TREE,ROOTID,1 ELSE STOP "ROOT LOST!"
080        CALL FKEYS(ROOT)
081        PAGE = PAGE+1
082      END
083      GOSUB 1000
084    UNTIL NOMORE DO REPEAT
```

The FKEYS Subroutine

The FKEYS subroutine, shown in Fig. 4-36, is the recursive routine that searches forward in each node keyed by NODEID.

```
       FKEYS
001 SUBROUTINE FKEYS(NODEID)
002 * Partial b-tree traversal -- forward
003 * Copyright 1983 William K. Meyer
004 * Modified 1988 Harvey E. Rodstein
005 *
006 COMMON TREEVARS(15)
007 *
008 EQU AM      TO CHAR(254)
009 EQU VM      TO CHAR(253)
010 EQU DELIM TO CHAR(0)
011 *
012 EQU TREE     TO TREEVARS(1)   ;* Tree file variable
013 EQU ROOTID   TO TREEVARS(2)   ;* Root identifier
014 EQU SKEY     TO TREEVARS(3)   ;* Search key
015 EQU INDAT    TO TREEVARS(4)   ;* Additional dat in the tree
016 EQU LOC.SEQ TO TREEVARS(5)    ;* The sorted sequence
017 EQU START    TO TREEVARS(6)   ;* Start value
018 EQU PREFIX   TO TREEVARS(7)   ;* Value prior to start key
019 EQU POSTFIX TO TREEVARS(8)    ;* Value after last key
020 EQU KEYS     TO TREEVARS(9)   ;* List of retrieved keys
021 EQU LINES    TO TREEVARS(10)  ;* Ongoing retrieval count
022 EQU NOMORE   TO TREEVARS(11)  ;* No more forward
023 EQU NOLESS   TO TREEVARS(12)  ;* No more backward
024 EQU RETFLG   TO TREEVARS(13)  ;* Flag of end of search
025 EQU MAX      TO TREEVARS(14)  ;* Max entries to retrieve
026 EQU DATS     TO TREEVARS(15)  ;* List of data values
```

FIG. 4-36. FKEYS subroutine listing (continues).

```
027 *
028 * The layout of each node
029 EQU NUM TO 1 ;* Number of entries in a node
030 EQU KEY TO 2 ;* Unique key list
031 EQU PTR TO 3 ;* Next node pointers
032 EQU DAT TO 4 ;* Additional data kept in the node
033 *
034 IF NODEID="" THEN RETURN
035 READ REC FROM TREE,NODEID ELSE RETURN
036 *
037 IF START="*" THEN
038   L1=1
039   L2=REC<NUM>+1
040 END ELSE
041   LOCATE(START,REC,KEY;L1;LOC.SEQ) ELSE NULL
042   LOCATE(POSTFIX,REC,KEY;L2;LOC.SEQ) THEN NULL
043 END
044 FOR I=L1 TO L2
045   IF REC<PTR,I>#"" THEN
046     CALL FKEYS(REC<PTR,I>)
047     NOMORE=0
048     IF RETFLG THEN RETURN
049   END
050   IF I<L2 THEN
051     KEYS<1,-1>=REC<KEY,I>
052     DATS<1,-1>=REC<DAT,I>
053     LINES=LINES+1
054     IF LINES=1 THEN
055       START=PREFIX
056       NOLESS=0
057     END ELSE
058       IF LINES>MAX THEN
059         LINES=LINES-1
060         RETFLG=1
061         RETURN
062       END
063     END
064   END
065 NEXT I
066 NOMORE=1
067 RETURN
068 *
069 END
```

FIG. 4-36 ends.

Program Highlights

The beginning and ending points in each node are determined. If the value of START is an asterisk, all values are to be reported.

```
037   IF START = "*" THEN
038     L1 = 1
039     L2 = REC<NUM> + 1
```

L2 is incremented by 1 because the pointer values are one more than the data values. For any case other than all the values being reported, the beginning and ending positions, indicated by L1 and L2, are determined using the LOCATE intrinsic function with L1 and L2 at the set variable position.

```
040   END ELSE
041      LOCATE(START,REC,KEY;L1;LOC.SEQ) ELSE NULL
042      LOCATE(POSTFIX,REC,KEY;L2;LOC.SEQ) THEN NULL
043   END
```

The node is processed from L1 to L2:

```
044   FOR I = L1 TO L2
         .....
065   NEXT I
066   NOMORE = 1
067   RETURN
```

As each value is extracted, the corresponding pointer value is also extracted. If this node has a child, then FKEYS is recursively called to handle the child node:

```
045      IF REC < PTR,I > #"" THEN
046         CALL FKEYS(REC < PTR,I >)
047         NOMORE = 0
048         IF RETFLG THEN RETURN
049      END
```

For all cases other than the last time through the loop, the current key and data values are extracted and added to the end of the KEYS and DATS multivalued lists:

```
050      IF I < L2 THEN
051         KEYS < 1, – 1 > = REC < KEY,I >
052         DATS < 1, – 1 > = REC < DAT,I >
053         LINES = LINES + 1
054         IF LINES = 1 THEN
055            START = PREFIX
056            NOLESS = 0
057         END ELSE
058            IF LINES > MAX THEN
059               LINES = LINES – 1
060               RETFLG = 1
061               RETURN
062            END
063         END
064      END
```

Assembler B-Trees

B-trees written in the Pick Assembler are hooked into the operating system as an integral part of the database. This means that no special files have to be set up for each new tree. The system grabs frames as they are needed. All tree references are stored as part of file defining D-pointer.

Each node is a frame, not an item. Therefore, node level pointers are frame addresses (FID's) and not item-ids. All tree maintenance is automatic. There is no special programming or interfaces in the application to update the tree each time the master file is altered. The system usually provides a single-called subroutine for list traversal.

There is one major disadvantage to maintaining trees in frames rather than items. On a system restore, B-tree nodes kept as items are placed in different frames, but as with all items, the item-ids remain the same. Therefore, the B-tree contents remain intact. However, when the level pointers are FIDs, they are forced to change on each restore. Therefore, all the pointers at every B-tree level must be rebuilt, regardless of whether or not the B-tree was saved. Rather than being able to restore the tree group by group, every node must be written and re-read multiple times. This means that for a million item file with several index keys, restoring the file can take several days.

A Word of Caution

The saying, "There is no such thing as a free lunch," applies here. B-trees take up in disk space, backup, and restore time what they save in access speed. In fact, B-trees with multiple keys and embedded data can grow larger than the file referenced. This tends to slow down the SAVE process. Rebuilding the trees on restore slows down the restore process. The choice is solely up to the user. Good luck!

Shopping for a B-Tree Package

The following is a list of software vendors who have a B-tree package available. They probably all have 100 great reasons why their packages are the best but hopefully, this section has clarified a few points about B-trees to make the choice a little easier:

Package: MISSING LINK
Company: Abacus
Contact: Dana Pittman
          2260 Redd Hooker Rd
          Memphis, Tn 38028
          (901) 278-6982

Package: SMART-TREE
Company: Modular Software
          P.O. Box 204
          Union City, Ga 30291
          (404) 964-7171

Package: B-TREE-P

Company: Semaphore Corp
          207 Coranda Dr
          Aptos, Ca 95003
          (408) 688-9200

In addition, the PICK/BASIC program listings for maintaining B-trees as presented in this text are available in back issues of Spectrum Tech magazine. The articles were written by William K. Meyers as a three part series dealing with the use and implementation of B-trees and can be found in the following issues:

Part 1, *Spectrum Tech*, January 1988
Part 2, *Spectrum Tech*, February 1988
Part 3, *Spectrum Tech*, March 1988

Process Control

PROCESS CONTROL ROUTINES HOLD TOGETHER AN APPLICATION BY DIRECTING the program flow. This chapter concentrates on ways of writing control routines that manage process initiation, parameter passing, and error recovery for unattended tasks such as reporting, data aging, and data archival and purge.

CHOOSING A LANGUAGE

The decision about which process control language to use is a major issue these days. A technical, bordering on philosophical, debate continues on whether PICK/BASIC or PROC should be the language of choice. As Henry Eggers said when discussing PROC vs PICK/BASIC on March 31, 1988, "When you had 32K of RAM and 16 users, you did things differently."

In the days when machines were the size of refrigerators, held less resources than today's laptops, and the state of PICK/BASIC made it a resource hog, PROC was the only efficient answer. In fact, for the first years that Pick was commercially available (Microdata Reality), it was the only procedural language implemented. Interactive file input-output was accomplished by assembler user exits, resulting in an application structured as the antithesis of a user-friendly system.

The Basic language was a latecomer to the Pick operating system. The original implementation of PICK/BASIC had more to do with standard Dartmouth Basic than with the modern form of the language. For years, PICK/BASIC was, as it is now, a powerful language for dealing with file input-output and data strings, but cumbersome, if not impossible, as a process control language.

The flow of most of the applications in use today, but developed prior to 1984, depends solely on PROC. Large, integrated applications written using PROC as the main thread of logic are potential support nightmares. PROC has only four major buffers to address. Only one of which, the primary input buffer, can be used to handle and pass common data between PROCs. Any new PROCs added to the package must be carefully interfaced to the remaining PROCs so that placement of data in the buffers does not disrupt the flow of the application (the familiar "house of cards" effect).

A way to get around this problem involves PICK/BASIC routines that issue PROC-WRITE statements that save the input buffer prior to transfer to the new PROC, and PRO-CREAD statements that retrieve the original buffer intact upon return. The question is, "If PICK/BASIC has to be used to get around the shortcomings of PROC, why not write the entire procedure in PICK/BASIC?"

This is a question that was asked and answered long before the EXECUTE statement became available on generic Pick implementations. The resulting packages ended up being a snarled mess of chained logic with routine after routine gallivanting here and there—sometimes actually returning to the main menu, other times terminating in oblivion. You might call it "Spaghetti City."

To allow PICK/BASIC control in the days before EXECUTE, many PICK/BASIC programs were designed to build PROCs to perform an ACCESS or TCL process, write the PROC item to some target PROC file, and chain to the just-created PROC via a predefined transfer PROC in the MD. The "on-the-fly" PROC would then transfer control back to the original program or to one of many other programs.

Writing PROCs "on-the-fly" and executing them is actually quite a good and efficient technique with certain provisions.

- PROCs keep pointers directly into the body of the PROC and abort if the group they reside in is modified.

- Therefore, do not write "on-the-fly" PROCs into the MD. Keep a standard PROC there which chains to the file where the PROC is written.

- Make sure the written PROC is just for the process that created it and no one else is likely to use it at the same time. (Many of these PROCs are given item-ids which include the current port number.)

The introduction of the EXECUTE statement to PICK/BASIC has expanded the language from a string and file IO handler to a sophisticated process controller. Applications can now be designed in a consistent style using the same language for all the procedural elements. Today's faster processors, faster disks, more efficient PICK/BASIC compilers, and the availability of the EXECUTE statement make PICK/BASIC the main choice of contemporary Pick programmers.

PROCESS INITIATION

Anarchical vs. Hierarchical Systems

The term anarchical is derived from the word anarchy meaning uncontrolled confusion and disorder. This is the state of applications programmed using chained logic. *Chained logic* is a one-way transfer of control from one program to another. There is no return because the original program terminates prior to initiating the targeted program.

When EXECUTE was not available in PICK/BASIC, application designers, who insisted upon writing all programs and process control in PICK/BASIC, depended solely on the CHAIN and ENTER statements, which were the only means of accomplishing the task without PROC.

The CHAIN command transfers control to any command that can be interactively entered at TCL. CHAIN can be likened to a system-wide GOTO. When invoked, PICK/BASIC runtime is terminated and the process indicated in the CHAIN command is initiated. Once this routine is complete, control returns to TCL.

```
CHAIN "LISTFILES"
```

or

```
CHAIN "RUN BP PROGB"
```

The ENTER command works similar to the CHAIN command, except that ENTER can only transfer control to a cataloged PICK/BASIC program. This is slightly more efficient than CHAIN since PICK/BASIC runtime does not have to be terminated and re-initiated. However, free workspace is re-initialized.

```
ENTER PROGB
```

or

```
ENTER "PROGB"
```

Notice that the ENTER command follows the same requirements as the CALL command. The program PROGB is invoked regardless of whether it is indicated as a literal or a program variable. In fact, it is handled in the descriptor table very much like the subroutine CALL. Like CHAIN, ENTER is a one-way transfer of control.

Never use ENTER or CHAIN from within a subroutine. It will probably abort the first time garbage collection is attempted.

Imagine how difficult it is to support "spaghetti" GOTO logic within a single program. Now compound this by following CHAINed logic within and between all the system elements. One change to a program anywhere in the system can cause a ripple effect which can cause problems in unpredictable locations.

A hierarchical approach allows the logical arrangement of programs and data with an application. The EXECUTE statement makes it possible to maintain a hierarchical design while remaining under the control of PICK/BASIC. EXECUTE allows any process which can be initiated from TCL, including any ACCESS or other PICK/BASIC program, to be invoked from a PICK/BASIC program. Upon completion of that process, control is returned to the controlling PICK/BASIC routine. The simple form of the PICK/BASIC

EXECUTE statement is as follows:

> EXECUTE *tclsentence*

The indicator *tclsentence* is any compound string expression. Of course, the resulting string must be a valid TCL sentence.

The EXECUTE statement needs to attach additional process workspace frames in order to perform the specified TCL command. Additional disk space is required for each new level of EXECUTE. The number of frames required differs between implementations. A PICK/BASIC program is allowed to recursively EXECUTE other programs. Unchecked, it is possible to run out of disk space.

EXECUTE levels are restricted to five on most of the implementations. The maximum number of levels can be altered by using the :TASKINIT verb. The general form of the: TASKINIT is:

> :TASKINIT *workspaces*{,*levels*}

The optional *levels* indicates the maximum number of EXECUTE levels allowed for active processes. The indicator *workspaces* specifies the number of pre-assigned workspaces attached to any process. Normally, each level of EXECUTE requires additional workspace frames to be retrieved from overflow and then linked into the current process. The overhead can become considerable. Using the: TASKINIT verb preallocates the workspace, thereby alleviating the need to attach and link these new frames for each new level. Please note that in generic Pick, each new workspace requires an average of 413 frames. The Ultimate form of :TASKINIT is as follows:

> :TASKINIT {*levels*} {(C)}

If the *levels* indicator is omitted, the system displays the current number of levels. The C option verifies that the workspace frames are properly linked.

The :TASKINIT verb may not be available on all generic Pick implementations. However, there is a way to programatically restrict the number of EXECUTE levels using the SYSTEM(16) function. SYSTEM(16) indicates the current EXECUTE level beginning with level 0. Restricting levels requires the following statement to be inserted or INCLUDEd in all EXECUTEd programs.

> IF SYSTEM(16) > MAX THEN STOP

The variable MAX is any numeric integer.

Parameter Passing

This section describes methods to pass data to and from performed routines. Before the discussion concentrates on the preferred hierarchical methods, here is a brief insight into how parameters have been historically (hysterically is probably better) passed from PICK/BASIC using the CHAIN and ENTER commands. Parameter passing in the anarchical world is quite a bit more difficult than in the hierarchical world.

In the dark days before EXECUTE, there needed to be a way for CHAINED PICK-.BASIC programs to share data. The COMMON directive was, and in some cases still is, used to perform this system subterfuge.

In the cases of ENTER or CHAIN, the workspace is normally re-initialized between the routines, losing any data setup in the originating routine. The shared data can be placed in free workspace and the re-initialization overridden by using the following techniques:

- Use an identical COMMON statement at the beginning of both routines.
- Use the option (I) on the command sentence invoked from the CHAIN or ENTER commands. Option (I) indicates that the variable workspace is NOT to be re-initialized when the new process is initiated.

For example:

```
CHAIN "RUN BP PROGB (I"
```

or if cataloged,

```
CHAIN "PROGB (I"
```

WARNING: *Forget this!* Although this technique may still be used on some older software packages (mostly on firmware machines), this method may (and does) prove fatal to many newer software-based systems.

Rules for coding in today's world;

- Don't use CHAIN or ENTER unless the destination and return path is absolutely clear!

  CHAIN "OFF" There is no question what this does.
- Never use the (I) option. This can cause unpredictable results and may, in some cases, abort the process.
- Never CHAIN or ENTER another program from an external subroutine. Not only can this create unforeseen runtime problems, but it is also a sloppy coding practice.
- Use EXECUTE the rest of the time.

The Data Statement

Another way that data can be passed between routines is with the PICK/BASIC DATA statement. DATA stores the responses in a LIFO (last-in, first-out) stack to be used as input in subsequent processes (quite like the PROC STON command.) Each INPUT statement "pops" the top entry off the stack. The general form of the DATA statement is:

```
DATA element{,element,element...}
```

The braces indicate optional specifications. Each element, separated by a comma, is a new entry on the input stack. Alternatively, each element can be part of a separate DATA statement to produce the same results:

DATA *element*
DATA *element*

...

Figure 5-1 shows simple uses of DATA which are valid in any implementation of the Basic language. The result in either case is 50.

```
DATA 5,10
INPUT A
INPUT B
PRINT A*B

or

DATA 5
DATA 10
INPUT A
INPUT B
PRINT A*B
```

·FIG. 5-1. The DATA statement.

The DATA statement elements in PICK/BASIC can be complex expressions as well as constants, in the form:

DATA *expression*{,*expression*,...}

In Pick R83, DATA not only stacks responses within the same program, but also for any routine EXECUTED or CHAINED. The use of the DATA statement is another way that programs can CHAIN and pass data to another routine without the use of the COMMON statement.

Figure 5-2 copies the item 'OLDID' in the STAFF file to a new item, NEWID, and deletes on the copy. Again EXECUTE is preferable because program control is not lost when the COPY is complete.

Using the CHAIN statement:

```
DATA 'NEWID'
CHAIN 'COPY STAFF OLDID (D'
```

Using the EXECUTE statement:

FIG. 5-2. Using the DATA statement to pass parameters.

```
DATA 'NEWID'
EXECUTE 'COPY STAFF OLDID (D'
```

A series of responses can be stacked, as described above, by separating each entry with a comma, or specifying each response in a subsequent DATA statement. However, a little cheating may be in order. When a DATA statement indicates a list of responses as follows:

DATA *data1,data2,data3*

the response stack is stored internally as a string delimited by attribute marks. (The attribute marks are indicated by carets.)

data1^data2^data3

An alternative method of specifying multiple data elements is to place these elements as attributes in a dynamic array variable. The variable ARRAY is then used in the following data statement, as in Fig. 5-3.

```
ARRAY = ''
ARRAY<1> = data1
ARRAY<2> = data2
ARRAY<3> = data3
DATA ARRAY
```

FIG. 5-3. DATA dynamic array reference.

or better yet:

```
ARRAY = data1:AM:data2:AM:data3
DATA ARRAY
```

The DATA statement is also useful for passing a TCL command to follow any statement that generates an active list. (See Chapter 4, "List Processing.") For example:

```
DATA 'SAVE-LIST CA.STAFF'
EXECUTE 'SELECT STAFF WITH STATE = "CA"'
```

Within the single EXECUTE, the STAFF file is selected and the active list is saved.

Although the DATA statement can be used to stack responses for the EXECUTE statement on Pick R83 compatible machines, it fails on Ultimate implementations. In order to pass stacked responses to another EXECUTE level in Ultimate, a redirection clause must be used in the following general form:

EXECUTE *tclstatement,//*IN. < *inputstack*

The indicator *tclstatement* is any literal statement or any variable or compound string statement resulting in a valid TCL sentence. The indicator *inputstack* is any literal string or multi-attributed dynamic array.

The SP-File Program

The program example listed in Fig. 5-4 of the DATA statement is used in conjunction with EXECUTE to automatically drive SP-EDIT. The goal is to transfer a print image file to a series of standard items in the default target file, SPOOL-FILE.

Program Highlights

The code up through and including line 015 is standard setup of program constants and deserves no further discussion. The main functional code begins after the operator is

```
      SP-FILE
001 * PROGRAM SP-FILE
002 * Drives SP-EDIT to file print image to SPOOL-FILE
003 * Harvey Eric Rodstein
004 *
005 * Initialization
006 *
007 PROMPT '>'
008 *
009 EQU BELL TO CHAR(7)
010 EQU FF   TO CHAR(12)
011 EQU AM   TO CHAR(254)
012 EQU ESCC TO CHAR(251)
013 EQU ESC  TO CHAR(27)
014 *
015 ESCAPE = ESC:ESCC:'X'
016 *
017 * Get the Spooler Job number and EXECUTE SP-EDIT
018 *
019 INPUT JOB
020 IF JOB = '' THEN STOP
021 INPUT ITEMNAME
022 ITEMNAME = OCONV(ITEMNAME,'MCU')
023 RESPONSE = 'S':AM:'F':AM:'SPOOL-FILE':AM:ITEMNAME:AM:'Y'
024 DATA RESPONSE
025 EXECUTE 'SP-EDIT ':JOB
026 STOP
027 *
028 END
```

FIG. 5-4. SP-FILE program listing.

prompted for the spooler job number and the target item name. The stacked responses to the SP-EDIT command interaction are defined as follows:

```
023 RESPONSE = 'S':AM:'F':AM:'SPOOL-FILE':AM:ITEMNAME:AM:'Y'
```

The dynamic array is built in a single statement using standard concatenation. The string contained in RESPONSE is stacked via the DATA statement just prior to invoking SP-EDIT.

```
024 DATA RESPONSE
025 EXECUTE 'SP-EDIT ':JOB
```

Each attribute in RESPONSE satisfies the next input request in SP-EDIT:

SP-EDIT request.......	Stacked response
DISPLAY? (Y/N/S/D/X/<CR>)	S
SPOOL (Y/N = CR/T/TN/F)	F
FILE NAME	SPOOL-FILE
INITIAL ITEM NAME	ITEMNAME
DELETE (Y/N = CR)	Y

Capturing the TCL Sentence

The next way to pass data to a process, rather than stack input, is to capture and parse the TCL command line. The ability to capture the TCL sentence in PICK/BASIC is being implemented in many different flavors as part of enhanced versions of R83 and in Advanced Pick. However, this does not have to stop the intrepid programmer on the systems that do not currently have this feature. The TCL line can be grabbed using, dare it be said, PROC. Both techniques are discussed in this section.

The Intrinsic TCL Sentence Function

The function (currently available on CIE, ALTOS, ICON and any other implementation using utilities from ACCUSOFT) for capturing the TCL sentence is:

    SENTENCE( )

Notice that there are no arguments. The SENTENCE( ) function retrieves the entire TCL sentence whether the program is invoked from TCL, PROC, the PICK/BASIC CHAIN command, or the EXECUTE statement. The TCL sentence is retrieved intact, including the option string containing the parentheses.

There are a couple of precautionary warnings that must be made clear about the SENTENCE( ) function. First, the SENTENCE( ) function should be performed in the initiation section of the PICK/BASIC program. If the function is invoked after an EXECUTE of another TCL sentence, the original TCL line is lost. However, the ENTER statement does not affect the SENTENCE( ) function and leaves the original sentence intact.

Second, any TCL options that are valid for PICK/BASIC runtime are in effect even if SENTENCE( ) is used. There is away to override this by modifying the catalogued PICK/BASIC verb in the master dictionary. Unfortunately, this modification is not consistent. In one implementation, the P on attribute one is changed to a PO, while on others, the P is changed to a PG. To be safe, look it up before forging ahead.

Finally, be aware that each implementation may have a maximum number of characters, typically 300, which can be retrieved from the initiating sentence.

Each word in the retrieved TCL sentence is delimited by a space and must be extracted via the FIELD function. Figure 5-5 shows the main portion of the previous program, SP-FILE, written using the SENTENCE( ) function.

```
016 *
017 * Get the Spooler Job number and EXECUTE SP-EDIT
018 *
019 TCL      = SENTENCE( )
020 JOB      = FIELD(TCL,' ',2)
021 ITEMNAME = FIELD(TCL,' ',3)
022 ITEMNAME = OCONV(ITEMNAME,'MCU')
023 IF JOB   = '' THEN STOP
024 RESPONSE = 'S':AM:'F':AM:'SPOOL-FILE':AM:ITEMNAME:AM:'Y'
025 DATA RESPONSE
026 EXECUTE 'SP-EDIT ':JOB
027 STOP
```
FIG. 5-5. Using SENTENCE( ) in the SP-FILE program.

For those who speak Ultimate, a "slightly" more cumbersome function is available to retrieve the TCL sentence. The general syntax is as follows:

GET(ARG.{,*expression*}) *variable* {THEN..} {ELSE..}

The braces ({}) indicate an optional specification. In the simplest form of the command, each word or argument in the TCL sentence is, in turn, retrieved and placed in the "variable." The THEN.. ELSE construct allows handling of a successful or unsuccessful retrieval of an argument. Both THEN and ELSE are optional. Ultimate also provides the following function:

EOF(ARG.)

This function is set true if the previous GET(ARG.) successfully retrieves the message and false if it doesn't.

The routine in Fig. 5-6 builds an attribute marked list of all the arguments found in the TCL sentence. As each word is retrieved, it is added to the end of the dynamic array, TCL. The LOOP is terminated when the end of the argument list is encountered, EOF(ARG.). The JOB and ITEMNAME used in SP-FILE are extracted via standard intrinsic functions. The indicator *expression* in the general form of GET(ARG.,*expression*) represents the numeric value of a particular argument. Figure 5-7 demonstrates its use.

```
TCL = ''
LOOP
 GET(ARG.) WORD
UNTIL EOF(ARG.) DO
 TCL<-1> = WORD
REPEAT
*
JOB      = TCL<2>
ITEMNAME = TCL<3>
ITEMNAME = OCONV(ITEMNAME,'MCU')
IF JOB   = ''  THEN STOP
```

FIG. 5-6. Parsing the TCL sentence on Ultimate.

```
GET(ARG.,2) JOB ELSE STOP
GET(ARG.,3) ITEMNAME ELSE ITEMNAME = ''
ITEMNAME = OCONV(ITEMNAME,'MCU')
```

FIG. 5-7. GET(ARG.) retrieving specific arguments.

Capturing TCL without Special Functions

There is still a way to retrieve a TCL sentence when the previous functions are not available. The only drawback is that the process must be initiated from a PROC. However, this isn't so bad because the only PROCs used are relegated to simple two-line items in the master dictionary.

Some ground rules about PROCs must be established. First and foremost, whenever a PROC is initiated from TCL, the entire TCL sentence is placed in the PROC primary input buffer, (PIB.). This can be tested by entering this simple PROC into the master dictionary as follows:

```
ID: SIMPLE
001 PQ
002 DO
```

The command DO displays the currently active input buffer in its entirety. Consider the following sentence:

```
>SIMPLE MAKES LIFE EASY
```

The verb is SIMPLE. The rest of the TCL line is treated as excess baggage. The contents of the active input buffer are:

```
SIMPLE MAKES LIFE EASY
```

Any PICK/BASIC program initiated from a PROC can retrieve the primary input buffer by using the PROCREAD statement in the general form:

```
PROCREAD variable {THEN...} {ELSE..}
```

The THEN clause indicates that the primary input buffer is successfully retrieved (the program has indeed been initiated from a PROC), and the ELSE clause indicates that the primary input cannot be retrieved (the program has not been initiated from a PROC).

PROCREAD is valid on both generic Pick and Ultimate implementations. The only difference is that generic Pick uses spaces as delimiters for the elements in the primary input buffer, while Ultimate Proc and McDonnell Douglas New Proc use attribute marks.

In Fig. 5-8, the SP-FILE routine is re-written using a PROC-driven PICK/BASIC program. Figure 5-9 is the same PICK/BASIC routine containing modifications for the Ultimate Proc and McDonnell Douglas New Proc environments.

The PROC in the MD looks like this:

```
ID: SP-FILE
001 PQ
002 HRUN BP SP-FILE
```

The business part of the program looks like this:

```
016 *
017 * Get the Spooler Job number and EXECUTE SP-EDIT
018 *
019 PROCREAD TCL ELSE
020     PRINT 'MUST BE RUN FROM A PROC'
021     STOP
022 END
020 JOB      = FIELD(TCL,' ',2)
021 ITEMNAME = FIELD(TCL,' ',3)
022 ITEMNAME = OCONV(ITEMNAME,'MCU')
023 IF JOB   = '' THEN STOP
```

FIG. 5-8. Using PROCREAD to capture the TCL sentence.

```
016 *
017 * Get the Spooler Job number and EXECUTE SP-EDIT
018 *
019 PROCREAD TCL ELSE
020     PRINT 'MUST BE RUN FROM A PROC'
021     STOP
022 END
020 JOB      = TCL<2>
021 ITEMNAME = TCL<3>
022 ITEMNAME = OCONV(ITEMNAME,'MCU')
023 IF JOB   = '' THEN STOP
```

FIG. 5-9. PROCREAD in Ultimate.

The Getsentence Subroutine

The listing in Fig. 5-10 is a generic subroutine which allows parameters to be passed to a program regardless of whether the program is initiated from TCL, PROC, CHAINED or EXECUTED. It is designed to check for one of three possible methods by which data can be passed. First, the sentence may exist in the PROC primary input buffer. Second, the sentence elements may be stacked for INPUT via the PROC STON command. Third, the operator may choose to enter the sentence interactively from the terminal keyboard. The first alternative requires the use of the PROCREAD command. The second and third are handled identically via the PICK/BASIC INPUT statement.

Program Highlights

The use of the included common item in the initialization section is optional unless the subroutine is part of an integrated application.

```
011 INCLUDE COMMONS
```

The program must first determine whether or not the sentence is waiting in the PROC input buffer. An attempt is made to PROCREAD the primary input buffer.

```
015 PROCREAD SENTENCE THEN
016 * Run from a PROC
017 IF SYSTEM(10) THEN SENTENCE = '';* STON is used
018 END ELSE
019 * No PROC
020 SENTENCE = ''
021 END
```

If the program is initiated by a PROC, there are two possibilities; the TCL sentence is already in the primary input buffer or the data is stacked for INPUT. The SYSTEM(10) function is used to determine whether the PROC has issued a STON, (stack on). The result has two states, true (1) or false (0.) It is important to note that SYSTEM(10) is also true for the case where the program has been initiated by another PICK/BASIC program using the EXECUTE statement and the sentence data is stacked as a result of the DATA statement.

```
001 SUBROUTINE GETSENTENCE(SENTENCE)
002 * Get A Sentence from PROC PIB or PROC STON
003 * DATE STARTED : February 1987
004 * AUTHOR: Harvey Eric Rodstein
005 * COPYRIGHT: H.E.RODSTEIN Computer Consulting 1986,7,8
006 *
007 * Initialization
008 *
009 PROMPT ''
010 *
011 INCLUDE COMMONS
012 *
013 * Get the arguments and options
014 *
015 PROCREAD SENTENCE THEN
016    * Run from a PROC
017    IF SYSTEM(10) THEN SENTENCE = '' ;* STON is used
018 END ELSE
019    * No PROC
020    SENTENCE=''
021 END
022 IF SENTENCE='' THEN
023    LOOP
024     INPUT ISENTENCE
025    UNTIL ISENTENCE='' DO
026     SENTENCE = SENTENCE : TRIM(ISENTENCE) : ' '
027    REPEAT
028 END ELSE
029    SENTENCE = TRIM(SENTENCE)
030    * Strip off the verb
031    VERB = FIELD(SENTENCE,' ',1)
032    SENTENCE = SENTENCE[COL2()+1,LEN(SENTENCE)-COL2()]
033 END
034 *
035 RETURN
```

FIG. 5-10. The GETSENTENCE subroutine listing.

After a successful PROCREAD, the variable, SENTENCE, contains either the entire sentence or only the verb. However, if the stack is active, the program assumes that the PROC has issued a STON and the input buffer should be ignored. Therefore, the variable SENTENCE is initialized to null.

```
IF SYSTEM(10) THEN SENTENCE = ''
```

A null value for SENTENCE indicates that the variable string SENTENCE should be built by looping on INPUT until a null value is entered (a carriage return is pressed at INPUT ISENTENCE).

```
022 IF SENTENCE = '' THEN
023 LOOP
024  INPUT ISENTENCE
025 UNTIL ISENTENCE = '' DO
```

```
026  SENTENCE = SENTENCE : TRIM(ISENTENCE) : ' '
027 REPEAT
028 END ELSE
029 SENTENCE = TRIM(SENTENCE)
030 * Strip off the verb
031 VERB = FIELD(SENTENCE,' ',1)
032 SENTENCE = SENTENCE[COL2( ) + 1,LEN(SENTENCE) – COL2( )]
033 END
```

If the sentence already has a value (from PROCREAD), it is trimmed of leading, trailing and excess embedded blanks. The resulting string is passed back to the calling PICK/BASIC program.

Please note that, unlike the SENTENCE( ) function, the GETSENTENCE subroutine does not include the verb as part of the retrieved sentence. The verb is removed to ensure consistency between the INPUT data and the data retrieved from the PROC primary input buffer.

The verb is stripped in the following manner. The FIELD statement identifies the verb and provides the columnar position (COL2( )) of the space following the verb. The sentence is rebuilt using the string extract syntax.

```
031 VERB = FIELD(SENTENCE,' ',1)
032 SENTENCE = SENTENCE[COL2( ) + 1,LEN(SENTENCE) – COL2( )]
```

Other Uses of PROCREAD and PROCWRITE

Before continuing look at Fig. 5-11. Here are a couple of routines which are commonly used in PROC oriented packages. These programs, SAVEIBUF and GETIBUF, provide a method to save and restore the PROC input buffers so that any new PROCS can be added to the application package without affecting the state of the primary input buffer.

Program Highlights

These routines save and restore the primary input buffer in the file PBUFS (PROC BUFFERS). The item containing the PROC buffer is identified by port number. Look closely at line 009 of the SAVEIBUF routine:

```
009 PORT = FIELD(OCONV(0,'U50BB'),' ',1)
```

The output of a WHO can be captured by the following:

```
OCONV(0,'U50BB')
```

The port number is extracted using the FIELD statement.

Please note that many enhanced R83 implementations can retrieve the port number and the account name via the SYSTEM(18) and SYSTEM(19) functions, respectively:

```
PORT = SYSTEM(18)
ACCOUNT = SYSTEM(19)
```

```
        GETIBUF
001 * PROGRAM GETIBUF
002 * Retrieves the PROC PIB
003 * Harvey Eric Rodstein
004 *
005 * Initialization
006 *
007 OPEN 'PBUFS' TO PBUFS.FILE ELSE STOP 201,'PBUFS'
008 *
009 PORT = FIELD(OCONV(0,'U50BB'),' ',1)
010 READ BUFFER FROM PBUFS.FILE,PORT ELSE BUFFER = ''
011 PROCWRITE BUFFER
012 STOP
013 *
014 END

        SAVEIBUF
001 * PROGRAM SAVEIBUF
002 * Saves the PROC PIB
003 * Harvey Eric Rodstein
004 *
005 * Initialization
006 *
007 OPEN 'PBUFS' TO PBUFS.FILE ELSE STOP 201,'PBUFS'
008 *
009 PORT = FIELD(OCONV(0,'U50BB'),' ',1)
010 PROCREAD BUFFER THEN WRITE BUFFER ON PBUFS.FILE,PORT
011 STOP
012 *
013 END
```

FIG. 5-11. GETIBUF and SAVEIBUF program listings.

The PROCWRITE statement overwrites the current PROC primary input buffer. The general form is:

PROCWRITE *variable* {ELSE ...}

The ELSE clause is optional and is active only if the program is not initiated from a PROC:

011 PROCWRITE BUFFER

Capturing Output

Print output from the standard system processes, TCL, ACCESS (or RECALL) and PICK/BASIC can be redirected to and captured by a PICK/BASIC variable via the EXECUTE statement.

The general syntax for out redirection in Pick is the following:

EXECUTE *tclsentence* CAPTURING *variable*

The general syntax for the Ultimate compatible machines is as follows:

EXECUTE *tclsentence* ,//OUT. > *variable*

The indicator *tclsentence* represents any compound string expression that results in a valid TCL command sentence. The indicator *variable* represents the variable into which the data is captured, one attribute per print line. Standardly, the capture routine converts the carriage return, line feed (CHAR(13), CHAR(10)) combination into an attribute mark (CHAR(254)), and form feeds (CHAR(12)) into null strings.

Within PICK/BASIC, only the results of a PRINT can be captured. The output of the CRT (in Pick) and the DISPLAY (in Ultimate) command are not captured and always display on the terminal screen. Some TCL verbs cannot be captured by EXECUTE because they do not follow the conventions of the virtual environment. The tape attachment and spooler entry numbers fall into this class on many systems. Always perform a test before relying on them.

A simple example of output redirection can be demonstrated for the WHO command. As previously shown, the user exit "U50BB" may be used to generate a WHO. But, availability of this user-exit is not guaranteed for all implementations. The following statement works on the generic Pick implementations:

```
EXECUTE 'WHO' CAPTURING WHO
PORT = FIELD(WHO,' ',1)
ACCOUNT = FIELD(WHO,' ',2)
```

A more powerful example of output capturing is provided in the program STATUS found in Chapter 8, "The Virtual Machine." In this example, the output of a WHERE command is captured and each line parsed to determine its content.

The Scroll Program

The SCROLL program, shown in Fig. 5-12, captures output from any command sentence and provides a generic method for paging backward and forward through the resulting listing. This is quite powerful, since standard system output allows paging in a single direction, forward.

The way in which the capture routine deals with page headings differs between implementations. Some generate and capture the heading of the first page and strip the rest, regardless of the current TERM setting. Others generate a heading for each page, based on the current TERM setting.

```
    SCROLL
001 * PROGRAM SCROLL
002 * Scrolls backward and forward through any listing
003 * Harvey Eric Rodstein
004 *
005 * Initialization
006 *
007 EQU BELL TO CHAR(7)
008 EQU FF   TO CHAR(12)
009 EQU AM   TO CHAR(254)
010 EQU ESCC TO CHAR(251)
011 EQU ESC  TO CHAR(27)
```

FIG. 5-12. The SCROLL program listing (continues).

```
012 *
013 ESCAPE = ESC:ESCC:'X'
014 *
015 CLS = @(-1)
016 EOS = @(-3)
017 EOL = @(-4)
018 RON = @(-13)
019 ROF = @(-14)
020 *
021 * Get and EXECUTE the sentence
022 *
023 LOOP
024   PROMPT '>' ; CRT 'ENTER TCL ':
025   INPUT SENTENCE
026 UNTIL SENTENCE = '' OR INDEX(ESCAPE,SENTENCE,1) DO
027   EXECUTE SENTENCE CAPTURING LISTING
028   * Trim leading null attributes
029   LOOP WHILE LISTING<1> = '' DO
030     LISTING = DELETE(LISTING,1)
031   REPEAT
032   PROMPT ''
033   GOSUB 5000 ;* Paging routine
034   CRT CLS:
035 REPEAT
036 STOP
037 *
038 5000 * - Paging Routine
039 *
040 PMAX = 18
041 MAX = DCOUNT(LISTING,AM)
042 IF PMAX >=  MAX THEN
043   MSG = '(H)ardcopy, E(X)it'
044 END ELSE
045   MSG = '(T)op, (B)ottom, (P)revious, (N)ext, (H)ardcopy, or E(X)it'
046 END
047 CNT = 1
048 PAGENO  = 1
049 MAXPAGE = INT(MAX/PMAX)+1
050 CRT @(-1):
051 *
052 GOSUB 6000 ;* Display the Screen
053 *
054 * Prompt for Command
055 *
056 LOOP
057   EXITFLAG =0
058   CRT @(0,22):@(-4):RON:MSG:ROF:' ':
059   CRT @(0,23):'[ ] ':MORE:@(1,23):
060   INPUT ANS,1:
061   ANS = OCONV(ANS,'MCU')
062   BEGIN CASE
063     CASE ANS # '' AND INDEX(ESCAPE,ANS,1) ;* Exit
064       EXITFLAG = 1
```

FIG. 5-12 continues.

```
065    CASE (ANS='N' OR ANS='')        ;* Next Page
066     IF (PAGENO<MAXPAGE) THEN
067      CNT = CNT + 1
068      PAGENO = PAGENO + 1
069      GOSUB 6000
070     END
071     CASE ANS = 'P' AND PAGENO>1   ;* Previous Page
072      PAGENO = PAGENO - 1
073      CNT = (PAGENO-1)*PMAX+1
074      GOSUB 6000
075     CASE ANS = 'T'                 ;* Top
076      CNT = 1
077      PAGENO = 1
078      GOSUB 6000
079     CASE ANS = 'B'                 ;* Bottom
080      PAGENO = MAXPAGE
081      CNT = (PAGENO-1)*PMAX+1
082      GOSUB 6000
083     CASE ANS = 'H'                 ;* Hardcopy
084      CRT @(0,22):EOL:@(0,20):
085      PRINTER ON
086      IX=1
087      FOR XCNT = 1 TO MAX
088        XLINE = LISTING<XCNT>
089        IX = IX + 1
090        NEWPAGE = IX>PMAX
091        PRINT XLINE
092        IF NEWPAGE THEN IX=1;PRINT FF:
093      NEXT XCNT
094      PRINTER CLOSE ; PRINTER OFF
095    END CASE
096 UNTIL EXITFLAG DO REPEAT
097 RETURN
098 *
099 *
100 6000 * Display the screen
101 *
102 CRT @(0,0):RON:'Scroll':ROF:' ':EOL:
103 CRT
104 CRT STR('-',79)
105 *
106 I = 1
107 PCOL = 0
108 PROW = 3
109 CRT @(70,0):'Page ':PAGENO:EOL:
110 ENDPAGE = 0
111 MORE = ''
112 LOOP
113   LINE = LISTING<CNT>
114   PRINT @(PCOL,PROW):LINE:EOL:
115   ENDPAGE = (CNT>=MAX) OR (I>=PMAX)
116 UNTIL ENDPAGE DO
117   I = I + 1
```

FIG. 5-12 continues.

202

```
118   CNT = CNT + 1
119    PROW = PROW + 1
120 REPEAT
121 CRT EOS:
122 IF ENDPAGE AND I>=PMAX THEN MORE = 'More.'
123 RETURN
124 *
125 END
```

FIG. 5-12 ends.

Program Highlights

The first task of this program is to accept the input of a variable TCL command sentence and EXECUTE it. Instead of letting the output scroll by on the terminal screen, it is captured as a variable string so that the standard array and string handling techniques can be used to scroll through and display the results.

```
021 * Get and EXECUTE the sentence
022 *
023 LOOP
024 PROMPT '>'
025 INPUT SENTENCE
026 UNTIL SENTENCE = '' OR INDEX(ESCAPE,SENTENCE,1) DO
027 EXECUTE SENTENCE CAPTURING LISTING
   ...
   ...
035 REPEAT
```

Any leading null attributes are stripped from the captured variable, LISTING, in the following manner:

```
028 * Trim leading null attributes
029 LOOP WHILE LISTING<1> = '' DO
030  LISTING = DELETE(LISTING,1)
031 REPEAT
```

It is probably a good idea to generate a listing without page headings because paging is now a function of the PICK/BASIC program and not the output processor. The display headings and footings can be coded as an integral part of the PICK/BASIC program.

Subroutine 5000 is the main logic for paging forward, backward, top, bottom and providing a hard copy of the listing to the printer. The current page limits in the listing are controlled by two main variables; PMAX, the maximum number of lines per page, and MAX, the total number of lines in the LISTING. The current line count, CNT, and page number, PAGENO are initialized to 1, but are recalculated based on the PAGENO and PMAX for each page requested. The maximum number of pages (used for positioning to the bottom of the listing), is determined by the following calculation:

```
049 MAXPAGE = INT(MAX/PMAX)+1
```

Subroutine 6000 displays the current page based on the initial value of CNT. The end of a page occurs when either the temporary line counter, I, is at the end of the page, I > = PMAX, or the end of the LISTING is reached, CNT > = MAX.

```
112 LOOP
113 LINE = LISTING<CNT>
114 PRINT @(PCOL,PROW):LINE:EOL:
115 ENDPAGE = (CNT> = MAX) OR (I> = PMAX)
116 UNTIL ENDPAGE DO
117 I = I + 1
118 CNT = CNT + 1
119 PROW = PROW + 1
120 REPEAT
```

Prior to each call of 6000, the starting CNT position must be calculated. Take a look at each of the paging functions in subroutine 5000.

Next Page   The current value of CNT is always left at the last line of the current page by subroutine 6000. Scrolling to the next page is accomplished by simply incrementing the current CNT and the PAGENO.

```
066  IF (PAGENO<MAXPAGE) THEN
067  CNT = CNT + 1
068  PAGENO = PAGENO + 1
069  GOSUB 6000
070  END
```

Previous Page   Scrolling to the previous page requires that the starting CNT be calculated based on the requested page number and the maximum number of lines per page, PMAX.

```
072  PAGENO = PAGENO − 1
073  CNT = (PAGENO−1)*PMAX+1
074  GOSUB 6000
```

Top and Bottom   Positioning the scroll to the first page is trivial. All it requires is setting the CNT and PAGENO to 1.

```
076  CNT = 1
077  PAGENO = 1
078  GOSUB 6000
```

Scrolling to the bottom requires the page number be set to the maximum page value and the CNT be calculated based on that number.

```
080  PAGENO = MAXPAGE
081  CNT = (PAGENO−1)*PMAX+1
082  GOSUB 6000
```

ERROR RECOVERY

In order to implement effective process control routines, it is imperative that errors be trapped and dealt with before allowing any other process to continue. In an interactive routine, error recovery may be as simple as displaying a message to the terminal screen and requesting operator response. In unattended processes, error recovery requires a much more programmatic approach. An unattended process must be able to determine whether an error has occurred, record the error in some sort of error log, and make a logical decision about the continuation of the process.

Trapping Errors

ACCESS, TCL, RUNOFF and the rest of the Pick processes terminate by passing through a routine called WRAPUP. WRAPUP as its name implies, "wraps up" the current system routine before returning to TCL, the controlling PROC, or controlling PICK/BASIC program. WRAPUP also calls the system PRTERR subroutine which is used to print the contents of specified error message items from the ERRMSG file. Whether the process control language is PROC or PICK/BASIC, the ERRMSG item-id's which have been passed to WRAPUP are available to the control routine.

In PROC, the error message generated by the processed command sentence can be interrogated using the PROC specification E as follows:

IF E = ERRMSG*id proc-command*

Each time a command is processed from the PROC output buffers, the resulting ERRMSG item-ids are placed in the PROC secondary input buffer. The E specification addresses the first entry of the PROC secondary input buffer.

If more detail is needed, the Set Secondary Active (SS) command can be used. When the secondary buffer is active, each entry can be addressed by the standard PROC A*n* command, where the *n* stands for the position in the active input buffer. An example of using PROC to trap error messages is shown in Fig. 5-13.

The use of the SS command has its advantages, because processes can generate more than a single error. Some processes retrieve and print multiple items from the ERRMSG

```
HLIST STAFF WITH STATE = "AZ"
P
IF E = 401 X

or

HLIST STAFF WITH STATE = "AZ"
P
SS
IF A1 = 401 X
```

ERRMSG 401 is the NO ITEMS PRESENT error message.

FIG. 5-13. Trapping ERRMSGs in PROC.

file. Each item-id reference, delimited by a space on generic Pick and an attribute mark on Ultimate, is stored in the secondary input buffer in the order of occurrence.

A simple demonstration of this can be accomplished by executing the WHAT verb and displaying the errors that occur. The DO command displays the entire contents of the currently active input buffer.

```
001 PQ
002 HWHAT
003 P
004 SS
005 D0
```

This PROC displays the following ERRMSG item-ids:

```
999 1200 1210 1213 1214 1217 1221 1240 1243 1204
```

Figure 5-14 demonstrates how a series of ERRMSG item-ids can be checked in a PROC. The premise is that a QSELECT that references a nonexistent item generates both ERRMSG [201] NOT ON FILE and ERRMSG [404] 0 ITEMS SELECTED. The error string looks as follows:

```
201 404
```

If the controlling PROC simply checks for the occurrence of ERRMSG [401] NO ITEMS PRESENT in the first position of the error string, the error will not be trapped. ERRMSG 201 is the fatal message since the item does not exist. ERRMSG [404] n ITEMS SELECTED, usually considered a successful condition, is generated by both the successful and the above failure cases.

```
HQSELECT LISTS TEST
STON
H<
P
SS
S1
10 C
IF A = 401 X
IF A = 202 X
F
IF A G 10
```

FIG. 5-14. Checking multiple ERRMSG item-ids in PROC.

There are two fatal conditions that may result from a QSELECT. The controlling program must check for either ERRMSG [202] NOT ON FILE, or [401] NO ITEMS PRESENT.

The IF conditionals check for the possible bad error message items. The operator F is used to move the input buffer pointer forward one position. The existence of the next input buffer entry is checked before the value is compared to the possible fatal ERRMSG item-ids. (Is this cryptic enough?)

Figure 5-15 is an easier way to check for a successful completion of a SELECT or QSELECT statement without muddling through all the possible ERRMSGs. Instead,

FIG. 5-15. Checking for an
active list in PROC.

```
HQSELECT LISTS TEST
STON
H<
P
IF # S X
```

check for an active list with the PROC specification S. S is true if the list is active and false if not. (The equivalent in PICK/BASIC is the SYSTEM(11) function.) Enough with PROC. Not bad for a subject that was supposed to be skipped.

Error messages can also be trapped from the PICK/BASIC EXECUTE statement. Within generic Pick, there are two methods for returning the ERRMSG item-ids; the EXECUTE modifier, RETURNING, and the SYSTEM function, SYSTEM(17).

The RETURNING modifier is used within the syntax of the EXECUTE statement as follows:

EXECUTE *tclsentence* RETURNING *errorlist*

The indicator *errorlist* is a list of the ERRMSG item-id's delimited by a space. The PICK/ BASIC examples in Fig. 5-16 produce the same result as the PROCs above.

```
EXECUTE 'LIST STAFF WITH STATE = "AZ"' RETURNING ERR
IF ERR = '401' THEN STOP
```

or

```
EXECUTE 'QSELECT LISTS TEST' RETURNING ERR
ERRCNT = DCOUNT(ERR,' ')
BAD = 0
FOR I = 1 TO ERRCNT UNTIL BAD
   ANERR = FIELD(ERR,' ',I)
   BAD = (ANERR='401') OR (ANERR='202')
NEXT I
IF BAD THEN STOP
```

FIG. 5-16. *Trapping ERRMSGs in PICK/BASIC using RETURNING.*

The second method for returning the ERRMSG item-id's does not require any modification of the EXECUTE statement. The function SYSTEM(17) contains the list of ERRMSG's trapped from the previous EXECUTE statement. The difference is that SYSTEM(17) holds the ERRMSG's delimited by attribute marks, not spaces.

As before, the examples in Fig. 5-17 can check for an active list rather than checking all the possible ERRMSG item-ids. The SYSTEM(11) function is true when a list is active and false when a list is not active, as in Fig. 5-18.

In the Ultimate world, shown in Fig. 5-19, ERRMSG item-ids must be retrieved using the GET(MSG.) statement in the following general form:

GET(MSG.{,*expression*}) *variable* {THEN...} {ELSE..}

The operation of this statement is identical to the GET(ARG.) statement. Each GET(MSG.) invoked retrieves the next error message in the list of returned errors, or

```
EQU AM TO CHAR(254)
EXECUTE 'QSELECT LISTS TEST'
ERR = SYSTEM(17)
ERRCNT = DCOUNT(ERR,AM)
BAD = 0
FOR I = 1 TO ERRCNT UNTIL BAD
    ANERR = ERR<I>
    BAD = (ANERR='401') OR (ANERR='202')
NEXT I
IF BAD THEN STOP
```

FIG. 5-17. Trapping ERRMSGs in PICK/BASIC using SYSTEM(17).

```
EQU AM TO CHAR(254)
EXECUTE 'QSELECT LISTS TEST'
IF NOT(SYSTEM(11)) THEN STOP
```

FIG. 5-18. Checking for an active list in PICK/BASIC.

```
EXECUTE 'QSELECT LISTS TEST'
LOOP
GET(MSG.) ERR THEN BAD = (ERR='401') OR (ERR='202')
UNTIL (EOF(MSG.) OR BAD) DO REPEAT
IF BAD THEN STOP
```

FIG. 5-19. Trapping ERRMSGs on Ultimate.

retrieves the error message in the position indicated by the results of "expression." In addition, Ultimate provides the following function:

EOF(MSG.)

This function is true if the previous GET(MSG.) successfully retrieves designated error message and false if the message does not exist.

The Error Recovery Process

The mechanics of trapping, logging, and subsequently reporting runtime errors is quite straightforward. However, the programmatic decision on recovery and subsequent process flow can get complex when multiple error conditions are possible, unless one simple rule is followed:

Always test for successful completion first

It is quicker and easier to make a decision about the successful completion of a process than it is to handle the myriad of possibilities that can cause an abort. The main process flow should only be concerned about whether the performed routine has an error-free completion. Any unexpected results should be handled by a specialized error recovery routine. This routine not only determines which errors have occurred, but also reports the errors, logs the errors, and determines their severity.

Most system routines pass a predictable series of ERRMSG item-ids upon a successful run. For example, when a successful select is performed, both a QSELECT and a

SELECT pass ERRMSG 404 (*n* items selected) in the first position of the error string. The code segment in Fig. 5-19 can be rewritten as follows:

```
EXECUTE 'QSELECT LISTS TEST'
IF SYSTEM(17)<1> # '404' THEN
      CALL ERRORSUB(PORT,EXIT)
      IF EXIT THEN STOP
END
```

The ERRORSUB Subroutine

The subroutine ERRORSUB, shown in Fig. 5-20, contains the specific code for dealing with the multiple conditions of unattended process failure. This example is intended as a skeletal program which can be elaborated upon by the programmer.

```
001 SUBROUTINE ERRORSUB(PORT,EXITFLAG)
002 EQU AM TO CHAR(254)
003 FATALERRORS = '3':AM:'10':AM:'201'
004 ERRLIST = SYSTEM(17)
005 ERRCNT  = DCOUNT(ERRLIST,AM)
006 OPEN 'ERRORLOG' TO ERRORLOG THEN
007     WRITE ERRLIST ON ERRORLOG,PORT:'.':TIME():'.':DATE()
008 END
009 FATAL = 0
010 FOR I = 1 TO ERRCNT UNTIL FATAL
011     ERR = ERRLIST<I>
012     LOCATE(ERR,FATALERRORS;FOUND) THEN
013         FATAL = 1
014     END
015 NEXT I
016 IF FATAL THEN STOP ELSE RETURN
```

FIG. 5-20. ERRORSUB subroutine listing.

Program Highlights

The subroutine ERRORSUB uses two passed parameters, PORT and EXITFLAG. However, in most integrated applications one one need be passed, EXITFLAG. The EXITFLAG notifies the main program that a fatal application error was found and processing should be terminated. The PORT can either be part of an application COMMON block, or retrieved "on-the-fly" by the subroutine.

In this case, three messages are considered fatal. These are arbitrary choices for the purposes of demonstration.

```
ID: 3  VERB?
ID: 10 FILE NAME MISSING
ID: 201 'filename' IS NOT A FILENAME
```

The dynamic string, FATALERRORS, is defined using attribute marks as delimiters.

```
003 FATALERRORS = '3':AM:'10':AM:'201'
```

This is later used within a LOCATE statement to determine whether any of the ERRMSG item-ids are considered fatal. The list of ERRMSG item-ids need not be passed in the argument list because they are already available with SYSTEM(17):

```
004 ERRLIST = SYSTEM(17)
```

The number of errors is counted, followed by an attempt to OPEN the ERRORLOG file. The existence of ERRLOG triggers the save of the current ERRMSG list. The log entry item-id consists of the PORT concatenated to the internal time-date.

```
005 ERRCNT = DCOUNT(ERRLIST,AM)
006 OPEN 'ERRORLOG' TO ERRORLOG THEN
007 WRITE ERRLIST ON ERRORLOG,PORT:'.':TIME( ):'.':DATE( )
009 END
```

This need not be the only information saved in the ERRORLOG file. Other data might include the controlling process name, the current program name, and the operator identifier. Next, the entries in the error list are checked for fatal errors.

```
009 FATAL = 0
010 FOR I = 1 TO ERRCNT UNTIL FATAL
011     ERR = ERRLIST<I>
012     LOCATE(ERR,FATALERRORS;FOUND) THEN
013        FATAL = 1
014     END
015 NEXT I
016 IF FATAL THEN STOP ELSE RETURN
```

The FOR..NEXT loop continues searching each error until a fatal condition occurs. An error, ERR, is extracted from ERRLIST and an attempt is made to locate the error within the FATALERRORS list. If ERR is located (the THEN statement), the FATAL flag is set and the loop is immediately terminated.

Capturing Spool Entry Numbers

Here is an example of using the RETURNING clause or SYSTEM(17) to capture the Spooler ENTRY #*n* message. Consider the following ACCESS statement:

```
LIST STAFF LPTR
```

The process responds with the following message:

```
ENTRY #2
```

In this case, the print job is assigned the second entry in the job queue. If this ACCESS command is EXECUTEd from PICK/BASIC as follows:

```
EXECUTE 'LIST STAFF LPTR'
ERRLIST = SYSTEM(17)
```

The variable string ERRLIST from SYSTEM(17) is as follows:

1099^2

The "^," caret, represents an attribute mark. The general form of the error list is:

1099 *attribute-mark entry-number*

This number can be extracted and either used to immediately process the spool job or filed for later use. In release R83, the returned error list is identical whether a hold entry is generated or not.

Figure 5-21 is a sample program that generates a spooler hold item, passes the spool job number to the program SP-FILE (see above), and, subsequently, transfers the print image to a standard item format.

```
        SP-MOVEJOB
001 * PROGRAM SP-MOVEJOB
002 * Generate STAFF report and move job to SPOOL-FILE
003 * Harvey Eric Rodstein
004 *
005 * Initialization
006 *
007 PROMPT '>'
008 *
009 EQU BELL TO CHAR(7)
010 EQU FF   TO CHAR(12)
011 EQU AM   TO CHAR(254)
012 EQU ESCC TO CHAR(251)
013 EQU ESC  TO CHAR(27)
014 *
015 * EXECUTE the STAFF Report and Move the Job
016 * to SPOOL-FILE item STAFF.REPORT via SP-FILE
017 *
018 EXECUTE 'SP-ASSIGN HS'
019 EXECUTE 'SORT STAFF LPTR'
020 DATA SYSTEM(17)<2>,'STAFF.REPORT'
021 EXECUTE 'SP-FILE'
022 *
023 END
```

FIG. 5-21. SP-MOVEJOB program listing.

Program Highlights

The important section of this program is between lines 018 and 021. The spooler is assigned to a Hold and Suppress mode just prior to generating the STAFF file report. Line 020 extracts the second error message entry as a compound part of the DATA statement. The second parameter, 'STAFF.REPORT' is the initial item-id used by SP-FILE.

```
020 DATA SYSTEM(17)<2>,'STAFF.REPORT'
021 EXECUTE 'SP-FILE'
```

The entire SP-FILE PICK/BASIC program is provided earlier in this chapter in Fig. 5-20.

PICK/BASIC ERRMSG WRAPUP

All Pick processes, by default, generate standard system error messages. PICK/BASIC runtime has a full set of low-level warnings and aborts. These can be found in the ERRMSG file under items with item-id's beginning with a B. A few can provide warnings about garbage in the database. These include:

[B16] NON-NUMERIC DATA WHEN NUMERIC DATA REQUIRED; ZERO USED!

or

[B24] DIVIDE BY ZERO ILLEGAL; ZERO USED!

Any of these "non-fatal" runtime warning methods can occur if the database is corrupted either by system problems or insufficient validation in data entry. These messages should be considered fatal. As described in Chapter 3, the (E) runtime option is essential to prevent such occurrences of further corrupting the database. However, these messages are usually generated by program bugs and seldom indicate anything about application level problems.

At the application level, when a PICK/BASIC program attempts to OPEN a file that doesn't exist or attempts to read an item that should be there but is somehow missing, the error messages are generated by the PRINT statement. Or, if the program terminates successfully, the code simply indicates STOP, as in Fig. 5-22.

```
PRINT 'FILE ':FILENAME:' IS MISSING'
STOP
```

or

```
PRINT 'ITEM ':ITEMNAME:' IS MISSING'
STOP
```

FIG. 5-22. Typical PICK/BASIC termination and error generation.

This is sufficient if the process is run in an attended environment. But, it is inadequate in an unattended environment. This approach provides absolutely no indication of an error to the process control program.

It is possible for the programmer to specify a specific error message to be passed to WRAPUP at the termination of a PICK/BASIC program via the STOP command in the following form:

STOP {*errmsgid*{,*arg,arg,arg,...*}}

The braces ({w) indicate optional specifications. The indicator *errmsgid* is any valid item-id in the ERRMSG file. The indicators *arg,arg,..* represent an argument list of variable data elements passed to WRAPUP. The ERRMSGs used in Fig. 5-23 are as follows:

ID: 201 'filename' IS NOT A FILENAME
ID: 202 'item-id' NOT ON FILE.

FIG. 5-23. Preferred PICK/BASIC termination and error generation.   *or*

STOP 202,ITEMNAME

The parameters FILENAME and ITEMNAME are passed to the message handler and plugged into the printed message.

The STOP command passes a single error to WRAPUP. At present, the generic system provides no way to display and pass a series of error messages before the program terminates so they can be available to the controlling PROC or PICK/BASIC program. Don't be disheartened, there is hope on the horizon. Many Pick vendors are, or soon will be, providing an enhanced R83 which contains the ERROR statement. The general form of the ERROR statement is as follows:

ERROR *errmsgid*{,*argument,argument...*}

The syntax is similar to the STOP statement except that the PICK/BASIC program is not terminated. The specified error message is printed, with the optionally passed arguments, and the ERRMSG item-id is stacked for retrieval by the process controlling routine.

For those who speak Ultimate, a similar statement is currently provided in the form of the PUT function. The result of the PUT function is identical to the ERROR statement. The general form of the PUT function is as follows:

PUT(MSG.) *errmsgid*{*argument,argument..*}

Customizing ERRMSG Items

Programmers can define application specific messages and add them to the ERRMSG file. This allows a full range of application specific messages to be added to the system and handled through standard WRAPUP procedures.

Text alone is not sufficient to build an error message. There is a limited set of operators which controls output. Within the ERRMSG "language" these are operators for literal text strings, forced line feeds, and passed variable and system parameters.

The following ERRMSG operators have been divided into two major groups. First, those used for literal text and output formatting, and, second, those used for variable and system generated parameters.

Message Text and Format

Literal text is generated by the H operator in the following form:

H*textstring...*{ + }

The optional plus sign indicates to hold the cursor in case an INPUT follows the error display. The H operator outputs the literal text at the current screen cursor position and does not generate a carriage return and line feed. Therefore, H specifications on succeeding lines tend to concatenate the output.

New lines are indicated by the operator L in the following form:

L{(*n*)}

The braces ({ }) indicate an optional specification. An L by itself generates a single carriage return and line feed, an L(*n*) generates *n* carriage returns and line feeds.

A variation on the H operator is the E operator. The general form is:

E*textstring...*

The E operator outputs the ERRMSG item-id surrounded by brackets ([ ]), followed by the specified text string.

Text output may need to be centered or placed at column positions other than the left margin of the screen. Some enhanced versions of R83 allow absolute cursor positioning following the same standards used in the PICK/BASIC at-function.

@(*col,row*)

For the rest of the implementations, spacing must be controlled by the S operator in the following form:

S(*n*)

The indicator *n* represents the number of spaces to generate. (This is very much like the PICK/BASIC SPACE(*n*) function.) Figure 5-24 shows sample ERRMSG items and generated output.

Error item:

```
001 HThis is an
002 H error message
```

Displays:

```
This is an error message
```

Error item:

```
001 HThis is an
002 L
003 H error message
```

Displays:

```
This is an
 error message
```

Error item:

```
001 E VERB?
```

FIG. 5-24. Sample ERRMSG items and generated output (continues).

Displays:

```
[3] VERB?
```

Error item:

```
001 S(6)
002 HThis is an error message
003 L
004 S(6)
005 Hindented by 6 spaces
006 L
```

Displays:

```
:           This is an error message
:           indented by 6 spaces
```

```
(The colon (:) represents the left margin
and is not a part of the message.)
```

FIG. 5-24 ends.

Message Parameters

As previously demonstrated, ERRMSG items can accept variable parameters to be inserted into the final message. The A operator is used to specify the next argument in the passed parameter list. The general form is:

A{(*n*)}

Specifying A alone fills in the next argument, A(*n*) fills in the next argument left justified in a field length of *n*.

The following PICK/BASIC statement passes three arguments to the ERRMSG ARGS.

```
STOP 'ARGS','THIS','IS','EASY'
```

The results are illustrated in Fig. 5-25.

The ARGS item in ERRMSG looks like this:

```
ID: ARGS
001 HThese are passed arguments:
002 L
003 A
004 Hb
005 A
006 Hb
007 A
```

(The b is an embedded space.) This generates the following output:

```
These are passed arguments:
THIS IS EASY
```

FIG. 5-25. Variable arguments in an ERRMSG item.

Changing the A operators to A(5) generates the following:

```
003 A(5)
...
005 A(5)
...
007 A(5)
```

Each parameter is now left justified in a field of 5.

```
These are passed arguments:
THIS    IS    EASY
```

Arguments can also be right justified by using the R operator in the following form:

R(n)

The indicator n represents the field length. This is useful for columnarizing numeric arguments.

The following PICK/BASIC statements generate the arguments to be printed through ERRMSG ARGS.

```
A = '10'
B = '55'
C = '175'
STOP 'ARGS',A,B,C
```

The A parameters can be substituted with R(10) for the following results:

```
003 R(10)
...
005 R(10)
...
007 R(10)
```

Generates the following output:

```
These are passed arguments:
        10
        55
       175
```

Finally, system generated data can be inserted into an ERRMSG by using the following operators:

T   Outputs the current system time
D   Outputs the current system date

Neither of these generate a new line. The output is generated at the current screen cursor position and remains on the current line.

The Good Message

One of the most important entries should be the error item 'GOOD.' This is a quick and dirty entry for all PICK/BASIC routines to use upon error-free completion.

    STOP 'GOOD'

Combining all this information, a new ERRMSG item can be written. This is the ERRMSG item "GOOD," as shown in Fig. 5-26. Note that both attribute 003 and 005 have an embedded space at the end of the text string. Consider the following PICK/BASIC statement:

    STOP 'GOOD','AGING'

which generates the following output:

    [GOOD] 'AGING' Complete on 27 OCT 1988 at 23:10:00

The ERRMSG item-id GOOD is now available to the process control routine.

NOTE: It is a good idea to keep all user defined error messages in a separate USER.ERRMSG file. This eliminates the problem of losing application specific error messages every time the operating system is upgraded to a new release. The USER. ERRMSG file can be copied to the system ERRMSG file after any system rebuild is performed.

FIG. 5-26. The "GOOD" ERRMSG item.

```
ID: GOOD
001 E '
002 A
003 H' Completed on
004 D
005 H at
006 T
```

Input-Output Error Recovery

Process error recovery is not solely a function of the EXECUTE statement or the PROC E command. There exists a growing number of PICK/BASIC functions that can be used to recover from errors generated internally by PICK/BASIC input and output statements.

The PICK/BASIC READ commands contain a THEN..ELSE conditional process. The THEN represents a successful READ (the item exists), and the ELSE an unsuccessful READ (the item does not exist).

Traditionally, the WRITE statement has been unconditional. However, the newer implementations are providing an ELSE clause which modifies WRITE, DELETE, and CLEAFILE. The ELSE is taken if an update is attempted on a file which is write protected.

The INPUT statement, which has traditionally been unconditional, is also being fitted with an ELSE clause. The "classic" INPUT statement waits forever if there is no data on the line. The newer implementations are allowing a timeout condition. That is, INPUT waits only for so long before aborting. If a timeout occurs, the ELSE clause is taken.

Ultimate has extended both the file READ and WRITE. Files within Ultimate can exist locally or across a network link. Using communication links, the failure of a READ or WRITE is much more complex than deciding whether the item exists or not. The new logic wrinkle test for whether the communications link remains intact. This has led to the implementation of a new clause, ON ERROR. Ultimate users should consult the system provided manuals for the exact syntax and conditions of use.

Within all Pick systems, there is another condition by which a READ can "fail." This is not so much a failure as it is a possible process "hang." The statement is the READU, read for update. The READU locks the targeted item, or group, depending on the implementation. Any other READ or READU performed against a locked item or group takes neither the THEN or ELSE clause. The statement hangs and waits for the lock to be cleared. This can and does lead to performance problems if the lock is not cleared in a timely fashion.

READU, MATREADU, READ and READU statements on most new releases have the additional LOCKED clause available. The general form of a READ or READU using the LOCKED is as follows:

```
{MAT}READ{U} variable FROM filevar,item-id LOCKED stmts....
.... THEN stmts ELSE stmts
```

Many implementations allow the following multiple line structure for the same statement.

```
{MAT}READ{U} variable FROM filevar,item-id LOCKED
        stmts
        stmts
        ...

END  THEN
        stmts
        stmts
        ...
END ELSE
        stmts
        stmts
        ...
END
```

The LOCKED clause is taken only when the item or target group is locked. At this point, the programmer may include code which can either perform a pre-determined number of retries or generate an error. Either way, the process does not wait for the lock to clear. What the LOCKED clause does not make apparent is the port number that has set the lock. The LIST-LOCKS command must be used to provide this information.

Tape handling is a form of input-output which requires conditional performance regardless of whether the PICK/BASIC program is addressing the tape drive via the READT, WRITET, REWIND or WEOF statements.

```
READT variable THEN... ELSE...
```

```
WRITET variable THEN.. ELSE
REWIND THEN.. ELSE
WEOF THEN... ELSE...
```

The THEN clause indicates the action when the statement is performed successfully. The ELSE clause is only taken if the tape is "not attached" or an EOF (end of file) condition is encountered. Otherwise, the system prompts for an immediate action. After the action is taken, the code follows the THEN clause.

The PICK/BASIC SYSTEM(0) function, shown in Fig. 5-27, is designed as a catch-all for tape error handling. The following are values assigned to the generic Pick SYSTEM(0) function based on different tape handling conditions. Both generic Pick and Ultimate handle extended tape conditions, but the SYSTEM(0) results differ.

System (0) on Pick R83:

Value	Cause	
1		The tape is not attached.
2		An attempt was made to write a null variable.
11		The tape record was truncated.

SYSTEM(0) on Ultimate:

Value	Cause	
1		The tape is not attached.
2		An EOF mark was detected.
3		An attempt was made to write a null string.
4		An attempt was made to write a tape block larger than the current tape block size.
5		The tape is off line.
6		The tape cartridge is not formatted properly.

FIG. 5-27. The SYSTEM(0) function.

The SYSTEM(0) seems to be fair ground for enhancement and potential incompatibility. For example, some implementation dependent enhancements extend the tape handling error values more in-line with the Ultimate version. On other versions as a result of the LOCKED clause, SYSTEM(0) is being used to hold the port number of the process which set the item lock.

There is one more generic SYSTEM function for tape handling. SYSTEM(8) returns the current tape block size. This is the size specified by the last T-ATT command.

In summary, the SYSTEM(n) function is as powerful as it is inconsistent. Therefore, it is important to check the system manuals and release documentation to pinpoint any differences.

A PROCESS SHELL

This final section of "Process Control" concentrates on a specific application of process control known as a "User Shell." A *Shell* is a PICK/BASIC program environment that sits in between the user and the system. The major advantage of such a program is that it provides "single thread" process control and monitoring at the applications level, rather than at the systems level. It allows seemingly low-level features to be added without modification to the operating system. These features include:

Feature	*Description*
A TCL Stacker	TCL stackers keep track of all the command sentences entered. An arbitrary limit can be set so that the command stack does not grow too large and cumbersome. Commands are provided to retrieve, modify and EXECUTE any entry on the stack.
Security	This ties in with the TCL Stacker. The last *n* commands EXECUTEd can be reviewed and monitored. This routine can be easily modified so that every command is pre-parsed to ensure that certain sensitive routines are not invoked by an operator with an incompatible security clearance.
Stored Procedures	The SHELL program provides an easy method of storing and recalling a single command sentence or a series of command sentences through user-defined "paragraphs" and "batches." Unsophisticated users need not learn PROC or PICK/BASIC to store and perform ad hoc reports.

There are numerous other features that a User Shell allows. The limit is the programmer's imagination. The use of PICK/BASIC allows for a flexible and easily enhanced environment.

Program Highlights

The following is a discussion of functional highlights found in each routine of the SHELL program, shown in Fig. 5-28. It is by no means a detailed explanation of every line. That is left as an exercise for the reader. Please feel free to modify and enhance this program for your own use. Many people already have modified it.

```
        SHELL
001 PROGRAM SHELL
002 * TCL COMMAND STACK AND SHELL
003 * (c) 1986,87,88 H.E.Rodstein Computer Consulting
004 * Harvey Eric Rodstein
005 *
006 EQU STDP TO ':'
007 EQU DBP  TO '$'
008 EQU NILL TO CHAR(0)
```

FIG. 5-28. SHELL program listing (continues).

```
009 EQU LF    TO CHAR(10)
010 EQU CR    TO CHAR(13)
011 EQU ESC   TO CHAR(27)
012 EQU ESCC  TO CHAR(251)
013 EQU AM    TO CHAR(254)
014 EQU VM    TO CHAR(253)
015 *
016 PCHAR = STDP
017 *
018 TRACE.FLAG = 0
019 BATCH.FLAG = 0
020 STACK.FLAG = 0
021 TERMINAL.OUTPUT = 0
022 ERROR      = ''
023 BATCHSTACK = ''
024 *
025 WHO     = OCONV(0,'U50BB')
026 PORT    = FIELD(WHO,' ',1)
027 ACCOUNT = FIELD(WHO,' ',2)
028 *
029 CAPTURE.FILENAME = 'STACK,CAPTURE'
030 CAPTURE.ID       = PORT
031 CAPTURE.BUFFER   = ''
032 CAPTURE.FLAG     = 0
033 UC.FLAG          = 0
034 STACK.FLAG       = 1
035 *
036 OPEN 'STACK' TO STACK.FILE ELSE STOP 201,'STACK'
037 OPEN 'PARAGRAPHS' TO PARAGRAPHS ELSE STOP 201,'PARAGRAPHS'
038 *
039 *STACK.ID = 'ST*':ACCOUNT:'*':PORT
040 STACK.ID = 'ST*':PORT
041 READ STACK FROM STACK.FILE,STACK.ID ELSE STACK = ''
042 READ STACK.MAX FROM STACK.FILE,'STACK.MAX' ELSE STACK.MAX = ''
043 IF STACK.MAX = '' OR NOT(NUM(STACK.MAX)) THEN STACK.MAX = 100
044 *
045 10 * Get a command sentence
046 *
047 EXT = ''
048 PROMPT PCHAR
049 *
050 IF NOT(BATCH.FLAG) THEN
051    STACK.FLAG = 1
052    CRT
053    INPUT TCL
054 END ELSE
055    LOOP
056       BATCH.FLAG = BATCH.FLAG + 1
057       TCL = BATCH<BATCH.FLAG>
058       T1 = TCL[1,1]
059    WHILE INDEX(':*',T1,1) AND (T1#'') DO REPEAT
060 END
061 *
```

FIG. 5-28 continues.

```
062 IF UC.FLAG THEN TCL = OCONV(TCL,'MCU')
063 *
064 GOSUB 100 ;* Process the Command Sentence
065 GOTO 10   ;* Get next command
066 *
067 *
068 *************************
069 *
070 * Subroutines
071 *
072 *
073 100 * Process the command
074 *
075 OTCL = TCL
076 TCL = TRIM(TCL)
077 COMMAND = FIELD(TCL,' ',1)
078 BOS = COL2()+1
079 IF NOT(UC.FLAG) THEN
080   COMMAND=OCONV(COMMAND,'MCU')
081 END
082 EXT = TCL[BOS,LEN(TCL)]
083 *
084 BEGIN CASE
085   CASE COMMAND=''
086     BATCH.FLAG=0
087   CASE COMMAND='SHELL'
088     CRT 'WISE GUY!'
089   CASE COMMAND='C'
090     GOSUB 9500
091   CASE COMMAND[1,1]='.'
092     GOSUB 5000
093   CASE NUM(COMMAND)
094     COMMAND = '.':COMMAND
095     GOSUB 5000
096   CASE COMMAND = 'TRACE'
097     IF TRACE.FLAG THEN
098       TRACE.FLAG = 0
099       PCHAR = STDP
100     END ELSE
101       TRACE.FLAG = 1
102       PCHAR = DBP
103     END
104   CASE COMMAND='TCL' OR COMMAND='END'
105     STOP
106   CASE COMMAND='STOP'
107     BATCH=''
108     BATCH.FLAG=0
109   CASE COMMAND='ERR' OR COMMAND='IFERR' OR COMMAND = 'ONERR'
110     ENO = FIELD(TCL,' ',2)
111     IF ENO = ERROR THEN
112       TCL = TCL[COL2()+1,LEN(TCL)]
113       GOSUB 100
114     END
```

FIG. 5-28 continues.

```
115    CASE COMMAND='DATA'
116     DVAR  = ''
117     FOR I = 1 TO DCOUNT(EXT,';')
118      DVAR<-1> = FIELD(EXT,';',I)
119     NEXT I
120     DATA DVAR
121     DVAR = ''
122    CASE COMMAND = 'PRINT'
123     PRINT EXT
124    CASE COMMAND = 'PRINTER'
125     BEGIN CASE
126      CASE EXT = 'ON'  ;PRINTER ON
127      CASE EXT = 'CLOSE'  ;PRINTER CLOSE
128      CASE 1  ;PRINTER OFF
129     END CASE
130    CASE COMMAND = 'PAUSE'
131     PROMPT ''
132     ECHO OFF
133     CRT 'Press any key to continue':
134     INPUT CONT,1
135     IF CONT = 'X' OR CONT = 'E' THEN
136       CRT 'Batch Exited!'
137       BATCH.FLAG = 0
138     END
139     ECHO ON
140    CASE COMMAND = 'BRANCH' OR COMMAND[1,2] = 'GO'
141     SRCH.CNT = INDEX(BATCH,':':EXT,1)
142     BATCH.FLAG = DCOUNT(BATCH[1,SRCH.CNT],AM)
143    CASE 1
144     GOSUB 200 ;* Pre-Parse and EXECUTE the sentence
145    END CASE
146    *
147    RETURN
148    *
149    *
150    200 * Pre-parse and Execute
151    *
152    * - Update the Stack
153    *
154    IF STACK.FLAG THEN
155      STACK = INSERT(STACK,1,0,0,TCL)
156      GOSUB 9000
157    END
158    *
159    * - Redirection Options
160    *
161    Z = INDEX(OTCL,'CAPTURING',1)
162    IF Z THEN
163      CAPTURE = OTCL[Z,LEN(OTCL)]
164      CAPTURE.FILENAME = FIELD(CAPTURE,' ',2)
165      IF CAPTURE.FILENAME = '' THEN CAPTURE.FILENAME = 'STACK,CAPTURE'
166      CAPTURE.ID = FIELD(CAPTURE,' ',3)
167      IF CAPTURE.ID = '' THEN CAPTURE.ID = PORT
```

FIG. 5-28 continues.

```
168    OTCL = OTCL[1,Z-1]
169    OPEN CAPTURE.FILENAME TO CAPTURE.FILE THEN
170        CAPTURE.FLAG = 1
171    END ELSE
172        CRT CAPTURE.FILENAME:' is not a file name'
173        OTCL = ''
174        TCL = ''
175        BATCH.FLAG = 0
176        RETURN
177    END
178 END
179 *
180 * - check for user '(P)rocess' or '(B)atch' commands
181 *
182 READ CHK FROM PARAGRAPHS,COMMAND ELSE CHK = ''
183 MPOS = ''
184 LOOP PAR = INDEX(CHK,'%',1) WHILE PAR DO
185   MPOS = OCONV(CHK[PAR+1,1],'MCU')
186   BEGIN CASE
187     CASE MPOS = 'E'
188       CHK = CHK[1,PAR-1]:EXT:CHK[PAR+2,LEN(CHK)]
189     CASE MPOS = 'I'
190       CRT 'ENTER PARAMETER(S) ':
191       INPUT PARAM
192       CHK = CHK[1,PAR-1]:PARAM:CHK[PAR+2,LEN(CHK)]
193     CASE NUM(MPOS)
194       CHK = CHK[1,PAR-1]:FIELD(TCL,' ',MPOS):CHK[PAR+2,LEN(CHK)]
195   END CASE
196 REPEAT
197 IF MPOS # '' THEN EXT = ''
198 *
199 TYPE = CHK[1,1]
200 BEGIN CASE
201   CASE TYPE = 'P'
202   TCL = ''
203   FOR I = 2 TO 100 UNTIL CHK<I>=''
204     ST = CHK<I>
205     IF ST[1,1] # '*' THEN TCL = TCL : ST
206   NEXT I
207   IF EXT # '' THEN TCL = TCL : ' ' : EXT
208   STACK.FLAG = 0
209   GOSUB 100
210   RETURN
211   CASE TYPE = 'B'
212   BATCH = CHK
213   BATCH.FLAG = 1
214   STACK.FLAG = 0
215   RETURN
216 END CASE
217 *
218 *
219 500 * Execute TCL statement
220 *
```

FIG. 5-28 continues.

```
221  IF TRACE.FLAG THEN CRT OTCL
222 *
223  IF COMMAND = 'LOGTO' OR COMMAND = 'OFF' THEN
224     CRT @(-1):
225     CHAIN TCL
226  END
227 *
228  IF CAPTURE.FLAG THEN
229   EXECUTE OTCL CAPTURING CAPTURE.BUFFER RETURNING ERROR
230   WRITE CAPTURE.BUFFER ON CAPTURE.FILE,CAPTURE.ID
231   IF NOT(BATCH.FLAG) THEN
232      CRT CAPTURE.ID:" Saved on File ":CAPTURE.FILENAME
233   END
234   CAPTURE.BUFFER = ''
235  END ELSE
236   EXECUTE OTCL RETURNING ERROR
237  END
238 *
239  CAPTURE.FLAG = 0
240  READ STACK FROM STACK.FILE,STACK.ID ELSE STACK = ''
241 *
242  RETURN
243 *
244 *
245  5000 *
246 *
247  COMMAND = COMMAND[2,LEN(COMMAND)]
248  BEGIN CASE
249   CASE COMMAND[1,1] = 'L'
250     CRT
251     OPTION = '(I,T)'
252     EXECUTE 'COPY STACK ':STACK.ID:' ':OPTION
253   CASE COMMAND[1,1] = 'X'
254     POS = TRIM(COMMAND[2,10])
255     IF POS = '' OR NOT(NUM(POS)) THEN POS = 1
256     TCL = STACK<POS>
257     IF EXT # '' THEN TCL = TCL : ' ' : EXT
258     STACK.FLAG = 0
259     GOSUB 100
260   CASE COMMAND[1,1] = 'T'
261     POS = TRIM(COMMAND[2,10])
262     IF POS = '' OR NOT(NUM(POS)) THEN POS = 1
263     TCL = STACK<POS>
264     STACK = INSERT(STACK,1,0,0,TCL)
265     GOSUB 9000 ;* WRITE THE STACK
266     CRT
267     OPTION = '(I,T)'
268     EXECUTE 'COPY STACK ':STACK.ID:' ':OPTION
269   CASE COMMAND[1,2] = 'DE'
270     POS = TRIM(COMMAND[3,10])
271     IF POS = '' THEN POS = 1
272     IF INDEX(POS,'-',1) THEN
273       POS1 = FIELD(POS,'-',1)
```

FIG. 5-28 continues.

```
274    POS2 = FIELD(POS,'-',2)
275    POS = POS1
276  END ELSE
277    POS2 = POS
278    POS1 = POS
279  END
280  IF NOT(NUM(POS1)) OR NOT(NUM(POS2)) THEN POS1=1;POS2=1
281  PDIF = POS2 - POS1 + 1
282  LOOP UNTIL NOT(PDIF) DO
283    STACK = DELETE(STACK,POS1,0,0)
284    PDIF = PDIF - 1
285  REPEAT
286  GOSUB 9000 ;* WRITE THE STACK
287 CASE COMMAND[1,1] = 'R'
288  COMMAND = OTCL[2,LEN(OTCL)]
289  DEL = OCONV(COMMAND,'MC/A':VM:'MC/N')[1,1]
290  COMMAND = COMMAND[2,LEN(COMMAND)-1]
291  POS = FIELD(COMMAND,DEL,1)
292  IF POS = '' OR NOT(NUM(POS)) THEN POS = 1
293  SRCH = FIELD(COMMAND,DEL,2)
294  REPL = FIELD(COMMAND,DEL,3)
295  LINE = STACK<POS>
296  Z = INDEX(LINE,SRCH,1)
297  IF Z THEN
298    LINE = LINE[1,Z-1]:REPL:LINE[Z+LEN(SRCH),LEN(LINE)]
299    PRINT POS 'R%3':' ':LINE
300    STACK<POS> = LINE
301    GOSUB 9000 ; * WRITE THE STACK
302  END ELSE
303    CRT 'Search string ':SRCH:' cannot be found'
304  END
305 CASE COMMAND[1,1] = 'V'
306  EXECUTE 'COPY ':CAPTURE.FILENAME:' ':CAPTURE.ID:' (I,S,T)'
307 CASE COMMAND = 'E'
308  EXECUTE 'JED STACK ':STACK.ID
309  READ STACK FROM STACK.FILE,STACK.ID ELSE STACK = ''
310 CASE COMMAND[1,1] = 'S'
311  POS = TRIM(COMMAND[2,10])
312  IF POS = '' OR NOT(NUM(POS)) THEN POS = 1
313  TCL = STACK<POS>
314  CRT TCL
315  CRT 'Enter Name':
316  INPUT SNAME
317  IF SNAME # '' THEN
318    WRITE 'P':AM:TCL ON PARAGRAPHS,SNAME
319    CRT "'":SNAME:"'" Saved!"
320  END ELSE
321    CRT 'Abort!'
322  END
323 CASE COMMAND = '?'
324  EXECUTE 'HELP STACKER'
325 CASE COMMAND = '??'
326  CRT 'UCase Flag   :':UC.FLAG
```

FIG. 5-28 continues.

```
327    CRT 'Batch Flag    :':BATCH.FLAG
328    CRT 'Capture Flag :':CAPTURE.FLAG
329    CRT 'Stack Flag   :':STACK.FLAG
330    CRT 'Trace Flag   :':TRACE.FLAG
331    CRT 'Last Error   :':ERROR
332    CRT
333  CASE COMMAND = 'UC'
334    IF UC.FLAG THEN
335      UC.FLAG = 0
336      CRT 'UC Off'
337    END ELSE
338      UC.FLAG = 1
339      CRT 'UC On'
340    END
341  CASE NUM(COMMAND)
342    POS = COMMAND
343    IF POS = '' OR NOT(NUM(POS)) THEN POS = 1
344    TCL = STACK<POS>
345    IF EXT # '' THEN TCL = TCL : ' ' : EXT
346    PROMPT NILL
347    XTCL = TCL
348    CRT PCHAR:TCL:
349    CALL EDLINE(TCL)
350    IF TCL = '' THEN RETURN
351    IF UC.FLAG THEN TCL = OCONV(TCL,'MCU')
352    PROMPT PCHAR
353    IF XTCL = TCL THEN STACK.FLAG = 0
354    GOSUB 100
355  CASE COMMAND = '.E'
356    EXECUTE 'JED ADVBP SHELL'
357  CASE COMMAND = '.B'
358    EXECUTE "BASIC ADVBP SHELL"
359  CASE 1
360    CRT
361    CRT 'STACK COMMAND?'
362 END CASE
363 *
364 RETURN
365 *
366 *
367 9000 * WRITE STACK
368 *
369 EOS = INDEX(STACK,AM,STACK.MAX)
370 IF EOS THEN STACK = STACK[1,EOS-1]
371 WRITE STACK ON STACK.FILE,STACK.ID
372 RETURN
373 *
374 *
375 9500 *
376 *
377 CRT @(-1):WHO
378 CRT TIMEDATE()
379 RETURN
```

FIG. 5-28 continues.

```
380  *
381  *
382  END
```

FIG. 5-28 ends.

The main functions of SHELL are:

- Retrieve the command sentence from either the terminal keyboard or from the next attribute in an active "batch" item. "Batch" items are a list of commands to be EXECUTEd in sequence.

- Process the command. Checks for any special "hard coded" commands. Most of these are specific to the internal "batch" processor.

- Pre-parse the command sentence. Checks for any special extended modifiers and options. This is where additional security measures can be added.

- EXECUTE the command.

SHELL Initialization   The initialization section sets up the program parameters including; the current port number and account name, the default capture parameters (used as a "pipeline" to direct output to any file and item), the main files and the TCL stack.

Please note that there are two command prompt characters used. The first is the colon (:), used for normal interaction. The second is the dollar sign ($), indicating TRACE mode is active. The TRACE mode is a simple debugging feature which displays every command sentence before processing.

The STACK and PARAGRAPH files are the main storage areas. The STACK file is used for the TCL stacks of each port. The PARAGRAPHS file is used to store user-defined "paragraphs" and "batches" containing command sentences for later retrieval and processing.

```
036 OPEN 'STACK' TO STACK.FILE ELSE STOP 201, 'STACK'
037 OPEN 'PARAGRAPHS' TO PARAGRAPHS ELSE STOP 201, 'PARAGRAPHS'
```

The item-id for the stack entry is currently based on the PORT number. Notice that line 039 is commented out. This allows the stack entry to be addressed by the account name and port number. The remaining code retrieves the maximum entries for the STACK.

```
039 *STACK.ID = 'ST*':ACCOUNT:'*':PORT
040 STACK.ID = 'ST*':PORT
041 READ STACK FROM STACK.FILE,STACK.ID ELSE STACK = ''
042 READ STACK.MAX FROM STACK.FILE, 'STACK.MAX' ELSE STACK.MAX = ''
043 IF STACK.MAX = '' OR NOT(NUM(STACK.MAX)) THEN STACK.MAX = 100
```

The MAIN Routine   The main routine retrieves the next command sentence to be processed based on whether or not a "batch" is active. Normally, the command sentence is prompted from the terminal keyboard. An active "batch" causes the command sentence to be retrieved from the next attribute in the "batch" item. BATCH.FLAG not only serves to signal an active "batch," but also as the attribute position pointer for the next command sentence.

```
055  LOOP
056      BATCH.FLAG = BATCH.FLAG + 1
057      TCL = BATCH<BATCH.FLAG>
058      T1 = TCL[1,1]
059  WHILE INDEX(':*',T1,1) AND (T1#'') DO REPEAT
```

The LOOP retrieves the next command sentence and checks for the first character. Lines beginning with ":" or "*" are skipped. The colon indicates a "batch" statement label and the asterisk represents a comment line.

There are two different item types stored in PARAGRAPHS. The first type is a "paragraph" and is stored in the following manner:

```
ID: paragraphname
001 P
002 command sentence
```

Whenever the *paragraphname* is entered at the SHELL command prompt, the stored command sentence is EXECUTEd. The command sentence can be spread across multiple lines, and comments can be included as long as the line begins with an asterisk,"*". A "paragraph" item would look as follows:

```
ID: STAFF.REPORT
001 P
002 * This is a simple STAFF report
003 SORT STAFF
004 BY STATE BY NAME
005 LPTR
```

The second type of item in the PARAGRAPHS file is a "batch." The general form is as follows:

```
ID: batchname
001 B
002 command sentence or paragraphs name
003 command sentence or paragraphs name
004 command sentence or paragraphs name
   .....
```

Each line is a separate command sentence or the name of a "paragraph" item. "Batch" items can include comments, lines beginning with an asterisk, statement labels, lines beginning with a colon, and a variety of other special commands. Here is a sample "batch" item:

```
ID: MAKE.STAFFLIST
001 B
```

```
002 SSELECT STAFF BY STATE BY NAME
003 ONERR 401 STOP
004 SAVE-LIST STAFFLIST
005 GET-LIST STAFFLIST
006 RUN BP PROCESS.STAFF
```

Process a Command This is where the special SHELL commands are checked and processed. The special SHELL commands are:

Command	Description
Dot "."	Stack processing commands
TRACE	Toggles TRACE.FLAG on and off.
END or TCL	Return to normal TCL. This may be password protected
STOP	Stop the current "batch" and return to the standard SHELL prompt
ONERR	Check for an error message from the previously EXECUTEd statement
BRANCH	Set Current BATCH.FLAG pointer to the attribute containing the statement label
DATA	Stack data for the next command in the "batch"
PRINT	Print the literal string following the PRINT command
PRINTER	Toggle the system printer on, off, or close the spooler
PAUSE	Press any key to continue

The dot commands and TRACE are designed to be interactively initiated. The remaining commands are specially suited for the "batch" language. The above commands are but a small subset of the commands which can be added to the SHELL.

```
075 OTCL = TCL
076 TCL = TRIM(TCL)
077 COMMAND = FIELD(TCL,' ',1)
078 BOS = COL2( ) + 1
079 IF NOT(UC.FLAG) THEN
080 COMMAND = OCONV(COMMAND,'MCU')
081 END
082 EXT = TCL[BOS,LEN(TCL)]
```

Before the TCL line is processed, the original is saved in the variable OTCL. OTCL is the string used by the EXECUTE statement. TCL is a "scratch" variable used for statement parsing. Notice that every command line is broken into two parts, the command, COMMAND, and the rest of the line, EXT or extension. The variable EXT is important for the processing of these special commands.

The ONERR "batch" command follows the general form:

ONERR *errmsgid command*

The ONERR "batch" command addresses the EXT as two more entities. First the error number:

```
ENO = FIELD(TCL,' ',2)
```

Then is the variable ENO matches the last ERROR, the remainder of the sentence becomes the entire new command line.

```
IF ENO = ERROR THEN
   TCL = TCL[COL2( )+1,LEN(TCL)]
   GOSUB 100
END
```

The COL2( ) function is a result of the previous FIELD statement. The command, GOSUB 100, recursively calls the command processing routine.

The DATA "batch" command causes the program to perform a DATA statement, using the values in DVAR, built from EXT. EXT may have separate DATA elements delimited by semi-colons, ";". The general form is:

```
DATA element{;element;element..}
```

or

```
DATA element
DATA element
```

...

The entries stacked in a PICK/BASIC DATA statement remain intact until the next INPUT statement.

Any PICK/BASIC command can be emulated as part of the SHELL's "batch" command language. The PRINT "batch" command initiates the PICK/BASIC PRINT statement. EXT provides the string to print. Also, the PRINTER "batch" command checks for an extension identical to the PICK/BASIC statement.

```
PRINTER ON      Initiates the PICK/BASIC code, PRINTER ON.
PRINTER OFF     Initiates PRINTER OFF.
PRINTER CLOSE   Initiates PRINTER CLOSE.
```

The BRANCH "batch" command is used to transfer control to a different statement line in the item. The general form is:

```
BRANCH label
```

Usually, the BRANCH command is used in conjunction with the ONERR command in the following format:

```
nnn SELECT STAFF WITH STATE = "CA"
mmm ONERR 401 BRANCH NOITEMS
```

The statement label in a "batch" begins with a colon and is designated as follows:

```
nnn :NOITEMS
```

If the command sentence has no special commands, the sentence is passed to subroutine 200, to be pre-parsed and EXECUTEd.

```
CASE 1
GOSUB 200
```

Pre-Parse and EXECUTE The first task, before EXECUTE, is to update the command STACK. STACK.FLAG indicates whether the STACK.FILE should be updated. Notice that STACK.FLAG is set to zero when a "batch" is active. This allows only the name to be inserted onto the stack without including every command line within the batch item.

Subroutine 9000 serves as the standard BATCH.FILE update routine.

```
368 9000 * WRITE STACK
369 *
370 EOS = INDEX(STACK,AM,STACK.MAX)
371 IF EOS THEN STACK = STACK[1,EOS – 1]
372 WRITE STACK ON STACK.FILE,STACK.ID
373 RETURN
```

The STACK is truncated at the position of the last attribute addressed by STACK.MAX. This routine efficiently truncates the dynamic array, STACK, using string handling functions rather than looping and performing intrinsic dynamic array DELETE's.

The CAPTURING Redirection Clause Any SHELL command sentence can be appended with a CAPTURING clause in the general form:

```
:commandsentence CAPTURING {filename itemid}
```

If found, the capturing clause is removed from the original command sentence, OTCL, and parsed. CAPTURE.FLAG is set to indicate that the CAPTURING modifier should be used in the EXECUTE phase. The following code determines whether the CAPTURING clause exits:

```
161 Z = INDEX(OTCL,'CAPTURING',1)
```

The CAPTURING phrase is stripped and the target file and item are determined.

```
163   CAPTURE = OTCL[Z,LEN(OTCL)]
164   CAPTURE.FILENAME = FIELD(CAPTURE,' ',2)
      .....
166   CAPTURE.ID = FIELD(CAPTURE,' ',3)
```

If "filename" and "itemid" are not specified, the default values are used.

```
CAPTURE.FILENAME = 'STACK,CAPTURE'
CAPTURE.ID = PORT
```

Before continuing, the CAPTURING clause is removed from the original command sentence.

```
168 OTCL = OTCL[1,Z – 1]
```

BATCH or PARAGRAPH Process Item Check When a "paragraph" is processed, the attributes are concatenated, excluding comments (ST[1,1] # '*',) and a single command sentence is built. This resulting command sentence is parsed by recursively calling the main parse subroutine, 100:

```
201   CASE TYPE = 'P'
202   TCL = ''
203   FOR I = 2 TO 100 UNTIL CHK<I> = ''
204     ST = CHK<I>
205     IF ST[1,1] # '*' THEN TCL = TCL : ST
206   NEXT I
207   IF EXT # '' THEN TCL = TCL : ' ' : EXT
208   STACK.FLAG = 0
209   GOSUB 100
210   RETURN
```

A "batch" simply sets the required flags and returns to the main routine for further processing:

```
211   CASE TYPE = 'B'
212   BATCH = CHK
213   BATCH.FLAG = 1
214   STACK.FLAG = 0
215   RETURN
```

The COMMAND is used as an item-id in the PARAGRAPHS file. If no item is read, the value of the item string, CHK, is null.

```
182 READ CHK FROM PARAGRAPHS,COMMAND ELSE CHK = ''
183 MPOS = ''
184 LOOP PAR = INDEX(CHK,'%',1) WHILE PAR DO

    .....

    ....

196 REPEAT
```

Prior to determining the PARAGRAPHS item type, the percent, "%", function is parsed. This allows variable data to be passed to the "paragraph" and "batch" item. Percent functions address the SHELL command line in the following manner:

%n   Where *n* is the position of the word to retrieve from the command line. The command is at %1.

%I   Prompt for the parameter from the keyboard.

%E   Use the entire extension, EXT, as the plug-in parameter.

Here is a short "paragraph" to allow the entry of other "paragraphs" and "batches."

```
ID: ENTER
```

```
001 P
002 ED PARAGRAPHS %2
```

The %2 reference retrieves the second entry on the SHELL command line. All subsequent "paragraphs" or "batches" can be created or altered by entering the following command line:

```
:ENTER name
```

EXECUTE the Sentence   The main logic of the EXECUTE routine centers on whether the CAPTURE.FLAG is set. If CAPTURE.FLAG is false, the statement is executed in a normal fashion. If the CAPTURE.FLAG is true, the CAPTURING clause is used to redirect the process output into the variable CAPTURE.BUFFER. The CAPTURE.BUFFER is then written to the targeted file and item.

```
228 IF CAPTURE.FLAG THEN
229   EXECUTE OTCL CAPTURING CAPTURE.BUFFER RETURNING ERROR
230   WRITE CAPTURE.BUFFER ON CAPTURE.FILE,CAPTURE.ID
231   IF NOT(BATCH.FLAG) THEN
232      CRT CAPTURE.ID:" Saved on File ":CAPTURE.FILENAME
233   END
234   CAPTURE.BUFFER = ''
235 END ELSE
236   EXECUTE OTCL RETURNING ERROR
237 END
```

Ultimate users beware. The EXECUTE code is far more extensive to emulate this routine. The most difficult logical problem is passing active lists from command to command. This is done by Generic R83 as a matter of fact, but it is not done by Ultimate. (Refer to Chapter 4, "List Processing" for details.)

Command Stack Processor   Subroutine 5000, which processes the stack elements, is initiated by any command beginning with a period or any numeric command. The supported stack commands are:

Command	Description
.L	Lists the STACK entries. This routine EXECUTEs a TCL COPY to the terminal.
.Xn	An immediate EXECUTE of STACK entry n.
.Tn	Place the nth STACK entry at the top of the STACK.
.DE$\{n\{-m\}\}$	Delete STACK entry n or n thru m.
.Rn/srch/repl	Replace the search string, *srch*, with the replace string, *repl*, at the nth STACK entry. This works very much like the standard EDIT replace command.

.E	Edit the STACK. This version uses JET-EDIT, but any editor command can be substituted.
.S*n*	Save the *n*th STACK entry as a "paragraph." This prompts for the "paragraph" name. The command sentence is stored in the PARAGRAPHS file.
.*n* or *n*	Display the *n*th STACK entry. Press Return to EXECUTE or Esc to abort.

Other dot commands:

.V	View the last CAPTURED item.
.?	Help
.??	Show the current flag values.
.UC	Force the entire command sentence to uppercase. This toggles case sensitivity.
..E	EDIT the SHELL program. (Development only!)
..B	Compile the SHELL program. (Development only!)

The .*n* or *n* stack commands allow the user to view the command line before handing it over to the EXECUTE. While viewing the command, the user has the capability to add to, change, or delete any portion of the command line via the external subroutine EDLINE. The Return key EXECUTEs the sentence and the Esc> key clears the command line. The Esc> key works like the Ctl-X in normal TCL.

The EDLINE Program

The EDLINE program is shown in Fig. 5-29. EDLINE allows "word processing" type edit functions on the displayed command sentence.

```
      EDLINE
001 SUBROUTINE EDLINE(STRING)
002 * Word Processing-Like String Edit Subroutine
003 * HER
004 * 10/01/88
005 *
006 EQU BELL        TO CHAR(7)
007 EQU BACKSPACE   TO CHAR(8)
008 EQU TAB         TO CHAR(9)
009 EQU LF          TO CHAR(10)
010 EQU CR          TO CHAR(13)
011 EQU ESC         TO CHAR(251)
012 EQU ESCC        TO CHAR(27)
013 EQU CTLX        TO CHAR(24)
014 EQU SP          TO CHAR(32)
015 EQU DEL         TO CHAR(127)
```

FIG. 5-29. The EDLINE program listing (continues).

```
016 EQU AM           TO CHAR(254)
017 EQU VM           TO CHAR(253)
018 EQU SVM          TO CHAR(252)
019 *
020 EQU HOME    TO CHAR(1)
021 EQU BAKKEY  TO CHAR(2)
022 EQU CLREOL  TO CHAR(3)
023 EQU DELKEY  TO CHAR(4)
024 EQU POSEOL  TO CHAR(5)
025 EQU FWDKEY  TO CHAR(6)
026 EQU NWORD   TO CHAR(14)
027 EQU PWORD   TO CHAR(16)
028 EQU INSSPC  TO CHAR(15)
029 EQU REPKEY  TO CHAR(18)
030 EQU TPOS    TO CHAR(26)
031 *
032 EQU MAXLENGTH TO 250
033 *
034 EOL = @(-4)
035 *
036 INSFLAG = 0
037 REPFLAG = 1
038 EXIT    = 0
039 DONE    = 0
040 *
041 ECHO OFF
042 POS = LEN(STRING)+1
043 MAXPOS = POS
044 LOOP
045   IN SKEY
046   KEY = CHAR(SKEY)
047   BEGIN CASE
048     CASE KEY = BACKSPACE OR KEY = BAKKEY
049       IF POS>1 THEN
050         POS=POS-1
051         CRT BACKSPACE:
052       END
053     CASE KEY = FWDKEY
054       CRT STRING[POS,1]:
055       IF POS<MAXPOS THEN POS = POS+1 ELSE CRT BELL:
056     CASE KEY = NWORD
057       STRING2 = STRING[POS,MAXLENGTH]
058       DELIM = OCONV(STRING2,'MC/N':VM:'MC/A')[1,1]
059       IF DELIM#'' THEN
060         OFFSET = INDEX(STRING2,DELIM,1)
061         POS = POS + OFFSET
062         CRT STRING2[1,OFFSET]:
063       END
064     CASE KEY = PWORD
065       TESTPOS = POS
066       LOOP
067         STRING1 = STRING[1,TESTPOS-1]
068         PCHAR   = STRING[TESTPOS-1,1]
```

FIG. 5-29 continues.

```
069             DELIM = OCONV(STRING1,'MC/N':VM:'MC/A')
070             DELIM = DELIM[LEN(DELIM),1]
071           UNTIL PCHAR#DELIM OR DELIM = '' DO
072             IF TESTPOS THEN TESTPOS=TESTPOS-1
073           REPEAT
074           IF DELIM # '' THEN
075             MAXDELIM = COUNT(STRING1,DELIM)
076             OFFSET = (POS-INDEX(STRING1,DELIM,MAXDELIM)) - 1
077             POS = POS - OFFSET
078             CRT STR(BACKSPACE,OFFSET):
079           END ELSE
080             CRT STR(BACKSPACE,POS-1):
081             POS = 1
082           END
083         CASE KEY = HOME
084           CRT STR(BACKSPACE,POS-1):
085           POS = 1
086         CASE KEY = POSEOL
087           CRT STR(BACKSPACE,POS-1):STRING:EOL:
088           POS = MAXPOS
089         CASE KEY = INSSPC
090           STRING1 = STRING[1,POS-1]
091           STRING2 = ' ':STRING[POS,MAXLENGTH]
092           STRING = STRING1:STRING2
093           CRT STRING2:EOL:STR(BACKSPACE,LEN(STRING2)):
094           MAXPOS = MAXPOS+1
095         CASE KEY = DELKEY OR KEY = DEL
096           STRING1 = STRING[1,POS-1]
097           STRING2 = STRING[POS+1,MAXLENGTH]
098           STRING = STRING1:STRING2
099           CRT STRING2:EOL:STR(BACKSPACE,LEN(STRING2)):
100           IF MAXPOS>1 THEN MAXPOS = MAXPOS-1
101         CASE KEY = TPOS
102           IF POS<MAXPOS-1 THEN
103             CHA21   = STRING[POS+1,1]:STRING[POS,1]
104             STRING = STRING[1,POS-1]:CHA21:STRING[POS+2,MAXLENGTH]
105             CRT CHA21:STR(BACKSPACE,2):
106           END
107         CASE KEY = CLREOL
108           STRING = STRING[1,POS-1]
109           MAXPOS=POS
110           CRT EOL:
111         CASE KEY = REPKEY
112           INSFLAG = NOT(INSFLAG)
113           REPFLAG = NOT(REPFLAG)
114         CASE INDEX(ESC:ESCC:CTLX,KEY,1)
115           EXIT = 1
116         CASE INDEX(CR:LF:TAB,KEY,1)
117           DONE = 1
118         CASE SKEY<32 OR SKEY>126
119           CRT BELL:
120         CASE REPFLAG
121           STRING1 = STRING[1,POS-1]
```

FIG. 5-29 continues.

```
122          STRING = STRING1:KEY:STRING[POS+1,MAXLENGTH]
123          POS = POS + 1
124          IF POS>MAXPOS THEN MAXPOS = POS
125          CRT KEY:
126       CASE INSFLAG
127          STRING1 = STRING[1,POS-1]
128          STRING2 = KEY:STRING[POS,MAXLENGTH]
129          STRING = STRING1:STRING2
130          POS = POS + 1
131          MAXPOS = MAXPOS + 1
132          CRT STRING2:EOL:STR(BACKSPACE,LEN(STRING2)-1):
133      END CASE
134 UNTIL EXIT OR DONE DO REPEAT
135 ECHO ON
136 IF EXIT THEN
137     CRT CR:EOL:
138     STRING = ''
139 END ELSE CRT
140 RETURN
141 *
142 END
```

FIG. 5-29 ends.

The EDLINE subroutine is initiated from the SHELL program by the following code:

```
349   CRT PCHAR:TCL:
350   CALL EDLINE(TCL)
351   IF TCL = '' THEN RETURN
```

The prompt character and the TCL line are displayed prior to calling the EDLINE routine. This is important, because the cursor must be sitting after the last character of the string before initiating EDLINE.

EDLINE contains no absolute cursor positioning. All cursor positioning is relative to the current screen position and is implemented by using cursor back and forward controls. Control characters—any character below decimal 32—are used for cursor positioning and line editing. Any other character is assumed to be text to be used, replaced, or inserted. The variables INSFLAG and REPFLAG indicate the current mode. Notice that REFLAG is initialized as the active default. The relative position in the string is determined by the following code:

```
042 POS = LEN(STRING) + 1
043 MAXPOS = POS
```

The special characters are defined as EQUATES in the initialization section of the program. However, many of these characters cannot be captured by the standard PICK/BASIC INPUT statement. These "shadow" characters include backspace, CHAR(8), carriage return, CHAR(13), and line feed, CHAR(10).

As of Pick R83 Release 2.2, a new INPUT statement is available. This is the PICK/BASIC IN statement in the general form:

IN *variable*

IN accepts a single character from the type ahead buffer, without stripping any control characters. Therefore, all the possible characters generated from an ASCII keyboard can be accepted. IN does one more thing: The characters are converted to their decimal equivalents. For example, carriage return is converted to a decimal 13. A similar feature is available on other enhanced R83 machines in the form:

    INPUT *variable*,0

This is an extension to the standard INPUT statement, except that the zero length indicates a single unedited character. This command retains the character in ASCII format, and does not convert it to the decimal equivalent. The only exceptions are Ctl-S, X-ON, and Ctl-Q, X-OFF.

The main program logic is as follows:

```
044 LOOP
045    IN SX
046    X = CHAR(SX)
047    BEGIN CASE
       ...
       Check for special characters
       ...
133    END CASE
134 UNTIL EXIT OR DONE DO REPEAT
```

The combination of lines 045 and 046 provide the same result as:

    INPUT X,0

There are three parts to the logic for any accepted character. First, if the command modifies the string contents, the string must be rebuilt. The string editing functions are performed using the standard methods of string extract, ([e), and concatenation, (:). Second, the current position, POS, and the maximum position, MAXPOS must be determined. The third and trickiest part is making sure that the cursor is at the correct position on the screen. The control key functions are:

Keys	*Keywords*	*Function/Description*
Backspace or Ctl-B	BACKSPACE or BACKKEY	*Cursor back.* Positions the cursor back one character. This is non-destructive.
Ctl-F	FWDKEY	*Cursor forward.* Positions the cursor one character forward.
Ctl-N	NWORD	*Next word.* Positions the cursor to the beginning of the next word.
Ctl-P	PWORD	*Previous word.* Positions the cursor to the beginning of the previous word.
Ctl-A	HOME	*Front of string.* Positions the cursor to the first character in the string.

Ctl-E	POSEOL	*End of string*. Positions the cursor to the end of the string.
Ctl-O	INSSPC	*Insert a space*. Opens the string by inserting a single space before the current cursor position.
Ctl-D or DEL key	DELKEY or DEL	*Delete a character*. Deletes a single character at the current cursor position.
Ctl-Z	TPOS	*Transpose*. Transposes the character at the current cursor position with the character immediately following.
Ctl-C	CLREOL	*Clear end of line*. Clears the string from the cursor position to the end.
Ctl-R	REPKEY	*Replace/Insert*. Toggles typeover and insert modes.
Ctl-X	ESC or ESCC or CTLX	*Abort*. Clears the string and aborts the edit.
Return or Line Feed	CR or LF or TAB	*Accept or Enter*. Passes the edited string back to the calling program.

The remaining CASEs are taken if none of the above control characters are present. Any other characters below CHAR(32) or above CHAR(126) are not accepted. Any other character is added onto the string depending on whether the REPFLAG or INSFLAG is currently active.

EDLINE can be used as an alternative to the INPUT statement for data entry screens so that entire lines do not have to be re-entered during an edit session. (See the INEDIT subroutine in Chapter 7, "Dictionary Driven Data Entry.")

6

Access Programming

ACCESS AND PICK/BASIC SHOULD PLAY SYMBIOTIC ROLES IN THE DEVELOPMENT OF AN application. Both ACCESS and PICK/BASIC have their strengths and weaknesses. However, beyond the ability to generate simple reports with ACCESS, its strengths aren't as obvious as its apparent weaknesses. Apparent is a good word because many of the advanced functions that are considered beyond ACCESS are not impossible. They are just not well documented.

Most programmers can appreciate the strengths of PICK/BASIC more easily than those of ACCESS because they are more likely to have been exposed to similar procedural languages in school or through other work experience. Many of the effective ACCESS programmers have been self taught or have found a patient guru.

The purpose of this chapter is to serve as that guru by explaining a bit more about what to be aware of when programming with ACCESS and by introducing techniques that should help make ACCESS a more prominent player in any application.

Application programming in a dictionary-driven non-procedural language, such as ACCESS, is not the same as programming with a procedural language such as PICK/BASIC, PROC or Assembler. *Procedural languages* allow the step-by-step control of the program. Any modifications or enhancements can be made at any position within the logical flow. Non-procedural languages require that specialized tasks be indicated in parameter tables, (dictionary items), which are activated at pre-determined points in the procedural flow. Parameter placement is as important as parameter contents. Therefore, effective dictionary programming requires some familiarity with the logical flow of ACCESS.

There are three main processing stages within ACCESS; 1) statement parsing and compilation, 2) data selection and sorting, and 3) data output.

The *compilation phase* converts the modifying clauses and data references used in the command sentence into a table of parameters which are interpreted during ACCESS runtime. Certain conversions and correlatives are partially evaluated at compilation. For example, the file name in a file translate conversion, (Tfile;option;;amc) is converted to the file base, modulo and separation. ACCESS effectively "opens" the file before runtime. The runtime tables can be displayed before processing by using the (Y) option on the command sentence. Try it and see.

The *data selection phase* walks through every frame in the specified file, building a list of item-ids based on the selection criteria. Once this list is assembled, it is sorted according to the sequence clause used in the ACCESS sentence.

The *print phase* performs all output conversions as it moves the sequenced data to the specified output device.

During each of these stages, the data is itself transformed between three states; 1) Stored format, 2) internal format, and 3) external format. *Stored data* is just as it implies, the format in which the data actually resides in the item. *Internal format data* is the form of the data during the selection process. *Externally formatted data* is how the data appears at print time.

Figure 6-1 demonstrates the active roles that correlatives and conversions in attributes 007 and 008 of the dictionary item play in the ACCESS process flow.

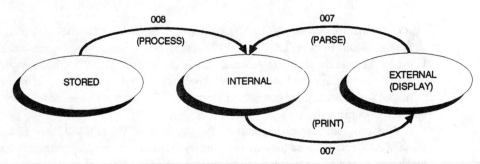

FIG. 6-1. Three states of the ACCESS process flow.

The contents of attribute 008 are processed during data selection. Inclusion of items at selection time based on the results of processing by correlatives or conversions, dictates their placement in attribute 008 of the dictionary item.

Attribute 007 is used at two separate times during ACCESS processing. The first time occurs during the parsing and compilation of the ACCESS sentence. Externally formatted data specified in a WITH clause is input converted so that it can be used for comparison during selection. Attribute 007 is used again at print time to convert the selected input converted data to its output format.

It is important for the programmer to keep these actions straight. For instance, correct results from break line totals cannot be attained unless the calculations are performed at print time and, therefore, specified in attribute 007.

ORGANIZING DICTIONARIES

The first and probably the most important task of ACCESS programming is the layout of the file dictionary. The dictionary should serve as the file "bible." It should clearly define all the data elements contained within or extrapolated from the data file.

The *dictionary* is the repository of all the data definition items which are used by a multitude of different ACCESS output reports and selection criteria. Requirements for new report formats are easily satisfied by cloning existing dictionary items and making the appropriate modifications. For example, if a report format requires the ADDRESS to be a field column 15 characters long instead of 25 characters long, the old dictionary item is copied to a new item under a slightly different item-id and then the length attribute (010), is altered. A dictionary item like ADDRESS may have any number of synonyms named ADDRESS1 thru ADDRESS*N*. This kind of proliferation of dictionary items creates a potential dictionary maintenance nightmare.

Dictionary Item Typing

Dictionary data definition items are typed at the system level, (attribute 001,) in three ways, A, S, or X. The *A type* is supposed to mean an attribute definition and the *S type* is supposed to be a synonym. However, whether an A or an S is used is inconsequential to the operating system. A and S data definitions are performed in the same way. As a result, most dictionaries are a hodgepodge of A's and S's which bear no rhyme or reason.

The only unique type is the X. An *X type* is treated as a protected attribute. Any attempt to request an X type results in an abort of the ACCESS process with the ERRMSG:

[E5] THE WORD 'data def name' IS ILLEGAL.

Any distinction between A and S typed definition items must be self-imposed. The following is a suggested standard for organizing file dictionaries based on the three major definition uses:

- *Real* Dictionary items that describe data as it physically exists at an attribute location within an item. This data may be in internal form, such as data or time, but is a whole entity without any string, arithmetic, or logical processing.

- *Synonym* Dictionary items that redefine existing real definitions using alternative output conversions and print formatting.

- *Virtual* Data that is not physically stored in the file, but is generated as a result of any string, arithmetic, or logical process.

Real Data Definitions

Real types are the only dictionary data definition items that use the A type code in attribute 001. As a standard policy, any dictionary should have a finite number of A's, one for each attribute. This makes it easier to distinguish between the physical and virtual data and subsequently assign unused attributes for new data fields.

Figure 6-2 is the suggested layout of an A type definition. Each attribute line is presented along with its default definition name as it exists in an account's master dictionary. Each A type contains only the bare bones of a definition. Conversions are limited to those that translate for readability data which is stored in internal format. The justification and length define the default values.

000 Itemid	Must clearly define the data.
001 D/CODE	Use an A.
002 A/AMC	Must be the attribute number.
003 S/NAME	Optional Column Heading
004 S/AMC	Optional Multivalue Association
005	Null
006	Null
007 F/CONV	SIMPLE Conversion (MR, ML, MT, D)
008 F/CORR	Null
009 V/TYP	Justification of field in report L - Left R- Right T - Text description U - Unconditional left
010 V/LEN	Maximum length of field

FIG. 6-2. Real data definition item layout.

The multivalue association is optional because it is fairly ineffectual in most cases. However, it is sometimes a good idea to specify controlling and dependent associations for the purposes of documentation alone.

Synonym and Virtual Definitions

Any data definition that is an alternate form for an existing definition, or generates virtual data should be created as an S definition type, as shown in Fig. 6-3.

Although all synonym and virtual definition items are S types, it is important to be able to further distinguish between simple synonyms and complex virtual definitions. This can be accomplished by extending the type field by adding a second value in the following manner:

001 S]extension

The right bracket (]) represents a value mark. This is an undocumented feature that seems

001 D/CODE	Should be an 'S'.	
002 A/AMC	The synonym attribute number or a 'dummy' attribute if a correlative is controlling output.	
003 S/NAME	Column Heading or data description.	
004 S/AMC	Multivalue Association.	
005	Null	
006	Null	
007 F/CONV	Print time conversion.	
008 F/CORR	Process time correlative.	
009 V/TYP	Justification of field in report. L - Left R - Right T - Text description U - Unconditional left	
010 V/LEN	Maximum length of field.	

FIG. 6-3. Synonym and Virtual data definition item layout.

to work on all implementations. The indicator "extension" can be any alphanumeric string. For this case, consider it to be a single alpha character as follows:

S   A true synonym
V   A virtual field
F   A virtual function used recursively in another correlative but never actually requested.
L   Logical comparison

Standards for the extension mnemonics can be quite varied but should be kept consistent within an application.

The following is a sample ACCESS statement to generate a report of the dictionary of any file which follows the above rules.

```
SORT DICT filename BY D/CODE BY A/AMC.....
... BREAK-ON D/CODE A/AMC F/CONV F/CORR V/TYP V/LEN
```

Attributes 007 and 008 are not the only positions where the placement of values can use the nuances of the ACCESS process flow. Attribute 002 is normally reserved for the amc count which extracts the addressed attribute from the source item. Virtual dictionary data definition items which derive data values from correlatives, override the attribute 002 amc indicator. For that reason, many definition items use a 0 or a dummy amc count, 99, in attribute 002.

However, attribute 002 does not only indicate the source attribute position, but also the data position in the "work item." As data is sampled and then prepared for printing, the output fields are placed in a temporary storage string or "work item." The amc value in attribute 002 dictates the position that the output field is placed in the string. Therefore, a dummy entry of 99 forces the system to pad to attribute 99 in the work item. Keep this in mind. Controlling the attribute position in work item is important when performing algebraic functions on break line values—a subject that is covered in more detail later in this chapter.

THE ALGEBRAIC CORRELATIVE

The discussion of ACCESS correlatives and conversions in this text centers around the use of the A correlative. The *A* or *Algebraic correlative* allows arithmetic, logical or string manipulation to be specified in an algebraic format.

There seems to be a disagreement as to whether the F correlative is preferable over the A correlative. The *F* or *Function correlative* requires that all processing be indicated in a stack oriented manner. Unfortunately, not every implementation handles the stack in the same manner. Some use postfixed Polish notation while others require "vanilla" Polish. Complex statements can get quite large and extremely unsupportable. More often than not, the programmer who spends hours writing a complex F correlative can forget what was done within a few weeks.

One argument against the A correlative is that it is slow compared to the F correlative. Time to put the record straight. The A correlative is a high level way of specifying an F correlative. During the ACCESS statement compilation, the A correlative is converted into an equivalent F correlative. ACCESS runtime is using the resultant F correlative. This can be verified by using the (Y) option in the ACCESS sentence. Therefore, the only extra time involved is at parse and compilation. This might add 3 seconds to an hour run. Big Deal.

Algebraic correlatives are easier to read and subsequently enhance. This makes support easier and thereby increases the efficiency of application maintenance. In addition, A correlatives can use recursive, symbolic references to other definition items allowing complex functions to be specified modularly rather than in long, never-ending structures.

Expressions in an algebraic correlative follow the similar rules of expressions used in PICK/BASIC. The general form is as follows:

A{;}*expression*

The semi-colon (;) is optional. Any expression can be a single operand or a compound algebraic formula which is used to perform an arithmetic, logical or string function. The valid *operands* are:

Operand	*Description*
amc	A numeric attribute reference. This is any valid amc reference which is usually found in attribute 002 of the definition item.
"literal"	Any literal alpha or numeric string.

N(datadef)	A recursive reference to any valid data definition item. The returned value is a result of attribute 008 of "datadef." Any conversions or correlatives in attribute 007 of "datadef" are not performed.
D	Internal System Date
T	Internal System Time
NB	Break level number. Break levels have a maximum value of 255.
ND	Number of detail lines leading up to the break. This information is available only at print time and, therefore, must be specified in attribute 007.
NI	Sequential item number being referenced.
NV	Value mark count being referenced.
NS	Sub-value mark count being referenced.

The amc designation in attribute 002 or within a correlative has a couple of special values. These special values are:

9999	The length of the item in bytes.
9998	A sequential item counter.

The amc 9999 generates the entire item length, excluding the item terminating segment mark. This value can be found in the default data definitions in an account's master dictionary under the item-ids *A9999 and SIZE. The amc 9998 keeps track of the running count of items processed in ACCESS. The default item *A9998 can be found in any account's master dictionary.

Arithmetic Expressions

The following are the valid arithmetic operators:

- +   add
- −   subtract
- *   multiply
- /   divide

Operator precedence in arithmetic expressions is similar to the precedence used in PICK/BASIC. Multiply and divide have precedence over addition and subtraction. Expressions are evaluated from left to right. However, to eliminate any ambiguities, parentheses can be used to force precedence in any arithmetic, logical or string expression.

Consider a file called STAFF, which stores general information about each staff member, including their date of birth (DOB). Figure 6-4 is an example of an arithmetic expression which calculates a staff member's age based on the date of birth. The number of days old is determined by:

D − N(DOB)

The recursive reference N(DOB) refers to the DOB definition item illustrated in Fig. 6-4.

The virtual definition item:

```
ID: AGE
001 S]V
002 00
003
004
005
006
007
008 A;((D-N(DOB))*"100")/"36525"
009 R
010 4
```

FIG. 6-4. Age calculation correlative.

The real DOB item referenced above:

```
ID: DOB
001 A
002 8
003
004
005
006
007 D2/
008
009 R
010 10
```

DOB, date of birth, addresses the internally formatted date kept in attribute 8 of the data item. The output conversion residing in attribute 007 of the definition item, DOB, is used at print time only and is not included as a functional step in the correlative.

Arithmetic calculation in ACCESS can only be performed on integers. Similarly, the result of any calculation is an integer value. Therefore, it is important to scale numbers by factors of 10 to ensure "decimal" precision. The result can be masked on output (MRn) to produce the correct decimal value.

In the AGE calculation, the number of days must be divided by the total number of days in a year, 365.25. The days in the year must be scaled by 100 to produce the integer value 36525. Since the denominator is scaled by a factor of 100, so must the numerator. Hence, the days alive is multiplied by the constant "100":

(D − N(DOB))*"100"

The final result is the integer value of years.

At this point it is helpful to demonstrate the (Y) option "just to prove a point." That is, A correlatives are no slower during processing than are F correlatives. Consider the following sentence:

LIST STAFF DOB (Y)

The display of the parsed version of the definition item DOB reveals the equivalent F correlative in use during runtime.

    F;D;8; – ;"100";*;"36525";/

A simple looking recursive A correlative could very easily result in a 10 line F correlative. It's a lot easier to let the system figure out the correlative.

Arithmetic Functions

The A correlative can also be used to perform the following arithmetic functions.

The remainder function   R(*expression1,expression2*)   This generates a remainder of the division of *expression1* by *expression2*. Either expression can be a single operand or a complex expression. However, the results of these expressions must be integer numerics.

The summation of multivalues   S(*expression*)   The *expression* targets any multivalued attribute and the function, S, sums all the values in the attribute. Again, the multivalued data or the results of the complex expression must be numeric.

Logical Expressions

Algebraic correlatives can also contain logical (Boolean) expressions. The logical operators are:

    =   equal
    #   not equal
    >   greater than
    <   less than
    > =   greater than or equal to
    < =   less than or equal to

The rules for the use of logical operators in ACCESS is similar to the rules in PICK/ BASIC. Some implementations allow these operators to be used in conditional IF.. THEN..ELSE statements in the A correlative. However, this is not consistent and not wholly required. There are ways to do quite sophisticated conditional logic by specifying pure Boolean algebraic expressions. The simple format is:

    A;*operand1* logicaloperator *operand2*

There are no embedded spaces in the command. Spaces are shown for readability. *Operand1* is compared to *Operand2*. If the comparison is true, the value of the expression is a 1. If the comparison is false, the value of the expression is 0. For example:

    A;N(AGE) > = "65"

The expression above compares the value of AGE to the literal numeric value 65. If age is greater than or equal to 65, then the expression evaluates as true, resulting in a value of 1.

```
ID: ELIGIBLE.FOR.RETIREMENT
001 S
002 0
003
004
005                              FIG. 6-5. Simple logical expression.
006
007
008 A;N(AGE)>"65"
009 R
010 1
```

If the age is less than 65, then the expression evaluates as false, resulting in a value of 0.
The above correlative can be used in a definition item as illustrated in Fig. 6-5.

This definition can be considered a logical phrase and used in an ACCESS sentence
as follows:

LIST STAFF IF ELIGIBLE.FOR.RETIREMENT = "1"

The = "1" must be used because the result is either a 1 or a 0, both of which are considered non-null values. Being able to say,

LIST STAFF IF ELIGIBLE.FOR.RETIREMENT

requires that the result is either null or non-null. See the Section entitled "Logical Conversions" for more information.

The logical connectives, AND and OR, are not available in the A correlative. Therefore, how can AND and OR conditions be emulated? Easily, by substituting the corresponding arithmetic operators, + and *.

+   represents OR
*   represents AND

For those who have taken Boolean Algebra, these operators are the standard indicators for
the logical connectives. The point to remember is that *0 is considered false and any other
positive integer is considered true*. Figure 6-6 shows a couple of simple truth tables for
OR and AND using the corresponding arithmetic operators. If eligibility for retirement is

```
OR
1     +     1     =     2 true
0     +     1     =     1 true
1     +     0     =     1 true
0     +     0     =     0 false
```

FIG. 6-6. Truth table using arithmetic connectives.

```
AND
1     *     1     =     1 true
0     *     1     =     0 false
1     *     0     =     0 false
0     *     0     =     0 false
```

250

not only based on N(AGE),but also N(SEX), (please no comments on discrimination), then the logical expression can be expressed as follows:

A;((N(SEX) = "M")*(N(AGE) > = "65")) + ((N(SEX) = "F")*(N(AGE) > = "60"))

This states that eligibility for males is 65 and up, while eligibility for females is 60 and up. Notice the grouping by parentheses of the logical expressions. The first half is true if the N(SEX) is male *and* the N(AGE) is greater than or equal to 65.

Conditional:

((N(SEX) = "M")*(N(AGE) > = "65"))

The second half is true if the N(SEX) is female *and* the age is greater than or equal to 60.

Condition2:

((N(SEX) = "F")*(N(AGE) > = "60"))

The first condition is ORed with the second condition.

condition1 + condition2

More complex Boolean expressions can be written in the abovemanner.

IF..THEN..ELSE Statements

Many of the implementations allow an IF..THEN..ELSE statement in an A correlative. The general form is:

A;IF *logical expression* THEN *expression* ELSE *expression*

The *logical expression* is any combination of operands and logical operators as described above. For example:

A;IF N(AGE) > "65" THEN "RETIRE" ELSE "KEEP"

If the age of the employee exceeds 65, then print RETIRE. If not, print KEEP. These are literal strings, but any valid expression can be used.

Concatenation

The A correlative can be used to build compound output strings or to extract substrings from any data string. The concatenation operator is a colon.

: *concatenation*

Figure 6-7 is an example of concatenation to build a virtual field using the CITY, STATE, and ZIP definitions in the dictionary of STAFF.

Any element used in concatenation can be the result of another compound expression. For example:

A;"The age of ":N(NAME):" is ":((D − N(DOB))*"100")/"36525"

Concatenation has the lowest precedence of all the operators. Arithmetic and logical expressions are evaluated prior to the final concatenation.

```
ID: CSZ
001 S]V
002 0
003
004
005                                    FIG. 6-7. Correlative string concatenation.
006
007
008 A;N(CITY):", ":N(STATE):" ":N(ZIP)
009 L
010 35
```

String Extraction

Substrings can be extracted from source strings by using the following general form:

expression[*expression1*,*expression2*]

The results of *expression1* and *expression2* must be numeric. *Expression1* is the beginning columnar position of the extract and *expression2* is the length of the extract. For example, if a field named N(PHONE) is always 10 digits, then the area code can be extracted as illustrated in Fig. 6-8. When the beginning and ending expressions are constants, as in this case, it is just as easy to use the text extract conversion, (Tbeg,len) instead:

```
008 A;N(PHONE)(T1,3)
```

```
ID: AREA.CODE
001 S]V
002 0
003
004
005                                    FIG. 6-8. Substring extraction.
006
007
008 A;N(PHONE)["1","3"]
009 R
010 3
```

Logical String Extraction

In some convoluted and strange way, the string extraction function can be used in conjunction with logical statements to generate an output string based on a logical comparison. The basis for how this works is dependent on the fact that any string of zero length is a null string. For example:

string["1","0"]

is a null string. A general form can be indicated as follows:

expression["1",length*logical]

When the result of the indicator "logical" is true, 1, the length expression remains intact. If the logical comparison is false, 0, then the length becomes zero and the result is a null string. For example, in the following correlative, the word "RETIRE" is generated based on whether the AGE is greater than or equal to "65."

A;"RETIRE"["1","6"*(N(AGE)>="65")]

The decision on whether to use the word "RETIRE" or "KEEP" can be made by concatenating two mutually exclusive conditions as follows:

A;"RETIRE"["1","6"*(N(AGE)>="65")]:"KEEP"]"1","4"*(N(AGE)<"65")]

Each side of the concatenation operator is "balanced." If the AGE is greater than or equal to "65" then the string "KEEP" is reduced to a null string and vice versa. Note, the string modified does not have to be a literal. It can be any valid expression.

Using Conversions in Correlatives

The results of an expression can be modified by passing it through any valid list of conversions in the following format:

A;*expression*(conv]conv]...)

The right bracket (]) represents a value mark. The result of this expression can be used as an element in any other compound algebraic expression. These are known as *nuclear tokens* in a similar fashion as in PICK/BASIC.

Consider the following example of one possible compound expression. In this case, the name field in attribute 1 of the data item follows the following format:

001 *lastname, firstname*

The attribute is addressed by the real data definition NAME. The full name can be expressed as a correlative which concatenates the last name to the end of the first name. The group extract conversion (G) is used to isolate the first and last names so that the positions can be changed. An example is shown in Fig. 6-9.

```
ID: NAME              ID: FULL.NAME
001 A                 001 S]V
002 1                 002 0
003
004
005
006
007
008                   008 A;N(NAME)(G1 1):" ":N(NAME)(G0,1)
009 L                 009 L
010 25                010 25
```

FIG. 6-9. Using conversions in complex correlative expressions.

Multivalued conversion lists can be used to perform multiple functions on a targeted attribute. The following correlative expression extracts the prefix from the PHONE field, and then uses the code to lookup the map coordinates of the phone number. These coordinates are kept in the first attribute of the items in the hypothetical code file called PRE-FIXES.

    A;N(PHONE)(T4,3]TPREFIXES;X;;1)

The text extract conversion, T4,3, addresses the prefix code and the results are then passed through the file translate conversion, TPREFIXES;X;;1.

String Output Formatting

The mask left or mask right, (ML or MR), output conversions prove quite useful for special formatting of compound output strings. A fixed length record can be generated through ACCESS by combining the functions of concatenation and output masking within an A correlative.

The following example demonstrates a trick that can be used to effectively override the output restrictions of ACCESS columnar reports. Normally, ACCESS columnar output is restricted to a single output value per column. However, a report may have page width restrictions, or simply must follow a specific output format that requires multiple fields to be placed in a single column. For example, the output requirements for a custom report of the STAFF file must follow the following format:

Column1	Column2
Full Name	Date of birth
Address	Age
City, State, Zip	Salary

Assume that each of these fields is previously defined using the definition item-ids:

Column1	Column2
FULL.NAME	DOB
ADDRESS	AGE
CSZ	SALARY

To meet the above output specifications, two separate virtual data definitions must be created. One for column 1 and one for column 2. These data definition items are shown in Fig. 6-10.

In the first column, COL1, each element of the concatenated string is a fixed length in a field of 30 characters. This produces a 90-character string. Pay attention to attributes 009 and 010, which define the output column characteristics as left justified in a field of 30 characters. *Left justification* automatically wraps to the next line those strings that are larger than the max length indicated in attribute 010. This effectively stacks the output, each field above the next.

The second column, COL2, deals with three numeric values. Hence the right justification throughout. The final output follows the same format as described above, except that the final width of each line is 12 characters. The SALARY field is the only difference.

```
ID: COL1
001 S]V
002 0
003 Column1
004
005
006
007
008 A;N(FULL.NAME)(ML#30):N(ADDRESS)(ML#30):N(CSZ)(ML#30)
009 L
010 30

ID: COL2
001 S]V
002 0
003 Column2
004
005
006
007
008 A;N(DOB)(MR#12):N(AGE)(MR#12):N(SALARY)(MR2,$#12)
009 L
010 12
```

FIG. 6-10. *String output formatting correlatives.*

The SALARY is stored with two implied decimals. The output mask takes advantage of the decimal scaling parameters available in the output mask.

LOGICAL CONVERSIONS

Not only may conversions be used to perform output formatting and string manipulation, but also to make logical decisions. The following are a group of conversions that test the data field being passed through the conversion. If the field matches the requirements of the conversion, then the field remains intact. On the other hand, if the field does not meet the requirements of the logical conversion, then the output is null.

Within the selection clause of an ACCESS command sentence, any dictionary data definition can be tested for a true condition, a non-null string, in the following manner:

WITH *datadef*

There is no logical operator or data value required in this clause. This is equivalent to saying:

WITH *datadef* # ''

A false or null string condition can be tested with either of the following clauses:

WITHOUT *datadef*
WITH NO *datadef*

Please note that the connective word IF is a synonym to the word WITH. Therefore, the existance of a field can be tested with the phrase:

> IF *datadef*

This opens up a wide range of possibilities for creating logical phrases as definition items. Logical phrases test for the state of the data rather than generate formatted output and eliminate the need for the sometimes confusing WITH..AND and WITH..OR structures in the ACCESS sentence.

Pattern Matching

The task of data pattern matching is traditionally part and parcel of the MATCHES operator within a PICK/BASIC program. This is no longer the only case where a pattern match is available or useful. The format for the pattern matching correlative is:

> P(*match*)[;(*match*);..]

The indicator "match" is a pattern match string which follows the same format as match strings in PICK/BASIC. Semi-colons indicate an OR condition. The data is passed through intact if it matches any of the match strings. The match operators are:

Operator	Description
*n*N	Match "n" numeric characters
*n*A	Match "n" alpha characters
*n*X	Match "n" alphanumeric characters
'literal'	Match any quoted literal string.

As in PICK/BASIC, if "N" is a zero (0) then the match is for any number of characters.

NOTE: The pattern match conversion must be used a stand-alone. It cannot be used to modify any expression in a correlative.

Figure 6-11 is a simple dictionary item that tests for a numeric item-id. This might prove handy when trying to select only those dictionary items used for automatic output formatting. This item can be placed in an account's master dictionary.

```
ID: NUMID
001 S]L      The L indicates a logical synonym.
002 0
003
004
005
006
007
008 P(0N)
009 R
010 3
```

FIG. 6-11. Pattern match conversion.

NUMID tests for attribute zero (the item id) and tests the value for any numeric. The ACCESS sentence to SELECT only those items that have numeric item-ids is as follows:

```
SELECT filename IF NUMID
```

The any number (0N) pattern match passes any string of numerics from none, a null string, to many. To ensure that the tested value contains a string of at least one numeric, the pattern match conversion must be: P(1N0N). This reads; match one numeric followed by any number of numerics.

Range Checking

The range check conversion tests whether a data value is between a specified minimum and maximum value. The general format is:

```
Rminimum,maximum{;minimum,maximum;...}
```

Range specifications can be alpha (RA,L;P,Z) or numeric. If the data is between the values, inclusive, it is passed through intact. Otherwise, a null string is reported. The semicolon is an OR specification. The data can be within any of the specified ranges. Please note that *multiple ranges* must be specified in *ascending sequence*. That is, the lower ranges must precede the higher range checks. (See Fig. 6-12.)

```
ID: ELIGIBLE.FOR.COMMISSION
001 S]L
002 15
003
004
005
006
007
008 R1000000,999999999
009 R
010 10
```

FIG. 6-12. Range check conversions.

```
ID: ELIGIBLE.FOR.RETIREMENT
001 S]L
002 0
003
004
005
006
007
008 A;N(AGE)(R65,999)
009 R
010 4
```

Range is useful for "hard coded" spans of time or money. For example, the logical definition item, ELIGIBLE.FOR.COMMISSION, checks that the total sales in attribute 15 of an item in the SALESMAN file is between $10,000.00 and $9,999,999.99. Notice that the range (100000,999999999) must reflect the internal format of the data, including the two implied decimal places. The range check for age (R65,999) should cover anyone alive today. (Unless Methuselah is working in your company.)

The selection statement can be expressed as follows:

SELECT SALESMAN IF ELIGIBLE.FOR.COMMISSION

The range conversion can also be used to modify expressions in an A correlative. For example, testing for the condition ELIGIBLE.FOR.RETIREMENT requires that the calculated value of AGE be used. This checks that the value of AGE is greater than or equal to 65 and less than or equal to 999. It's a safe bet that no one on staff is over 100 years old. The ACCESS select statement looks like this:

SELECT STAFF IF ELIGIBLE.FOR.RETIREMENT

Length Checking

The length conversion has two major functions. The first tests the length of the data string passed to it. The length to test can be specified in two ways. First, checking for a specific length is indicated as:

L*length*

The only strings that pass intact are those that match the indicated length. Second, a length range can also be specified in the following manner:

L*minlength,maxlength*

Only strings that are less than or equal to the *maxlength* and greater than or equal to the *minlength* are passed through intact. Otherwise, a null value is returned. This is probably helpful for weeding out garbage within a data file. One type of garbage might be an attribute which exceeds a maximum size limit. Consider the case illustrated in Fig. 6-13 where item-id's over 15 characters long must be identified.

```
ID: BIGID
001 S]L
002 0
003
004
005                 FIG. 6-13. Length checking conversion.
006
007
008 L16,100
009 L
010 15
```

Because the length range is inclusive, the *minlength* indicator of 16 is required to test for a length greater than 15. The *maxlength* indicator of 100 is an arbitrarily large number.

The culprit items can be selected using the following statement:

SELECT filename IF BIGID

Finally, the length function can also be used to count the number of characters in the string passed to it and is specified as:

LO

Used within an A correlative, the L0 conversion duplicates the LEN( ) function in PICK/BASIC. The following example extracts the last character from a variable length string in attribute 5 of a data item.

A;5[5(L0),"1"]

A string extract is performed against attribute 5:

5[startpos,length]

The value of the starting position is determined by:

5(L0)

This generates the length of attribute 5. The equivalent PICK/BASIC statement is:

LEN(ITEM(5))

Substitution

The substitution conversion is an implied IF..THEN..ELSE and can be used on systems that do not support the IF..THEN..ELSE construct in an A correlative. The substitution conversion is based on the condition of whether the data value passed to it is a null or zero, (that is, no value). The general form of the substitution conversion is as follows:

S;v1;v2

The indicators *v1* and *v2* are expressions that generate the substituted values. If the passed data has a value then v1 is used. If the passed data has no value then v2 is used. Substitution can be explained using the following pseudo-code statement:

if not(value = '') and not(value = 0) then *v1* else *v2*

The specifications for v1 and v2 are:

amc	A numeric attribute reference
"literal"	A literal string surrounded by quotes
*	The original value passed to the substitution conversion.

Here is a comparison of the substitution construct and the IF..THEN..ELSE construct used to produce the same results.

A;(N(SEX) = "M")(S;"MALE";"FEMALE")
   A;IF N(SEX) = "M" THEN "MALE" ELSE "FEMALE"

If the result of the logical expression, N(SEX) = "M", is true, the string "MALE" is printed. A true condition is a 1 and causes the "v1" substitution element to be used. If the condition is false, the string "FEMALE" is printed. A false condition is a zero and causes the "v2" substitution element to be used.

Substituting attribute for attribute is effective if the targeted attribute is null, but an alternative attribute should be reported. Consider the case of a ship-to address versus a billing address. In case there is no special ship-to, the billing address should be used. If the billing address is attribute 2 of the data item and the ship-to address is attribute 12, then the correlative on attribute 008 of the definition item would look like this:

008 A;2(S;*;12)

In pseudo-code:

if *amc2#''* and *amc2#0* then print *amc#2* else print *amc#12*

Sometimes, a zero result of an arithmetic calculation shouldn't be reported. This next example substitutes two dashes (-) if the calculation performed by the definition, BALANCE.DUE, is zero.

008 A;N(BALANCE.DUE)(S;*;"- -")

This can be explained as:

if BALANCE.DUE#0 then print BALANCE.DUE else print "- -"

Any attribute or result of a correlative can be used as a flag to determine which attribute in a data item will be reported. Consider the next correlative:

008 A;N(FLAG)(S;2;3)

The definition item FLAG is any calculation or comparison which results in a zero or positive integer. Stated as pseudo-code:

If FLAG#0 then print amc2 else print amc3

Also, testing for a zero or non-zero result can be used to modify logical statements in order to adjust a false, zero, result to a null output string. Earlier in this chapter, the following Boolean statement was used to determine eligibility for retirement.

A;((N(SEX) = "M")*(N(AGE) > = "65")) + ((N(SEX) = "F")*(N(AGE) > = "60"))

The three possible results of the above statement are 0, 1 or 2. Both 1 and 2 are considered true. Only 0 is considered false. However, a true-false test within an ACCESS sentence depends on true being a non-null string and false being a null string. Unfortunately, an ACCESS sentence selection clause, WITH datadef, considers all of the above, 0, 1 and 2, to be true because they are all not null.

The substitution conversion is used to modify the results of the Boolean expression in the following manner:

A;(*boolean expression*)(S;*;"")

This states:

if expression #0 then print expression else print ""

The entire Boolean phrase can be surrounded by parentheses to group it as a single element, and the result can be passed through the substitution conversion. Now, instead of having to say:

```
SELECT STAFF IF ELIGIBLE.FOR.RETIREMENT # 0
```

The statement can be specified as:

```
SELECT STAFF IF ELIGIBLE.FOR.RETIREMENT
```

Please note that the substitution conversion cannot "stand-alone." It must be used as part of an F or A correlative.

A COMPLEX CORRELATIVE EXAMPLE

The real power of the A correlative is the ability to combine expression types. The results of arithmetic and string expressions can be altered by using them as an integral part of a larger logical construct. Consider the case of a hypothetical INVENTORY file which contains items based on part number. The two main definition items used for this example are PRICE and product TYPE. The goal is to calculate a FINAL.PRICE based on the PRICE, the product TYPE and the TAX rate based on the STATE. Figure 6-14 shows the data definition items that are used to define PRICE and TYPE in the INVENTORY file.

```
                                   ID: PRICE          ID: TYPE
                                   001 A              001 A
                                   002 10             002 5
                                   003
                                   004
FIG. 6-14. PRICE and TYPE data definitions.   005
                                   006
                                   007 MR2
                                   008
                                   009 R              009 L
                                   010 12             010 1
```

Both PRICE and TYPE are real data pointers to attributes 10 and 5, respectively. The PRICE is stored with two implied decimal places as indicated by the output conversion in attribute 007. The FINAL.PRICE should be a simple calculation:

```
MARKDOWN.PRICE + TAX
```

Figuring the MARKDOWN.PRICE and the TAX on the MARKDOWN.PRICE requires most of the work. Notice that the calculations are performed in separate definition items avoiding the running-for-many-pages correlative and providing some degree of self-documentation.

The MARKDOWN.PRICE is calculated based on the TYPE field. If the TYPE is an A, the MARKDOWN should be 33 percent, and if the TYPE is B, then the markdown is 22 percent. Because the determination of the MARKDOWN.RATE can get complex, it is best defined as a separate data definition item, as in Fig. 6-15.

```
ID: MARKDOWN.RATE
001 S]F                          Defined as a virtual function
                                 that is not requested
                                 specifically in an ACCESS
                                 sentence.  It is used as a
                                 recursive call from another
                                 definition item, MARKDOWN.
002 0
003
004
005
006
007
008 A;(N(TYPE)="A")*"330")+(N(TYPE)="B")*"220")
009 R
010 10
```

FIG. 6-15. MARKDOWN.RATE definition item.

Because there is a possibility of fractional percent values and integer values must be used in ACCESS, the percent values are specified using three implied decimals. The number "330" represents 33.0 percent or the decimal value, .330, and "220" represents 22.0 percent or the decimal value, .220.

N(TYPE) is compared to the literal "A." If true, the result of (N(TYPE) = "A") is 1. This multiplied by "330" gives a result of "330." Conversely, the other logical comparison, (N(TYPE) = "B") must be false and evaluate to a 0. The expressions on either side of the plus sign (+) are mutually exclusive. The following is a simple truth table for this correlative.

TYPE	(N(TYPE) = "A")*"330") + (N(TYPE) = "B")*"220")
A	(1*"330") + (0*"220") = "330"
B	(0*"330") + (1*"220") = "220"

Any new exclusive value for TYPE can be added to the current expression making the correlative larger and more cumbersome than it is already.

As with all approaches in Pick, the previous correlative can be written in a number of different ways. The following are alternatives that work just as well:

A;IF N(TYPE) = "A" THEN "330" ELSE "220"
A;(N(TYPE) = "A")(S;"330";"220")

The value of MARKDOWN is then calculated based on the MARKDOWN.RATE as illustrated in Fig. 6-16.

The only trick involved is the placement of the decimal place for reporting. The PRICE has two implied decimal places. The MARKDOWN.RATE has three implied decimal places. Therefore, the internal value of MARKDOWN contains five implied decimal places. Both the scaling and precision must be used on the MR output mask. The general form is:

MR *precision scaling*

```
                            ID: MARKDOWN
                            001 S]V
                            002 0
                            003
                            004
FIG. 6-16. MARKDOWN definition item.    005
                            006
                            007 MR25
                            008 A;N(PRICE)*N(MARKDOWN.RATE)
                            009 R
                            010 12
```

Mismatched precision and scaling forces rounding. The output conversion, MR25, states that the decimal is moved five places to the left before rounding to a two decimal precision. This does not effect the internally formatted value. The output mask on attribute 007 is performed at print time only.

The next step is to calculate the MARKDOWN.PRICE, as shown in Fig. 6-17. This is accomplished by subtracting the value of MARKDOWN from the original PRICE. However, PRICE is held with two implied decimals, while the MARKDOWN contains five implied decimals.

```
                            ID: MARKDOWN.PRICE
                            001 S]V
                            002 0
                            003
                            004
FIG. 6-17. MARKDOWN.PRICE definition item. 005
                            006
                            007 MR25
                            008 A;(N(PRICE)*"1000")-N(MARKDOWN)
                            009 R
                            010 12
```

The PRICE must be scaled up by three decimal places to give it five implied decimals:

N(PRICE)*"1000"

The subtraction can now be performed. The resulting MARKDOWN.PRICE contains five implied decimals as is masked as such, MR25. The value of sales TAX must be calculated based on the MARKDOWN.PRICE and the current STATE. Unfortunately, hardcoding tax percentages by state in the form that the MARKDOWN.RATE is calculated is not a good solution.

(N(STATE) = "CA")*"060") + (N(STATE) = "TX")*"080") + ...

This gets even more difficult when taxes change by county and city within a state. (For the purposes of this example, taxes are by state only.) This kind of decision is more easily made as a table lookup from a code file based on the STATE.

Consider the code file called TAX.RATES as illustrated in Fig. 6-18. The tax rates are kept in attribute two with three implied decimal places. The TAX.RATES values can

TAX.RATES items:

```
ID: CA                    ID: TX
001 California            001 Texas
002 060                   002 080
```

TAX definition item:

```
ID: TAX
001 S]V
002 0
003
004
005
006
007 MR28
008 A;N(MARKDOWN.PRICE)*(N(STATE)(TTAX.RATES;X;;2))
009 R
010 10
```

FIG. 6-18. TAX definition and related TAX.RATES items.

be retrieved by using a file translate conversion modifying the STATE field. For the purpose of getting on with it, assume that a STATE field already exists. The sales tax is then determined by a file lookup in the TAX definition item.

The TAX is calculated by multiplying the MARKDOWN.PRICE by the tax rate. The tax rate is looked up on-the-fly by passing the value of STATE through the file translate as follows:

N(STATE)(TTAX.RATES;X;;2)

The result of multiplying a 5-implied decimal, MARKDOWN.PRICE by a 3-implied decimal, the retrieved tax rate, produces an integer with 8-implied decimal places. The MR28 output conversion scales the integer properly for reporting.

Finally, the MARKDOWN.PRICE and the TAX amount are at hand. To perform the addition that results in the FINAL.PRICE, the MARKDOWN.PRICE must be scaled up to 8 implied decimals, as shown in Fig. 6-19.

```
ID: FINAL.PRICE
001 S]V
002 0
003
004
005
006
007 MR28
008 A;(N(MARKDOWN.PRICE)*"1000")+N(TAX)
009 R
010 12
```

FIG. 6-19. FINAL.PRICE definition item.

TARGETING MULTIVALUES

Specific value positions in a multivalued attribute can be targeted via the use of specific conversions and correlative techniques. This section concentrates on the use of the A correlative to perform this function, but it is probably helpful to itemize the alternative methods before continuing.

Using File Translate

The only sanctioned and documented way to target a value is via the file translate conversion. The general form of the file translate is:

    Tfilename;option{vmc};inamc;outamc{;breakamc}

It is not the intention of this text to delve into the seldom used functions (inamc, breakamc) of the file translate. For this discussion, pay attention to the optional indicator for "vmc."

The file translate can be used to point to an attribute and value position in any file, provided the correct item-id is passed to the conversion. The only drawback is that this conversion must re-read the same item being used in the current ACCESS process.

Consider a file called INVOICE which contains part number line items in attribute 10 of each data item. A definition item can be created to report only the second value of the multivalued part attribute, as shown in Fig. 6-20.

```
ID: PART.LINE2
001 S
002 0
003
004
005
006
007
008 TINVOICE;X2;;10
009 L
010 10
```

FIG. 6-20. PART.LINE2 definition item using file translate.

Attribute 002 of the definition indicates that the item-id of the current item is to be used to re-read the current item and target attribute 10, value 2.

The amc value, 0, and the file translate can also be placed within an A correlative as follows:

    008 A;0(TINVOICE;X2;;10)

Special User Exits

There are also two user exits that can be used to address specific value positions. Please be careful. These may not work on all implementations and could cause problems. Again, caveat emptor.

The first is UC070;*n* where *n* is the multivalue being addressed. PART.LINE2 can be re-written as illustrated in Fig. 6-21.

```
ID: PART.LINE2          ID: PART.LINE
001 S                   001 S
002 10                  002 10
003
004                              FIG. 6-21. User exits for targeting
005                              multi-values.
006
007
008 UC070;2             008 UA070
009 L                   009 L
010 10                  010 10
```

The next user exit, UA070, requires the actual multivalue position to be indicated as a print limiter in the ACCESS sentence, allowing variable value addressing. To display only the second value of the 10th attribute requires the following ACCESS statement:

    LIST INVOICES PART.LINE "2"

Using A Correlatives

The A correlative can be used to target value positions. This is accomplished by the use of the NV operand within a logical expression. Again, PART.LINE2 is re-written, as shown in Fig. 6-22.

```
ID: PART.LINE2
001 S
002 0
003
004
005                              FIG. 6-22. PART.LINE2 using an A correlative.
006
007
008 A;10["1","10"*(NV="2")]
009 L
010 10
```

A logical string extraction is performed on the contents of attribute 10. The logical expression checks for the second multivalue:

    (NV = "2")

When the logical expression is true, the value length becomes 10 and the first 10 characters are extracted from attribute 10. If false, the value length becomes zero and a null string is extracted. This type of correlative designation allows a range of multivalues to be extracted:

    008 A;10["1","10"*((NV>"1")*(NV<"5"))]

The controlling logical expression tests for a range of 1 to 5, exclusively. Any logical expression based on value position can be substituted, including a test for the last value of the multivalued array.

Most of the time, the most recent occurrence of any data string is inserted at the top of the string (LIFO). Targeting the first multivalue is trivial. However, sometimes these lists are kept as FIFO stacks, adding the most recent occurrence to the end of the list. Therefore, it is the task of the correlative to determine the number of values present. This can be accomplished with the use of the summation (S) correlative function.

S(amc = amc)

The above function sums the number of multivalues by comparing each element against itself to obtain a true, 1, result. The final result is the total number of values. However, this exact syntax might not work on all implementations. An alternative that seems to work across the board tests that each value is non-null. (This only works if all value positions contain a value.) For example:

S(amc#" ")

Another variation test for a null OR non-null condition is:

S((amc = " ") + (amc#" "))

In any case, the value of NV is then tested against the result of the summation as follows:

NV = S(amc#" "))

The last value of attribute 10 can be extracted by the following correlative:

008 A;10["1","10"*(NV = S(10#" "))]

The use of string extracts creates a small aberration when using the definition items in an output list request. The address values are printed *n* number of lines displaced from the output line where *n* is the number of the value position. In Fig. 6-23 XXX, ZXY, and RRR are the second values of attribute 10 in each data item. This can be prevented by using the S( ), summation in the form:

A;S(*expression*)

LIST INVOICES PART.LINE2

INVOICES......... PART.LINE2......

FIG. 6-23. PART.LINE2 targeted value report.

INVOICES	PART.LINE2
001	
	XXX
002	
	ZXY
003	
	RRR

The previous examples can be written as:

008 A;S(10["1","10"*(NV = "2")])

or

008 A;S(10["1","10"*(NV = S(10#" "))])

Both the above cases retrieve a single value. The summation function works only for a single alphanumeric value. Otherwise, it attempts to add multiple alphabetic characters and produces a result of zero. However, numeric values can be handled for any range of value positions.

Numeric values can be reported using the summation (S) function in conjunction with the logical expression. If attribute 11 in the INVOICES item is the quantity (QTY) of each part sold, reporting the quantity for line two can be written as follows:

    008 A;S(11*(NV = "2"))

This indicates the sum of all values in attribute 11 is value 2. Only value 2 results in a non-zero value and is the only result reported.

A range of values can be summed by substituting a new logical expression. The following correlative sums values 2 through 5, exclusive:

    008 A;S(11*((NV > "2")*(NV < "5")))

The last numeric value of a value marked list can be reported using the following correlative:

    008 A;S(11*(NV = S(11#'')))

The comparison, NV = S(11#''), is the same as described above for the logical multivalued string extraction. Because summation always generates a single value, the aberration on output does not occur as before.

BREAK LINE CALCULATIONS

The following section demonstrates the calculation of results based on information available at the break line. The main rule for performing break line calculations is to use attribute 007 in the definition item. *Break line data* is determined during the ACCESS print pass rather than during data sampling. Any calculations specified on attribute 008 are performed too early.

Consider the SALESMAN file which contains both actual and projected income values for each salesman. The data item layout is as follows:

    ID: Salesman number
    001 Name
    002 Office
    003 Actual income
    004 Projected income

The office attribute can have a value of A, B or C to identify the office to which the salesman is assigned. The data definition items for the actual and projected income values are shown in Fig. 6-24. Both attributes are stored with two implied decimal places.

The first calculated value is the average income per office. This has to be calculated by dividing the total income per office by the number of detail lines generated in the report. The operand, ND, indicates the number of detail lines provided it is used in a correlative on line 007. Remember, the number of detail lines is not available until print time.

```
          ACTUAL                    PROJECTED
001  A                         001  A
002  3                         002  4
003  ACTUAL]INCOME
004
005
006
007  MR2,$                     007  MR2,$
008
009  R                         009  R
010  12                        010  12


AVG.INCOME
001  S
002  10
003
004
005
006
007  A;(3/ND)(MR2,$)
008
009  R
010  12
```

FIG. 6-24. AVG.INCOME and related data definitions.

The value residing in attribute three is divided by the number of details and the result is output masked to two decimal places.

The use of the direct amc reference is imperative at print time. The recursive N(data-def) function is only effective during the data sampling pass.

The ACCESS sentence to produce the report must request all associated definitions in order to produce the desired result shown in Fig. 6-25. The AVG.INCOME cannot be calculated without totaling both the ACTUAL income and the AVG.INCOME. The attribute 3 reference in AVG.INCOME does more than print the third attribute of the source item; it extracts the third attribute of the work item during processing. During the report break, the totals for each column are available in the designated attribute position of the work item.

Notice that the average income values are reported at the break line and not on the detail lines. This is influenced by yet another undocumented feature: The value in attribute 002 of the AVG.INCOME definition is the controlling factor. A non-zero attribute value in the amc position alters the detail line output of the report. If a zero is used in attribute 002 of the definition item, each detail value is displayed along with the break line values. In this case, the value 10 in attribute 002 is pointing to a "dummy" position in the work item.

It is important to use a "dummy" amc value which is not too far from the end of the last actually referenced amc position. Otherwise, the system must pad out the extra null attributes.

The next task is to calculate the percentage of ACTUAL income to PROJECTED income. This is broken into two parts; 1) calculating the percentage of the detail lines and 2) calculating the percentage of the total lines.

The ACCESS sentence:

```
SORT SALESMAN BY OFFICE BREAK-ON OFFICE.....
... TOTAL ACTUAL TOTAL AVG.INCOME
```

Outputs:

SALESMAN..	OFFICE	ACTUAL...... INCOME	AVG.INCOME..
006	A	$927.13	
008	A	$927.13	
012	A	$559.12	
	***	$2,413.38	$804.46
007	B	$927.13	
018	B	$927.13	
024	B	$555.55	
	***	$2,409.81	$803.27
009	C	$927.13	
010	C	$752.35	
044	C	$559.12	
	***	$2,238.60	$746.20
***		$7,061.79	$784.64

FIG. 6-25. Averaging income at report breaks.

The definition item PERCENT.GOAL1, shown in Fig. 6-26, calculates the percentage of the details. The calculation is specified using recursive references (N(datadef)) and is performed at selection time. The scaling is a bit tricky. Both ACTUAL and PROJECTED are 2 decimal implied values. To obtain the result as a percentage and not a decimal ratio, the numerator must be scaled up by two decimals (multiplied by 100.) To allow for a greater amount of precision in the division, the numerator is further scaled up by four additional decimal places. Hence, the numerator is scaled a total of 10 to the power of six.

```
        PERCENT.GOAL1
001 S
002 0
003 %GOAL1
004
005
006
007 MR24
008 A;((N(ACTUAL)*"1000000")/N(PROJECTED))
009 R
010 6
```

FIG. 6-26. PERCENT.GOAL1 definition item.

The printed result is scaled down by four decimals and printed with a two-decimal precision.

This division produces an accurate percentage at the detail lines, but fails at the break total lines. In fact, totaling such a definition produces a total of the percentages, not a percentage of the totals. Because breakline totals are only available at print time, an alternative definition, PERCENT.GOAL2, must be defined, as shown in Fig. 6-27.

```
                                    PERCENT.GOAL2
                              001 S
                              002 0
                              003 %GOAL2
                              004
FIG. 6-27. PERCENT.GOAL2 definition item.   005
                              006
                              007 A;((3*"1000000")/4)(MR24)
                              008
                              009 R
                              010 6
```

The same calculation is moved from attribute 008 to 007 with the following changes: 1) The data references must be replaced with direct amc operands in order to reference the proper position in the work item. 2) The output mask must be integrated as part of the A correlative in order to produce the correctly scaled result.

The ACCESS sentence in Fig. 6-28 generates totals for both percent calculations in order to provide a direct comparison. Compare the differences at the detail and total lines for PERCENT.GOAL1 and PERCENT.GOAL2. Notice that the detail lines are reported for PERCENT.GOAL2 as a result of the 0 in attribute 002 of the definition item.

The next and final task is to calculate average percentage at each break line. The final result depends on the detail percentages generated by PERCENT.GOAL1. This dictates that PERCENT.GOAL1 must be totaled in the ACCESS sentence so that the result is available in the work item at print time. In addition, the final report must not display the PERCENT.GOAL1 column. Consider the definition item in Fig. 6-29.

To ensure that the calculated results are available at print time, attribute 002 of PERCENT.GOAL1 is modified to point to "dummy" attribute 15 of the work item.

To allow the PERCENT.GOAL2 column to be specified in the ACCESS sentence, but not shown on the output report, the definition item is classified as a "hidden definition" by the following:

Parameter	Description
003 \	A backslash in attribute 003 of a definition indicates that the column heading is to be a null value.
007A;""	Hides the break total lines.
010 0	A zero in attribute 010 of the definition indicates a detail column width of zero.

These parameters used in conjunction effectively "hide" the output column.

271

The ACCESS command sentence:

```
SORT SALESMAN BY OFFICE BREAK-ON OFFICE TOTAL ACTUAL...
.... TOTAL PROJECTED TOTAL PERCENT.GOAL1......
.... TOTAL PERCENT.GOAL2
```

Generates:

SALESMAN..	OFFICE	ACTUAL...... INCOME	PROJECTED...	%GOAL1	%GOAL2
006	A	$927.13	$1,500.00	61.81	61.81
008	A	$927.13	$1,500.00	61.81	61.81
012	A	$559.12	$1,100.00	50.83	50.83
	***	$2,413.38	$4,100.00	174.45	58.86
007	B	$927.13	$1,234.00	75.13	75.13
018	B	$927.13	$1,500.00	61.81	61.81
024	B	$555.55	$987.00	56.29	56.29
	***	$2,409.81	$3,721.00	193.23	64.76
009	C	$927.13	$1,500.00	61.81	61.81
010	C	$752.35	$1,896.54	39.67	39.67
044	C	$559.12	$1,200.00	46.59	46.59
	***	$2,238.60	$4,596.54	148.07	48.70
***		$7,061.79	$12,417.54	515.75	56.87

9 ITEMS LISTED.

FIG. 6-28. Calculating percentages at detail and break lines.

```
      PERCENT.GOAL1
001 S
002 15
003 \
004
005
006
007 A; " "
008 A;((N(ACTUAL)*"1000000")/N(PROJECTED))
009 R
010 0
```

FIG. 6-29. PERCENT-GOAL1 hidden definition item.

The calculation of average percentage requires the total of the percent values generated by PERCENT.GOAL1 divided by the number of detail lines. The use of the ND operand dictates the correlative be placed in attribute 007 of the definition item, as in Fig. 6-30. The non-zero value in attribute 002 of AVG.PERCENT causes the details to be suppressed. PERCENT.GOAL1 is requested and available for processing, but is 'hidden' on output, as shown in Fig. 6-31.

```
                                          AVG.PERCENT
                                      001 S
                                      002 15
                                      003 %AVG
                                      004
         FIG. 6-30. AVG.PERCENT definition item.   005
                                      006
                                      007 A;(15/ND)(MR24)
                                      008
                                      009 R
                                      010 5
```

FIG. 6-30. AVG.PERCENT definition item.

The ACCESS command sentence:

```
SORT SALESMAN BY OFFICE BREAK-ON OFFICE TOTAL ACTUAL....
.... TOTAL PROJECTED SPACE8 TOTAL PERCENT.GOAL1 ......
.... TOTAL PERCENT.GOAL2 TOTAL AVG.PERCENT

(SPACE8 is a "dummy" definition for spacing using A"          ")
```

Generates:

SALESMAN..	OFFICE	ACTUAL...... INCOME	PROJECTED.....	%GOAL2..	%AVG
006	A	$927.13	$1,500.00	61.81	
008	A	$927.13	$1,500.00	61.81	
012	A	$559.12	$1,100.00	50.83	
	***	$2,413.38	$4,100.00	58.86	58.15
007	B	$927.13	$1,234.00	75.13	
018	B	$927.13	$1,500.00	61.81	
024	B	$555.55	$987.00	56.29	
	***	$2,409.81	$3,721.00	64.76	64.41
009	C	$927.13	$1,500.00	61.81	
010	C	$752.35	$1,896.54	39.67	
044	C	$559.12	$1,200.00	46.59	
	***	$2,238.60	$4,596.54	48.70	49.36
***		$7,061.79	$12,417.54	56.87	57.31

9 ITEMS LISTED.

FIG. 6-31. Averaging percentages at the break line.

ACCESS AS A BATCH UPDATE LANGUAGE

The output of ACCESS is not solely restricted to the terminal or the printer. While the verbs T-DUMP and T-LOAD allow for data archival and restoration of entire items to and from magnetic media (tape, diskette, cartridge), they do not allow attributes to be processed or the output format to be altered. The REFORMAT verb is used to direct the processed results of real, synonym and virtual definitions to another disk file or to magnetic media. Many batch data processing tasks that are currently being "brute-forced" in PICK/BASIC can be alternatively defined as a series of ACCESS directives.

REFORMAT generates new items to an initially empty work file. It is useful for doing data summary to an intermediate file for verification and reporting. The results can then be merged back into the on-line database via simple PICK/BASIC programs which are run only when the data is given the stamp of approval. REFORMAT can be used to format data records for non-Pick machines. The results can be later written to tape by a generalized PICK/BASIC program or transmitted across a communication line.

REFORMAT is not used for interactive updates because it does not provide or require user response during processing. REFORMAT is not used to target specific attributes in existing items because it always overwrites the targeted item. The general REFORMAT syntax is as follows:

>REFORMAT {DICT} *filename* {*itemlist*} {*sellist*}...
{*outlist*} {*modlist*} {(*option*)}

TO:destination file name or TAPE

REFORMAT or SREFORMAT works like all the command pairs available in ACCESS. REFORMAT moves the data in the order it is found on file. SREFORMAT orders the data in sequence controlled through a BY clause. All the sentence elements are the same as any LIST or SORT command sentence, except for the output list, *outlist*, specifications. The first descriptor in the outlist designates the item-id. Each subsequent descriptor targets the next attribute in sequence. The output list can be generalized as follows:

item-id attribute1 attribute2 attribute3 ... attributen

The system generated prompt TO: requests the name of the destination file. TAPE designation sends the record directly to the attached tape drive. In the case of TAPE output, the item-id is irrelevant and is designated as the first attribute in the output string.

Please note that the output fields generated to a target file are identical to those which are normally printed. The print pass simply moves the work item to another file rather than printing it on the terminal or sending it to the spooler. Therefore, both attributes 008 and 007 are performed before the data is moved to the file or tape.

Simple Data Reformatting

Items in the data file STAFF are to be moved to the file WORK under a different format. The only field to remain intact is the item-id. A single source item is used for this example.

```
ID: 101
001 SPADE, SAM
002 12 STOCKTON
003 SAN FRANCISCO
004 CA
005 92222
```

The new item layout to be generated in WORK is as follows:

```
ID: 101
001 firstname lastname
002 city, state
003 zip
```

The basic data elements for the REFORMAT must be defined in the DICT of STAFF. The CITY, STATE, and ZIP are actual attribute positions in a STAFF item and are, therefore, typed as real (A) definition items. The firstname and lastname, FNAME and LNAME, must extract the data from the first attribute and are, therefore, typed as synonym (S) definition items, as shown in Fig. 6-32.

FNAME	LNAME	CITY	STATE	ZIP
001 S	001 S	001 A	001 A	001 A
002 1	002 1	002 3	002 4	002 5
003	003	003	003	003
004	004	004	004	004
005	005	005	005	005
006	006	006	006	006
007	007	007	007	007
008 G1 1	008 G,1	008	008	008
009 L	009 L	009 L	009 L	009 L
010 10	010 10	010 20	010 2	010 10

FIG. 6-32. Definition items in the DICT of STAFF.

Additional virtual descriptor entries have to be created to handle the reformatted layout within the attributes for NAME and CITY, STATE, as shown in Fig. 6-33.

The REFORMAT statement can be expressed as follows:

```
>REFORMAT STAFF '101' *A0 NEWNAME CITYSTATE ZIP

TO:WORK
```

NEWNAME		CITYSTATE
001 S]V		001 S]V
002 0		002 0
003		003
004		004
005		005
006		006
007		007
008 A;N(FNAME):" ":A(LNAME)		008 A;N(CITY):", ":N(STATE)
009 L		009 L
010 10		010 10

FIG. 6-33. NEWNAME and CITYSTATE virtual definition items.

The item list indicates the single item, 101. The output list begins with the MD default definition item, *A0, indicating that the destination item-id is to be the same as the source item-id. Attribute 1 is NEWNAME, attribute 2 is CITYSTATE and attribute 3 is ZIP. The created item in the file WORK looks as follows:

```
ID: 101
001 SAM SPADE
002 SAN FRANCISCO, CA
003 92222
```

Reformat for Interface

This example generates a series of card image items which can be either dumped to tape via a generalized PICK/BASIC routine or transmitted across a communication line. The final destination is arbitrary. The ability to format the data without PICK/BASIC is the important issue. The fixed length record layout is the following:

```
         1         2         3         4         5         6
123456789012345678901234567890123456789012345678901234567890
<----First Last  Name---- > <----City-----> <--Zip-->-!<---------- 25 ------->
<-----15----> <--9-->-!End
```

A complex string expression is used to format the fixed record and placed in the definition item, CARD, as shown in Fig. 6-34.

```
CARD
001 S
002 0
003
004
005
006
007
008 A;(N(NEWNAME)(ML#25):N(CITY)(ML#15):N(ZIP)(ML#9))(ML#50)
009 L
010 50
```

FIG. 6-34. CARD definition item.

The ACCESS sentence to perform the data movement is illustrated on Fig. 6-35. CARD becomes the only attribute in the target item. To ensure a unique item-id for each record, a sequential count is used. The MD resident definition item, *A9998, uses the amc value 9998 to generate the sequential number.

When the new items need to be created in a particular order, the SREFORMAT verb is used. The sequential item-id defines the order in which the items will be retrieved from WORK. In Fig. 6-36, the generated tape records are in the order of the last name.

Destination Tape

Using TAPE as the destination generates a single tape block per data record. Prior to performing the REFORMAT, the tape drive must be attached at a block size equivalent to the record size.

The ACCESS sentence:

```
>REFORMAT STAFF *A9998 CARD
TO:WORK or TAPE
```

Generates:

```
ID: 1
001 JOHN WAYNE              AMARILLO       50505
ID: 2
001 HAROLD WASHINGTON       MISTY CLOUD    77777
ID: 3
001 HUNTER THOMPSON         LAS VEGAS      80808
ID: 4
001 SNOW WHITE              HOLLYWOOD      92713
ID: 5
001 RONALD REAGAN           WASHINGTON     20000
ID: 6
001 HARVEY RABBIT           SAN DIEGO      92777
```

FIG. 6-35. Card image generated by REFORMAT.

The ACCESS sentence:

```
>SREFORMAT STAFF BY LNAME *A9998 CARD
TO:WORK or TAPE
```

Generates:

```
ID: 1
001 HARVEY RABBIT           SAN DIEGO      92777
ID: 2
001 RONALD REAGAN           WASHINGTON     20000
ID: 3
001 HUNTER THOMPSON         LAS VEGAS      80808
ID: 4
001 HAROLD WASHINGTON       MISTY CLOUD    77777
ID: 5
001 JOHN WAYNE              AMARILLO       50505
ID: 6
001 SNOW WHITE              HOLLYWOOD      92713
```

FIG. 6-36. Card image by last name using SREFORMAT.

If more than one record is required per block, a generalized PICK/BASIC program can be developed to transfer the fixed records from a work file to the tape. The program reads the REFORMATed records from any file and builds a variable length string based on the current tape block size. This block can then be transferred to tape via the WRITET command.

Storage of records under sequential item-ids allows the PICK/BASIC program to retrieve each record in-turn via an incremented counter variable, rather than a SSELECT and READNEXT. The program terminates when the next item cannot be read. This sure beats waiting for a SSELECT on a potentially large file.

Break Line Summary

REFORMAT can be used to create items based on summarized values generated at the report break line. The BREAK-ON value must be specified as the first output list element as in the ACCESS command sentence in Fig. 6-37. The modifying phrase, BREAK-ON OFFICE, normally prints asterisks (*) at the break line unless used in conjunction with the (D) option, detail suppress. *Detail supress* causes the value controlling the break to be generated at the breakline, subsequently making the OFFICE code the item-id for each generated summary item. However, some implementations require that the BREAK-ON clause be modified with the 'V' option to force the value to be reported at the break as follows:

```
BREAK-ON OFFICE "'V'"
```

Attribute 1 of the new item contains the total of the ACTUAL income, attribute 2 is the total of the PROJECTED income, and attribute 3 is the PERCENT.GOAL2 calculation. The GRAND-TOTAL modifier generates a unique item-id of "TOT" for the grand total line values.

The ACCESS sentence:

```
SREFORMAT SALESMAN BY OFFICE BREAK-ON OFFICE TOTAL ACTUAL....
.... TOTAL PROJECTED TOTAL PERCENT.GOAL2 GRAND-TOTAL "TOT" (D
TO: WORK
```

Generates:

```
ID: A               ID: B               ID: C
001 $2,413.38       001 $2,409.81       001 $2,238.60
002 $4,100.00       002 $3,721.00       002 $4,596.54
003 58.86           003 64.76           003 48.70


ID: TOT
001
002 $7,061.79
003 $12,417.54
004 56.87
```

FIG. 6-37. Break line summary items generated by SREFORMAT.

Notice that the TOT item is shifted by one attribute. Also, the monetary values are generated in internal format due to the mask output conversions in attribute 007 of the definition items. (See the previous section, "Break Line Calculations.") If the generated data needs to be in an internal format, the output mask conversions must be left out of the defining item.

Exploded Sorts

Using SREFORMAT in conjunction with the BY-EXP modifier allows items with multivalues to be "staged" in the WORK file as individual items containing single values.

For example, consider the file, INV, which has two correlated multivalued attributes:

ID: Invoice number
001 multivalued part numbers
002 multivalued quantities

The DICT of INV has two "real" definition items defined as PART and QTY. The INV file data items and definition items are illustrated in Fig. 6-38. The right brackets represent value marks.

INV definition items:

```
ID: PART              ID: QTY
001 A                 001 A
002 1                 002 2
003
004
005
006
007
008
009 L                 009 R
010 5                 010 8
```

INV data items:

```
ID: 001               ID: 002
001 Z34]T35]A12       001 A12]Z34]Q111]U88
002 3]1]1             002 3]1]5]1

ID: 003
001 T55]Z34
002 1]2
```

FIG. 6-38. INV file definition and data items.

Each item generates a number of items equal to the number of entries it has in the exploded list. Therefore, each item creates one item for each value in the exploded attribute. For example, INV item 001 generates three separate items in the WORK file.

To avoid generated items from stepping on each other, each new item is given a unique sequential item-id. The body of the item contains a single-valued part number in attribute 1, an associated single-valued quantity in attribute 2, and the original item-id in attribute 3.

Now, the exploded information in WORK file can be reported using ACCESS with none of the shortcomings of multivalued handling, as shown in Fig. 6-39.

PICK/BASIC SUBROUTINES FROM DICTIONARIES

The next step in the evolution of ACCESS programming is the capability to call PICK/BASIC subroutines as a correlative process from either attributes 007 or 008 of a

The ACCESS sentence:

SREFORMAT INV BY-EXP PART *A9998 PART QTY *A0

Generates:

	1		2		3		4
001	A12	001	A12	001	Q11	001	T35
002	1	002	3	002	5	002	1
003	1	003	2	003	2	003	1

	5		6		7		8
001	T55	001	U88	001	Z34	001	Z34
002	1	002	1	002	3	002	1
003	3	003	2	003	1	003	2

	9
001	Z34
002	2
003	3

FIG. 6-39. *Exploded output using SREFORMAT.*

definition item. This feature has been available for years under PRIME Information, but has not been available until quite recently under Pick.

Again, each vendor has a unique standard for calling such routines. What seems to be the most popular, (available on enhanced R80 implementations and the Ultimate) is the B correlative:

B;*subname*

The subroutine must have a standard COMMON block included to be able to retrieve the related data and parameters that are normally available in the F or A correlatives. Under Advanced Pick (a.k.a. Open Architecture) from Pick systems, the PICK/BASIC subroutine retrieves the related information via a special ACCESS function.

There are so many differences, and so little settled at the time of this writing, it doesn't pay to go into too much detail about this capability, except to say that it is coming and should be used when it is available.

As a result of the ability to call PICK/BASIC subroutines from dictionaries, dictionary driven systems are soon at hand. Just imagine applications where all file update and retrieval are controlled through data definition items. The application is created as a by-product of defining the database.

Dictionary Driven
Data Entry

A S SOON AS NEW PICK PROGRAMMERS BECOME SOMEWHAT FAMILIAR WITH ACCESS AND
Pick/Basic, one of the first questions posed is, "Wouldn't it be nice to be able to define
data entry screens as easily as reports?" Of course it would. The most tedious and repetitive
programming task is writing data entry screens. The first couple of times is great fun, (it's
good practice), but the novelty soon wears off.

The ideal world would have an integrated database operating system where all database
update and reporting is inherently initiated through the file dictionaries. The advantage to
dictionary driven data entry is that it forces all database updates through a single "thread" of
logic resulting in an integrated system which is highly consistent, quickly modified and
easily maintained.

At present, the only way that interactive data entry can be written is by using
PICK/BASIC (or Assembler, if the developer has plenty of resources). This is where
enforced programming standards become imperative. (See Chapter 3 "A Closer Look at
PICK/BASIC," Section 3.3, "Programming Standards.") The main danger with extensive,
non-standardized use of PICK/BASIC is that the programs need not follow any of the rules
defined in the dictionary and, more often than not, end up using methods that are completely
obtuse to the layout of the database.

Under the current restraints of releases up to and including R83, dictionary driven data
entry must depend on a set of high level programs which create an "environment" for
development, dictating the structure of all the pieces of the application. Many third party
vendors are currently marketing screen drivers separately and as part of integrated applications generators that are entirely written in PICK/BASIC and/or assembler. However,
implementation philosophies vary.

Parameter Definition

The methods by which these parameters are defined can range from directly editing them into control items to the use of a sophisticated user interface. Here are the popular approaches for user interface:

- *Forms* A fill-in-the-blank approach. The user fills information in a group of data entry forms (screens.)

- *Prompted* A question-answer approach. The user is asked a series of leading questions, including, "Is this a required field?" and "What is the length of the field?" One of the final questions is usually, "Do you want to generate the screen?"

- *English* Data elements are defined as definition items in the file dictionary (entered via the editor or control programs), while screens and reports are defined by English imperative sentences, much in the same manner as ACCESS.

Data Entry Runtime

There are two major approaches to the handling of data entry screens during runtime based on the output of the parameter definition phase.

- *Table driven* Interpreted during runtime. The definition phase generates a series of tables that define all the operational elements. A limited set of programs reads these tables and interprets the information.

- *Code generators* A program is created for each screen. The definition phase generates PICK/BASIC source items. These source items are then automatically compiled and cataloged.

Due to the power of today's systems, comparative efficiency of table driven vs. code generated packages is a moot point. The main issue is now based solely on the application developer's functional requirements.

The advantage that code generators have is that the programs created can be directly modified to meet custom requirements. The disadvantage is that once the source code is modified, the generator can no longer be used. Some code generators only produce object code, thereby preventing direct modification to the generated routines. In order for object-code-only code generators to allow custom processing, user written code segments can be included during the compilation phase, or customized PICK/BASIC subroutines are called at pre-determined processing locations.

An advantage of table driven systems is that a limited set of programs is required during runtime, thereby reducing memory requirements. However, the disadvantage is that applications are completely dependent on these same control programs, which, in many cases, must be licensed for each user, whether or not the package is being used for development. Some table driven systems separate the development routines from the runtime interpreter, thereby freeing up the application to run on systems without development capabilities.

As with object-only code generators, custom processing is made available through PICK/BASIC subroutines which are called at pre-determined points in the process, (very much like ACCESS correlatives).

Every package available is a mix and match of the types described above. All of the above methods are in some way dictionary (table) driven. Even before a code generator can produce the first line of source code, all the controlling parameters must be organized and stored as tables in a related control file. Whether the package uses unique control tables or follows the standard layout of Pick file dictionaries; whether it interprets these tables or uses them to write programs; the overall result is basically the same a quick, easy, and consistent method for controlling data entry.

A SAMPLE DATA ENTRY SCREEN DRIVER

As demonstrated earlier in this text, the ability for PICK/BASIC to process any kind of data string, including a command statement, makes it a likely candidate for an interpreter or compiler of a higher level applications language. The programs presented in this chapter demonstrate a simple data entry screen driver written entirely in PICK/BASIC while taking advantage of some of the features of ACCESS.

The user interface requires definition items to be stored in the file dictionary. The screen layout is specified via an ACCESS-like command sentence which indicates the order and position of the data entry fields.

The main controlling program is called INPUT. The INPUT program is designed as a generalized "single thread" data entry routine. There are two major functional phases of INPUT. The first phase parses the command sentence into a series of control tables. The second phase is runtime. The assembled tables are interpreted during runtime by the main INPUT routine. INPUT is only the beginnings of a more complex package and therefore does not have all the features that can be found in commercially available packages. For example, INPUT handles only single valued attributes and there is no inherent data cross referencing. However, these programs are intended to demonstrate that sophisticated tasks can be implemented in routines that are a symbiosis of PICK/BASIC and ACCESS.

All the programs associated with INPUT are presented as a "boiler plate" for a home brewed version of a fourth generation data entry screen driver. This section is intended to explain the approach and functionality of the programs. Outside a few "Points of Interest," the code is left as an exercise for the reader.

The Subroutines

INPUT depends on the following group of external subroutines.

Subroutine	Description
GETSENTENCE	The same routine shown in Chapter 5, "Process Control." Allows the program to retrieve the command sentence.
ICOMPILE	Parses and compiles the command sentence into a series of data control tables.

INEDIT	Substitutes for the INPUT statement. Allows non-destructive back-space and keyboard string editing of the data fields. It also allows a timeout. (similar to EDLINE, previously presented)
FCORR	Emulates the ACCESS F correlative to allow simple arithmetic and string manipulation of data fields.
INPUTHELP	The HELP window processing subroutine (similar to the SCROLL program presented in Chapter 5, "Process Control").

The Command Sentence

The expected sentence layout follows the same general format as an ACCESS command sentence provided that the entire TCL is available to the program via the SENTENCE( ) function:

INPUT *filename output-list options*

Unfortunately, in standard R83 this is not the case. This program must rely on the GETSENTENCE subroutine. The GETSENTENCE subroutine does not include the verb as part of the passed command string. Using the GETSENTENCE subroutine, INPUT can be initiated from TCL, another PICK/BASIC program (with the INPUT sentence stacked) or a PROC (also with the input statement stacked.) The retrieved command sentence is then passed to the ICOMPILE subroutine.

After initiating INPUT, the subroutine expects entry from the keyboard or from the PROC stack. A sample initiating PROC is illustrated in Fig. 7-1.

```
      INPUTSTAFF
001  PQ
002  HINPUT
003  STON
004  HSTAFF ID NAME ADDRESS<        FIG. 7-1. INPUT process initiating PROC.
005  HCITY STATE<
006  HZIP<
007  H<
008  P
```

The stacked response on lines 004 through 006 can be specified on any number of lines or on the same line. The only requirement is that the sentence input must be terminated by a null input line as indicated on line 007. The stacked input is built into a single command string.

Because the GETSENTENCE subroutine can also retrieve the PROC primary input buffer, INPUT can be initiated by a generalized PROC, INP. The command sentence can be specified at TCL as illustrated in Fig. 7-2. In either case, the string passed by GETSENTENCE must follow the format:

{DICT} *filename output-list options*

The PROC INPUTSTAFF passes the following command sentence to the INPUT program:

STAFF ID NAME ADDRESS CITY STATE ZIP

PROC in the MD:

```
ID: INP
001 HINPUT
002 P
```

Sample INP command sentence:

```
>INP STAFF ID NAME ADDRESS CITY STATE ZIP
```

FIG. 7-2. Generalized INP PROC and sample command sentence.

STAFF is the file name to be updated. ID, NAME, ADDRESS, CITY, STATE, and ZIP make up the "output-list." The indicator "output-list" represents a list of definition item names as follows:

{item-id-def{ {{modifier} def} {{modifier} def}...

The indicator "item-id-def" is the first definition item name in the output-list. It is used to describe the item-id input field, but is not required. If the ICOMPILE routine finds that the first definition does not have an amc value of zero and, therefore, is not an item-id reference, a hard-coded default item is used.

The indicator "def" represents the definition item names; NAME, ADDRESS, CITY, ZIP etc. The indicator "mod" represents a modifier which allows variable features to be associated with each definition.

The Tables

The internal tables are allocated in the COMMONS code segment. The common area is used to allow exception processing through external subroutines without having to pass miles of parameters. Each array is allocated 75 elements creating a defacto maximum of 75 data fields per screen. This of course can be extended by patching the COMMONS items and recompiling all the programs. The common arrays are:

Array	*Description*
DATADEF (75)	ICOMPILE reads each definition item into a subsequent entry in the DATADEF array. The sequence is determined by the order in which the definition items are specified in the command sentence.
DSPFIELD (75)	The display format of each data field. Used for to refresh the data field after external windows are printed. Synonym names are assigned via an EQUATE statement within the COMMONS item.
ITEM (75)	The current data item.
LAST.ITEM (75)	The last written data item.
CURRENTDEF (75)	The parsed definition item for the current input field.

The simple COMMON variables are:

ITEMID	The current item-id

IDDEF	The definition item for the item-id entry.
DATAFILE	The file variable referencing the data level.
DICTFILE	The file variable referencing the dictionary level.

In addition, the COMMONS items contains standardized EQUATES and variables containing the standard @ terminal control functions.

Input Field Definitions

The INPUT definition items reside in the file dictionary along with all the definition items used by ACCESS. The format of the definition items, shown in Fig. 7-3, follows closely to that of an ACCESS definition item except for a few extensions.

ID: Definition Name

001 Type	Usually an S]U. The U extension stands for update.
002 Amc	The retrieved and updates attribute pointer.
003 Label	The screen label for the data field
005 n/a	
005 n/a	
006 Iconv	Used for input conversions. If not specified, defaults to same as output conversion. This does not seem to effect ACCESS at all.
007 Oconv	Output conversion.
008 Correlative	Generates default output values. At the present time, only the substitution (S) conversion is allowed.
009 Just	(L)eft or (R)ight justified on display.
010 Max	The Maximum display length of the field. All input is variable with no maximum.
011 Internal use	
012 Valid	Conversion used to validate input. If the result of the ICONV is null, the data is invalid.
013 n/a	
014 Error Message	Invalid entry error message text.
015 Help Message	Quick help text.
016 Help item-id	Help text item-id stored in the INPUT.HELP.FILE.

FIG. 7-3. INPUT process field definition item layout.

When ICOMPILE encounters a definition name in the command sentence, it first attempts to read the related definition item from the current file dictionary. If that fails, it attempts the read from the account master dictionary. If both fail, ICOMPILE aborts with the error message:

[202] 'word' NOT ON FILE

The code is as follows:

```
READ DATADEF(FIELDNUM) FROM DICTFILE,AWORD ELSE
    READ DATADEF(FIELDNUM) FROM MD,AWORD ELSE STOP 202,AWORD
END
```

As the data definitions are read into the DATADEF array, the label fields are given sequence numbers for display and the longest label is determined. After the statement is parsed, DATADEF is passed through a second time and the final screen positions of the data fields is calculated. By keeping track of the longest label length, all the other labels can be padded to force alignment of the input positions. An example is shown in Fig. 7-4. Assume that because each definition does not have a value in attribute 003, the ICOM-PILE subroutine uses the definition item-ids as the screen input labels. Because ADDRESS is the longest label, all the data display fields are automatically aligned based on its length.

INP command sentence:

>INP STAFF ID **NAME ADDRESS CITY**

FIG. 7-4. INPUT process automatic field alignment.

Formats the screen fields as:

```
Name.... FINK, SAM
Address. 12 MAIN ST
City.... LOS ANGELES
```

Input Modifiers

Modifier words usually effect the data definition name immediately following in the command sentence. The simplest modifications are made when the REQUIRED or DIS-PLAY modifiers are used. Attribute 11 of the DATADEF is set to a 1 if it is required, a 0 if not. Attribute 1, the type field, is set to an alpha "O" if the field is display only, and left alone if not.

The following modifiers are hard-coded in the ICOMPILE subroutine.

Modifier	Description
@(col,row)	Any definition can be placed at a specific column and row on the screen. If this modifier is not used, each input field is prompted on the next available line. For example: STAFF @(0,12) NAME ADDRESS @(55,12) CITY

DISPLAY	Display describes a definition as display only. The field cannot be modified on the screen. For example:

STAFF NAME CITY STATE DISPLAY STATE.NAME

The STATE.NAME is displayed only and not available for modification. This is a useful modifier if the definition output is a virtual value and not an actual data field.

REQUIRE	Requires that a field be input, (non-skip). For example:

STAFF NAME ADDRESS CITY REQUIRE ZIP

PAGE	An INPUT screen can be made up of multiple pages. Paging occurs automatically when the number of definitions exceeds the number of rows on the screen. Paging can also be forced with this option as follows:

STAFF NAME ADDRESS CITY STATE PAGE SALARY HIRE.DATE

NAME, ADDRESS, CITY and STATE are on page 1, and SALARY and HIRE.DATE are on page 2.

USING	INPUT definition items normally use correlative and conversion extensions that cannot normally be understood by ACCESS. USING helps alleviate confusion by allowing INPUT definition items to be stored in a file other than the targeted file dictionary. The general form is:

STAFF USING SCREENDICT

The file to be updated is STAFF, but the input data definitions are to be read from SCREENDICT.

PROTECT	This indicates that the entire screen is display only. The change prompt only allows pagination and exit. The PROTECT modifier must be used just prior to the file name in the command sentence as follows:

STAFF NAME ADDRESS CITY STATE ZIP

If ICOMPILE does not find the above modifiers in the hard-coded area, then it checks if the modifier exists in the master dictionary. Any modifier defined as a CZ type in the MD is considered a throwaway and skipped. Therefore, any valid throwaway can be used. In addition, groups of input fields can be aligned by using the @ modifier. Each new @ modifier begins a new alignment group, as shown in Fig. 7-5.

The INP command sentence:

        INP STAFF ID @(0,11) NAME ADDRESS @(45,11) CITY STATE

Produces aligned output as follows:

        Name.... FINK,SAM   City.. LOS ANGELES
        Address. 12 MAIN ST   State. CA

FIG. 7-5. Group field alignment using the @ modifier.

ADDRESS is the longest label in the first group and CITY is the longest label in the second group.

Options

The indictor "options" is any special modifier used at the end of the sentence. The valid options are:

Option	*Description*
DBL-SPC	If the sentence is not a form-type, using @ function modifiers, each automatically positioned input field is double spaced from the previous.
COMPILE	The syntax of the COMPILE modifier is:

COMPILE *subname*

After the command sentence parsing is complete, an initialization subroutine is built consisting of explicit statements setting each table entry to the indicated parameters.

When the COMPILE option is used, the created subroutine is written to the file name indicated in the variable, SUBFILENAME, "ADVBP" for the purposes of the above example. The initialization subroutine is then compiled and catalogued. The associated screen can be initiated by using the "subname" as the only argument in the INPUT command sentence as follows:

>INP *subname*

For example:

>INP STAFF NAME CITY STATE ZIP COMPILE STAFF.SCREEN

Creates a subroutine called STAFF.SCREEN. The same screen can be initiated by using STAFF.SCREEN as the only argument in the INPUT command sentence:

>INP STAFF.SCREEN

If the "subname" is not used, a subroutine is created using the format:

SCR.*filename*

In this case, the subroutine would be called:

SCR.STAFF

The INPUT program determines whether or not the first word of the sentence is a subroutine name as follows:

```
028 SUBNAME = FIELD(ARGS,' ',1)
029 SUBOK = (OCONV(SUBNAME, 'TMD;X;;2 ') = 'E6')
030 IF SUBOK THEN
031     CALL @(SUBNAME)
032 END ELSE
```

```
033    CALL ICOMPILE(ARGS)
034 END
```

The variable SUBNAME is passed through a file translate which reads the second attribute of the possible SUBNAME verb in MD.

```
029 SUBOK = (OCONV(SUBNAME,' TMD;X;;2') = 'E6')
```

If this attribute is an "E6", then SUBNAME is a subroutine, otherwise, the statement must be parsed via ICOMPILE.

Conversions and Correlatives

Conversions and correlatives are carried as baggage by the ICOMPILE subroutine. All interpretation is performed within the INPUT main program during runtime.

The data definition item is extended beyond the output conversion, 007, and correlative, 008, attributes. Additions have been made in attribute 006, input conversions, and attribute 012, validation. Each of these attributes can contain standard ACCESS conversions, which are used to process data variables via the ICONV and OCONV PICK/BASIC functions. In addition, extended "conversions" are parsed and interpreted by the PICK/BASIC program to allow for special processing.

Correlative Parameters

The correlative specification in attribute 008 allows field default values to be generated. It is an integral part of INPUT subroutine 2000. Subroutine 2000 parses the field definition parameters for the current field into the CURRENTDEF table, retrieves the data from the specified attribute, and performs any functions indicated by a correlative. The special correlative functions in attribute 008 can be:

Correlative	*Description*
S	The substitution conversion in the form:
	S;v1;v2
	This follows the same format as the standard substitution conversion discussed in the previous chapter except that this version is interpreted by the PICK/BASIC code, allowing special extensions. The *v* values can be:

Value	*Description*
D	Internal date
"literal"	A literal string
"*"	The original value
amc	The data item attribute number

F	The F correlative follows the postfix polish notation of the generic Pick implementations. However, it is actually interpreted by the

FCORR subroutine using the following form:

F;*element*;*element*;...

Elements are operand or operators. The operands can be:

Operand	Description
amc	The data item attribute
Cnum	A numeric constant
"literal"	A literal string
(conv)	Any access conversion
D	The internal system date.
T	The internal system time.

The operators can be:

Operator	Description
+	Add
–	Subtract
*	Multiply
/	Divide
:	Concatenate

Please note that all operations are performed in the following form: S1 = S2 op S1

B   A PICK/BASIC subroutine call of the form:

B;*subname*

If the first character of attribute 008 is none of the above, the program attempts to pass the data field through an OCONV using the value of attribute 008. Any user defined PICK/BASIC subroutine specified in an INPUT field definition item must follow the general form illustrated in Fig. 7-6.

FIG. 7-6. INPUT process user subroutine general form.

```
SUBROUTINE subname(DATAFIELD)
INCLUDE IBP,S COMMONS
* body of the subroutine
RETURN
```

The correlative field found in the item-id definition item indicates a function to be performed just prior to the item being filed. For example, a special subroutine can be called to do other processing or validation just before performing the MATWRITE, as shown in Fig. 7-7.

FIG. 7-7. Sample INPUT item-id definition subroutine.

```
SUBROUTINE subname(REPROMPT)
INCLUDE IBP,S COMMONS
* body of the subroutine
IF ITEM(1)='' AND ITEM(5)='' THEN
  ERRORMSG = 'Real BAD!'
  REPROMPT = 0
END
RETURN
```

The parameter passed to the subroutine is the REPROMPT flag. If for any reason, the update is not to be allowed, the subroutine simply has to set the REPROMPT flag to zero to prevent the MATWRITE.

Input and Output Conversion Parameters

Input conversions are specified in attribute 006 of the definition item and are processed by subroutine 5000 within the INPUT main program. The only special conversion allowed is the B, PICK/BASIC subroutine, which follows the same format as above. Any other conversion causes the input data field to be passed through the ICONV function. If no input conversion is specified, the input conversion field defaults to the output conversion.

Output conversion in attribute 007 are used by INPUT subroutine 2500, output convert and display. Again the only special conversion allowed is the B, PICK/BASIC subroutine call.

Validation

The validation parameter in attribute 012 is used to validate field input and is processed by subroutine 5500 in the program, INPUT. Validation can be specified by any ACCESS logical conversion. If value of DATAFIELD is intact after subroutine 5500, then it is valid data. If DATA FIELD is null, the input data is not valid.

Subroutine 5500 uses the ICONV function, which produces a null string if the data value does not meet the requirements of the conversion. For example:

```
LOOP
  INPUT DD
UNTIL ICONV(DD,"D")#'' DO REPEAT
```

This is basically all that is needed to validate the entry of a date. If the value of DD is not in a recognizable format, the ICONV passes back a null. The validation parameter can be any of the following conversions; D (date), MT (mask time), P (pattern match), R (range check), L (length check), or S (substitution), as shown in Fig. 7-8.

```
SUBROUTINE CHECKIT(DATAFIELD)
INCLUDE IBP,S COMMONS
IF NOT(DATAFIELD MATCHES "1A' '2N") THEN DATAFIELD=''
RETURN
```

FIG. 7-8. Sample INPUT validation subroutine.

In addition, the extended B conversion is made available. The PICK/BASIC subroutine should pass back a null string if the data value does not meet the coded criteria.

Keyboard Field Editing

Accepting any input from the keyboard, is controlled by the INEDIT subroutine. This includes the item-id prompt, field editing, and the "change or file" prompt. The INEDIT routine is quite similar to the EDLINE routine previously discussed. Most of the keystrokes are handled the same except for a few nuances. Some keystrokes are strictly used for string editing and are processed internally by INEDIT. Other keystrokes activate special functions in INPUT and are passed intact to the INPUT program.

The following functions are controlled by keystrokes internally interpreted by the INEDIT subroutine. These are used to visually edit the data string. The EQUATED key names are displayed along with the function and required keystrokes.

Keys	*Keywords*	*Function/Description*
Backspace or Ctl-B	BACKSPACE or BACKKEY	*Cursor back*. Positions the cursor back one character. This is non-destructive.
Ctl-F	FWDKEY	*Cursor forward*. Positions the cursor one character forward.
Ctl-N	NWORD	*Next word*. Positions the cursor to the beginning of the next word.
Ctl-P	PWORD	*Previous word*. Positions the cursor to the beginning of the previous word.
Ctl-A	HOME	*Front of string*. Positions the cursor to the first character in the string.
Ctl-E	POSEOL	*End of string*. Positions the cursor to the end of the string.
Ctl-O	INSSPC	*Insert a space*. Opens the string by inserting a single space before the current cursor position.
Ctl-D or DEL key	DELKEY or DEL	*Delete a character*. Deletes a single character at the current cursor position.
Ctl-Z	TPOS	*Transpose*. Transposes the character at the current cursor position with the character immediately following.
Ctl-C	CLREOL	*Clear end of line*. Clears the string from the cursor position to the end.
Ctl-R	REPKEY	*Replace/Insert*. Toggles typeover and insert modes.

EDLINE passes back specific characters needed by INPUT. Some of these characters are triggered at any position within the edited string. Others must be only specified at the first position of the string. The functions that can be initiated at any point in the string are:

Keys	*Keywords*	*Function/Description*
Esc	ESC or ESCC	*Abort*. Abort editing the field and leave the current field intact.
Return or Line feed or Tab keys.	CR or LF or TAB	*Accept or Enter*. Pass the edited string back to the calling program.
"?"		*Help*. The question mark at any position in

the input field passes a single question mark to the INPUT program. The single line help is displayed. A second question mark calls the INPUTHELP subroutine and displays the full HELP window.

"^"   *Back Field*. The caret, "^" tells INPUT to go back one field, leaving the original data field unaffected.

The following functions use keys which are considered data unless entered at the first position of the input field. At which point, the single keystrokes are passed to the INPUT program.

Key	*Function/Description*
Space or minus sign (−)	*Clear a field*. This is rejected if the field is REQUIRED.
A period, (.)	*Duplicate a field*. Indicates the field value is to be retrieved from the corresponding field in the last written item. The array LAST.ITEM in INPUT is used to keep track of the last item written.

The remaining CASEs are taken if none of the above control characters are present. Any other characters below CHAR(32) or above CHAR(126) are not accepted. Any other character is added onto the string depending whether the REPFLAG or INSFLAG is currently active.

The INEDIT subroutine requires that the main program passes a variable argument list. The arguments are as follows:

INEDIT(STRING,TIMER)

STRING is the edited version of the data string. TIMER is the timeout length. (The number of seconds to wait with no input.)

Reviewing the INEDIT subroutine, the loop that accepts keystrokes is as follows:

```
045 T = TIME( )
046  LOOP
047    TIMEOUT = (TIME( ) − T) > TIMER
048  UNTIL TIMEOUT OR SYSTEM(14) DO REPEAT
049  IF NOT(TIMEOUT) THEN
050    IN SKEY
051    KEY = CHAR(SKEY)
052  END ELSE KEY = ESC
```

The LOOP keeps processing until either the SYSTEM (14) function detects a character waiting in the input type ahead buffer or TIMEOUT becomes true. The TIMEOUT flag is set when the number of elapsed seconds between the current time, TIME( ) and the initial time, T, is greater than the passed TIMER value.

```
047    TIMEOUT = (TIME( ) − T) > TIMER
```

When a TIMEOUT condition occurs, an <escape> response is plugged into the KEY variable. This is useful for preventing an item from remaining locked. Both the INPUT program field input and change prompt subroutines, 400 and 4000, use INEDIT and designate a timeout of 90 seconds.

The prompt for the item-id in subroutine 100 requires a less critical timeout. Therefore, the timeout is set at 300 seconds, or 5 minutes:

```
CALL INEDIT(RESP,300)
```

The Main Input Procedure

The main procedural section of the INPUT program consists of two main tasks; 1) getting the item-id and, subsequently, reading the item, and 2) editing the contents of the item. These tasks are controlled by subroutines 100 and 200, respectively.

The highest level controlling LOOP is as follows:

```
059 LOOP
060     LOOP
061         LOCKFLAG = 0
062         GOSUB 100 ; * Get the ID and the item
063     WHILE LOCKFLAG DO REPEAT
064 UNTIL EXITFLAG DO
065     GOSUB 200 ; * Edit the item
066 REPEAT
```

Without belaboring the details, here are the INPUT program's internal subroutines and a brief explanation of their functions: Subroutine 100 handles input and validation of the item-id and MATREADUs the ITEM array. The flag, LOCKFLAG, is set only if the LOCKED clause is taken in the MATREADU statement.

```
153 MATREADU ITEM FROM DATAFILE,ITEMID LOCKED
154         CRT @(0,2):ROF:'The item is locked!':ROF:BELL:EOL:
155         LOCKFLAG = 1
156 END ELSE
157         MAT ITEM = ''
158         CHANGEFLAG = 1
159         NEWFLAG = 1
160 END
```

This indicates that the item is being used by another process and forces re-prompting for the item-id.

```
060     LOOP
061         LOCKFLAG = 0
062         GOSUB 100 ; * Get the ID and the item
063     WHILE LOCKFLAG DO REPEAT
```

The item-id can be retrieved from one of two places; the terminal keyboard or the next item-id on an active list. The ACTIVELIST flag is retrieved as follows:

```
021 ACTIVELIST = SYSTEM(11)
```

The SYSTEM(11) function is true when a SELECT, GET-LIST, QSELECT has been successfully performed just prior to initiating the INPUT routine. (Pick R83 only!) INPUT retrieves every item in the active list until the end of the list is reached or the operator enters an XK, exit and kill, or FK, file and kill, at the "change or file" prompt.

Item-id entry from the keyboard allows a few special keystrokes:

Esc   Terminate the INPUT process.

+   Retrieve the next available, unused, sequential item-id.

?   Display the help screens using the INPUTHELP subroutine.

*   Perform an internal PICK/BASIC SELECT on all the items in the file.

Subroutine 200 handles the data field editing functions after the item has been retrieved. The main procedural flow is further broken into two functions; the "change and file" prompt handled in subroutine 400, and data input handled by subroutine 300. The controlling LOOP is as follows:

```
170 LOOP
171    EXITFLAG = 0
172    IF NOT(NEWFLAG) THEN GOSUB 400;* Change, File, and Exit Prompt
173 UNTIL EXITFLAG DO
174    GOSUB 300 ;* Input field data
175 REPEAT
176 RETURN
```

Subroutine 300 is a controlling loop which handles a single input field based on the incremented (or decremented) counter, FIELDNUM. The BACKFIELD flag indicates whether the previous field is to be processed instead of the next field.

```
179 300 * Input field data
182 LOOP
185    LOOP
186       VMC = 1
187       GOSUB 2000 ;* Get Field data
191          GOSUB 4000 ;* Get Input
194       IF BACKFIELD THEN
196          FIELDNUM = FIELDNUM − 1
207       END ELSE
208          FIELDNUM = FIELDNUM + 1
209       END
210    UNTIL (FIELDNUM > FIELDEND) DO REPEAT
211       *
212 WHILE NEWFLAG AND PAGENO < PAGES DO
```

```
213    PAGENO = PAGENO + 1
219 REPEAT
```

Subroutine 300 calls two other subroutines, 2000 and 4000. Subroutine 2000 retrieves the field data parameters and the value of the DATAFIELD. Subroutine 4000 prompts each data field referenced by the current value of FIELDNUM.

The details for data field editing, validation and movement are covered above in the above sections titled, Correlatives, Input and Output Conversions, Validation, and Keyboard Field Editing.

Subroutine 400 is the "change and file" prompt. It allows the contents of any input field to be changed, multiple pages to be scrolled, and the item to be written or deleted. The valid responses are:

Response	*Description*
?	Displays the help screens controlled by INPUTHELP.
Esc	Exit the item without filing changes. X can be used also.
XK	Exit the item without filing changes and "kill" the active list.
P	Forward one page.
B	Back one page.
C*n*	Change all the fields (C by itself) or a single field where the optional *n* is the field number.
F	File and exit to the item-id prompt. FI can be used also.
FK	File the item, "kill" the active list, and exit to the item-id prompt.
FD	Delete the current item. There is an "Are you sure?" prompt which goes along with this.

The other miscellaneous INPUT internal subroutines are:

Subroutine	*Description*
1000	Print the screen header.
1100	Display the screen labels.
1200	Output convert and display all the data fields. (Uses subroutine 2500.)
2001	A subset of subroutine 2000. Get the field data and perform any correlative functions.
2500	Output convert and display a single data field.
5000	Input convert a data field
5500	Validate data entry.
6000	Redisplay the current page. (Used to repaint the screen from the DSPFIELD matrix after the help screen has been displayed.)
6055	Redisplay a segment of the screen data.
6100	The "are you sure?" prompt.
6500	Bleed the remaining entries off an active list. This performs the "kill" function.
8000	The automatic single line help display routine.

The Listings

More can be learned by looking at one line of code versus reading three paragraphs. With that in mind, the remainder of this chapter is devoted to the program listings. The only listing not found here is GETSENTENCE, which is provided in Chapter 5. Feel free to use, modify, critique, bombast, enjoy, etc. these programs. The challenge is to add the other important features that must exist in a complete screen generator. Here are some suggested features:

- Multivalue handling
- Automatic data cross referencing, including cross-reference reporting and maintenance.

All of the following programs (Fig. 7-9 through 7-14) should be placed in a file called IBP,S. This is the S data section of the IBP dictionary. In addition, the ISUB dictionary should be created with its own S data section. The suggested commands for doing this are:

```
>CREATE-FILE DICT IBP 3,1
>CREATE-FILE DATA IBP,S 11,5
>CREATE-FILE DICT ISUB 3,1
>CREATE-FILE DATA ISUB,S 11,5
```

```
      COMMONS
001 * Common variables
002 *
003 COMMON DATADEF(75),DSPFIELD(75),ITEM(75),LAST.ITEM(75)
004 COMMON CURRENTDEF(25),ITEMID,IDDEF
005 COMMON ACTIVELIST,FORMFLAG,COMPILE,PAGELIMITS
006 COMMON DATAFILE,DICTFILE,FILENAME,PROTECTED
007 COMMON FIRSTROW,LASTROW
008 COMMON TERMDEPTH,TERMWIDTH,TERMTYPE
009 COMMON PAGENO,PAGES,FIELDNUM
010 *
011 * CURRENTDEF Synonyms
012 *
013 EQU TYPE        TO CURRENTDEF(1)
014 EQU ATTRIBUTE   TO CURRENTDEF(2)
015 EQU LABEL       TO CURRENTDEF(3)
016 EQU FIELDCOL    TO CURRENTDEF(4)
017 EQU FIELDROW    TO CURRENTDEF(5)
018 EQU INCONV      TO CURRENTDEF(6)
019 EQU OUTCONV     TO CURRENTDEF(7)
020 EQU CORRELATIVE TO CURRENTDEF(8)
021 EQU JUST        TO CURRENTDEF(9)
022 EQU LENGTH      TO CURRENTDEF(10)
023 EQU REQUIRED    TO CURRENTDEF(11)
024 EQU VALID       TO CURRENTDEF(12)
025 EQU ERRORMSG    TO CURRENTDEF(13)
026 EQU HELPMSG     TO CURRENTDEF(14)
```

FIG. 7-9. INPUT process COMMONS code segment listing (continues).

```
027 EQU HELPID      TO CURRENTDEF(15)
028 EQU DISPLAYONLY TO CURRENTDEF(16)
029 EQU LABLEN      TO CURRENTDEF(17)
030 EQU FORMAT      TO CURRENTDEF(18)
031 *
032 * Default constants
033 *
034 EQU BELL        TO CHAR(7)
035 EQU BACKSPACE   TO CHAR(8)
036 EQU TAB         TO CHAR(9)
037 EQU CR          TO CHAR(13)
038 EQU FF          TO CHAR(12)
039 EQU LF          TO CHAR(10)
040 EQU ESCC        TO CHAR(27)
041 EQU SP          TO CHAR(32)
042 EQU ESC         TO CHAR(251)
043 EQU AM          TO CHAR(254)
044 EQU VM          TO CHAR(253)
045 EQU SVM         TO CHAR(252)
046 *
047 * Terminal Controls
048 *
049 CLS      = @(-1)
050 HOME     = @(-2)
051 EOS      = @(-3)
052 EOL      = @(-4)
053 RON      = @(-13)
054 ROF      = @(-14)
055 UON      = @(-15)
056 UOF      = @(-16)
057 CRLF     = CR:LF
058 ESCAPE = ESCC:ESC:'X'
059 TERMWIDTH = SYSTEM(2)
060 TERMDEPTH = SYSTEM(3)
061 TERMTYPE  = SYSTEM(7)
```

FIG. 7-9 ends.

```
    ICOMPILE
001 SUBROUTINE ICOMPILE(ARGS)
002 * Parse and Compile Input Statement
003 * DATE STARTED : February 1987
004 * AUTHOR: Harvey Eric Rodstein
005 * COPYRIGHT: H.E.RODSTEIN Computer Consulting 1986,7,8
006 *
007 * Initialization
008 *
009 PROMPT ''
010 *
011 INCLUDE COMMONS
012 *
013 OPEN 'MD' TO MD ELSE STOP 201,'MD'
014 *
```

FIG. 7-10. INPUT process ICOMPILE subroutine listing (continues).

```
015 * Init work variables
016 *
017 MAT DATADEF = ''
018 PAGENO       = 1
019 PAGES        = 1
020 SUBNAME      = ''
021 DBLSPC       = 0
022 PROTECTED    = 0
023 FORCEPAGE    = 0
024 FORCELIST    = ''
025 *
026 D.IDDEF = 'A':AM:'0':AM:AM:AM:AM:'MCU':AM:AM:AM:'R':AM:'5'
027 *
028 * Find and Open the File
029 *
030 FILEFLAG = 0
031 DICTFLAG = 0
032 CNT = DCOUNT(ARGS,' ')
033 FOR I = 1 TO CNT UNTIL FILEFLAG
034  FILENAME = FIELD(ARGS,' ',I)
035  BEGIN CASE
036     CASE FILENAME = 'DICT'
037        DICTFLAG = 1
038     CASE FILENAME = 'DISPLAY' OR FILENAME = 'PROTECT'
039        PROTECTED = 1
040     CASE 1
041        OPEN 'DICT',FILENAME TO DICTFILE THEN FILEFLAG = I
042  END CASE
043 NEXT I
044 *
045 IF FILEFLAG THEN
046    IF DICTFLAG THEN
047       DATAFILE = DICTFILE
048       OPEN 'MD' TO DICTFILE ELSE STOP 201,'MD'
049       DICTNAME = 'MD'
050    END ELSE
051       OPEN FILENAME TO DATAFILE ELSE STOP 201,FILENAME
052       DICTNAME = FILENAME
053    END
054 END ELSE
055    FILENAME = FIELD(ARGS,' ',1)
056    STOP 201,FILENAME
057 END
058 *
059 WORDPOS = FILEFLAG+1
060 *
061 * Check for using clause and item-id def
062 *
063 AWORD=FIELD(ARGS,' ',WORDPOS)
064 IF AWORD='USING' THEN
065    WORDPOS=WORDPOS+1
066    UFILE=FIELD(ARGS,' ',WORDPOS)
067    IF UFILE='DICT' THEN
```

FIG. 7-10 continues.

```
068     WORDPOS=WORDPOS+1
069     UFILE=FIELD(ARGS,' ',WORDPOS)
070     OPEN 'DICT',UFILE TO USEDICTFILE ELSE STOP 201,'DICT ':UFILE
071   END ELSE
072     OPEN UFILE TO USEDICTFILE ELSE STOP 201,UFILE
073   END
074   WORDPOS=WORDPOS+1
075   IDNAME=FIELD(ARGS,' ',WORDPOS)
076 END ELSE
077   USEDICTFILE=DICTFILE
078   IDNAME=AWORD
079 END
080 *
081 * Parse item-id defintion
082 *
083 IDDEF = ''
084 READ IDDEF FROM USEDICTFILE,IDNAME THEN
085     IDATT = IDDEF<2>
086     IF NUM(IDATT) THEN IDATT=IDATT+0
087     IF IDATT=0 THEN
088         WORDPOS = WORDPOS+1
089     END ELSE IDDEF = ''
090 END
091 IF IDDEF = '' THEN
092     READ IDDEF FROM USEDICTFILE,'ID' ELSE IDDEF = D.IDDEF
093 END
094 LABEL = IDDEF<3>
095 IF LABEL = '' THEN
096     IDLABEL = 'Item Id'
097 END ELSE IDLABEL = OCONV(LABEL,'MCT')
098 IDDEF<3> = IDLABEL
099 *
100 * Parse the rest to a matrix
101 *
102 WORD          = ''
103 DEFINITIONS   = ''
104 FIRSTROW      = 6
105 LASTROW       = TERMDEPTH
106 MAXLABLEN     = 0
107 FIELDNUM      = 1
108 LASTFIELDNUM = FIELDNUM
109 ROW           = FIRSTROW
110 CURSORLIST    = ''
111 PAGELIMITS    = ''
112 VMBEG         = 0
113 REQUIRED      = 0
114 DISPLAYONLY   = 0
115 *
116 IF LASTROW > 23 THEN LASTROW = 23
117 *
118 FORMFLAG = INDEX(ARGS,'@',1)
119 COMPILE  = INDEX(ARGS,'COMPILE ',1)
120 *
```

FIG. 7-10 continues.

```
121 IF COMPILE THEN CRT 'Parsing arguments...':
122 CRT
123 *
124 * Special modifiers
125 *
126 LOOP
127   AWORD=FIELD(ARGS,' ',WORDPOS)
128 UNTIL AWORD='' DO
129   BEGIN CASE
130     CASE AWORD[1,1]='@'
131       PARAMS = FIELD(FIELD(AWORD,'(',2),')',1)
132       COL = FIELD(PARAMS,',',1)
133       ROW = FIELD(PARAMS,',',2)
134       OK  = NOT(COL='') * NOT(ROW='') * NUM(COL:ROW)
135       IF NOT(OK) THEN STOP AWORD
136       CURSORLIST<FIELDNUM,1> = COL
137       CURSORLIST<FIELDNUM,2> = ROW
138       ALIGNFIELD = FIELDNUM-1
139       GOSUB 1000 ;* Align grouped labels
140       MAXLABLEN = 0
141     CASE AWORD[1,4] = 'REQU'
142       REQUIRED = 1
143     CASE AWORD = 'PAGE' OR AWORD = 'FORCEPAGE'
144       FORCEPAGE = 1
145     CASE AWORD[1,7] = 'DISPLAY' OR WORD[1,7]='PROTECT'
146       DISPLAYONLY = 1
147     CASE AWORD[1,7]='COMPILE'
148       COMPILE=1
149       WORDPOS=WORDPOS+1
150       SUBNAME = FIELD(ARGS,' ',WORDPOS)
151     CASE AWORD='DBL-SPC'
152       DBLSPC = 1
153     CASE 1
154     READ DATADEF(FIELDNUM) FROM USEDICTFILE,AWORD ELSE
155         READ DATADEF(FIELDNUM) FROM MD,AWORD ELSE STOP 202,AWORD
156     END
157     TYPE = DATADEF(FIELDNUM)<1>
158     BEGIN CASE
159       CASE TYPE#'' AND INDEX('AS',TYPE[1,1],1)
160           DEFINITIONS<-1> = AWORD
161           FORCELIST<FIELDNUM>=FORCEPAGE
162           IF FORCEPAGE THEN
163               FORCEPAGE=0
164               ALIGNFIELD=FIELDNUM-1
165               GOSUB 1000 ;* Align grouped labels
166               MAXLABLEN=0
167           END
168           LABEL = TRIM(DATADEF(FIELDNUM)<3>)
169           IF LABEL = '' THEN LABEL = AWORD
170           LABEL = (FIELDNUM:')') "L#3":" ":OCONV(LABEL,'MCT')
171           DATADEF(FIELDNUM)<3>=LABEL
172           LABLEN = LEN(LABEL)
173           IF LABLEN > MAXLABLEN THEN MAXLABLEN = LABLEN
```

FIG. 7-10 continues.

```
174              ASSOCIATE = DATADEF(FIELDNUM)<4>
175              AFIELD = ASSOCIATE[1,1]
176              LENGTH = DATADEF(FIELDNUM)<10>
177              DATADEF(FIELDNUM)<11> = REQUIRED
178              REQUIRED = 0
179              IF DISPLAYONLY THEN
180                  DATADEF(FIELDNUM)<1>='O'
181                  DISPLAYONLY = 0
182              END
183              DSPFIELD(FIELDNUM) = ''
184              FIELDNUM = FIELDNUM + 1
185          CASE TYPE = 'CZ' ; NULL ;* Throwaway connective
186          CASE 1            ; STOP 202,AWORD
187        END CASE
188    END CASE
189    WORDPOS=WORDPOS+1
190 REPEAT
191 *
192 * Check for screen position inconsistancies
193 *
194 IF ROW>LASTROW THEN STOP 'ROW ':ROW:' GREATER THAN ':LASTROW
195 IF ROW<FIRSTROW THEN STOP 'ROW ':ROW:' LESS THAN ':FIRSTROW
196 FIELDMAX = FIELDNUM - 1
197 IF NOT(FIELDMAX) THEN STOP 'DATA DEFINITIONS MISSING'
198 *
199 ALIGNFIELD = FIELDMAX
200 GOSUB 1000 ; * Align grouped labels
201 *
202 * Calculate Screen Positions
203 *     LABCOLROW is the LABEL position
204 *     FIELDCOLROW is the Data FIELD position
205 *
206 COL = 0
207 ROW = FIRSTROW-1
208 BEGPAGE = 1
209 LASTLEN = 1
210 *
211 * Screen position parsing
212 *
213 FOR FIELDNUM = 1 TO FIELDMAX
214    LABEL = DATADEF(FIELDNUM)<3>
215    LABLEN = LEN(LABEL)
216    ASSOCIATE = DATADEF(FIELDNUM)<4>
217    ATYPE = ASSOCIATE<1,1>[1,1]
218    LENGTH = DATADEF(FIELDNUM)<10>
219    IF NOT(FORMFLAG) AND ATYPE='' THEN
220      LABLEN = MAXLABLEN + 1
221      MAXFIELDLEN = TERMWIDTH-LABLEN-5
222      IF DATADEF(FIELDNUM)<10> > MAXFIELDLEN THEN
223          DATADEF(FIELDNUM)<10> = MAXFIELDLEN
224      END
225    END
226    *
```

FIG. 7-10 continues.

```
227     FORCEPAGE = FORCELIST<FIELDNUM>
228     IF CURSORLIST<FIELDNUM>='' THEN
229        ROW = ROW+1+DBLSPC
230        IF ROW>LASTROW THEN
231           FORCEPAGE = 1
232           ROW = FIRSTROW
233        END
234     END ELSE
235        COL = CURSORLIST<FIELDNUM,1>
236        ROW = CURSORLIST<FIELDNUM,2>
237     END
238     *
239     * Mark multiple pages
240     *
241     IF FORCEPAGE THEN
242        PAGELIMITS<-1> = BEGPAGE:VM:FIELDNUM-1
243        BEGPAGE = FIELDNUM
244     END
245     *
246     * Update Input Field Screen Positions
247     *
248     LABCOLROW = COL:SVM:ROW
249     FIELDCOLROW = ''
250     FIELDCOLROW = COL+LABLEN+2:SVM:ROW
251     DATADEF(FIELDNUM)<3> = LABCOLROW:VM:LABEL
252     DATADEF(FIELDNUM)<5,-1> = FIELDCOLROW
253 NEXT FIELDNUM
254 *
255 IF PAGELIMITS='' THEN
256     PAGELIMITS = '1':VM:FIELDMAX
257     PAGES = 1
258 END ELSE
259     PAGELIMITS<-1> = BEGPAGE:VM:FIELDMAX
260     PAGES = DCOUNT(PAGELIMITS,AM)
261 END
262 *
263 *
264 IF NOT(COMPILE) THEN RETURN
265 *
266 * Build and Compile Init Code
267 *
268 SUBFILENAME = 'ADVBP'
269 OPEN SUBFILENAME TO IBPS ELSE STOP 201,SUBFILENAME
270 READ COMREC FROM SUBFILE,'COMMONS' ELSE STOP 202,'COMMONS'
271 *
272 IF SUBNAME = '' THEN SUBNAME = 'SCR.':FILENAME
273 *
274 CRT 'Building Init Subroutine ':SUBNAME:
275 *
276 PREC = 'SUBROUTINE ':SUBNAME
277 PREC<-1> = 'INCLUDE ':SUBFILENAME':' COMMONS'
278 PREC<-1> = 'FIELDMAX = ':FIELDMAX
279 PREC<-1> = 'FIRSTROW = ':FIRSTROW
```

FIG. 7-10 continues.

```
280 PREC<-1> = 'LASTROW   = ':LASTROW
281 PREC<-1> = 'PAGENO    = 1'
282 PREC<-1> = 'PAGES     = ':PAGES
283 PREC<-1> = 'PAGELIMITS = ""'
284 PREC<-1> = 'PROTECTED = ':PROTECTED
285 *
286 PREC<-1> = 'FILENAME = "':FILENAME:'"'
287 PREC<-1> = 'DICTNAME = "':DICTNAME:'"'
288 PREC<-1> = 'OPEN "DICT",DICTNAME TO DICTFILE ELSE STOP 201,DICTNAME'
289 PREC<-1> = 'OPEN FILENAME TO DATAFILE ELSE STOP 201,FILENAME'
290 *
291 CRT
292 CNT = DCOUNT(PAGELIMITS,AM)
293 FOR I = 1 TO CNT
294   PREC<-1> = 'PAGELIMITS<':I:'> = "':PAGELIMITS<I>:'"'
295   CRT '-':
296 NEXT I
297 CRT '+':
298 *
299 CNT = DCOUNT(IDDEF,AM)
300 JREC = 'IDDEF = \':IDDEF<1>:'\'
301 FOR I = 2 TO CNT
302   JREC = JREC:':AM:\':IDDEF<I>:'\'
303   CRT '-':
304 NEXT I
305 PREC<-1> = JREC
306 CRT '+':
307 FOR I = 1 TO FIELDMAX
308    CNT = DCOUNT(DATADEF(I),AM)
309    JREC = 'DATADEF(':I:') = \':DATADEF(I)<1>:'\'
310    FOR J = 2 TO CNT
311       JREC = JREC:':AM:\':DATADEF(I)<J>:'\'
312    NEXT J
313    PREC<-1> = JREC
314    CRT '-':
315 NEXT I
316 PREC<-1> = 'MAT DSPFIELD = ""'
317 PREC<-1> = 'RETURN'
318 WRITE PREC ON SUBFILE,SUBNAME
319 CRT
320 CRT 'Compiling Init Subroutine ':SUBNAME
321 EXECUTE 'BASIC ':SUBFILENAME:' ':SUBNAME
322 EXECUTE 'CATALOG ':FIELD(SUBFILENAME,',',1):' ':SUBNAME
323 RETURN
324 *
325 *
326 * Subroutines
327 *
328 1000 * Align grouped labels
329 *
330 IF MAXLABLEN THEN
331    FOR I = LASTFIELDNUM TO ALIGNFIELD
332       IF DATADEF(I)<4> = '' THEN
```

FIG. 7-10 continues.

```
333          LABEL = DATADEF(I)<3>
334          DATADEF(I)<3> = LABEL:STR('.',MAXLABLEN-LEN(LABEL))
335        END
336     NEXT I
337 END
338 LASTFIELDNUM=FIELDNUM
339 RETURN
340 *
341 END
```

FIG. 7-10 ends.

```
    FCORR
001 SUBROUTINE FCORR(CORR,RESP)
002 * F CORRELATIVE EMULATOR
003 * DATE STARTED : February 1987
004 * AUTHOR: Harvey Eric Rodstein
005 * COPYRIGHT: H.E.RODSTEIN Computer Consulting 1986,7,8
006 *
007 * Initialization
008 *
009 PROMPT ''
010 *
011 INCLUDE COMMONS
012 *
013 STACK = ''
014 *
015 OPCNT = DCOUNT(CORR,';')
016 FOR I = 2 TO OPCNT
017   OP = FIELD(CORR,';',I)
018   OPT= OP[1,1]
019   BEGIN CASE
020     CASE NUM(OP)
021       IF OP<=75 THEN
022           STACK = INSERT(STACK,1;ITEM(OP))
023       END ELSE STOP 'ATTRIBUTE ':OP:' IS OUT OF RANGE'
024     CASE INDEX(\C"'\,OPT,1)
025       STACK = INSERT(STACK,1;FIELD(OP,OPT,2))
026     CASE OPT='('
027       STACK<1> = OCONV(STACK<1>,FIELD(FIELD(OP,'(',2),')',1))
028     CASE OPT='D'
029       STACK = INSERT(STACK,1;DATE())
030     CASE OPT='T'
031       STACK = INSERT(STACK,1;TIME())
032     CASE OPT='+'
033       STACK<1> = STACK<2>+STACK<1>
034       STACK = DELETE(STACK,2)
035     CASE OPT='-'
036       STACK<1> = STACK<2>-STACK<1>
037       STACK = DELETE(STACK,2)
038     CASE OPT='*'
039       STACK<1> = STACK<2>*STACK<1>
```

FIG. 7-11. INPUT process FCORR subroutine listing (continues).

```
040        STACK = DELETE(STACK,2)
041     CASE OPT='/'
042        STACK<1> = STACK<2>/STACK<1>
043        STACK = DELETE(STACK,2)
044     CASE OPT=':'
045        STACK<1> = STACK<2>:STACK<1>
046        STACK = DELETE(STACK,2)
047   END CASE
048 NEXT I
049 RESP = STACK<1>
050 RETURN
051 *
052 END
```

FIG. 7-11 ends.

```
    INEDIT
001 SUBROUTINE INEDIT (STRING,TIMER)
002 * Interactive string edit
003 * DATE STARTED : February 1988
004 * AUTHOR: Harvey Eric Rodstein
005 * COPYRIGHT: H.E.RODSTEIN Computer Consulting 1988
006 *
007 * Initialization
008 *
009 PROMPT ''
010 *
011 INCLUDE COMMONS
012 *
013 EQU HOMKEY TO CHAR(1)
014 EQU BAKKEY TO CHAR(2)
015 EQU CLREOL TO CHAR(3)
016 EQU DELKEY TO CHAR(4)
017 EQU POSEOL TO CHAR(5)
018 EQU FWDKEY TO CHAR(6)
019 EQU NWORD  TO CHAR(14)
020 EQU PWORD  TO CHAR(16)
021 EQU INSSPC TO CHAR(15)
022 EQU REPKEY TO CHAR(18)
023 EQU CTLX   TO CHAR(24)
024 EQU TPOS   TO CHAR(26)
025 EQU DEL    TO CHAR(127)
026 *
027 EQU MAXLENGTH TO 240
028 *
029 EOL = @(-4)
030 INEOL = ']':EOL
031 *
032 INSFLAG = 0
033 REPFLAG = 1
034 IF STRING = '' THEN INDISP = SPACE(LENGTH) ELSE INDISP = STRING
035 MAXPOS = LEN(STRING)+1
```

FIG. 7-12. INPUT process INEDIT subroutine listing (continues).

```
036 DONE = 0
037 POS  = 1
038 ICOL = LEN(LABEL)+2
039 *
040 CRT @(0,4):EOL:
041 CRT @(0,3):EOL:LABEL:@(ICOL-1,3):'[':INDISP:']':@(ICOL,3):
042 *
043 ECHO OFF
044 LOOP
045   T = TIME()
046   LOOP
047     TIMEOUT = (TIME()-T)>TIMER
048   UNTIL TIMEOUT OR SYSTEM(14) DO REPEAT
049   IF NOT(TIMEOUT) THEN
050     IN SKEY
051     KEY=CHAR(SKEY)
052   END ELSE KEY=ESC
053   BEGIN CASE
054     CASE KEY = BACKSPACE OR KEY = BAKKEY
055       IF POS>1 THEN
056         POS=POS-1
057         CRT BACKSPACE:
058       END
059     CASE KEY = FWDKEY
060       CRT STRING[POS,1]:
061       IF POS<MAXPOS THEN POS = POS+1 ELSE CRT BELL:
062     CASE KEY = NWORD
063       STRING2 = STRING[POS,MAXLENGTH]
064       DELIM = OCONV(STRING2,'MC/N':VM:'MC/A')[1,1]
065       IF DELIM#'' THEN
066         OFFSET = INDEX(STRING2,DELIM,1)
067         POS = POS + OFFSET
068         CRT STRING2[1,OFFSET]:
069       END
070     CASE KEY = PWORD
071       TESTPOS = POS
072       LOOP
073         STRING1 = STRING[1,TESTPOS-1]
074         PCHAR   = STRING[TESTPOS-1,1]
075         DELIM = OCONV(STRING1,'MC/N':VM:'MC/A')
076         DELIM = DELIM[LEN(DELIM),1]
077       UNTIL PCHAR#DELIM OR DELIM = '' DO
078         IF TESTPOS THEN TESTPOS=TESTPOS-1
079       REPEAT
080       IF DELIM # '' THEN
081         MAXDELIM = COUNT(STRING1,DELIM)
082         OFFSET = (POS-INDEX(STRING1,DELIM,MAXDELIM)) - 1
083         POS = POS - OFFSET
084         CRT STR(BACKSPACE,OFFSET):
085       END ELSE
086         CRT STR(BACKSPACE,POS-1):
087         POS = 1
088       END
```

FIG. 7-12 continues.

```
089        CASE KEY = HOMKEY
090          CRT STR(BACKSPACE,POS-1):
091          POS = 1
092        CASE KEY = POSEOL
093          CRT STR(BACKSPACE,POS-1):STRING:EOL:
094          POS = MAXPOS
095        CASE KEY = INSSPC
096          STRING1 = STRING[1,POS-1]
097          STRING2 = ' ':STRING[POS,MAXLENGTH]
098          STRING = STRING1:STRING2
099          CRT STRING2:INEOL:STR(BACKSPACE,LEN(STRING2)+1):
100          MAXPOS = MAXPOS+1
101        CASE KEY = DELKEY OR KEY = DEL
102          STRING1 = STRING[1,POS-1]
103          STRING2 = STRING[POS+1,MAXLENGTH]
104          STRING = STRING1:STRING2
105          CRT STRING2:INEOL:STR(BACKSPACE,LEN(STRING2)+1):
106          IF MAXPOS>1 THEN MAXPOS = MAXPOS-1
107        CASE KEY = TPOS
108          IF POS<MAXPOS-1 THEN
109            CHA21 = STRING[POS+1,1]:STRING[POS,1]
110            STRING = STRING[1,POS-1]:CHA21:STRING[POS+2,MAXLENGTH]
111            CRT CHA21:STR(BACKSPACE,2):
112          END
113        CASE KEY = CLREOL
114          STRING = STRING[1,POS-1]
115          MAXPOS=POS
116          CRT INEOL:
117        CASE KEY = REPKEY
118          INSFLAG = NOT(INSFLAG)
119          REPFLAG = NOT(REPFLAG)
120        CASE INDEX('?^',KEY,1)
121          DONE = 1
122          STRING = KEY
123        CASE ((POS=1) AND INDEX(' .-',KEY,1))
124          DONE = 1
125          STRING = KEY
126        CASE INDEX(ESC:ESCC,KEY,1)
127          DONE = 1
128          STRING = ESC
129        CASE INDEX(LF:CR:TAB,KEY,1)
130          DONE = 1
131          STRING = TRIM(STRING)
132        CASE SKEY<32 OR SKEY>126
133          CRT BELL:
134        CASE REPFLAG
135          STRING1 = STRING[1,POS-1]
136          STRING = STRING1:KEY:STRING[POS+1,MAXLENGTH]
137          POS = POS + 1
138          IF POS>MAXPOS THEN MAXPOS = POS
139          CRT KEY:
140        CASE INSFLAG
141          STRING1 = STRING[1,POS-1]
```

FIG. 7-12 continues.

```
142          STRING2 = KEY:STRING[POS,MAXLENGTH]
143          STRING = STRING1:STRING2
144          POS = POS + 1
145          MAXPOS = MAXPOS + 1
146          CRT STRING2:INEOL:STR(BACKSPACE,LEN(STRING2)):
147    END CASE
148 UNTIL DONE DO REPEAT
149 *
150 ECHO ON
151 RETURN
152 *
153 END
```

FIG. 7-12 ends.

```
    INPUTHELP
001 SUBROUTINE INPUTHELP(HELP.ITEM)
002 * Input Help Screens
003 * DATE STARTED : February 1988
004 * AUTHOR: Harvey Eric Rodstein
005 * COPYRIGHT: H.E.RODSTEIN Computer Consulting 1988
006 *
007 * Initialization
008 *
009 INCLUDE COMMONS
010 *
011 PROMPT ''
012 *
013 OPEN 'INPUT.HELP.FILE' TO HELP.FILE ELSE RETURN
014 *
015 VAL.FLAG = 0
016 DESCVALS = ''
017 OLEN     = 79
018 ANS      = ''
019 *
020 *
021 100 *
022 *
023 TITLE = 'INPUT HELP'
024 MSG   = '(T)op, (P)age or (B)ack page, (H)ardcopy, or <ESC>ape'
025 MSG   = '(?) more help, ':MSG
026 READ LISTING FROM HELP.FILE,HELP.ITEM ELSE
027    LISTING = 'NO HELP AVAILABLE'
028 END
029 GOSUB 5000 ;* Setup and paint the screen
030 GOSUB 6000 ;* Scroll
031 RETURN
032 *
033 *
034 5000 * Setup
035 *
036 POS  = 0
037 CMAX = 18
```

FIG. 7-13. INPUT process INPUTHELP subroutine listing (continues).

```
038 PMAX = CMAX
039 MAX  = DCOUNT(LISTING,AM)
040 CNT  = 1
041 *
042 PAGEMARKS = ''
043 HPAGENO   = 1
044 *
045 CRT @(-1):
046 GOSUB 5500 ;* Paint the screen
047 *
048 RETURN
049 *
050 *
051 5500 * Paint the screen
052 *
053 CRT @(0,0):RON:TITLE:ROF: ' ':HELP.ITEM :EOL:
054 CRT
055 CRT STR('-',79)
056 *
057 I = 1
058 PAGEMARKS<HPAGENO> = CNT
059 PCOL = 0
060 PROW = 3
061 CRT @(70,0):'Page ':HPAGENO:EOL:
062 FORCEPAGE = 0
063 ENDPAGE = 0
064 MORE = ''
065 LOOP
066    LINE = LISTING<CNT>
067    FORCEPAGE = (LINE[1,3]= '!BP')
068    IF FORCEPAGE THEN
069       I = PMAX
070    END ELSE
071       CRT @(PCOL,PROW):LINE:EOL:
072    END
073    ENDPAGE = FORCEPAGE OR (CNT>=MAX) OR (I>=PMAX)
074 UNTIL ENDPAGE DO
075    I = I + 1
076    CNT = CNT + 1
077    PROW = PROW + 1
078 REPEAT
079 CRT EOS:@(0,23):
080 CRT @(0,23):RON:MSG:ROF:
081 IF ENDPAGE AND I>=PMAX THEN MORE = 'More.'
082 RETURN
083 *
084 *
085 6000 * Scroll
086 *
087 EXIT = 0
088 LOOP
089    CRT @(0,22):@(-4):RON:'Enter':ROF:' ':
090    CRT @(20,22):'[ ] ':MORE:@(21,22):
```

FIG. 7-13 continues.

311

```
091    INPUT ANS,1:
092    ANS = OCONV(ANS,'MCU')
093    BEGIN CASE
094      CASE ANS # '' AND INDEX(ESCAPE,ANS,1)
095        CRT @(-1):
096        EXIT = 1
097      CASE (ANS='P') OR (ANS=' ')
098        IF I >=  PMAX THEN
099          CNT = CNT + 1
100          HPAGENO = HPAGENO + 1
101          GOSUB 5500
102        END
103      CASE ANS = 'T' ;* Top
104        CNT = 1
105        HPAGENO = 1
106        GOSUB 5500 ;* Paint the screen
107      CASE ANS = 'B'
108        HPAGENO = HPAGENO -1
109        IF NOT(HPAGENO) THEN HPAGENO = 1 ELSE
110          CNT = PAGEMARKS<HPAGENO>
111          GOSUB 5500 ;* Paint Screen
112        END
113      CASE ANS = '?'
114        EXIT = 0
115        LOOP
116          CRT @(0,22):@(-4):RON:'Enter Letter of the Option':ROF:
117          CRT @(28,22):'[ ]':@(29,22):
118          INPUT ANS,1:
119          ANS = OCONV(ANS,'MCU')
120          IF ANS = '' OR INDEX(ESCAPE,ANS,1) THEN EXIT = 1
121        UNTIL EXIT OR ALPHA(ANS) DO REPEAT
122        IF NOT(EXIT) THEN
123          CALL INPUTHELP(HELP.ITEM:'.':ANS)
124          CNT = PAGEMARKS<HPAGENO>
125          GOSUB 5500 ;* Paint the screen
126        END ELSE
127          EXIT = 0
128        END
129      CASE ANS = 'H'
130        CRT @(0,22):EOL:@(0,20):
131        LINES = DCOUNT(LISTING,AM)
132        PRINTER ON
133        FOR LINE = 1 TO LINES
134            PRINT LISTING<LINE>
135            IF NOT(MOD(LINE,50)) THEN PRINT FF:
136        NEXT LINE
137        PRINTER OFF; PRINTER CLOSE
138      CASE ANS = '+'
139        EXECUTE 'JED INPUT.HELP.FILE ':HELP.ITEM
140        READ LISTING FROM HELP.FILE,HELP.ITEM ELSE
141            LISTING = 'NO HELP AVAILABLE'
142        END
143        GOSUB 5000
```

FIG. 7-13 continues.

```
144   END CASE
145 UNTIL EXIT DO REPEAT
146 RETURN
147 *
148 *
149 END
```

FIG. 7-13 ends.

```
    INPUT
001 * PROGRAM INPUT
002 * Main Input Routine
003 * DATE STARTED : February 1987
004 * AUTHOR: Harvey Eric Rodstein
005 * COPYRIGHT: H.E.RODSTEIN Computer Consulting 1986,7,8
006 *
007 * Initialization
008 *
009 PROMPT ''
010 *
011 INCLUDE COMMONS
012 *
013 DRAWLINE=STR('-',TERMWIDTH)
014 *
015 * Parse Data Definitions
016 *
017 * Get the arguments and options
018 *
019 CALL GETSENTENCE(ARGS)
020 *
021 ACTIVELIST=SYSTEM(11)
022 IF ACTIVELIST THEN SELECTED=1 ELSE SELECTED=0
023 *
024 * Parse / Compile Subroutine
025 * Parses for both interpretive and compiled statements
026 *
027 FILENAME=''
028 SUBNAME=FIELD(ARGS,' ',1)
029 SUBOK=(OCONV(SUBNAME,'TMD;X;;2')='E6')
030 IF SUBOK THEN
031     CALL @SUBNAME
032 END ELSE
033     CALL ICOMPILE(ARGS)
034     IF COMPILE THEN STOP
035 END
036 *
037 * Check Run Time File Control Parameters
038 *
039 * Delete is OK?
040 *
041 READ TEMP FROM DICTFILE,'DELETEOK' THEN DELETEOK=1 ELSE DELETEOK=0
042 *
```

FIG. 7-14. INPUT process INPUT program listing (continues).

```
043 * Check for Last Changed Date Field
044 *
045 READV LASTCHANGED FROM DICTFILE,'LASTCHANGED',2 ELSE LASTCHANGED=0
046 IF NOT(NUM(LASTCHANGED)) OR LASTCHANGED='' THEN LASTCHANGED=0
047 *
048 IF NOT(PROTECTED) THEN
049    CMESSAGE='(C)hange, (F)ile, (P)age, (B)ack page, or <ESC>ape '
050 END ELSE
051    CMESSAGE='(P)age, (B)ack page, or <ESC>ape '
052 END
053 *
054 * Main INPUT Procedure
055 *
056 MAT LAST.ITEM=''
057 CRT CLS: ;* Clear The Screen
058 *
059 LOOP
060   LOOP
061     LOCKFLAG=0
062     GOSUB 100 ; * Get the ID and the item
063   WHILE LOCKFLAG DO REPEAT
064 UNTIL EXITFLAG DO
065   GOSUB 200 ; * Edit the item
066 REPEAT
067 CRT CLS:
068 STOP
069 *
070 *
071 ****************************************************
072 * Subroutines
073 ****************************************************
074 *
075 100 * Get item-id and ITEM
076 *
077 PAGENO     =1
078 REPROMPT   =0
079 NEWFLAG    =0
080 EXITFLAG   =0
081 ITEMID     =' '
082 VMC        =1
083 CHANGEFLAG  =0
084 MAT DSPFIELD=''
085 *
086 IDFLAG=1
087 GOSUB 1000 ;* Header Screen
088 IDFLAG=0
089 CRT EOS:
090 *
091 * Get Id parameters
092 *
093 INCONV   = IDDEF<6>
094 IF INCONV='' THEN INCONV=IDDEF<7>
095 IDCORR   = IDDEF<8>
```

FIG. 7-14 continues.

314

```
096 LENGTH    = IDDEF<10>
097 VALID     = IDDEF<12>
098 HELPMSG   = IDDEF<15>
099 ERRORMSG  = IDDEF<15>
100 HELPID    = IDDEF<16>
101 FIELDBEG  = PAGELIMITS<1,1>
102 FIELDEND  = PAGELIMITS<1,2>
103 LABEL     = 'Enter ':IDDEF<3>
104 IF NOT(ACTIVELIST) THEN
105    LOOP
106      REPROMPT=0
107      GOSUB 8000
108      RESP=''
109      LOOP
110         CALL INEDIT(RESP,300)
111      WHILE RESP='' DO REPEAT
112      CRT @(0,2):EOL:
113      URESP=OCONV(RESP,'MCU')
114      BEGIN CASE
115        CASE INDEX(ESCAPE,URESP,1)
116          EXITFLAG=1
117          RETURN
118        CASE RESP='+'
119          READU NEXTID FROM DICTFILE,'NEXT#' ELSE NEXTID='1'
120          RESP=NEXTID
121          WRITE NEXTID+1 ON DICTFILE,'NEXT#'
122        CASE RESP='?'
123          CALL INPUTHELP(HELPID)
124          CRT CLS:
125          GOSUB 1000
126          REPROMPT=1
127        CASE RESP ='*'
128          SELECT DATAFILE
129          READNEXT RESP THEN ACTIVELIST=1 ELSE REPROMPT=1
130        CASE 1
131          NEXTID=0
132          GOSUB 5500 ;* Validate Entry
133      END CASE
134    WHILE REPROMPT DO
135      CRT BELL:
136    REPEAT
137 END ELSE
138    READNEXT RESP ELSE
139       IF SELECTED THEN
140          CRT @(0,23):
141          STOP 403
142       END ELSE
143          CRT @(0,2):ROF:'End of List':ROF:BELL:EOL:
144          ACTIVELIST=0
145          RETURN
146       END
147    END
148 END
```

FIG. 7-14 continues.

```
149 *
150 GOSUB 5000 ;* Input Convert
151 ITEMID=INFIELD
152 *
153 MATREADU ITEM FROM DATAFILE,ITEMID LOCKED
154     CRT @(0,2):ROF:'The item is locked!':ROF:BELL:EOL:
155     LOCKFLAG=1
156 END ELSE
157     MAT ITEM=''
158     CHANGEFLAG=1
159     NEWFLAG=1
160 END
161 RETURN
162 *
163 *
164 200 * Data Entry and Validation
165 *
166 GOSUB 1000 ;* Display Heading
167 GOSUB 1100 ;* Display Labels
168 GOSUB 1200 ;* Display Data, All Fields
169 *
170 LOOP
171     EXITFLAG=0
172     IF NOT(NEWFLAG) THEN GOSUB 400;* Change, File, and Exit Prompt
173 UNTIL EXITFLAG DO
174     GOSUB 300 ;* Input field data
175 REPEAT
176 RETURN
177 *
178 *
179 300 * Input field data
180 *
181 BACKFIELD=0
182 LOOP
183     ESCFLAG=0
184     FIELDNUM=FIELDBEG
185     LOOP
186         VMC=1
187         GOSUB 2000 ;* Get Field data
188         IF NOT(DISPLAYONLY) THEN
189             BACKFIELD=0
190             NEXTFIELD=0
191             GOSUB 4000 ;* Get Input
192             IF ESCFLAG THEN NEWFLAG=0 ;RETURN
193         END
194         IF BACKFIELD THEN
195             IF FIELDNUM>1 THEN
196                 FIELDNUM=FIELDNUM - 1
197                 IF FIELDNUM<FIELDBEG THEN
198                     IF FIELDNUM<PAGELIMITS<PAGENO,1> THEN
199                         FIELDNUM=FIELDBEG
200                     END ELSE
201                         FIELDBEG=FIELDNUM
```

FIG. 7-14 continues.

316

```
202             END
203               END
204            END ELSE
205                IF DISPLAYONLY THEN RETURN
206            END
207         END ELSE
208             FIELDNUM=FIELDNUM+1
209         END
210    UNTIL (FIELDNUM>FIELDEND) DO REPEAT
211      *
212 WHILE NEWFLAG AND PAGENO<PAGES DO
213    PAGENO=PAGENO + 1
214    FIELDBEG=PAGELIMITS<PAGENO,1>
215    FIELDEND=PAGELIMITS<PAGENO,2>
216    GOSUB 1000
217    GOSUB 1100
218    GOSUB 1200
219 REPEAT
220 NEWFLAG=0
221 RETURN
222 *
223 *
224 400 * Change/File Prompt
225 *
226 FIELDBEG=PAGELIMITS<PAGENO,1>
227 FIELDEND=PAGELIMITS<PAGENO,2>
228 LOOP
229    REPROMPT=0
230    LENGTH = 10
231    LABEL   = CMESSAGE
232    ANS=''
233    LOOP
234      CALL INEDIT(ANS,90)
235    WHILE ANS='' DO REPEAT
236    ANS=OCONV(ANS,'MCU')
237    EXT=TRIM(ANS[2,4])
238    ANS=ANS[1,1]
239    CRT @(0,2):EOL:
240    KILLIST=INDEX(EXT,'K',1)
241    BEGIN CASE
242      CASE ANS[1,1]='?'
243        CALL INPUTHELP('CHANGEFILE')
244        GOSUB 6000
245        REPROMPT=1
246      CASE INDEX(ESCAPE,ANS[1,1],1)
247        EXITFLAG=1
248        RELEASE DATAFILE,ITEMID
249        CRT @(0,2):EOL:ROF:ITEMID:' Exited!':ROF:BELL:
250      CASE ANS='P' OR ANS=' '
251        THISPAGE=PAGENO
252        IF EXT='' OR NOT(NUM(EXT)) THEN
253            PAGENO=PAGENO+1
254        END ELSE
```

FIG. 7-14 continues.

```
255              PAGENO=EXT
256          END
257          IF PAGENO>PAGES THEN PAGENO=PAGES ELSE
258              IF PAGENO<1 THEN PAGENO=1
259          END
260          IF THISPAGE # PAGENO THEN
261              FIELDBEG=PAGELIMITS<PAGENO,1>
262              FIELDEND=PAGELIMITS<PAGENO,2>
263              GOSUB 1000
264              GOSUB 1100
265              GOSUB 1200
266          END
267          REPROMPT=1
268      CASE ANS='B'
269          IF PAGENO>1 THEN
270              PAGENO=PAGENO-1
271              FIELDBEG=PAGELIMITS<PAGENO,1>
272              FIELDEND=PAGELIMITS<PAGENO,2>
273              GOSUB 1000
274              GOSUB 1100
275              GOSUB 1200
276          END
277          REPROMPT=1
278      CASE PROTECTED
279          CRT BELL:
280          REPROMPT=1
281      CASE ANS='C'
282          IF EXT='' THEN
283              CHANGEFLAG=1
284          END ELSE
285              IF NUM(EXT) THEN
286                  IF EXT>=FIELDBEG AND EXT<=FIELDEND THEN
287                      FIELDBEG=EXT
288                      FIELDEND=EXT
289                      CHANGEFLAG=1
290                  END ELSE REPROMPT=1
291              END ELSE REPROMPT=1
292          END
293      CASE ANS='F'
294          BEGIN CASE
295          CASE INDEX(EXT,'D',1)
296              IF DELETEOK THEN
297                  GOSUB 6100 ;* Sure
298                  IF ANS='Y' THEN
299                      DELETE DATAFILE,ITEMID
300                      CRT @(0,2):EOL:ROF:ITEMID:' Deleted!':ROF:BELL:
301                      EXITFLAG=1
302                  END ELSE REPROMPT=1
303              END ELSE
304                  CRT @(0,2):ROF:'Delete Not Allowed!!':ROF:BELL:EOL:
305                  REPROMPT=1
306              END
307          CASE 1
```

FIG. 7-14 continues.

```
308              IF IDCORR[1,1]='B' THEN
309                SUBNAME=FIELD(IDCORR,';',2)
310                CALL @SUBNAME(REPROMPT)
311              END
312              IF NOT(REPROMPT) THEN
313                IF LASTCHANGED THEN
314                  ITEM(LASTCHANGED)=DATE():' ':OCONV(0,'U50BB')
315                END
316                MATWRITE ITEM ON DATAFILE,ITEMID
317                MAT LAST.ITEM=MAT ITEM
318                CHANGEFLAG=0
319                CRT @(0,2):ROF:ITEMID:' Filed.':ROF:EOL:
320                IF NOT(INDEX(EXT,'S',1)) THEN EXITFLAG=1 ELSE
321                  REPROMPT=1
322                END
323              END
324          END CASE
325      CASE 1
326          CRT BELL:
327          REPROMPT=1
328      END CASE
329 WHILE REPROMPT DO REPEAT
330 IF KILLIST THEN
331    EXITFLAG=1
332    GOSUB 6500
333 END
334 RETURN
335 *
336 *
337 1000 * Print HEADER
338 *
339 CRT @(0,1):ROF:' ':HOME:EOL:
340 IF NEWFLAG THEN CRT 'New ':
341 CRT 'Item ':RON:ITEMID:ROF:" in File '":FILENAME:"'":
342 CRT ' at ':OCONV(TIME(),'MTH'):' on ':OCONV(DATE(),'D'):
343 IF NOT(IDFLAG) THEN CRT @(68,0):'Page ':PAGENO:' of ':PAGES:
344 CRT @(0,1):EOL:DRAWLINE:@(0,5):DRAWLINE:
345 RETURN
346 *
347 1100 * Display Labels
348 *
349 FBEG=PAGELIMITS<PAGENO,1>
350 FEND=PAGELIMITS<PAGENO,2>
351 CRT @(0,FIRSTROW):EOS:
352 FOR I=FBEG TO FEND
353    SPOS=DATADEF(I)<3,1>
354    CRT @(SPOS<1,1,1>,SPOS<1,1,2>):ROF:DATADEF(I)<3,2>:ROF:
355 NEXT FIELDNUM
356 RETURN
357 *
358 *
359 1200 * Convert and Display Data Fields
360 *
```

FIG. 7-14 continues.

```
361 FIELDNUM=FIELDBEG
362 LOOP
363     VMC=1
364     GOSUB 2000 ;* Get Field Data
365     DSPVMC=VMC
366     GOSUB 2500 ;* Display the Data
367     FIELDNUM=FIELDNUM+1
368 UNTIL FIELDNUM>FIELDEND DO REPEAT
369 RETURN
370 *
371 *
372 2000 * Get Field Data
373 *
374 TYPE        = DATADEF(FIELDNUM)<1>
375 ATTRIBUTE   = DATADEF(FIELDNUM)<2>
376 LABEL       = DATADEF(FIELDNUM)<3,2>
377 LABEL       = FIELD(LABEL,'.',1)
378 FIELDCOL    = DATADEF(FIELDNUM)<5,1,1>
379 FIELDROW    = DATADEF(FIELDNUM)<5,1,2>
380 INCONV      = DATADEF(FIELDNUM)<6>
381 OUTCONV     = DATADEF(FIELDNUM)<7>
382 CORRELATIVE = DATADEF(FIELDNUM)<8>
383 JUST        = DATADEF(FIELDNUM)<9>
384 LENGTH      = DATADEF(FIELDNUM)<10>
385 REQUIRED    = DATADEF(FIELDNUM)<11>
386 VALID       = DATADEF(FIELDNUM)<12>
387 ERRORMSG    = DATADEF(FIELDNUM)<14>
388 HELPMSG     = DATADEF(FIELDNUM)<15>
389 HELPID      = DATADEF(FIELDNUM)<16>
390 DISPLAYONLY = INDEX(TYPE,'O',1)
391 LABLEN      = LEN(LABEL)
392 FORMAT      = 'L#':LENGTH
393 IF ERRORMSG = '' THEN ERRORMSG = 'Unexpected Format!'
394 IF INCONV   = '' THEN INCONV = OUTCONV
395 IF NOT(NUM(REQUIRED)) OR REQUIRED='' THEN REQUIRED =0
396 *
397 *
398 2001 * Get data and perform correlative
399 *
400 IF ATTRIBUTE THEN
401     DATAFIELD=ITEM(ATTRIBUTE)<1,VMC>
402 END ELSE
403     DATAFIELD=ITEMID
404 END
405 OVERLENGTH=LEN(DATAFIELD)>LENGTH
406 DSPFIELD(FIELDNUM)<2>=FORMAT
407 *
408 IF CORRELATIVE # '' THEN
409     CORRTYPE=CORRELATIVE[1,1]
410     BEGIN CASE
411       CASE CORRTYPE='S'
412         IF DATAFIELD#'' AND DATAFIELD#0 THEN
413             SFIELD=FIELD(CORRELATIVE,';',2)
```

FIG. 7-14 continues.

320

```
414          END ELSE
415              SFIELD=FIELD(CORRELATIVE,';',3)
416          END
417          STYPE=SFIELD[1,1]
418          BEGIN CASE
419            CASE SFIELD='*'
420                NULL
421            CASE NUM(SFIELD)
422                DATAFIELD=ITEM(SFIELD)
423            CASE INDEX(\"'\,STYPE,1)
424                RESP=FIELD(SFIELD:STYPE,STYPE,2)
425                GOSUB 5000
426                DATAFIELD=INFIELD
427            CASE SFIELD='D'
428                DATAFIELD=DATE()
429            CASE 1
430                DATAFIELD=''
431          END CASE
432      CASE CORRTYPE='F'
433          CALL FCORR(CORRELATIVE,DATAFIELD)
434      CASE CORRTYPE='B'
435          SUBNAME=FIELD(CORRELATIVE,';',2)
436          CALL @SUBNAME(DATAFIELD)
437      CASE 1
438          RESP=OCONV(DATAFIELD,CORRELATIVE)
439          GOSUB 5000 ;* Input Convert It
440          DATAFIELD=INFIELD
441    END CASE
442    IF ATTRIBUTE THEN ITEM(ATTRIBUTE)<1,VMC>=DATAFIELD
443    DSPVMC=VMC
444    GOSUB 2500 ;* Display the field
445 END
446 RETURN
447 *
448 *
449 2500 * Perform Output Convert and Display
450 *
451 IF OUTCONV#'' THEN
452    IF OUTCONV[1,1]='B' THEN
453        SUBNAME=FIELD(OUTCONV,';',2)
454        CALL @SUBNAME(DATAFIELD)
455    END ELSE DATAFIELD=OCONV(DATAFIELD,OUTCONV)
456 END
457 DSPFIELD(FIELDNUM)<1,DSPVMC>=DATAFIELD
458 CRT @(FIELDCOL,FIELDROW+DSPVMC-1):ROF:DATAFIELD FORMAT:ROF:
459 *
460 RETURN
461 *
462 *
463 4000 * Get Input for a field
464 *
465 LOOP
466    GOSUB 8000
```

FIG. 7-14 continues.

```
467    REPROMPT=0
468    OFIELD=DSPFIELD(FIELDNUM)<1,VMC>
469    IF JUST='R' THEN OFIELD=TRIM(OFIELD)
470    IF OFIELD='' THEN OFIELD=SPACE(LENGTH)
471    IF DATAFIELD='' THEN
472        RESP=''
473    END ELSE
474        RESP=OFIELD
475    END
476    OFIELD=OFIELD FORMAT
477    CRT @(FIELDCOL,FIELDROW+VMC-1):RON:OFIELD:ROF:
478    CALL INEDIT(RESP,90)
479    CRT @(0,2):EOL:
480    URESP=OCONV(RESP,'MCU')
481    BEGIN CASE
482      CASE RESP # '' AND INDEX(ESCAPE,URESP,1)
483        ESCFLAG=1
484        RESP=''
485        CRT @(FIELDCOL,FIELDROW+VMC-1):ROF:OFIELD:ROF:
486      CASE RESP='^'
487        BACKFIELD=1
488        CRT @(FIELDCOL,FIELDROW+VMC-1):ROF:OFIELD:ROF:
489      CASE RESP='' OR RESP=' '
490        IF DATAFIELD='' AND REQUIRED THEN
491            CRT @(0,2):EOL:ROF:'Required Entry':ROF:BELL:
492            REPROMPT=2
493            RQM;RQM
494        END ELSE
495            NEXTFIELD=1
496            CRT @(FIELDCOL,FIELDROW+VMC-1):ROF:OFIELD:ROF:
497        END
498      CASE RESP='?'
499        CALL INPUTHELP(HELPID)
500        GOSUB 6000
501        REPROMPT=1
502      CASE RESP='-'
503        IF REQUIRED THEN
504            CRT @(0,2):EOL:
505            CRT ROF:"A REQUIRED field cannot be cleared!":ROF:BELL:
506            REPROMPT=1
507            RQM;RQM
508            CRT @(FIELDCOL,FIELDROW+VMC-1):RON:OFIELD:ROF:
509        END ELSE INFIELD=''
510      CASE RESP='.'
511        INFIELD=LAST.ITEM(ATTRIBUTE)<1,VMC>
512      CASE 1
513        GOSUB 5500 ;* Validate Entry
514        IF NOT(REPROMPT) THEN
515            GOSUB 5000 ;* Input Convert
516        END
517    END CASE
518 WHILE REPROMPT DO REPEAT
519 IF NEXTFIELD OR BACKFIELD OR ESCFLAG THEN RETURN
```

FIG. 7-14 continues.

```
520 *
521 IF ATTRIBUTE THEN ITEM(ATTRIBUTE)<1,VMC>=INFIELD
522 DATAFIELD=INFIELD
523 DSPVMC=VMC
524 GOSUB 2500 ;* Output Convert and Display
525 *
526 RETURN
527 *
528 *
529 5000 * Input Convert a Field
530 *
531 IF INCONV # '' THEN
532    IF INCONV[1,1]='B' THEN
533       SUBNAME=FIELD(INCONV,';',2)
534       CALL @SUBNAME(RESP)
535    END ELSE RESP=ICONV(RESP,INCONV)
536 END
537 INFIELD=RESP
538 RETURN
539 *
540 5500 * Validate Entry
541 *
542 REPROMPT=0
543 IF VALID # '' THEN
544    IF VALID[1,1]='B' THEN
545       SUBNAME=FIELD(VALID,';',2)
546       CALL @SUBNAME(RESP)
547       TEMP=RESP
548    END ELSE TEMP=ICONV(RESP,VALID)
549    IF TEMP='' THEN
550       REPROMPT=1
551       CRT @(0,2):EOL:ROF:ERRORMSG:ROF:BELL:
552       RQM;RQM;RQM
553    END
554 END
555 RETURN
556 *
557 *
558 6000 * Redisplay Current Page
559 *
560 GOSUB 1000
561 GOSUB 1100
562 *
563 6055 * Redisplay a screen segment
564 *
565 FOR I=FBEG TO FEND
566    OUTFIELD=DSPFIELD(I)
567    FIELDCOLROW=@(DATADEF(I)<5,1,1>,DATADEF(I)<5,1,2>+VMC-1)
568    CRT FIELDCOLROW:ROF:OUTFIELD<1,VMC> OUTFIELD<2>:ROF:
569 NEXT I
570 RETURN
571 *
572 *
```

FIG. 7-14 continues.

```
573 6100 * Are You Sure?
574 *
575 CRT @(0,2):EOL:ROF:'Are You Sure? ':ROF:
576 INPUT ANS,1:
577 CRT @(0,2):EOL:
578 ANS=OCONV(ANS,'MCU')
579 RETURN
580 *
581 *
582 6500 * Bleed Active List
583 *
584 BLED=0
585 LOOP
586    READNEXT ID ELSE BLED=1
587 UNTIL BLED DO REPEAT
588 ACTIVELIST=0
589 RETURN
590 *
591 *
592 8000 * Help Processor
593 *
594 CRT @(0,2):EOL:HELPMSG<1,1>:
595 RETURN
596 *
597 END
598 *
599 RETURN
```

FIG. 7-14 ends.

The Virtual Machine

THE PICK SYSTEM IS A VIRTUAL INFORMATION MANAGEMENT MACHINE DESIGNED independently of hardware. The virtual machine existed before the first hardware implementation. The result is an environment where the tasks of system memory, process and database management are integrated into a coherent, "single-thread" entity which is transparent to the applications programmer/analyst.

However, the environment in its many forms does have a few traps. These pitfalls are not swiftly and mercifully apparent. They lay like a quagmire, waiting to slowly drag under and suffocate system throughput. With this in mind, it is useful to provide some insight into the internal working of the operating system without giving away the shop. It is important to convey what goes on "behind the scenes," but not belabor the issue by revealing the exact contents of every word, byte and nibble. Besides, each licensee has made enough detailed changes to make such an endeavor worth an encyclopedia rather than a humble text.

VIRTUAL MEMORY

Virtual memory is a term used to describe the fact that programs and data are not restricted to the size of physical space in RAM. Memory resources are allocated to each process on a demand page basis. Physical memory is used as a "desktop," where active data is temporarily moved for review or alteration.

Buffers in physical memory are the same size as disk frames. Frames are retrieved from the disk, processed in physical memory, and, if altered, re-written to the disk. Depending upon system usage, the same frame may be assigned to a different memory buffer between process activations. The actual memory buffer location is transparent and consequently not important to the applications programmer. What is not transparent is the time it takes to continually page to and from memory if the memory resources are insufficient. This can become true quite quickly when a single large string is sorted by using the Pick ACCESS language and/or multiple user requests exceed available memory.

The Monitor

The brain of the Pick system is the Monitor. The *Monitor* is the driving process of the virtual machine. It is memory resident software that manages process timesharing, device reads and writes, and, most importantly, the resources of physical memory.

The size of the Monitor depends on whether the system is implemented under software or hardware control. The difference between a hardware and a software implementation is that the virtual Pick instructions are microcoded as a firmware system, and written in the computer's native assembler language on a software system.

Microcode is typically stored in static RAM (SRAM) and is usually harder to write and maintain than native assembler code. However, nowadays the differences are almost totally insignificant as far as performance goes.

Firmware based systems are still manufactured by McDonnell Douglas with their REALITY, SPIRIT and SEQUEL based systems and by Ultimate on their Honeywell and DEC systems. The Pick OS does not run on these machines without the presence of the firmware set. Software implementations operate on a wide range of hardware based on the Intel 8088 (IBM XT's), 80286, 80386, Motorola 68000, 68020 and 68030, and many others. The Monitor on a software machine requires more physical memory than the monitor on a firmware machine.

Virtual and physical memory are illustrated in Fig. 8-1.

Process Control

The Monitor uses a memory resident set of tables to keep track of process status and memory usage. The tables for keeping track of process (port) status are the Process Identification Blocks or PIB's. A process status may be one of the following:

Status	*Description*
INPUT ROADBLOCKED	The process is accepting input from a port.
OUTPUT ROADBLOCKED	The process is sending to a port.
AWAITING DISK IO	The process is probably experiencing a frame fault.
PROCESS ROADBLOCKED	This is sometimes called the COMA bit. It is used by the operating system to suspend processing.
SLEEPING	The process is sleeping.

The PIB status bytes can be displayed using the WHERE command. It is important to become familiar with these status bytes and the WHERE command in order to determine the current state of a process. This is a great help in determining whether a line is process-

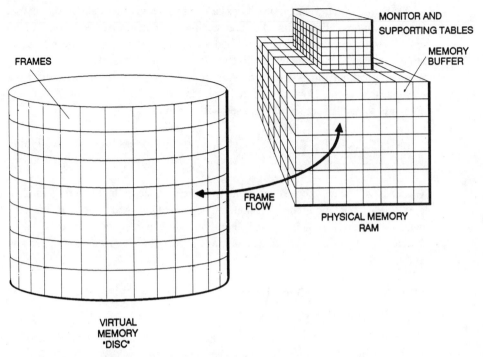

FRAMES

MONITOR AND
SUPPORTING TABLES

MEMORY
BUFFER

FRAME
FLOW

PHYSICAL MEMORY
RAM

VIRTUAL
MEMORY
"DISC"

FIG. 8-1. Virtual and physical memory.

ing, printing, sleeping, in the debugger, or X-OFF'ed by someone who inadvertently typed in Ctrl-S on the attached terminal keyboard. See the section entitled "Process Status Verbs" for more details.

Timesharing

The Monitor timeshares processes. Each process is activated based on its position in an activation queue. This queue is called the Select Next User queue (SNU). A process on the SNU queue is not activated in a "round robin." A process is bubbled up the SNU queue using a priority schema heavily dependent on the number of input interrupts from the port.

It should be understood that only the monitor is interrupt driven, not the virtual machine. A received interrupt is basically queued by the Monitor to be handled when the virtual machine is good and ready.

Keystrokes received from the async line are given priority. The OS inherently relegates a "batch" process (one which is stepping through data without terminal input, such as an ACCESS SELECT), to a lower priority than an interactive process.

A process remains active for a period of time called a *timeslice*. The length of a process timeslice can also affect system throughput. Timeslice ranges vary on different machines. Small, slow machines usually give interactive tasks a timeslice of between 30 and 50 milliseconds, while the larger, faster systems maintain an 8 to 16 millisecond range. The optimum number varies between implementations.

On the other hand, batch processes can be given higher timeslices to help make up for fewer activations. Higher timeslices on stand-alone batch runs may serve to optimize the time allotted. However, this is not a good idea if your system use is heavily dependent on interactive tasks. Fiddling with the timeslice beyond what has been initially provided serves no great purpose when trying to optimize throughput. In fact, it causes more problems than it's worth. However, be that as it may, the TIMESLICE or SLICE verb is usually made available, but should be used with discretion.

>TIMESLICE 30   Sets the current process timeslice to 30 milliseconds.
>TIMESLICE 50 (4   Sets the process at port 4 to 50 milliseconds.

A process will be deactivated before its timeslice is used up by executing a Release Quantum (RQM) command in the virtual assembler or PICK/BASIC, or by referencing a frame that is not in physical memory and, therefore, must be read from the disk.

During PICK/BASIC runtime, the process timeslice is given up if the following conditions occur:

- The process is IO roadblocked
- The process is waiting for the disk
- The process is sleeping
- The process finds a disk record locked

THE PHANTOM OF THE OPERATING SYSTEM

A process may or may not have a physical port attached to it. It depends on the number of processes for which a system is configured versus how many physical async ports exist. Any unused port may potentially be used to run a "phantom process." Phantom processes run in the background with no interactive requests.

The system always has at least one phantom process. This process is the Spooler and is assigned a process location 1 higher than the last configured port. The spooler phantom is displayed on the last line of the WHERE.

The Spooler is an underused process. The Spooler can potentially perform a number of functions, depending on the implementation. The Spooler's major tasks are linking process workspace during system coldstart, handling printing on parallel ports, and logging disk errors. Certain implementations also use the Spooler for handling GFEs and monitoring the status of background processes. The Spooler sleeps the rest of the time.

Print image is spooled to print event files by the process running the application. The job of de-spooling to port attached serial printers is performed by the process on that port. This has already changed for several implementations. The parallel print tasks are handled by a separate process, just like the serial printers, and not by the Spooler. The phantom Spooler ends up having very little work to do that is directly related to print spooling and de-spooling.

Memory Management

The Monitor establishes memory resident tables for memory resource management. The actual number of tables and specific makeup may vary from implementation to implementation. However, the generic parts are the Hash Address Table (HAT), the Hash Link Table, Frame Identifier tables (FID tables), and Buffer Status Tables.

A group of frame id's will uniquely hash to an entry in the HAT table. The HAT tables are a set of pointers to a linked chain of entries in the FID tables that specify whether a frame is in memory or not and the Buffer Status Tables indicate buffer usage and status in physical memory.

Figure 8-2 is a conceptualization of memory lookup tables.

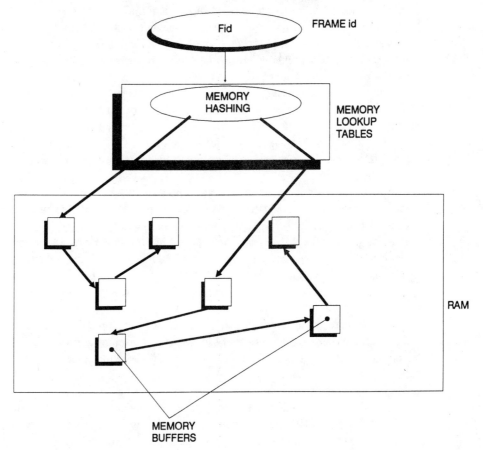

FIG. 8-2. Memory buffer lookup.

The Buffer Status Tables, or BST, indicate whether a memory buffer is AVAILABLE, IO BUSY, MEM LOCKED, or WRITE REQUIRED. They indicate:

Status	*Description*
AVAILABLE	the buffer is free to be used for a frame from disk.

IO BUSY	the buffer has a frame being read from or written to disk.
MEM LOCKED	the buffer is locked in memory and not available for virtual paging. This may also be called CORE LOCKED as a left-over from bygone days.
WRITE REQUIRED	the contents of the buffer have changed and are ready to be updated to the disk. More on this when talking about frame faults.

Frame Faults

It might be said that "The fault.. is not in ourselves but in our frames." A *frame fault* occurs whenever a process references data that is not already in physical memory. The Monitor performs the physical memory management tasks. Without a quick memory search technique, the amount of time it would take to search through the entire RAM for that frame would be extremely detrimental to system performance. The Monitor uses the combination of the HAT and FID tables to look for the referenced FID in memory. The FID is hashed to a unique entry in the HAT table. This entry contains a pointer to the first in a linked list of entries that indicate the FID and its corresponding memory location. If the FID is not found within the linked list, the frame is not currently memory resident.

If the frame is already memory resident, the FID and Buffer address should be found in the FID tables. The physical location is attached and the process continues until its timeslice is used up.

If the frame is not in memory, the system has some work to do. Any time that a frame is referenced and is not in memory, the Monitor has to find an available buffer in which to deposit it. If a buffer is found AVAILABLE, a disc read is scheduled. At this point, the monitor terminates the process timeslice and activates another process on the queue. It doesn't matter if the process has a timeslice of 30 milliseconds and only 3 milliseconds have transpired. The requirement of disk IO cuts short the process timeslice. On completion of the disk read, the corresponding memory management tables are set up and the process is available to be reactivated.

What if there are no available buffers in memory? The monitor must find the least recently used buffer that is not memory locked. Each machine has some kind of schema for determining the activity of a buffer in memory and will indicate the most inactive buffer.

When looking for a free buffer, the system takes the oldest frame not marked as WRITE REQUIRED. A non write required buffer is immediately available to be used. When a WRITE REQUIRED frame is encountered, it is scheduled to be written, but the system goes on looking for a free buffer and does not wait for the write to complete.

Anytime the content of a frame is changed, the corresponding memory buffer is flagged WRITE REQUIRED. The system does not immediately write that frame to disk. If that were so, then system throughput would be alarmingly slow. WRITE REQUIRED indicates that the frame is ready to be written when time or necessity allows. At what point? In general, there are three situations where a write occurs. First, is the *automatic frame write*. Automatic frame writes occur when the system stands idle. Idle means that no terminal IO requests have occurred within a reasonable period of time. The term "reasonable" is purposely vague. The Monitor uses the time on its "hands" to force WRITE REQUIRED buffers to disk. This definitely doesn't occur during peak use hours.

The second instance is a result of *demand paging* when the Monitor is searching for a free memory buffer. If a buffer has the WRITE REQUIRED status, the contents are written to disk.

The third instance is when *disk writes are forced at predetermined intervals*. This is usually coded in the Monitor by the Pick OEM. Basically, the Monitor will attempt to write a single or set of write required frames at predetermined times between process activations. McDonnell Douglas has a verb called SET-WRITES. SET-WRITES tells the monitor to force frame writes after a number of passes through the SNU queue. For example:

>SET-WRITES 100000

is a typical setting which designates a forced write every 10,000 times through the queue.

>SET-WRITES 3

Designates every 3 times through the queue and creates massive system degradation.

CAUTION: Don't trip the juggler! Current systems use Metal Oxide Semiconductor (MOS). This RAM is fast but volatile. When power is lost, so is memory.

During normal operation, the portions of the database may exist in a state of flux. Frames are constantly moving from disk to memory and from memory to disk. The Monitor can be likened to a juggler. If your system goes down because of a power failure, or hangs due to an internal system bug or hardware problem, then it is quite possible that the Monitor has been caught in mid-juggle. This can corrupt the database. This corruption is called a *group format error* (GFE). More later on GFE's.

The virtual machine must be given a chance to perform a graceful shutdown. The verb for this may be POWER-OFF, or SHUTDOWN or :WARMSTOP, depending on the implementation. These processes make sure there are no active users and subsequently flush all WRITE REQUIRED buffers so that the system can be powered down with no data corruption. Certain Uninterruptable Power Supplies (UPSs) will detect a power problem and signal the machine to initiate a shutdown before everything goes to the dogs.

Virtual frames are re-entrant. Data frames, ABS code (the virtual assembler,) and PICK/BASIC object code frames are shared among processes thereby reducing memory requirements. When several processes address the same disk frame, the frame is shared in memory. When the frame is initially paged into memory and memory resources are sufficient, it is quite possible that it will already be there without the Monitor having to schedule another disk read.

Thrashing

A serious bottleneck can occur when there is insufficient physical memory to handle many user data requests. The scenario goes like this:

A process addresses a frame which is not already in memory, forcing a frame fault. The monitor terminates the process timeslice, schedules the IO and goes off to service another process. At some point while the monitor is activating another process, the requested frame is placed in a memory buffer. However, there are too many processes making too many disk requests. So, by the time your process is activated, the memory buffer used to read the frame has become the least recently used and has been used by a different frame. This forces your process into another frame fault and everything happens all over again. At some point down the long road, your frame will be there when your process is reactivated. But, this may be 5 minutes later.

The situation where frames are being paged in and out without being accessed is called *thrashing*. The system is like a beached flounder, thrashing around and going nowhere. The simplest way to prevent thrashing and increase system throughput is to add enough memory. Here are some suggestions for determining the operational memory requirements for a system.

First, you should know the minimum requirements per attached user. The monitor and all its associated tables requires a different amount of memory depending on whether this is a firmware or software implementation:

Firmware: 32 to 64k, depending on the manufacturer.
Software: 256k

A reasonable minimum amount of memory for each active process is calculated by multiplying the data frame size in kbytes by 16.

Memory per process = *framesize* * 16

Therefore, for a system with 512 byte frames, the minimum RAM requirement for each process is 8k (.5 x 16). For a system with a frame size of 2k, the minimum requirement is 32k.

Sixteen frames are enough for a typical process to do data entry with a fairly simple PICK/BASIC data entry program. Large items and complex validation requires a little more. Batch ACCESS and updates require a lot more. As a simple rule-of-thumb, if the process load is moderate, then double this figure. If the process load is heavy, multiply the figure times 4, or 8. The additional RAM overhead increases the probability that data referenced by a process will remain memory resident.

Connectability is a misleading term. It means one thing to a system's analyst and another to a system salesman. As any good engineer would do, calculate for the worst case. For instance, consider Pick R83 on the PC AT. The best case memory requirements per process is 8K. Figuring out the memory requirement for a 10 user PC AT (11 processes counting the Spooler), as follows:

Monitor overhead   =   256K
User requirement   =   11 * 8K
                        ————
                        344K

The worst case scenario for the same machine uses 64k per user.

Monitor Overhead   =   256K
User requirement   =   11 * 64K
                        ————
                        960K

This is not a good number for those of you using R83 on the PC AT. The maximum amount of RAM is restricted to 640k bytes. All other implementations do not have this restriction.

VIRTUAL WORKSPACE

Disk space does not actually begin with frame 1, as you can see in Fig. 8-3. The low end of disk space, not addressable through standard Pick applications, contains the boot block and the monitor allowing the Pick operating system to be bootstrapped automatically when the machine is powered up.

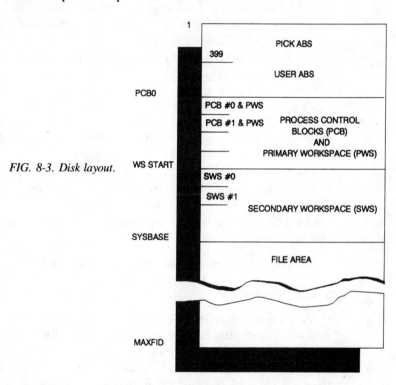

FIG. 8-3. Disk layout.

ABS Region

The first section of the addressable disk is called the ABS region. ABS stands for *Absolute code*. This has classically been the first 511 frames (1-511) but is well beyond that in most modern systems. The ABS region is now on the average 1023 frames (1-1023).

The ABS region is where the virtual assembler code resides. The virtual code is the meat and potatoes of the system. It is the code that runs all the higher level system processes including TCL, the ACCESS language (ACCESS, ENGLISH, RECALL), PICK/BASIC runtime, PICK/BASIC compiler, PROC etc. The standard Pick system ABS takes up the first 400 frames. The remaining frames are available for specialized applications such as JET, ACCUPLOT, COMPUSHEET and any user developed assembler routines.

The virtual assembler looks like any assembler language, but contains a very powerful macro instruction set for handling strings. On a firmware implementation, assembled virtual code is a set of high level opcodes which are interpreted by the firmware set. On software implementations, the virtual assembler mnemonics are treated as macros by the assembly process. The resulting object code is the processor's native assembler code. Because of this, assembled modes on a software machine take up between two and four times as much space as assembled modes on a firmware machine.

Process Control Blocks

The Process Control Blocks contain the counters to accumulators, registers and workspace pointers for each process to keep track of where it is and what it is doing. Each port has a set of Process Control Blocks and workspace. Do not confuse the Process Control Blocks with the *Process Identification Blocks* (PIB's). PIB's help the Monitor keep track of process status and activations.

In the generic system, there are 32 frames per process control block. The first frame in each process control block is called the *Primary Control Block* or the PCB. The PCB contains the accumulator, index registers and a few counters and storage registers. For efficiency, some implementations play a trick and will MEMLOCK a port's PCB at LOGON.

The PCB is followed by the *Secondary Control Block (SCB),* and the secondary is followed by other control blocks (try to obtain a virtual assembler manual for more specific details) and the bare minimum of linked workspace.

The disk space overhead for the process control blocks can be determined with the following formula:

Process Control Space = (*number of ports* + 1) * 32

Process Work Space

The process work space follows immediately after the Process Control Blocks. Called "free workspace," these traditionally come in triplets (designated as the HS, IS, and OS; possibly Larry, Moe, and Curly) of 127 frames a piece. The size and number of workspace blocks varies between implementations and according to the data frame size. For example, some systems with 2K data frames use 40 frames for each workspace block. There are no guarantees for what your implementation might contain.

All programs that manipulate data must use the workspace. For example, Editor copies the specified item into the IS workspace. The flip command (F) in the Editor copies the working item between the IS and OS buffers in workspace. Each flip includes the changes indicated since the last flip.

Virtual Overhead

To calculate the overhead for the Process Work Spaces, be aware that each work space triplet takes up 127 times 3 per port. Use the following formula:

Process workspace = (*number of ports* + 1) * 127 * 3

The total virtual workspace overhead on the disk is determined as follows:

Total = *ABS frames* + *Process Control Space* + *Process Workspace*

The "new age" systems are now allowing floating workspace. Within most of the history of the Pick system, when a process used all there was in its workspace, any program running would abort with the message "NOT ENOUGH WORKSPACE." Very soon, this will no longer be the case. When the process runs out of its allocated workspace, it will simply grab some more. In fact, if a program is written that requires more and more workspace, it will keep grabbing workspace until there is no more disk available.

The File Data Area

Finally, the meat and potatoes of any application, is the data area of the disk. The first file is allocated space following the last block of Process Work Space. This file is the system dictionary, SYSTEM. There are a core of accounts and files that must exist for the higher level system applications to function. Items in the SYSTEM file define both account master dictionaries and system level files. The accounts and account level files usually include:

Account	Description
SYSPROG	The system programmers account Usually the only account definition
BLOCK-CONVERT	An account level file to define characters for the BLOCK-PRINT process
ACC	The system accounting file
PROCLIB	The system PROC library
ERRMSG	The system error message file
EXECUTE-CONTROL	System level file used by the PICK/BASIC EXECUTE command

These accounts seem to be the core of many systems. There are probably other accounts that must reside on your system, but these vary between implementations. For example, some implementations require an additional SECURITY account, ULTIMATE for one. Others keep the system ERRMSG file as a System dictionary level file. On generic systems which use the EXECUTE statement in PICK/BASIC, there must be a SYSTEM level file called EXECUTE-CONTROL. Each account has a set of files and items that must exist for the system to operate.

PROCESS STATUS VERBS

This section discusses the verbs related to the process status.

The WHAT Command

The WHAT command displays the current system configuration including the amount of physical memory, the size of ABS, the PCB for line zero (start of the process control blocks), the workspace size, and the base of the system dictionary.

In addition, WHAT performs a series of other system status related commands which display group locks, execution locks, perform a system WHERE, and finally spooler status via SP-STATUS. The standard syntax of WHAT and a sample report are shown in Fig. 8-4.

```
>WHAT

10:35:46 09 JUN 1988
CORE LINES PCB0 WSSTART  WSSIZE  SYSBASE/MOD/SEP MAXFID AVAIL.OVERFLOW
640K     7  800     1024     127     3691  11   1 111502        69282

     32049 (07D31)- 01
     00 00 00 00 00 00 00 00 00 00 00 00 00 00 00 00
     00 00 00 00 00 00 00 00 00 00 00 00 00 00 00 00
     00 00 00 00 00 00 00 00 00 00 00 00 00 00 00 00

     00 00 00 00 00 00 00 00 00 00 00 00 00 00 00 00
     00 00 00 00 00 00 00 00 00 00

     *00    0320  FF30    T      121.000      121.1AB
     01     0340  FF30           228.5FD
     02     0360  BF30           170.219      170.097
     03     0380  7DB0             1.20D        9.2B5     71.57C     72.107
     04     03A0  6D30           351.0DB
     06     03E0  BF30           170.219      170.142

     THE SPOOLER IS INACTIVE.

     PRINTER # 0 IS PARALLEL, INACTIVE, AND ON LINE.
     THE PRINTER IS DEFINED AS PARRALLEL PRINTER # 0.
     ASSIGNED OUTPUT QUEUES: 0.
     THE NUMBER OF INTER-JOB PAGES TO EJECT IS 0.
     The SPOOLER is in an unambiguous state.
```

FIG. 8-4. Sample WHAT output.

WHAT Options

The output of the WHAT verb is made up of four different sections. These are:

- The configuration table
- System lock tables
- The output of the WHERE command
- The spooler status output of the SP-STATUS command

These tables may be excluded by using the available options for WHAT.

Options	Description
>WHAT L	Exclude the system locks
>WHAT W	Suppress the WHERE display
>WHAT S	Exclude SP-STATUS
>WHAT P	Send the WHAT display to the spooler

The SYSTEM Configuration Line

The system configuration line consists of:

Input	Description
CORE	The amount of physical memory on the machine. *Core* is an outdated term meaning physical memory. Core was a memory that used magnetic "donuts" for bits in memory. Core memories were not volatile (they did not lose information if power was lost) but slow. Modern memories are based on MOS technology. MOS is *metal oxide semiconductors*. MOS is fast but highly volatile. Be that as it may, this system currently has 640 thousand bytes of MOS.
LINES	The number of processes for which the system is configured. The number of LINES may be less than the physical number of ports on the system.
PCB0	The decimal frame number for line 0's primary control block. This is the first frame of the process control blocks. Because the first PCB begins immediately after the ABS region, it is probably correct to assume that the system is configured for 800 ABS frames (0-799).
WSSTART	The frame address of the first frame in additional process workspace. These frames are important for any higher level application to run, including anything written in PICK/BASIC.
WSSIZE	The number of frames in each block of process workspace. Remember, each process must use a triplet of these blocks to make up its workspace.
SYSBASE MOD/SEP	The first frame, the base, of the primary space of the system dictionary file. Also included are the current modulo and separation of the system file.
MAXFID	The maximum addressable frame on disk.
OVERFLOW	The total number of unused frames on the disk.

System Locks

The next group of status indicators are the system locks. There are many flavors of system level locks and each are displayed by the WHAT command. The lock information can also be displayed by entering the LIST-LOCKS command, as shown in Fig. 8-5.

```
>LIST-LOCKS

(group/item locks)

     32049 (07D31)- 01

(PICK/BASIC execution locks)

     00 00 00 00 00 00 00 00 00 00 00 00 00 00 00 00
     00 00 00 00 00 00 00 00 00 00 00 00 00 00 00 00
     00 00 00 00 00 00 00 00 00 00 00 00 00 00 00 00

(System locks)

     00 00 00 00 00 00 00 00 00 00 00 00 00 00 00 00
     00 00 00 00 00 00 00 00 00 00
```

FIG. 8-5. LIST-LOCKS output.

The first lock indication is any active group or item locks. This varies with each implementation. *Group locks* prevent any port other than the initiating port from accessing items within a file group. *Item locks* prevent only the item from being shared. The other items in the group are still available. The following example is Pick PC XT/AT R83 and therefore indicates a group lock:

    32049 (07D31) - 01

The general format is:

   decimal group FID (*hex group* FID) – *initiating port number*

In this case, the group beginning at primary frame 32049 is locked by the application on port 1. The first block of zeros indicates the PICK/BASIC execution locks. These are locks set by the PICK/BASIC runtime command, LOCK. Some implementations allow 64 reserved locks (0-63), while others allow only 48 locks (0-47). Such is the case with my AT running Pick 2.1.

Each entry represents an execution lock, 0-47, and indicates the port number which initiated the lock. The 00 indicates an available lock. "How can anyone tell the difference between an empty lock and one set by port 0?" This dilemma has been solved by some of the vendors by using the double pound sign (##) or period (..) to indicate an unused lock.

The next group of locks indicate the other system lock bytes. 00 indicates available and the channel number indicates the lock is set. Each position in the table represents a different system lock.

Position	Description
0	The lock table lock. A process must lock the lock table before it can update it.
1	Overflow table lock. Only a single process at a time can alter the overflow table. Many problems still exist with peripherally written software which attaches and alters the table without first checking for a lock.

2	Group lock table. Even when a group lock is set, a table of group locks must be maintained.
3	The MESSAGE processor lock. Only one process at a time can send a message.
4-the end	Reserved for undocumented system use.

Locks 2, 3, 4 and the rest do not exist on every implementation. On some systems, group locks are handled directly by the monitor and no locks are needed. Some systems send messages using IO redirection, not the system debugger, and no locks are needed.

The final display of the WHAT verb is the spooler status (SP-STATUS). This system has two printers attached. Printer 0 is parallel and does not show up on the WHERE output. Printer 1 is a serial printer attached to a standard serial port. Serial printers do show up on the WHERE output and usually will be seen with a BF PIB status, sleeping, and a return stack in ABS frame 170, the spooler control code.

LISTU and WHO

Rather than discuss the WHERE command as part of the WHAT, WHERE should be dealt with separately. An important fact to realize about WHERE is that it interrogates the PIB's in memory. WHERE gives an accurate report of active ports.

In contrast, the command LISTU activates a PROC which performs a Pick ACCESS language request on the system's ACC file. The ACC file is used by the system when a process is logged on and off. An item is written to ACC at logon time and deleted when the process is logged off. The layout of the ACC port is shown in Fig. 8-6.

FIG. 8-6. ACC port LOGON item layout.

ID: *Process PCB in hex.*

001 *Account name*

002 *Internal Date*

003 *Internal time*

PCB stands for *primary control block*. PCB's are discussed later in this chapter under the heading, "Process Workspace."

The problem with LISTU arises when the system crashes or is brought down before processes have a chance to log off. At system coldstart time, the ACC items are still there. A LISTU can be quite misleading under these circumstances. That is why it is a good idea to "clean up" the ACC as part of the standard coldstart procedure.

The verb WHO retrieves the account and line information displayed from the logon item in the ACC file. The syntax is:

>WHO {*line#*}

or

>WHO {*}

This outputs the account name being used on the specified line# or the current account name if no line# is specified. The asterisk (*), displays the account name for all lines.

The WHERE Command

Back to the WHERE command. Here is the syntax. An output example of WHERE is shown in Fig. 8-7. At this time, the discussion concentrates the first 3 columns, process status. The process return stacks are discussed later in this chapter.

>WHERE

-1-	-2-	-3-	-4-	-5-	-6-	-7-	-8-
*00	0320	FF30	T	121.000	121.1AB		
01	0340	FF30		228.5FD			
02	0360	BF30		170.219	170.097		
03	0380	7DB0		1.20D	9.2B5	71.57C	72.107
04	03A0	6D30		351.0DB			
06	03E0	BF30		170.219	170.142		

FIG. 8-7. WHERE output.

The Port Number

The first column of WHERE displays the process port number. The second displays the location in hexadecimal of the process's PCB.

The PCB Location

Column 2 is the port Primary Control Blocks (PCB). For example, the PCB for line 0 (the line on which the WHERE was performed, indicated by an asterisk) is hex 0320. Using the facilities of the system:

>XTD 0320   800

The command XTD means convert hex to decimal. The decimal 800 was echoed by the system as the result of the conversion request. So, the primary control block for port 0 is in frame 800.

PIB Status Bytes

The third column of the WHERE displays the two PIB status bytes. The following are typical values in the generic Pick world, but may be different on your implementation. To get familiar with the status bytes, use the two terminal method. Run a known process on one terminal and look at it with a WHERE on the other terminal. I know this sounds tedious, but this method is very effective for getting to know your system.

To eliminate the frustration of interpreting these bytes, some vendors have provided a new verb, PIB-STATUS or simply STATUS. PIB-STATUS interrogates the active process PIB's and displays their statuses in English. If your system does not have this, demand it or write one yourself. When we discuss the EXECUTE statement in PICK/BASIC, the latter solution will seem less intimidating.

Within the first PIB byte, there are 6 bits which indicate:

Status	Description
INPUT	Receiving characters from the async line.
OUTPUT	Transmitting characters on the async line.
DISCIO	Waiting for a frame fault.
SLEEPING	Inactive for a period of time.
ECHO	Character echo on or off
PROCESS	meaning the process is active or comaed.

The bit positions can vary between implementations. Here are some typical values observed on the XT/AT implementation. These are the typical results of PIB byte 1.

Result	Description
7B or FB	Indicates an output roadblocked process. That is, the process is in the act of outputting to the communications line.
7D or 6D	Indicates an input roadblocked process. The process is accepting characters from the communications line.
5F	Indicates that the process is waiting for a disk IO. Usually the indication of a frame fault.
7F or FF	Indicates the process is active or ready to be activated.
3F or BF	Indicates the process is sleeping.

Byte 2 of the PIB statues uses 2 major bits to indicate:

Status	Description
DEBUGGER	The bit is high when the process is in the debugger.
LOGGED	Set high if the process is logged on.

As before, the position of these bits can vary. Typical values are:

Result	Description
30	Indicating normal operation.
B0	Indicating that the process is in the debugger.

Device Attachment

Column 4 indicates whether the tape (T) is attached to this process. McDonnell Douglas use a (P) to indicate a port attached printer.

The Return Stack

Columns 5 and higher are the *virtual assembler return stack*. The number preceding the period is a decimal frame identifier (FID). The number following the period is the hexadecimal number of bytes the process has displaced within the frame. Column 5 indicates the current active execution location of the process. Each subsequent column is where the process "came from." For example, port number 3 is sitting in frame 1, the debugger, which interrupted the code in frame 9, which was called from frame 71, which in turn was called from frame 72. In other words, the break key was pressed while an ACCESS report was running:

Frame	Process Name
1	System Debugger
2,5	TCL
6	Terminal IO
7	Disk IO
13-16	EDITOR
33,34	Overflow Handling
35,36	Tape IO
40	LOGON
41-46	PROC
48	Group Locks
53-70	ACCESS compiler
70-120	ACCESS LIST
121	WHERE
127	Overflow Table
165-183	Spooler
190-199	PICK/BASIC Compiler
200-220	File SAVE
220-260	PICK/BASIC Runtime
300-400	Usually JET

The Pick system usually takes up to frame 300 in the ABS region. Following frame 300 is where user purchased or written assembler applications are stored. These may include JET, ACCU/PLOT, COMPUSHEET and a multitude of other packages.

Taking a closer look at the WHERE reveals the following information:

Port	Description
0	The current port executing the WHERE.
1	PICK/BASIC runtime.
2	A terminal attached printer.
3	ACCESS and was broken into the system debugger.
4	Using the JET editor
6	The phantom spooler.

With experience, one can look at any line of the WHERE output and determine the type of task the process is currently running. For example, if one terminal after another is starting to "hang," a WHERE executed on a free terminal may provide clues to the problem if not the answer. Should the return stack show these ports sitting at frame 48, then the problem is group lock contention. The WHAT should also show the group locks that are set.

CAUTION: The return stack entries can vary from machine to machine. I only provide the generic or "vanilla" layout.

To determine the exact locations of your system code, either call your vendor for some documentation (a likely story), or do as I have done. Sit down with two terminals at the same desk. Let's call these terminals A, the one performing the WHERE, and terminal B, the one executing known tasks. On terminal A, constantly execute a WHERE of terminal B. If terminal B is on port 9, then the command would be:

```
>WHERE 9
```

As terminal B performs a PROC, study the results of the WHERE on terminal A. This is how I have laid out the ABS locations presented here.

Most of the ABS frame locations can be traced through the verb definition items found in an account master dictionary. *Verbs* are dynamic pointers to ABS frames. The initiating frames are indicated in the body of the item. For more information on verb layouts, refer to the section entitled "Items in the System Hierarchy" in Chapter 1, "The Pick Database."

WHERE Options

The following lists the options available with the WHERE command:

>WHERE 9	For a single port.
>WHERE 9-20	For a range of ports.
>WHERE 'SYSPROG'	Show all process logged onto a specific account.
>WHERE Z	Show all the processes, logged on or not.

The Status Program

Figure 8-8 is a PICK/BASIC routine for interpreting the WHERE command. STATUS executes a WHERE, captures the output into a variable, parses the information, looks up the meanings of the ABS frames and displays the results. Here is where a manual should be handy to verify the command syntax.

```
    STATUS
001 *STATUS
002 * Execute WHERE and interpret return stack
003 *
004 PROMPT ''
005 EQU AM TO CHAR(254)
006 OPEN 'ACC' TO ACC ELSE STOP 201,ACC
007 OPEN 'ABS' TO ABS ELSE STOP 201,'ABS'
008 *
009 ECHO OFF
```

FIG. 8-8. STATUS program listing (continues).

```
010 CRT @(-1):
011 LOOP
012   CRT @(-2):
013   EXECUTE 'WHERE' CAPTURING WHERE
014   C = DCOUNT(WHERE,AM)
015   FOR I = 1 TO C
016     WLINE = TRIM(WHERE<I>)
017     PORT = FIELD(WLINE,' ',1)
018     PCB  = FIELD(WLINE,' ',2)
019     READ AREC FROM ACC,PCB ELSE AREC = 'UNKNOWN'
020     ACCOUNT = AREC<1>
021     MAXSTACK = DCOUNT(WLINE,' ')
022     LASTFID = ''
023     CRT PORT "L#3": " " : ACCOUNT "L#10" : " =====> ":@(-4):
024     FOR J = 4 TO MAXSTACK
025       RTNENTRY = FIELD(WLINE,' ',J)
026       ABSFID = FIELD(RTNENTRY,'.',1)
027       IF ABSFID = LASTFID THEN
028           FUNC = ''
029       END ELSE
030           READ FUNC FROM ABS,ABSFID ELSE FUNC = ABSFID
031           CRT FUNC : ' ':
032       END
033       LASTFID = ABSFID
034     NEXT J
035     CRT
036   NEXT I
037 UNTIL SYSTEM(14) DO
038   CRT @(-3):
039   RQM
040 * SLEEP 2
041 REPEAT
042 INPUT DUMMY,SYSTEM(14)
043 ECHO ON
```

FIG. 8-8 ends.

Program Highlights

After performing a minimal amount of setup, the two driving programs must be opened.

```
006 OPEN 'ACC' TO ACC ELSE STOP 201, 'ACC'
007 OPEN 'ABS' TO ABS ELSE STOP 201, 'ABS'
```

The ACC file is used to retrieve the current account name to which the process is logged. ABS frames are defined in a file called ABS. ABS is used as a lookup table. The item layout is as follows:

```
ID: ABSFID
001 Description
```

The system echo is turned off and the screen is cleared. The echo is disabled for a good reason. This entire process keeps running until any key is received from the keyboard.

```
009 ECHO OFF
010 CRT @( – 1):
```

The function SYSTEM(14) retrieves the count of characters waiting in the "typeahead" buffer. ULTIMATE uses the equivalent function, SYSTEM(11). This eliminates the need for the operator to hit the break key to terminate a program.

```
011 LOOP
012    CRT @( – 2): ;* Home the cursor
013    EXECUTE 'WHERE' CAPTURING WHERE
          ....

          ....
037 UNTIL SYSTEM(14) DO
038    CRT @( – 3): ;* Clear to the end of the screen
039    RQM
040 * SLEEP 2
041 REPEAT
042 INPUT DUMMY,SYSTEM(14)
043 ECHO ON
```

If the result of SYSTEM(14) remains zero (false), the timeslice is given up via RQM to serve as a delay, and the process is repeated. If sampling is not required every second, a longer delay can be indicated. Notice the SLEEP 2 commented out.

When the routine exits the LOOP, the INPUT strips the stray character or characters typed, and ECHO is re-enabled. Here is the code which captures the WHERE.

```
013 EXECUTE 'WHERE' CAPTURING WHERE
```

The CAPTURING clause is discussed at length in Chapter 3. Suffice it to say; all output, which normally would go to the terminal display, is directed to a named program variable. Carriage returns are converted to attribute marks. That is CHAR(13) is converted to CHAR(254). Form feeds, CHAR(12), and line feeds, CHAR(10), are stripped. By the way, the ULTIMATE world must indicate the same capture in this manner:

```
013 EXECUTE 'WHERE',//OUT. > WHERE
```

The result must now be parsed. Re-examine a single line of WHERE output. The column positions are marked in Fig. 8-7. The number of lines is counted and placed into the variable MAXSTACK. The counter, I, begins at 1 because the first line of the WHERE output is the first logged on line. Be aware that some of the implementations place column headers on the first 1 to 3 lines of the WHERE display. If this is true, you must compensate for it.

```
014    MAXSTACK = DCOUNT(WHERE,AM)
015    FOR I = 1 TO MAXSTACK
016       WLINE = TRIM(WHERE<I>)

          ......
036    NEXT I
```

Each line, in turn, is extracted from WHERE and immediately trimmed. TRIM reduces the embedded spaces to a single blank between the entries. All leading and trailing spaces are stripped. The resulting string WLINE looks like this:

```
1- 2---  3---  4----  5----  6-----   7----  8- 9-  ...
03 0380 7DB0 1.20D 9.2B5 71.57C 72.107
```

Each field of data is separated by a space and may be isolated using the FIELD function.

```
017   PORT = FIELD(WLINE,' ',1)
018   PCB = FIELD(WLINE,' ',2)
```

The PCB can be used to read the current ACC logon item. Read the item and get the account name. Count the number of data positions. In this case, there are seven. Next, display what is there so far.

```
019   READ AREC FROM ACC,PCB ELSE AREC = 'UNKNOWN'
020   ACCOUNT = AREC<1>
021   MAXSTACK = DCOUNT(WLINE,' ')
023   CRT PORT "L#3": " " : ACCOUNT "L#10" : " = = = = = > ":@(-4):
```

Now, address each entry from position 4 to the maximum. Extract the FID for the ABS frame, read the description and display it. The related items in ABS are:

```
ID:   1       71      72
001   DEBUG ACCESS  ACCESS
```

The LASTF logic prevents the same process description from being displayed more than once in a repeated sequence.

```
024   FOR J = 4 TO MAXSTACK
025      RTNENTRY = FIELD(WLINE,' ',J)
026      ABSFID = FIELD(RTNENTRY,'.',1)
027      IF ABSFID = LASTFID THEN
028        FUNC = ''
029      END ELSE
030        READ FUNC FROM ABS,ABSFID ELSE FUNC = ABSFID
031        CRT FUNC : ' ':
032      END
033      LASTFID = ABSFID
034   NEXT J
```

The resulting output line looks like this:

```
03 CLASS = = = = = > DEBUG 9 ACCESS
```

In this case, FID's 1, 71, and 72 are defined in the file ABS. FID 9 does not have a corresponding entry in the ABS file.

9

Working in the Virtual Environment

"The first thing to understand about a virtual environment is that things can get very strange. It's like being Alice in Wonderland."

—Ian Sandler, April 25, 1988

THE MAD HATTER, MARCH HARE AND DOOR MOUSE WOULD HAVE MADE EXTRA-ordinary Pick programmer/analysts. They understood the concepts of variable reality. Rather than pour from the pot, they simply shifted one chair to the left for a fresh cup of tea.

PROGRAMMING CONSIDERATIONS

In the Pick Operating System, things are not always what they seem. And if you've been working with the system for a while, you've probably already realized that there are no hard and fast rules for efficient design and implementation, except to keep all options open and remain as flexible as possible.

If the applications programmer has a better feeling for the moving boundaries of the Wonderland within the Pick Operating System, his other ability to analyze application performance, maintenance and design problems will be greatly enhanced. In a virtual environment, the best way to do things is almost always the simplest. The reason is that you can't anticipate the way that the virtual environment will perform in any particular case. When faced with this sort of situation, there are some methods for testing designs that are likely to work well.

The first method is to experiment If you have a particular problem and you can see several ways of solving it, mock up a test case and try the different methods to see which one seems to work best for you. However, don't bother investing the time and effort in extensive experimentation with a case that does not occur frequently. There is no point in optimizing a routine that doesn't occur very often.

The primary concern of application design is *to make the code as maintainable and as intelligible as possible*. Never let efficiency constraints bother the initial application layout, with one exception. The design of the database. The database is crucial. However, if the database is already in place, and the goal is to maintain and enhance the code, then the code should be readable and maintainable.

The next step is to look at the code and determine places that are likely to create execution bottlenecks Optimize only those lines of code that are repeatedly and frequently executed. It is reasonable to invest the time and effort to make this code run faster.

Monitor size of the data The next and probably most important thing you have to watch out for in an application is the size of the data. If there is a particular field of data which must be processed, the answer to the efficient processing problem differs greatly if that field is 10 or 100 or 10,000 or 100,000 bytes long. If you have found a place in an application where you think efficiency is important and you are modeling it, that model is absolutely useless unless the data you are working on is about the right length.

There are a few ways to speed up the system. The monitor can be rewritten or modified to work more efficiently. The hardware can be made faster. However, neither of these alternatives are within the reach of the applications programmer. The programmer must find ways using the high level resources at his disposal to increase system efficiency.

An efficient application is a symbiosis of coding practices and database design. "You can't have one without the other." Ok, Ok, you caught me, you can have one without the other. It might even work. Not very well, but it will work. At least a steady support job is guaranteed!

APPLICATION DESIGN CONSIDERATIONS

There are certain things to be aware of when designing a Pick-based application. The first is that the size of the data items is crucial. The size of any string is crucial. The more segments that a string is broken into by crossing multiple frame boundaries, the slower the handling of that string. *String size* is the limiting factor in designing an efficient application. It's definitely worth a few more words to understand why.

The one thing that affects performance more than anything else on a Pick system is a piece of code running into a frame boundary while processing data, and having to cross over it. The way the machine crosses a frame boundary, is that it bumps into the last byte of the existing frame, schedules a disk read for the next frame and goes away. It will not come back to your process until the frame is in memory. Depending on system resources, this could be seconds later.

One of the things that you try to optimize on the machine is *frame faults*. The best way to optimize frame faults is to not do them unnecessarily. The best way to achieve this is not to do anything artificial. The second best way is to keep strings down to manageable sizes.

A construct is *artificial* if it doesn't represent the way you would naturally think about doing the application on paper. Imagine a manual system with a fairly intelligent person doing the paper work. The constructs that seem alien to them are probably alien to the virtual environment. One of the major strengths of Pick is that you can design things more or less for a manual system so that it makes it very easy to understand. Provided you keep track of the "hot" spots for efficiency, you can design 95% of your system with this method and produce an extremely maintainable, efficient system.

For example, if you have an order that has ten lines, it makes sense to include the lines of the order as part of the order. If the order has a thousand lines, including it within the order makes no sense whatsoever.

If unlimited string sizes happen to be available, what of it? Unlimited item size is in a family of features which Dick Pick has dubbed, "Rope." It allows bad design without fault. Improper use might go so far as to tie the knot and kick out the stool.

Design for the worst case. That is, normalize the database hierarchically as far as it will go. As far as you can, use small items in a structured file schema where details reside as separate items in DETAIL files, all keyed from a master record in the MASTER file.

Now here's the catch. If you have very big files where the related data must be retrieved as an entity, using many small items is the worst possible thing you can do for performance. On very big files with the amount of data being at least a thousand times the size of physical memory, the only significant enemy is disk IO, *unnecessary frame faults*.

If large amounts of related data must be retrieved, the data must be grouped together in big items. The contrary would be retrieving the same information by requiring the separate request for the many subsidiary files and items associated with it. Every time an order is updated, several hundred critical IO's must be performed.

There is the ever-present overhead of the CPU processing a long string and waiting for the disk to get the string into memory. When the CPU is waiting for the disk, there isn't much it can do anyway.

The major rule is to look at a few important facts about the application and the usage of the data. If this is a very large file containing related data that logically must reside together, stick everything into one big item. If the file is not frequently used, who cares? Normalize the design as far as it will go. If it is a file that has only a few detail lines with one order, look at how this item will be used with the rest of the world. In this case, normalize to smaller items. If, on the other hand, you tend to report the data together at one time, build the related data into the same item.

Contrary to what you are probably thinking so far, designing a database for the virtual machine should normally be very easy. First, find or dream up a good manual system. Now, design your database as close to that as you possibly can. Look at your application, group together the data by frequency of use, and try to design your files to the best of your ability so that no element of any item is more than a frame size.

Remember, there is no right or wrong. Don't restrict yourself with unrealistic restraints. The data design must fit the requirements of the application. Within that, try to keep string sizes with some manageable limit and reduce frame faults, but don't strangle yourself. The resulting application will probably be a hybrid of normalized hierarchical design, where it is efficient, and monolithic design where it is more effective. The key is to design the application so that it is easy to move between the different methods, when the amount of data stored in the files changes radically. By the way, give my regards to the Cheshire Cat.

Index

SAVEIBUF program, process control, 198-199
screen driver, 283-313
SCROLL program, process control, 200-204
searches, literal, 56
secondary control blocks, 334
secondary lock codes, 61
sector, 7
security, 58-71
  account security parameters, 58-60
  CHARGE-TO verb, 60
  encrypted data fields, 71
  encrypted program source, 71
  flags, 59, 70
  hidden program source, 71
  level setting for, 64
  logon security programs, 66-70
  passwords, 59
  problems with, 64-65
  process shell and, 220
  synonym accounts, 62-64
  system privilege, 59
  update/retrieval locks, 60-65
  users and directories, 65
SELECT, 55, 56, 137, 138, 139, 141, 164, 206, 209
SELECT...TO, 138, 139, 143
semicolons, PICK/BASIC, 113
SENTENCE(), 193, 197, 198, 284
separation, 7, 32, 33, 42-47, 49, 57
SEQUEL firmware, 326
shared runtime, PICK/BASIC, 74
SHELL program, process control, 144, 220-228, 230
SIMPLE, 195
simple variables, 82
SIMPLE.LINK.LIST program, list processing, 153-154
SIMPLE.LIST program, list processing, 151
simultaneous updates, 58
size limitations, data storage, 10-12
size review period, 37
SIZER program, 49-57
sizing and resizing files, 36, 39-49
  SIZER program, 49-57

SLEEP, 77
Smart-Tree, B-tree package, 182
SORT, 6, 274
sorted lists, 146-147
sorts, exploded, 135-137, 278
SP-EDIT, 191, 192
SP-FILE program, process control, 191-192
SP-MOVEJOB program, process control, 210-211
SP-STATUS, 339
SPIRIT firmware, 326
spool entry numbers, capturing, 210-211
Spooler, virtual environment, 328
SREFORMAT, 274, 276, 277, 278
SSELECT, 136, 277
stack lists, 144
stackers, TCL, 220
stacks, push and pop, 146, 189
standard deviation, 29
STAT verb, 24
STAT-FILE, 30, 31, 32, 54, 55
STATELIST, 134
statement labels, 112
static files, 35, 42-43
static pointers, 4
statistics, 23-34, 54
status bits, 13
STATUS program, virtual environment, 342-346
STON, 135, 189, 196, 197
STOP, 213, 230
stored data, 242
strings, 10, 86, 98-111
  ASCII, 79
  descriptor table and, 77-78
  dynamic array, 87
  extraction, 252
  length of, 14
  logical, extraction of, 252
  output formatting, 254
  size of, virtual environment, 348
  trimming, 105
structured loops, 113
sub fields, 10
sub-values, 10-11
SUBLEVELS program, 126
subroutines, 79, 125-129

calling, 83
data entry, dictionary, 283
parameter passing, 83
PICK/BASIC, from dictionaries, 279-280
recursive, 172
repetitive calls, 126
testing levels of, 125
usage rules for, 128-129
substitution, 259
SUBTEST program, 127
SUMMARY files, 38-39
summation of multivalues, 249
symbol table, PICK/BASIC, 84
synonym accounts, 62-64
synonym dictionary item, 243-246
SYS-GEN file, 31
SYSPROG, 59
SYSTEM configuration line, 337
SYSTEM dictionary, 3
system
  linkage errors 17-19, 17
  locks, 337
  privilege, 58, 59
  statistics on, 30-31
SYSTEM(), 219, 294, 345

T

T-ATT, 219
T-DUMP, 134, 273
T-LOAD, 273
table driven data entry, 282
target account/file name, 4
TCL, 4-6, 193-196, 220, 230
TERM setting, 200
terminal echo, disable, 70
terminating segment mark, 11, 24
THEN, 90, 149, 194, 195, 218, 219
THEN...ELSE, 147, 217
thrashing, 331-333
TIME(), 294
timesharing, virtual memory, 327
TRACE mode, 228, 230
transaction files, 57
transient GFEs, 14
trapping errors, 205
traversal program, B-tree, 173-179
trees, 168-183

TRIM, 105, 346
TRNLIST, 134
truth tables, 250

U

ULT.LINK program, list processing, 156
Ultimate, 13, 195
unaccessible frame faults, 349
unbalanced loops, 114
unlinked frames, 14-16, 18
UNTIL, 115, 149
updates, 58
  attribute, 57
  batch items, ACCESS for, 273-279
  locking, 58, 60-65
  simultaneous, 58
user defined functions, 129-130
user exits, 265
user security, 65
utilization, 32-33

V

validation, data entry, dictionary, 292
value marks, 10, 11, 110, 136
variables, 77-86
  ASCII strings, 79
  CASE statement, structured conditional, 118-120
  common, 82
  data conversions and, 80
  declaration and typing, 78-81
  descriptor allocation, 82-84
  descriptor table for, 77-78
  dimensioned, 82
  file variables, 79
  nontyped, 79, 80
  numerics, 79
  reporting descriptor allocation, 84-86
  simple, 82
  subroutines, 79
variance, 29
verbs, 3-5
  parsing, 106
  process status, 335-346
  statistic gathering (see statistics)

TCL, 5-6
virtual assembler routines, 3
virtual dictionary item, 243-246
virtual environment, 325-346
  application design considerations, 348-350
  demand paging, 331
  device attachment, 341
  forced disk writes, 331
  frame faults, 330
  LISTU and WHO command, 339
  memory management, 329
  operating system, 328-333
  PIB status bytes, 340
  process status verbs, 335-346
  programming considerations for, 347-348
  return stack, 341
  STATUS program, 342-346
  SYSTEM configuration line, 337
  thrashing, 331-333
  virtual memory, 325-328
  virtual workspace, 333-335
  WHAT command, 336
  WHERE command, 340, 343
  working in, 347-350
virtual memory, 325-328

W

warning messages (see also error recovery), 80, 212
WEOF, 218
WHAT command, 336, 337, 343
WHERE, 200, 339, 340, 343, 345, 346
WHILE, 114, 115
WHO command, 5, 339
WITH, 242, 255
workspace, virtual, 333-335
WRAPUP error message, 212-219
WRITE, 89, 98, 159, 172, 217, 218
WRITET, 218, 277

X

xFF item-terminating segment mark, 24
XTD command, TCL, 5

354